Gender and the Environment

BUILDING EVIDENCE AND POLICIES TO ACHIEVE THE SDGS

OECD
BETTER POLICIES FOR BETTER LIVES

This document, as well as any data and map included herein, are without prejudice to the status of or sovereignty over any territory, to the delimitation of international frontiers and boundaries and to the name of any territory, city or area.

The statistical data for Israel are supplied by and under the responsibility of the relevant Israeli authorities. The use of such data by the OECD is without prejudice to the status of the Golan Heights, East Jerusalem and Israeli settlements in the West Bank under the terms of international law.

Please cite this publication as:
OECD (2021), *Gender and the Environment: Building Evidence and Policies to Achieve the SDGs*, OECD Publishing, Paris, *https://doi.org/10.1787/3d32ca39-en*.

ISBN 978-92-64-96413-6 (print)
ISBN 978-92-64-89763-2 (pdf)

Photo credits: Cover © Fahkamram/Shutterstock.

Corrigenda to publications may be found on line at: *www.oecd.org/about/publishing/corrigenda.htm*.

Preface

Protecting the planet and its biodiversity is the single most important intergenerational responsibility we face. Moreover, the impacts of environmental and climate change are not gender neutral. In developing and advanced economies alike, women are more vulnerable to the effects of climate change than men. Through climate change and severe environmental hazards, millions of people are placed at risk of displacement, 75% of whom are women. Despite women's role in agriculture and farming, women farmers have limited rights to inherit, access and use land and other productive resources, due mainly to deep-rooted social norms. Lower access to finance and education further restricts their ability to prepare for and respond to environmental shocks. Women tend to be overrepresented in low-income groups, which are most affected by pollution in cities and environmental damage from industry. Furthermore, during and after an environmental crisis or a pandemic, women and girls are exposed to an increased risk of gender-based violence. Discrimination and violence also affect women's mobility patterns and transport choices, which can have negative environmental impacts.

Throughout the world, women tend to display a higher sensitivity to environmental concerns, but they are largely under-represented in the decision-making processes of global climate leadership –whether in finance, economy, energy or infrastructure ministries, or in business. These factors all add to the structural challenges faced by women and girls in the legal and social framework. Significant gender gaps remain in labour force participation (especially in higher paying jobs), wages, and access to finance and natural resources. Furthermore, the COVID-19 crisis has exacerbated pre-existing gender inequalities, highlighting the intersection of climate and gender justice.

Women are not only victims but also powerful agents of change, and come with knowledge and skills to contribute to climate change adaptation and mitigation.

While UN processes have long recognised the interlinkages between climate and gender justice through the UNFCCC Gender Action Plans and the UN Convention on Biological Diversity, more needs to be done to support countries in systemically integrating gender analysis into data collection efforts, as well as climate change, budget and development cooperation policies.

This OECD report brings together, for the first time, all the existing evidence from OECD countries on the differential impacts of environmental factors on men and women's health, such as air pollution, water and soil contamination, exposure to chemicals, climate change and natural disasters. It demonstrates that understanding and effectively taking into account the gender dimension of climate change is key to achieving sustainable development and the Sustainable Development Goals (SDGs).

This timely publication also looks into how to foster the economic opportunities that could emerge for women in greener economies. The green recovery and transition, informed by policies that support gender-sensitive job reallocation, could create a virtuous circle of gender equality and sustainable development, while offering opportunities for women's economic empowerment.

Ensuring gender equality and addressing the various intersectional concerns that affect the most vulnerable population not only strengthens social justice, it also contributes to managing the economic and environmental imperatives. Through this work, the OECD emphasises the need for an integrated approach to gender equality and environmental sustainability in all policy areas and sectors. The proposed policy measures support governments in gathering systematic evidence on gender-differentiated environmental impacts, and provide a way forward for more effective policy action.

A missing and unheralded part of climate solution is gender equality. Let us work together to make the gender-environment nexus a force for transforming our economies and societies to be more resilient, inclusive and sustainable.

Angel Gurría

OECD Secretary General

Foreword

This report was prepared following a call from OECD Member countries during the 2019 Ministerial Council Meeting (MCM) to integrate gender mainstreaming into all policy areas of the OECD. The OECD subsequently launched a "Gender Policy Platform: Accelerating Mainstreaming through the Sustainable Development Goals" with a particular focus on areas where the OECD had yet to apply a gender lens, environment being one of these policy areas. The work was financed through a Central Priorities Fund allocation and Voluntary Contributions.

The report provides an overview of the gender-environment nexus, looking into data and evidence gaps, economic and well-being benefits as well as governance and justice aspects. The analysis is conducted using the Sustainable Development Goal (SDG) Framework. Nine environment-related SDGs are examined under a gender-environment lens, covering topics such as sustainable agriculture and fisheries, biodiversity protection, ecosystem management, clean water and sanitation, affordable and clean energy, sustainable infrastructure and inclusive cities, responsible consumption and production, and climate action. This mapping exercise aims at building the evidence and help countries identify possible future work on gender mainstreaming in environmental policies.

The report benefited from comments from the following OECD Committees and Working Parties for information and comments: Environment Policy Committee (EPOC), Committee on Statistics and Statistical Policy (CSSP), Development Assistance Committee (DAC), Employment, Labour and Social Affairs Committee (ELSAC), Health Committee (HEA), Regional Development Policy Committee (RDPC), Public Governance Committee's Working Party on Gender Mainstreaming and Governance, and Investment Committee's Working Party on Responsible Business Conduct.

The report was prepared under the supervision of Sigita Strumskyte, Head of the Sustainable Development, Gender and Partnerships Team in the Environment Directorate, and under the guidance of Rodolfo Lacy, OECD Environment Director. The first version of the report was drafted by Sigita Strumskyte in close collaboration with Romina Boarini, Director of the OECD's Centre for Well-Being, Inclusion, Sustainability and Equal Opportunity (WISE). Dimitra Xynou, Policy Analyst, researched and drafted subsequent parts of the report, with contributions from Addie Erwin, Alina Manrique de Lara and Sara Ramos Magaña, members of the Environment Directorate's Sustainable Development, Gender and Partnerships Team. Valuable comments were provided by Shardul Agrawala, Simon Buckle, Bob Diderich, Nathalie Girouard and Kumi Kitamori of the Environment Directorate. Special thanks go to Naoko Kawaguchi (SGE) and Céline Folsché (LEG) for their insights. Enrico Botta, Amy Cano Prentice, Justine Garrett, Alexander Mackie, Miguel Rodriguez Cardenas, and Cecilia Tam (ENV), Stina Heikkilä, Stefano Marta and Debra Mountford (CFE), Michelle Harding, Hannah Simon and Kurt Van Dender (CTP), Rena Hinoshita, Shivani Kannabhiran, Jennifer Schappert and Cristina Tebar Less (DAF), Juan Casado Asensio and Jenny Hedman (DCD), Pierre de Boisséson, Gaelle Ferrant and Alejandra Maria Meneses (DEV), Caitryn Guthrie (EDU), Willem Adema, Michele Cecchini and Shunta Takino (ELS), Cayenne Chachati, Juliane Jansen, Edwin Lau, Carina Lindberg, Scherie Nicol, Guven Pinar, Ana Maria Ruiz Rivadeneira, Toni Rumpf, Tatyana Teplova, Yola Thuerer and Laura Völker (GOV), Graham Pilgrim (SDD), Kelsey Burns (STI), Claire Delpeuch, Guillaume Gruère and Jane Korinek (TAD), Carlotta Balestra, Guillaume

Cohen, Grainne Dirwan, Lara Fleischer and Michal Shinwell (WISE), Liliana Suchodolska (Paris 21), Mechthild Wörsdörfer, Sara Moarif and Amrita Dasgupta (IEA), Magdalena Olczak and Wei-Shieun Ng (ITF), as well as other OECD colleagues, contributed with comments and suggestions which are gratefully acknowledged.

Amy Plantin provided valuable guidance on aligning the report with the work of EPOC. Elizabeth Corbett, Carole Guerrier, Dominique Haleva, Annette Hardcastle, Deborah Holmes Michel, Ines Reale, Anna Rourke of the OECD Environment Directorate provided administrative support and formatted the report. Marie-Claude Gauhier and Ricardo Sanchez Torres helped administratively to prepare previous versions of the report. The report benefited from editing by Amelia Smith. Elizabeth Del Bourgo and Stéphanie Simonin-Edwards provided communications and publication production support.

The authors would like to thank the Environmental Policy Committee (EPOC) Delegates and other OECD Committees and Working Parties for useful comments and suggestions on earlier versions of the report.

Table of contents

Tables

Figures

Boxes

Acronyms and Abbreviations

ADIMA : Analytical Database on Individual Multinationals and Affiliates

AFOLU : Agriculture, Forestry and other Land Use

APEC : Asia-Pacific Economic Cooperation

BRIICS : Brazil, Russian Federation, India, Indonesia, China and South Africa

BSR : Basel, Rotterdam and Stockholm Conventions

C3E : Clean Energy Education and Empowerment

CBD : Convention on Biological Diversity

CEDAW : Convention on the Elimination of All Forms of Discrimination Against Women

CEFIM : Clean Energy Finance and Investment Mobilisation

CEO : Chief Executive Officer

CGD : Citizen-generated data

COP : Conferences of the Parties

COVID-19 : Coronavirus Disease

CSSP: Committee on Statistics and Statistical Policy

CSW : Commission on the status of Women

DAC : Development Assistance Committee

EBRD : European Bank for Reconstruction and Development

EDC : Endocrine Disrupting Chemical

EIB : European Investment Bank

ELSAC : Employment, Labour and Social Affairs Committee

EMFF : European Maritime and Fisheries Fund

EPA : United States Environment Protection Agency

EPIC : Environmental Policy and Individual Behaviour Change

EPOC : Environmental Policy Committee

EU : European Union

FAO : Food and Agriculture Organization of the United Nations

FDI : Foreign Direct Investment

GAP : Gender Action Plan

GBA+ : Gender-Based Analysis Plus

GBD : Global Burden of Disease

GBV : Gender-based violence

GDP : Gross Domestic Product

GGRETA : Governance of Groundwater Resources in Transboundary Aquifers

GHG : Greenhouse gas

GIA : Gender Impact Assessment

GIPC : Gender Inclusive Cities Programme

GRI : Global Reporting Initiative

HEA: Health Committee

HIC : High index country

IAEG-GS : Inter-Agency and Expert Group on Gender Statistics

ICT : Information and Communication Technology

IEA : International Energy Agency

IFC : International Finance Cooperation

IG : Inclusive Growth

ILO : International Labour Organization

IRC : International Water and Sanitation Centre

IRENA : International Renewable Energy Agency

IUCN : International Union for Conservation of Nature

LDN : land degradation neutrality

LIC : Low income country

LMIC : Lower Middle Income Country

LUC : land use change

MCM : Ministerial Council Meeting

MNE : Multinational Enterprises

NAP : National Adaptation Plan

NBSAP : National Biodiversity Strategies and Action Plan

NDC : Nationally Determined Contribution

NGO : Non-governmental organization

ODA : Official Development Assistance

OECD : Organisation for Economic Co-operation and Development

PCSD : Policy Coherence for Sustainable Development

PEER : Partnerships for Enhanced Engagement in Research

PM : Particle Matter

POP : Persistent Organic Pollutants

R&D : Research and Development

RDPC : Regional Development Policy Committee

REDD+ : Reducing emissions from deforestation and forest degradation

SDG : Sustainable Development Goal

SEEA : System of Environmental-Economic Accounting

SEMARNAT : Mexican Ministry of Environment and Natural Resources

SIDS : Small Island Developing States

SIGI : Social Institutions Gender Index

SME : small and medium sized enterprise

SNA : System of National Accounts

SRD : sewage related debris

STEM : Science, technology, engineering and mathematics

TCFD : Task Force on Climate-related Financial Disclosures

UMIC : Upper middle income country

UN : United Nations

UN ESCAP : United Nations Economic and Social Commission for Asia and the Pacific

UNCCD : United Nations Convention to Combat Desertification

UNCED : UN Conference on Environment and Development

UNDESA : United Nations Department of Economic and Social Affairs

UNDRR : United Nations Office for Disaster Risk Reduction

UNECE : United Nations Economic Commission for Europe

UNEP : UN Environment Programme

UNESCO : United Nations Educational, Scientific and Cultural Organization

UNFCCC : National Focal Points for the United Nations Framework Convention on Climate Change

UNSD : United Nations Statistics Division

US : United States

VCs : Voluntary Contributions

W4C : Wireless for Communities

WASH : Water, Sanitation and Hygiene

WHO : World Health Organization

WTO : World Trade Organization

WTP : willingness-to-pay

WWAP : World Water Assessment Programme

WWF : World Wide Fund for Nature

Executive Summary

Gender equality and the empowerment of all women and girls are universal goals in their own right, as explicitly set out in Sustainable Development Goal (SDG) 5 in the United Nations' Agenda 2030 for Sustainable Development (2030 Agenda), the Convention on the Elimination of All Forms of Discrimination Against Women (CEDAW), and the 1995 Beijing Declaration and Platform for Action. The OECD has issued two recommendations on gender: the *2013 Recommendation of the Council on Gender Equality in Education, Employment, and Entrepreneurship*, and the *2015 Recommendation of the Council on Gender Equality in Public Life*. Yet a 2017 progress report on these recommendations shows that gender disparities and biases against women and girls persist in all fields, and calls for effective actions to remove obstacles to ensure equal and equitable opportunities. Addressing gender inequalities is a social, and economic, imperative.

This report uses the SDG framework to explore links between gender equality and environmental sustainability in the nine environment-related SDGs (2, 6, 7, 9, 11, 12, 13, 14 and 15). It provides evidence and rationale for the need to embed gender equality in economic, social, and environmental goals, by identifying trade-offs and complementarities among different policies in the context of Agenda 2030.

Recognising the multiple dimensions of and interactions between gender equality and the environment, this report applies an integrated policy framework taking into account both inclusive growth and environmental considerations. The framework draws on recent OECD guidance including the Policy Framework for Inclusive Growth, the Green Growth Strategy, the Recommendation on Policy Coherence for Sustainable Development, the two gender Recommendations, and related work on gender equality, governance and gender mainstreaming, including the OECD Toolkit on Implementing and Mainstreaming Gender Equality.

Chapters 1 to 3 outline the need to apply the environment-gender nexus to policy making and highlight potential benefits of merging both agendas. These chapters note the limitations of the current SDG framework in this area – e.g. out of the 231 unique SDG indicators, only 20 provide a gender dimension of environmental factors – and considerable lack of data on the gender-environment nexus despite numerous international and national initiatives even beyond the SDG framework. More systematic evidence gathering on gender-differentiated environmental impacts and initiatives emerges as a priority, especially on the differential impacts of environmental factors on men's and women's health, economic opportunities that could emerge for women in greener economies, and women's role in accelerating the shift towards sustainable consumption patterns.

Chapter 4 acknowledges the roles of women, youth and various vulnerable groups (e.g. indigenous peoples and people from small island developing states) in pursuing environmental and climate justice, while calling attention to their environment-related needs at local, national and international levels.

Chapter 5 presents a set of policy measures that could support more systematic evidence gathering on gender-differentiated environmental impacts. Leveraging the gender-environment nexus requires (i) gender equality and women's empowerment through policies that ensure equal access to quality education and health, as well as gender parity in decision making bodies; (ii) environment-related domestic policies that apply gender a lens in the design of national environmental policies and specific plans on climate change, biodiversity, oceans, and circular economy, including the establishment of environmental standards that account for differential impacts of environmental hazards and risks for men and women (iii) mainstreaming gender in transboundary policies, including trade, foreign direct investments, responsible business conduct, and development co-operation. Implementation could use a number of available OECD standards, and assessment and evaluation mechanisms.

Chapters 6 to 14 examine the nine environment-related SDGs (2, 6, 7, 9, 11, 12, 13, 14 and 15) through a gender-environment lens, supported by comparative data (in the few cases where it is available), case studies, surveys and other evidence. These chapters illustrate that women around the world are disproportionately affected by climate change, deforestation, land degradation, desertification, growing water scarcity and inadequate sanitation. This is especially the case in developing countries and in some rural communities, where women may have more limited access to land, natural commons, and other assets than men; may face barriers to decent work and finance, compounded with a skills gap and lack of information; and are more likely to shoulder an over-proportionate share of unpaid work, including household and family chores. Some of these challenges are also present – though on a different scale – in developed countries, especially where women face greater opportunity costs from inadequate and unsafe transport and infrastructure, adverse environmental health outcomes from air pollution, climate change and toxic chemicals entering food chains. The report upholds that a gender-responsive approach to land use, water, energy and transport management policies would allow societies to support and enhance the role of women in promoting more sustainable and inclusive economic development, and increase well-being. Each chapter proposes possible actions that governments and other stakeholders could take into consideration when designing and applying environmental policies.

Across all chapters, the report recognises women as agents of change in the transition to a low-carbon economy, and identifies their role as part of the labour force, as consumers, and as decision makers. Integrating gender equality is essential for the successful implementation of a circular economy, management of natural resources, and digital innovation, among other key areas. Barriers preventing the full participation of women in this transition – such as the gender gap in science, technology, engineering and mathematics (STEM) subjects – are also identified. More broadly, prevailing social and cultural norms, and their extension to societal and economic structures, limit women's access to economic opportunities in environmentally sustainable activities and in environmental leadership positions in both the public and private sectors. The just transition should include a gender perspective that actively promotes women's empowerment, to guarantee equal opportunities for both men and women in the workforce.

1 Gender equality and sustainable development

Progress towards achieving the Sustainable Development Goals calls for targeted responses. Gender equality and environmental goals are mutually reinforcing, yet their complementarities and trade-offs are not adequately presented nor considered in the 2030 Agenda. Acknowledging and addressing the gender-environment nexus could provide for policy coherence, a focus on well-being, and a turn to green and inclusive growth.

1.1. Key findings

This chapter presents the interlinkages between gender equality and environmental sustainability, and the extent of their inclusion in the Sustainable Development Goals framework. The key messages raised are:

- Gender equality and environmental goals are mutually reinforcing. Women experience differentiated effects from environmental factors, and are often most affected by environmental degradation due to socio-economic and discriminatory factors. At the same time, women express more "green" attitudes in their personal choices, and could greatly contribute to the transition to a low-carbon economy.
- The gender-environment nexus can be understood by recognising, on the one hand, the extent to which slow progress on environmental goals affects the condition of women and men differently and hampers gender equality; and on the other, how gender equality and women's empowerment can deliver positive impacts on the environmental aspects of the 2030 Agenda.
- The SDG framework provides adequate coverage on gender equality (SDG 5) and on environmental goals (the five Planet goals), while gender- and environment- related issues are also separately present in other SDGs. However, the gender-environment nexus is not sufficiently present in the SDG framework overall.
- The OECD Policy Coherence for Sustainable Development Framework and OECD's work on Going for Growth could provide a basis for identifying trade-offs, complementarities and links between gender-environment policies and outcomes in terms of well-being, in line with the SDGs and the OECD's Well-being framework.
- There is a need to apply a gender equality lens to the nine environment-related SDGs (SDGs 2, 6, 7, 9, 11, 12, 13, 14, and 15). This is provided in this report through analysis, case studies and policy recommendations.

1.2. Gender equality and environmental goals are mutually reinforcing

Meeting the Sustainable Development Goals (SDGs) requires urgent, targeted action. Addressing multiple objectives in the context of the gender-environment nexus is therefore key in advancing towards a fairer and more sustainable form of development. Environmental factors have gender-differentiated effects, due to men's and women's different roles and behaviours in various societies, as well as their different physiological characteristics. Whether one looks at energy, water, transport, urban design, agriculture, or consumption patterns, a gendered lens is key to understanding differences in environmental impacts.

Gender inequalities have increased as the COVID-19 pandemic has continued to deteriorate economies and populations' overall well-being. The recovery process is a crucial and timely opportunity for countries to embark on a more sustainable and gender-equal development path (OECD, 2019[1]).

Gender equality and women's empowerment are central to development, environmental sustainability and achievement of the SDGs, as discussed in Chapters 6 to 14 of this report. Globally, women play a central role in community support, resilience building and conservation efforts, thereby ensuring the well-being of current and future generations. Eco-feminist and "women and environment" approaches in particular reflect this unique understanding of nature and women's role as stewards of the environment (d'Eaubonne and Paisain, 1999[2]); (Dankelman, 2010[3]); (UNDP, 2019[4]). Men and women do not necessarily have the same experiences and responses to environmental occurrences. The integration of gender equality matters when it comes to expressing grievances about, as well as defining, framing and prioritising, environmental issues and what policy prescriptions are chosen (Taylor, 2002[5]).

The green economy affords great potential for women to engage in green jobs and participate in green innovation, but only if there is an enabling policy and social framework in place. More generally, giving women greater access to leadership positions in both the public and private sectors and at all levels of decision-making can help focus priorities on environmental goals (Bonewit and Shreeves, 2015[6]); (Hossain et al., 2017[7]); (Ben-Amar, Chang and McIlkenny, 2017[8]).

To help build a coherent approach to the 2030 Agenda, these and other interlinkages between gender equality and environmental sustainability requires analysing possible trade-offs and complementarities between different goals and policy interventions. Achieving gender equality calls for looking beyond social and economic inequalities and diving deep into the disproportionate effects of systemic issues – including environment-related inequalities – which could further exacerbate the former. This requires an integrated policy framework that brings together the three facets of inequalities: economic, social and environmental.

The gender-environment nexus can be understood by recognising, on the one hand, the extent to which slow progress on environmental goals affects the condition of women and men differently and hampers gender equality, and on the other, how gender equality and women's empowerment can deliver positive impacts on the environmental aspects of the 2030 Agenda (Figure 1.1).

Figure 1.1. The Gender-Environment Nexus

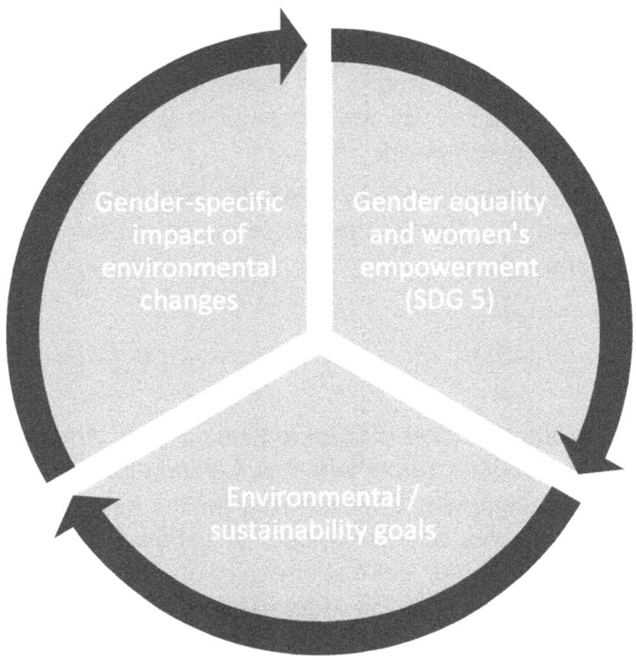

Source: OECD

1.3. Gender equality and the environment in the SDG Framework

The United Nations' 2030 Agenda for Sustainable Development provides an overarching set of goals, targets and indicators to track humanity's progress towards fundamental well-being for all. The SDGs encompass economic, social and environmental ambitions, and to some extent identify inherent complementarities and trade-offs among different goals as well as transmission channels.

The SDGs are grouped into five main categories: People, Planet, Prosperity, Peace and Partnerships. Gender equality and empowering women and girls (SDG 5) is a goal in and of itself in the People category. The legislative conditions for gender equality are referenced in the Peace, People and Prosperity categories (SDG 16, SDGs 1 to 4 and SDGs 7 to 11 respectively). Women's and girls' empowerment is referenced in five Planet goals and their targets and indicators (SDG 6 and SDGs 12 to 15), all of which are directly related to the environment. But two Planet goals (SDGs 14 and 15) have no gender-related indicators, despite many links.

With respect to environmental sustainability, five goals comprise the Planet category: SDG 6 (Clean water and sanitation), SDG 12 (Responsible consumption and production), SDG 13 (Climate change), SDG 14 (Life below water) and SDG 15 (Life on land). The environment is also an important aspect of three Prosperity goals: SDG 7 (Affordable and clean energy), SDG 9 (Industry, innovation, and infrastructure) and SDG 11 (Sustainable cities and communities). In addition, promoting sustainable agriculture is part of SDG 2 (Zero hunger). Thus, a total of nine SDG goals are linked to the environment. (Figure 1.2).

Both gender equality and environmental sustainability have a prominent role in the 2030 Agenda. Yet, as described in detail in Chapter 2, the SDG framework only recognises a few of their interlinkages and is silent on many important ones. Annex A maps the SDG indicators that are considered gender-related, environment-related or both. Across all the SDGs, only 20 unique indicators (out of a total of 231) incorporate both gender and environment. Only 14 of these cover the 9 environment-related SDGs analysed in depth in this report. Effectively, the SDG framework includes a strong but largely separate focus on gender equality and environmental sustainability, only marginally touching upon the interplay between these two objectives.

Figure 1.2. Environmental SDGs in the SDG framework

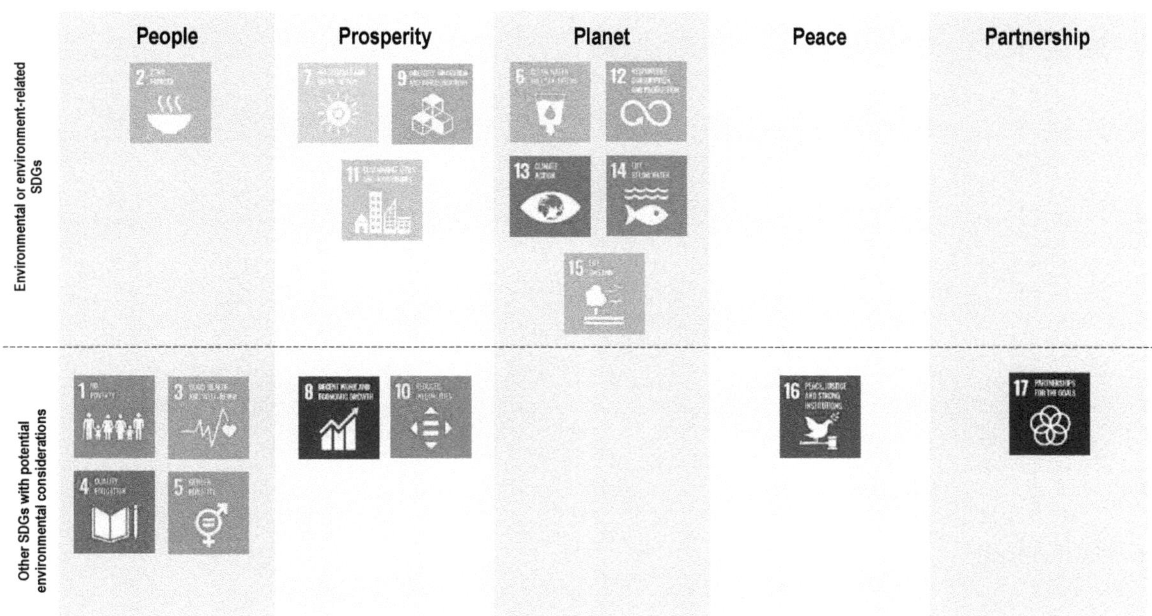

Source: OECD

1.4. Policy Coherence for Sustainable Development and its application to the gender-environment nexus

Identifying and understanding the interactions between SDGs and targets will help policy makers maximise synergies and exploit win-wins (pursue multiple objectives at the same time); avoid potential policy conflicts (pursue one policy objective without undermining others); manage trade-offs (minimise negative impacts on other policies); and ultimately design policies that generate multiple co-benefits for sustainable development (Figure 1.3).

SDG 17 (Partnerships for the goals) includes Target 17.14, to "enhance policy coherence for sustainable development". Policy coherence for sustainable development (PCSD) is an approach and policy tool to integrate the economic, social, environmental and governance dimensions of sustainable development at all stages of domestic and international policy making.

The OECD PCSD Framework identifies three interactional impacts of the SDGs: immediate (impacts on people's well-being today); transboundary (impacts of domestic actors on the population of other countries, e.g. as a result of trade, foreign investment or multinational firm operations); and intergenerational (impacts affecting natural, human or social capital, and thereby future well-being). To assess these interactions, the OECD's work on Going for Growth and the Policy Framework for Inclusive Growth (OECD, 2018[9]) provide approaches for identifying trade-offs, complementarities and links between policies, as well as possible outcomes in terms of well-being, in line with the SDGs and the OECD's Well-being framework.

Figure 1.3. Mapping goal and policy interactions in the PCSD framework

Source: (OECD, 2015[10])

1.5. The need to apply a gender equality lens to the environment-related SDGs

This report provides an overview of the available evidence on the gender-environment nexus. It applies an integrated policy framework to better understand the trade-offs and complementarities between gender and environmental goals, including transboundary and inter-generational effects. All 17 SDGs are interrelated; hence, all could be considered relevant for the gender-environment nexus. However, for the sake of analysis and advancing research and the policy agenda, this report focuses on the nine SDGs that have direct environmental implications.

Progress on SDG 5 and other SDGs in the People category, such as equal access to quality education (SDG 4), can boost actions to achieve all the environmental SDGs, especially if such education integrates an environmental focus that acknowledges all subjects in society as agents of change, including women (Melero and Solis-Espallargas, 2012[11]). Women impact natural resource management through their various roles in households, the economy, and society. Therefore, gender equality is crucial to ensuring a balanced approach to the economic, social and environmental dimensions of sustainable development and achieving all SDGs. Furthermore, given women's role in many societies, progress made on the nine environment-related SDGs can boost women's well-being, particularly their health (SDG 3) and economic opportunities (SDG 8).

Understanding the interlinkages between gender equality and the environment via these SDGs helps uncover a number of underlying systemic and structural gender inequalities and biases, generally related to ownership and use of natural resources, energy, transport, water, digital, urban design, housing, land-use, environment and agriculture in both advanced and developing countries (Table 1.1). When such ingrained biases are not disclosed or addressed, they perpetuate in environment-related decisions and policy design, further exacerbating gender inequalities.

Table 1.1. Interactions between SDG 5 and the nine environmental SDGs

Interactions between SDG5 and the nine environmental SDGs	
Goal	**Links with SDG5**
SDG 2. Zero hunger	Eliminating gender discrimination (in particular in land ownership and inheritance rights) and promoting women's engagement in sustainable agriculture could help drive action to meet all the relevant targets under SDG 2, in particular 2.3 on small-scale farming, 2.4 on resilient and sustainable agriculture, and 2.5 on conservation of plant and animal genetic resources, especially those under extinction. Introducing gender-sensitive and gender-inclusive aspects in agricultural investment, trade and value chains, and rural infrastructure policies could support achieving Targets 2.a and 2.b. SDG 2, in line with the 2012 Rio+20 UN Conference on Sustainable Development, which sets the ground for promoting sustainable agriculture and transitioning to more sustainable agricultural production methods. The SDGs refer to women's (and other groups') role as small-scale farmers, acknowledge their knowledge (Target 2.3) and support equal ownership of and access to agricultural land (Target 5.a).
SDG 6. Clean water and sanitation	Clean water and sanitation has a gender dimension in many developing countries, as women are the main resource gatherers. Ensuring easy, safe access to clean water would allow women more time to exploit economic opportunities and better access to education. Access to sanitation is critical to women's health and well-being (SDG 3), and also affects girls' schooling. Women can also contribute in the governance of water and sanitation at international, national and local community levels.
SDG 7. Affordable and clean energy	Accessible, clean energy can empower women by reducing the opportunity cost of collecting biofuels and reducing barriers to child education in developing countries. Energy poverty also affects many women in advanced countries. Women's empowerment and leadership in the energy sector may play a catalytic role in promoting clean energy and more efficient energy use. The just transition should include a gender perspective to guarantee equal opportunities for both men and women in the workforce.
SDG 9. Industry, innovation and infrastructure	Industrialisation and rural-urban migration policies need to take into account women's role in families, communities and the environment. Infrastructure is key not only to achieving environment-related objectives, but must include a gender dimension that secures access to all. Biases and other barriers that reduce access to STEM education, in particular in relation to sustainable development, hamper women's role in science and research.
SDG 11. Sustainable cities and communities	Women and men relate to urban and settlement design and transport infrastructure differently due to different social roles, occupational patterns and preferences. Urban and settlement planning and transport infrastructure that do not take into account the needs of different users can significantly reduce the economic opportunities and well-being of these users by increasing the time and means spent on commuting, and, at the same time, contribute to air pollution and inefficient resource use. Urban and settlement development sectors - housing, transport, and land use – have marked implications on gender equality goals through three key dimensions: user patterns (accessibly, safety and affordability), labour market participation (employment and participation in decision-making), and spillover effects (social and environmental). Women's greater involvement in decision making in these sectors could help reduce the overall environmental footprint of infrastructure.
SDG 12. Responsible consumption and production	Women make more purchasing decisions on household perishables but have less of a say in production chains. Unsustainable production, waste generation and pollution often have distinct harmful impacts on women, in particular on those who are socially disadvantaged, through various channels – from straining natural goods on which they depend for subsistence, to poor labour conditions in the "feminised" workforce, to an increasing amount of unpaid work related to waste management, and greater involuntary and uninformed exposure to harmful products and chemicals. At the same time, due to cultural norms, occupational and physical differences and distinct preferences and attitudes, men's and women's consumption patterns differ and have different environmental footprints.

Interactions between SDG5 and the nine environmental SDGs	
SDG 13. Climate action	There are gender differences stemming from the cumulative economic, social and health impacts of climate change. Because of their role in recovery and household management, and their traditional knowledge, women are particularly impacted by climate change and related natural hazards such as the increased frequency of floods and droughts. Natural disasters disproportionately affect women and girls. Women and girls could be proactive and experienced agents, engaging in climate change action. UNFCCC discussions have been integrating gender equality considerations since 2001, and gender equality has been a stand-alone item in the COP since 2012. The 2015 Paris Agreement emphasised the contribution of gender equality and empowerment of women to fighting climate change as well as the specific impact of climate change on women.
SDG 14. Life below water	SDG 14 is inherently related to the health of the environment; and progress toward its indicators can be buttressed by empowering and engaging women as agents of change. Women-led initiatives targeting the cleanup and protection of coastal areas demonstrate that women could contribute to more sustainable management of maritime ecosystems. Empowering women in the fisheries sector and building on their role as small-scale fishers could support sustainable fisheries. Yet, none of the targets of SDG 14 address gender equality or the relation of marine resources to the livelihoods of women and men, including the role they can play in food security, employment and poverty reduction.
SDG 15. Life on land	Of the Aichi Biodiversity Targets, only Target 14 overtly addresses gender equality, calling for the needs of women, indigenous peoples and local communities, and the poor and vulnerable to be taken into account in the restoration and safeguarding of ecosystems. Yet Aichi Target 14 does not include a specific indicator on gender equality, and identified indicators are not sex-disaggregated. Only Aichi Target 18 (traditional knowledge) includes gender relevant indicators, in respect to trends in land use change and tenure in traditional territories of indigenous and local communities, differentiated by sex. These are the same indicators as for SDG Targets 5.a and 1.4. In addition, a gender-sensitive target could be added on ensuring access to "commons" such as forests, mountain resources and rivers for local and indigenous communities that depend on them for their living and manage them on a sustainable basis. Alternatively, this target could be included in SDG 1 (e.g. under 1.4).

Source: Based on Authors' analysis of the UNstats Global indicator framework for the Sustainable Development Goals and targets of the 2030 Agenda for Sustainable Development.

According to General Recommendation No. 37 of the Committee on the Elimination of Discrimination against Women (CEDAW), in many contexts, gender inequalities limit the control that women and girls have over decisions governing their lives, as well as their access to resources such as food, water, agricultural input, land, credit, energy, technology, education, health services, adequate housing, social protection and employment. As a result of these inequalities, women and girls are more likely to be exposed to disaster-related risks and losses to their livelihoods, and are less able to adapt to changes in climatic conditions.

The combination of gender inequalities, biases, and social norms dictating specific roles for women and men, lead to a differential impact of environmental factors by gender. In particular, some of women's biological markers, such as their reproductive role or their physical traits, can make them differentially and/or disproportionately impacted to environmental harm such as air pollution or toxic industrial chemicals (Arbuckle, 2006[12]); (Street et al., 2018[13]). Exposure to environmental harm can also vary between men and women, as well as their respective roles in addressing the consequences of natural hazards (Neumayer and Plümper, 2007[14]).

The other aspect of the gender-environmental sustainability nexus is the role of women in promoting sustainable production and consumption, protecting biodiversity and ensuring climate–compatible human activity. Women already play an active environmentalist role at the community and grassroots level, yet a gap in knowledge and awareness of gendered consumption patterns linked to some of the most polluting activities (heating, eating, mobility) may lead to less effective climate policies which do not tailor the need of all genders (UN WomenWatch, 2009[15]).

In addition, women's contribution to the government and business sectors is hampered by a structural governance gender gap, with few women in leadership positions. Where they are able to reach such positions, women are likely to integrate sustainability considerations into their organisation's vision and strategy (Homsy and Lambright, 2021[16]).The gender gap is largest when it comes to governance and decision-making in the sectors most determinant for achieving the nine SDGs covered in this report. For example, the infrastructure sector (water, energy, transport, housing and digital, among others), both public and private, has the highest gender employment gaps and the lowest representation of women in senior management positions (OECD, 2019[1]); (Wilson Center, 2018[17]); (IRENA, 2019[18]); (Kersley et al., 2019[19]). Given women's positive attitudes to conservation and environmental protection, this governance gap requires urgent attention if we are to accelerate progress towards the 2030 Agenda. Determined action is needed to tackle possible discrimination and bias. A greater effort to bridge gender gaps in the Science, Technology, Engineering, Mathematics (STEM) sectors is critical to its modernisation and 'greening'.

This report brings together several strands of OECD analysis to show that each of the environment-related SDGs has a different but complementary role in achieving gender equality as set out in SDG 5. It also identifies the reverse effects, i.e. how advances on gender equality, which require efforts across all SDGs, can help progress on sustainability related goals. By applying a gender equality lens, this report recognises the gender-environment nexus as a key component of the 2030 Agenda and its overarching goal of "shifting the world onto a sustainable path" and "leaving no one behind".

The report can be divided in two parts. The first part, consisting of Chapters 1-5, provides a general overview of the gender-environment nexus, looking into data and evidence gaps, economic and well-being benefits and governance and justice aspects, and includes tentative policy recommendations. The second part, consisting of Chapters 6-14, illustrates the nexus through a thematic lens by looking at each of the nine environment-related SDGs.

Each thematic chapter is structured as followed: (i) key complementarities and trade-offs that need to be taken into account to achieve gender equality and environmental sustainability goals; (ii) key challenges for gender equality due to lack of progress on environmental sustainability goals; (iii) how gender equality and women's engagement can boost environmental sustainability; and (iii) key actions to advance the gender-environment agenda and ongoing work.

Countries (OECD and non-OECD members) do not have a commonly agreed definition of "gender" nor specific categories that the term comprises. Providing such a definition is beyond the scope of this report. The report relies largely on available empirical analysis with reference to the differentiated rights, roles and attributes that women and men have in relation to environmental issues. Additional analysis on the differentiated impact of environmental factors on indigenous and other vulnerable groups are also included in some parts of the report, and stated explicitly in such cases. It is acknowledged that countries may use different terminology to describe sex- and gender- disaggregated data/statistics or indicators. For the purposes of this report, reference to sex-disaggregated data covers data acquired based on biological differences between sexes. Gender-disaggregated data refers to data that may require gender analysis beyond biological and physiological comparisons. The terms are used without prejudice to national or sub-national terminology.

It is also worth noting that intersectionality has been considered while drafting this report, as women and girls may face diverse and multiple exclusions on the basis of disability, age, race, ethnicity, religion or belief, sexuality, location, socio-economic status or other characteristic. Certain case studies in the report cover such intersectionality challenges, delving at specific situations where multiple inequalities occur, which create an even tighter link with environmental factors, for example in the case of indigenous populations. However, due to limited data availability, an intersectional approach could not be applied in all of this report's analysis.

References

Arbuckle, T. (2006), "Are there sex and gender differences in acute exposure to chemicals in the same setting?", *Environmental Research*, Vol. 101/2, http://dx.doi.org/10.1016/j.envres.2005.08.015. [12]

Ben-Amar, W., M. Chang and P. McIlkenny (2017), "Board Gender Diversity and Corporate Response to Sustainability Initiatives: Evidence from the Carbon Disclosure Project", *Journal of Business Ethics*, Vol. 142/2, pp. 369-383, http://dx.doi.org/10.1007/s10551-015-2759-1. [21]

Ben-Amar, W., M. Chang and P. McIlkenny (2017), "Board Gender Diversity and Corporate Response to Sustainability Initiatives: Evidence from the Carbon Disclosure Project", *Journal of Business Ethics*, Vol. 142/2, pp. 369-383, http://dx.doi.org/10.1007/s10551-015-2759-1. [8]

Bonewit, A. and R. Shreeves (2015), *The Gender Dimension of Climate Justice In-Depth Analysis*, http://www.europarl.europa.eu/supporting-analyses. [6]

Dankelman, I. (2010), *Gender, Environment and Sustainable Development: Understanding the Linkages*. [3]

d'Eaubonne, F. and J. Paisain (1999), *What Could an Ecofeminist Society Be?*, Indiana University Press, https://muse.jhu.edu/article/370400/pdf. [2]

Homsy, G. and K. Lambright (2021), "Beyond community characteristics: a leader's gender and local government adoption of energy conservation practices and redistributive programmes", *Local Environment*, Vol. 26/2, pp. 297-312, http://dx.doi.org/10.1080/13549839.2021.1886068. [16]

Hossain, M. et al. (2017), "Women in the boardroom and their impact on climate change related disclosure", *Social Responsibility Journal*, Vol. 13/4, pp. 828-855, http://dx.doi.org/10.1108/SRJ-11-2016-0208. [20]

Hossain, M. et al. (2017), "Women in the boardroom and their impact on climate change related disclosure", *Social Responsibility Journal*, Vol. 13/4, pp. 828-855, http://dx.doi.org/10.1108/SRJ-11-2016-0208. [7]

IRENA (2019), *Renewable Energy: A Gender Perspective*, http://www.irena.org. [18]

Kersley, R. et al. (2019), *The CS Gender 3000 in 2019: The changing face of companies*. [19]

Melero, N. and C. Solis-Espallargas (2012), "Género y Medio Ambiente: el Desafío de Educar Hacia una Dimensión Humana del Desarrollo Sustentable", https://www.researchgate.net/publication/256093864_Genero_y_medio_ambiente_el_desafio_de_educar_hacia_una_dimension_humana_del_desarrollo_sustentable?enrichId=rgreq-d2f3e0693d2bb4d574fddff4e49b397e-XXX&enrichSource=Y292ZXJQYWdlOzI1NjA5Mzg2NDtBUzoxMDIwNzcw. [11]

Neumayer, E. and T. Plümper (2007), "The Gendered Nature of Natural Disasters: The Impact of Catastrophic Events on the Gender Gap in Life Expectancy, 1981–2002", *Annals of the Association of American Geographers*, Vol. 97/3, pp. 551-566, http://dx.doi.org/10.1111/j.1467-8306.2007.00563.x. [14]

OECD (2019), "Sustainable connectivity: Closing the gender gap in infrastructure", *OECD Environment Policy Papers*, No. 15, OECD Publishing, Paris, https://dx.doi.org/10.1787/6350ba66-en. [1]

OECD (2018), *Opportunities for All: A Framework for Policy Action on Inclusive Growth*, OECD Publishing, Paris, https://dx.doi.org/10.1787/9789264301665-en. [9]

OECD (2015), *Better Policies for Development 2015: Policy Coherence and Green Growth*, OECD Publishing, Paris, https://dx.doi.org/10.1787/9789264236813-en. [10]

Street, M. et al. (2018), *Current knowledge on endocrine disrupting chemicals (EDCs) from animal biology to humans, from pregnancy to adulthood: Highlights from a national italian meeting*, MDPI AG, http://dx.doi.org/10.3390/ijms19061647. [13]

Taylor, D. (2002), *Race, Class, Gender, and American Environmentalism*, United States Department of Agriculture, Forest Service, https://www.fs.fed.us/pnw/pubs/gtr534.pdf. [5]

UN WomenWatch (2009), "Women, Gender Equality and Climate Change", *The UN Internet Gateway on Gender Equality and Empowerment of Women*. [15]

UNDP (2019), *Women Women as Environmental Stewards : The Experience of the Small Grants Programme*, https://www.undp.org/content/undp/en/home/librarypage/environment-energy/sgp/Women_as_Environmental_Stewards.html. [4]

Wilson Center (2018), *Roadmap to 50x50*, http://www.wilsoncenter.org/program/global-womens-leadership-initiative (accessed on 11 September 2020). [17]

2 Recent progress in mapping the gender-environment nexus

In recent decades, much progress has been made on the gender equality agenda. Likewise, some important decisions and actions have been taken on the environmental sustainability agenda. Yet these processes have only occasionally been brought together. The full range of interlinkages between gender and environmental goals has not been sufficiently visible or adequately prioritised in areas such as infrastructure, urban development, green jobs, innovation, and sustainable consumption. Ensuring women's presence in leadership positions in the public and private sector will be key to driving a more integrated agenda. While women often play important roles in environmental action, they are often underrepresented in the decision-making of environment-related matters and even less so areas such as finance, which ultimately define environmental outcomes. The COVID-19 pandemic has also been a dramatic reminder of how systemic gender inequalities can be exacerbated by global shocks and crises, and how closely environmental factors are linked to people's well-being. To bring together the gender and environmental sustainability agendas, the massive shortage of gender-disaggregated data needs to be addressed as a matter of urgency.

2.1. Key findings

This chapter provides a description of the state of affairs in evidence gathering and policy actions with respect to the gender-environment nexus, including the following findings:

- The United Nations SDG framework provides ample focus on stand-alone gender equality issues and environmental goals, but falls short in embedding gender equality in the nine environment-related SDGs. More could be included on the specific impact of climate change, environmental damage and biodiversity loss on women, and on the role of women in sustainable consumption. Out of the 231 unique indicators in the SDG framework, 114 have an environmental angle, and only 20 of those provide for gender-specific and/or sex disaggregation, constituting a meagre 9% of the total. The current SDG indicator framework falls short in supporting policy makers in designing gender-responsive policies and measures.
- No gender data is systematically available, even for OECD countries, for the indicators under eight of the nine environment-related SDGs. This is either because no indicator has been identified as gender-related in the SDG framework – as is the case for oceans (SDG 14) and biodiversity (SDG 15) – or because no data is available for a sufficient number of countries - as for water, sustainable production, climate, energy and cities. Data is systematically available for only one of the two unique gender-environment indicators, under SDG Target 9.5, on the share of women inventors, and on researchers per million inhabitants.
- There are a number of international initiatives to further develop gender-disaggregation of environmental data. Many of them focus on developing countries where data availability is more limited. The lack of data is a key challenge to overcome if policy makers are to leverage and address the gender-environment nexus. Further efforts are also needed in advanced economies, and there is an important role for the OECD to play.
- There is a wide spectrum of efforts across OECD countries to integrate the gender-environment nexus in policy making. Seventeen out of thirty OECD countries who replied to a survey on the nexus said they consider gender aspects in environmental policy making, either systematically or occasionally. Gender equality and women's empowerment considerations are most integrated into policies relating to climate change, green entrepreneurship and jobs (including the agricultural and forestry sectors), and women's participation and leadership in environment-related decision making.
- There are a number of policy areas that need better and more effective integration of the nexus, such as taxation, budgeting, regulatory impact assessments, development cooperation, trade and investment. As an example, and despite "women and the environment" being one of the twelve critical areas under the Beijing Platform for Action, the link is slowly being picked up by OECD DAC Members. On average, about 19.4% of total aid allocated to environment for the period 2002-2017 had a focus on gender equality. The trend is improving and the share exceeded 34% in 2017 (OECD, 2020[1]).

2.2. Parallel advances on the gender equality and environmental sustainability agendas

Collective awareness of gender inequality and its importance in public policy has grown, both nationally and internationally. There is a similar if not greater increase in awareness of environmental emergencies such as climate change, pollution, shrinking biodiversity and the growing damage to oceans and seas. These two agendas have occasionally been brought together, especially at the international level, but more could be done to enhance the interaction between gender equality and environmental sustainability.

The 2030 Agenda has laid out gender mainstreaming in the interlinkages between gender equality and all other SDGs, and as such provides an opportunity to integrate gender equality and environmental sustainability goals more systematically. Governments around the world are stepping up their sustainability actions, but the implications for and role of women are not always sufficiently addressed.

Many gender equality initiatives to address inequality have looked at the issue from an economic and social angle, focusing on discrimination, education, labour and health policies (OECD, 2017[2]). Clearly, these are *sine qua non* conditions to address and leverage the gender-environment nexus. However, the differential environment impacts on women and the effects of gender inequality on environmental outcome, as well as the specific behaviours and preferences of women, have not always been the subject of adequate research or policy focus. The full range of interlinkages between gender equality and the environmental SDGs have not been sufficiently visible or adequately prioritised. For example, gender equality perspectives are rarely a priority in infrastructure or urban development,[1] green jobs and innovation, or sustainable consumption, yet gender equality could play a significant role in delivering more sustainable outcomes and achieving the SDGs.

The COVID-19 pandemic has demonstrated how systemic gender inequalities can be exacerbated by global shocks and crises. As the OECD paper "Women at the core of the fight against the COVID crisis" shows, women make up almost 70% of the health care workforce and are exposed to a greater risk of being infected with the virus (OECD, 2020[3]). Women shoulder much of the burden at home, with school and childcare facility closings coupled with longstanding gender inequalities vis à vis unpaid work. Women also face a high risk of job and income loss, and an increased risk of violence, exploitation, abuse or harassment, in times of crisis and quarantine. Climate change and drivers of biodiversity loss such as deforestation and wildlife trade may increase the risk of further pandemics, as well as vector-borne or water-borne infections. As women and vulnerable groups are often affected most by such environmental degradation – especially in developing countries where women and girls are often responsible for providing water, food and fuel for their families using surrounding environmental resources – it is important that countries integrate a gender equality and inclusiveness perspective in their environmental action.

The socio-economic stresses of the COVID-19 pandemic and restrictions on movement have also significantly increased the risk of gender-based violence (GBV) (IUCN, 2020[4]). Women and girls are at greater risk of human and transnational sex trafficking, and child marriage. GBV is a pervasive barrier to (i) improving women's overall disproportionate vulnerability to environmental degradation, and (ii) enhancing their ability to realise their rights as leaders in conservation and environmental stewardship (Table 2.1). Programmes such as USAID's Resilient, Inclusive and Sustainable Environments (RISE) Challenge promote greater awareness of the intersection between environmental degradation and GBV. The RISE Challenge funds organisations to adapt and implement promising or proving practices to prevent and respond to GBV in other sectors to environmental programmes. It incentivises partnerships between environmental organisations, local and indigenous communities and gender and GBV experts to build an evidence base of effective interventions (USAID, 2020[5]).

Table 2.1. Interlinkages between gender-based violence and environmental issues

Environmental issues and threats that exacerbate tensions	Associated effects exacerbating gender-inequality	Gender-based violence dimensions
• Resource scarcity • Restricted access to/control over natural resources	• Food insecurity • Household stress • Inter-communal conflict	• Intimate partner violence • Child marriage • Coerced transactional sex Abduction and rape
• Deforestation • Land degradation • Land-use change • Desertification • Droughts	• Women and girls travel longer distances to collect resources, particularly when increasingly scarce/restricted • Decrease in life expectancy and quality of life	• Women and girls exposed to sexual violence and *abduction en route* • Women lose direct access to natural resources, driving economic Gender Based Violence • Child brides (Chamberlain, 2017[6])
• Unsustainable extraction • Environmental crimes • Biodiversity loss	• Land grabbing and dispossession • Militarisation • Abuse of drugs and alcohol • Migration/displacement	• Sexual violence Sex trafficking (including forced prostitution) • Women lose direct access to natural resources, driving economic Gender Based Violence
• Weather-related disasters • Sea level rise • Climate change • Climate-related conflict	• Destruction of natural resources that underpins livelihoods (driving scarcity and poverty) • Damage to infrastructure services • Displacement and disruption of /communities	• Women and children exposed to sexual and intimate partner violence in and outside of evacuation camps Inequitable access to (or availability of) recovery services, information or support • Coerced transactional sex
• Increase in ocean pollution (plastics) • Increase in land waste • Lack of clean water and sanitation	• Irreversible destruction of biodiversity • Worsened health • Lower quality of life and life-expectancy • Perpetuating social reproduction of poverty	• Women lose direct access to natural resources, driving economic Gender Based Violence
• Energy poverty • Increase in air pollution (from agriculture, transport and energy) • Pollution from Industrial processes • Increased density in cities	• Increased conflict for resources due to unsustainable resource depletion • Increase in poverty • Barriers for education (Specially for young girls - Decrease in women's empowerment due to lower education rates d • Exposure to dangerous chemicals • Lower quality of life • Lower quality of health	• Increase in gender based violence • Continued subjugation of women due to low education rates
• Unsustainable consumption and production chains	• Women's increased poverty • Lower quality of health	• Increased exploitation • Abuse of labour • Women lose direct access to natural resources, driving economic Gender Based Violence
• Discrimination in the workplace • Discrimination in environmental work	• Multiple layers of discrimination based on gender, age, ethnicity and sexual orientation • Ineffective implementation of projects Economic violence through inequity of pay, advancement and opportunity	• Sexual harassment • Sexual violence • Women lose direct access to natural resources, driving economic Gender Based Violence
• Gender-blind conservation projects	• Worsened livelihoods for local communities • Abuse of power, particularly in relation to control and management over resources • Increased community violence	• Sexual and physical violence • Sexual exploitation • Economic gender-based violence • Intimate partner violence

There are three main action channels for leveraging the gender-environment nexus: (i) enhancing more mechanisms at all levels for assessing the impact of environmental policies on women; (ii) advancing gender-responsive programming and policies to achieve sustainable development; and (iii) engaging women more in environmental decision making. This chapter reviews recent progress on the gender equality and environmental agendas, comments on the main available evidence on the gender-environment nexus, and identifies the main policy actions taken by high-income and developing countries to support the three action channels mentioned above.

2.2.1. Cross-country progress on gender equality and women's empowerment

The year 2020 marked the 25th anniversary of the Beijing Declaration and Platform for Action. Approved in 1995 by 189 countries at the Fourth World Conference on Women, the agreed text set a global policy framework for achieving gender equality and empowering women and girls around the world. The 12 critical areas of concern covered under the Beijing Declaration and Platform for Action are more pertinent than ever today. Progress has been achieved, with one billion fewer people trapped in extreme poverty since 1995, and parity in education being reached on average at the global level (UNWomen, 2020[7]). However, in the context of COVID-19, newly released data from UNDP and UN Women shows that 435 million women and girls will be living on less than USD 1.90 a day by 2021, 47 million of those as a direct result of the pandemic (Azcona et al., 2020[8]). Given that no country has achieved gender equality, recovery efforts and stimulus should be gender-inclusive. As countries reorient their priorities, it is important to embed gender equality in longer-term strategies such as environmental policies.

On a global scale, women aged 25 to 34 continue to be 25% more likely to live in extreme poverty than men. Women continue to spend over 4 hours per day on unpaid care and domestic work, whereas men only spend 1.7 hours per day on such tasks (UNWomen and UNDESA, 2019[9]). Existing gender wage gaps and glass ceilings exacerbate a persisting gender gap in labour force participation. Women all over the world experience violence, discrimination and fewer opportunities for gainful employment. Even when they have more opportunities – for example, in agriculture, forestry and fisheries women account for 39% of the workforce – women are rarely owners. Only 14% of agricultural landholders are women, making them less able to fight the effects of climate change and environmental degradation (OECD, 2019[10]); (UNWomen, 2020[7]).

The gender gap in global labour force participation came to 27% in 2019, a decrease compared to the 1990 figure of 29.1% (ILO, 2020[11]); (ILO, 2018[12]). The gender gap is widest in greenhouse gas (GHG) emissions- and energy-intensive economic sectors such as energy, transport, construction, and manufacturing processes (Section 3.4).

Women's welfare across different economic sectors could worsen as a result of the COVID-19 crisis. Not only do women make up almost 70% of the healthcare workforce, but they are also generally concentrated in lower-level health sector jobs. They represent 25% of decision-making and leadership roles and face a gender pay gap of 28% (WHO, 2019[13]); (OECD, 2020[14]).

Women make up roughly 47% of employees in the air transport industry, 53% in food and beverage services, 60% in accommodation services, and 62% in the retail sector. Such sectors that have been hit hardest by the pandemic. Women are more likely than their male counterparts to be in temporary and precarious employment. To make matters worse, the International Labour Organisation (ILO) estimates that almost 25 million jobs could disappear worldwide due to COVID-19, leading not only to a surge in overall poverty but also to a sharp increase in gender inequality (ILO, 2020[15]) .

To support the gender equality agenda, G20 countries agreed in 2014 to the "25 x 25" goal: to reduce the gap in labour force participation rates between men and women by 25% by the year 2025. The OECD, together with the ILO, has been monitoring progress on this goal. The report "Women at Work in G20 countries: Policy action since 2019", found that while the gender gap in participation has declined in almost all G20 economies, these gains are threatened by challenges associated with the COVID-19 crisis, such as the added burden of unpaid care work (ILO and OECD, 2020[16]).

Another important aspect is the gender digital divide. The OECD report "Bridging the Digital Gender Divide: Include, Upskill, Innovate" (OECD, 2018[17]) identified this divide as complex as it requires different interventions according to the specific digital technology barriers faced by women and girls.

OECD research on the social and economic facets of gender inequality has been advancing, supported by mainstreaming gender into various work streams under the OECD Gender Initiative. Work has also advanced on integrating gender equality in OECD databases, including through gender indicators on employment, education, entrepreneurship, health, development and governance tracked within the OECD Gender Data Portal and OECD.Stat for OECD Member countries and selected non-Members. This data enables tracking progress on the OECD Gender Recommendations: the 2013 *Recommendation on Gender Equality in Education, Employment, and Entrepreneurship* and the 2015 *Recommendation on Gender Equality in Public Life* (Box 2.1). In 2017, the OECD Ministerial Council meeting identified three urgent gender equality issues: violence against women, the gender wage gap, and unequal sharing of household tasks (OECD, 2017[2]).

Box 2.1. The OECD Gender Recommendations

The OECD Gender Recommendations are rooted in the OECD Gender Initiative, which started in 2010, the All on Board for Inclusive Growth initiative, launched in 2012, and the understanding that, despite existing policies, "significant gender disparities and biases nevertheless remain in educational and occupational choices; earning levels and working conditions; career progression; representation in decision-making positions; in public life; in the uptake of paid and unpaid work; in entrepreneurial activities; in access to finance for entrepreneurs; and in financial literacy and financial empowerment" (OECD, 2017[18]).

The *Recommendation on Gender Equality in Education, Employment, and Entrepreneurship*, adopted in May 2013, sets out a number of measures that Adherents should consider implementing in order to address gender inequalities in education, employment and entrepreneurship (OECD, 2017[18]). In particular, it recommends that Adherents should – through appropriate legislation, policies, monitoring, and campaigning – ensure equal access to education; better enable female labour force participation; promote family-friendly policies; foster greater male uptake of unpaid work; work toward better gender balance in positions of public and private sector leadership; and promote entrepreneurship among women.

The *Recommendation on Gender Equality in Public Life*, adopted by the OECD Council in 2015, is grounded upon the understanding that government actions have an enormous capacity to strengthen or weaken gender equality and diversity in OECD economies and societies (OECD, 2016[19]). The Recommendation focuses on effective governance and the implementation of gender equality objectives and gender mainstreaming measures, including gender budgeting, inclusive public procurement and regulatory cycles. It recommends that Adherents strengthen accountability and oversight mechanisms for gender equality and mainstream initiatives across and within government bodies. It also recommends actionable guidelines to enhance women's equal access to opportunities in service and judicial appointments. The 2018 "Toolkit on Implementing and Mainstreaming Gender Equality" presents a palette of policy options, tools, self-assessment questions and good practices as a practical road map to support countries in the implementation of the 2015 Gender Recommendation.

Important progress has been made following the OECD Gender Recommendations: two-thirds of adhering countries have implemented new equal pay policies, including transparency measures and wage gaps analyses. Nine Member countries have introduced compulsory gender quotas in board membership positions, and many countries have implemented quotas to increase women's participation in politics. Some countries, such as Austria and France, have reinforced their anti-harassment laws, while others, such as Greece and Korea, are increasing awareness-raising campaigns about sexual harassment, its prevention, and victims' rights. Initiatives to extend the length of paternity leave have been introduced in some countries, for instance in Spain (OECD, 2017[20]).

Nevertheless, major gender gaps persist. In OECD countries, in 2018, women at the median still earned 13% less than men (OECD, 2020[21]); the gender wage gap has not evolved much since 2010 (OECD, 2020[14]). Women only hold 21.4% of land assets (OECD, 2019[10]) and their pension payments are about 25% lower than men's (OECD, 2019[22]). Women in OECD Member countries held 30% of seats in Parliament in 2019, showing a slow increase in representation since 2012 (OECD, 2019[23]). Women represented 31.2% of ministers, 33% of Supreme Court judges (OECD, 2019[23]), and on average 5% of mayors in nine OECD countries – ranging from 0% to 32%. Clearly, women's voices in designing national and local policies and ensuring equality in the judicial system is lacking (OECD, 2017[24]).

Following the G20/OECD Principles of Corporate Governance, OECD, G20 and Financial Stability Board member countries adopted measures to ensure more equal gender composition in corporate boards and senior management positions. Almost half of the 49 jurisdictions examined by the OECD 2019 Corporate Governance Factbook have introduced requirements or regulatory measures for disclosing gender composition of boards, yet only 22% require such disclosures for the gender composition of senior management. Jurisdictions that have introduced mandatory or voluntary quotas for more gender diversity remain the minority. Data from 2017 on the actual participation of women on boards show that in some cases quotas or targets are still not met. Women tend to be more present in senior management positions, occupying over 15% of managerial positions in 37 of the 49 jurisdictions covered, and over 15% of board positions in only 26 of the 49 jurisdictions covered (OECD, 2019[25])

Across OECD countries, women disproportionately bear the burden of unpaid domestic work and caregiving. They spend on average almost 18% of their time on such work, whereas the equivalent time spent by men is about 9% (OECD, 2020[14]). With paid and unpaid work time combined, women work on average 25 minutes more per day than men (OECD, 2020[14]). Despite a stable decrease in the average gender employment gap over the last decade, women still have lower employment rates than men in OECD countries (61% versus 76% in 2019, employment ratio for population aged 15 to 64), (OECD, 2017[2]). The gap appears to be wider in developing countries (Ferrant and Thim, 2019[26]).

Women are 1.5 times more likely to be denied financing to start a business in seven EU states (Halabisky, 2018[27]). Women-led start-ups are systematically less likely to attract venture capital funding (Breschi, Lassébie and Menon, 2018[28]). The 2018 OECD survey *Risks that Matter* found that women were more likely than men to believe that government does not incorporate their views when designing or reforming public benefits, and were less satisfied overall with access to public services and income support (OECD, 2019[29]).

With few exceptions, women and girls in low and middle income countries are subject to a much higher degree of discrimination, more legal constraints and limited economic opportunities, compared to those in OECD countries. Discrimination against women is greater overall for access to land assets, when compared to access to non-land assets and formal financial services. Access to land and non-land assets is most limited in lower middle income countries (LMICs), followed by low income countries (LICs), upper middle income countries (UMICs) and high income countries (HICs). Discrimination against women accessing formal financial services is highest in LICs, followed by LMICs, UMICs and HICs (Figure 2.1).

Figure 2.1. Women face restricted access to land and non-land assets, and to formal financial services

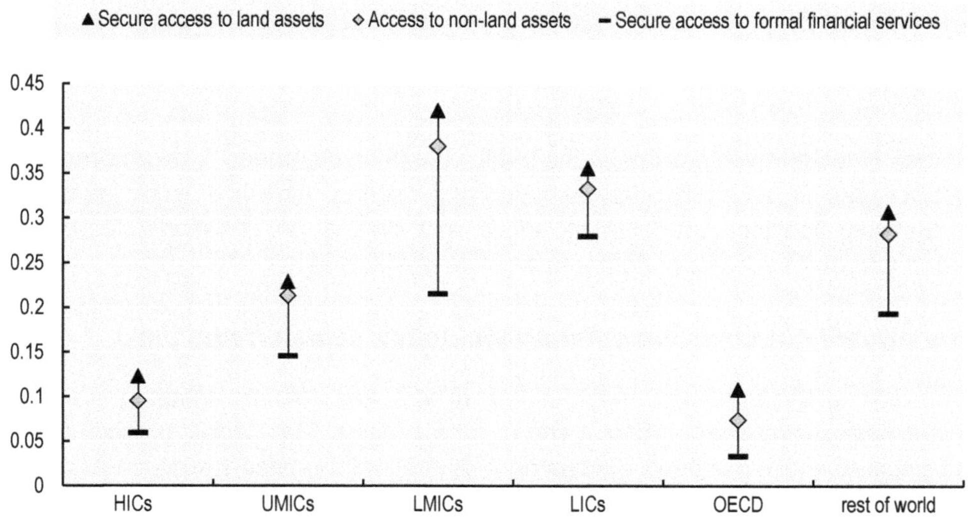

Note: Restricted Access to Productive and Financial Resources sub-index information on three indicators: secure access to land assets, secure access to non-land assets and secure access to formal financial services. Ranking range from 0 for no discrimination to 1 for very high discrimination.
Source: (OECD, 2019[10]), Gender, Institutions and Development Database, accessed 23 May 2020.

The OECD, together with UN Women and the World Bank, is a co-custodian of SDG indicator 5.1.1: whether or not legal frameworks are in place to promote, enforce and monitor equality and non-discrimination on the basis of sex. As such, it manages a database of discriminatory social institutions affecting women's and girls' lives. The Social Institutions Gender Index (SIGI) describes such institutions as "restricting [women's and girls'] access to justice, rights and empowerment opportunities," thus "undermining their agency and decision-making authority" (OECD, 2020[30]). This affects women's status and perpetuates gender gaps in important areas such as education, employment, health, politics and access to credit.

Based on the latest SIGI Global Report, discrimination is higher where women's integration in the labour market is more limited (OECD, 2019[31]). Although 164 countries acknowledge women's right to own, use and manage land, only 52 countries meet their legal requirements by putting such a right into practice. Strong customary laws and weak law enforcement and implementation perpetuate this gap, as women tend not to exercise their rights (OECD, 2019[31]). In developing countries, women account for only 15% of agricultural landholders (OECD, 2019[31]) but represent 43% of the agricultural labour force.

Trends are similar for non-land assets. In 42% of the 180 countries examined, women are guaranteed equal property rights, yet in 34 countries, men are the sole administrators of a couple's marital property. In 29% of countries, women face restricted legal rights to property and other non-land assets after a divorce or separation. Moreover, many women suffer from multiple forms of discrimination, including discrimination against women living with HIV/AIDS, women with disabilities, rural women, older women, female-headed households, indigenous women and women belonging to minority groups. The legal frameworks governing property and assets of 27 countries do not apply to all groups of women. For instance, in Latin America and the Caribbean, indigenous women are less likely to access legal documentation such as birth certificates, which are a prerequisite for purchasing property and other non-land assets (OECD, 2019[32]).

Women's access to formal financial services is widely guaranteed by law. In 98% of countries, women have equal access to credit and opening a bank account. But in practice, varying levels of discrimination persist in countries where customary laws prevent women from getting a financial education, accessing credit by themselves, and or making household financial decisions (OECD, 2019[31]).

2.3. Women in the driver's seat – leading the debate and decisions in the public and private spheres

Advancing women in leadership positions in the public and private spheres is paramount to ensuring that gender equality is mainstreamed in policy and decision making. And vice-versa: gender equality and diversity can provide additional benefits to public and private organisations, leading to improved performance and productivity levels (Offermann and Foley, 2020[33]).

2.3.1. Gender equality in environmental public policy decision making

Public decision-making systems and mechanisms play a key role in ensuring that all voices are represented when discussing environmental and climate policies. More equal participation of women in public life and decision making around environment- and climate-related issues could result not only in more gender-sensitive and gender-responsive policies, but also in women's greater economic empowerment and more effective solutions to climate change (Bonewit and Shreeves, 2015[34]).

The 2014 OECD Report "Women's Access to Public Life" shows that gender diversity in decision-making bodies enhances the promotion of women's and children's interests and generates more public trust. Gender diversity in the judicial system also improves the quality of decisions taken, and upholds the legitimacy of courts. Women jurists more typically advance gender-responsive decisions on actions directed against women (OECD/CAWTAR, 2014[35]).

Women are increasingly represented in high-level public policy positions linked to environmental decision making in OECD countries. In May 2020, women occupied more than 40% of positions (OECD average) as Ministers of Environment, National Focal Points for the United Nations Convention to Combat Desertification (UNCCD), and National Focal Points for the United Nations Framework Convention on Climate Change (UNFCCC) (Figure 2.2). Women exceeded men as National Focal Points for the Convention on Biological Diversity (CBD), supporting the argument that women are more active in issues relating to biodiversity, both on the ground and in decision making.

Figure 2.2. Environment-related high-level representation by gender in OECD countries, 2020

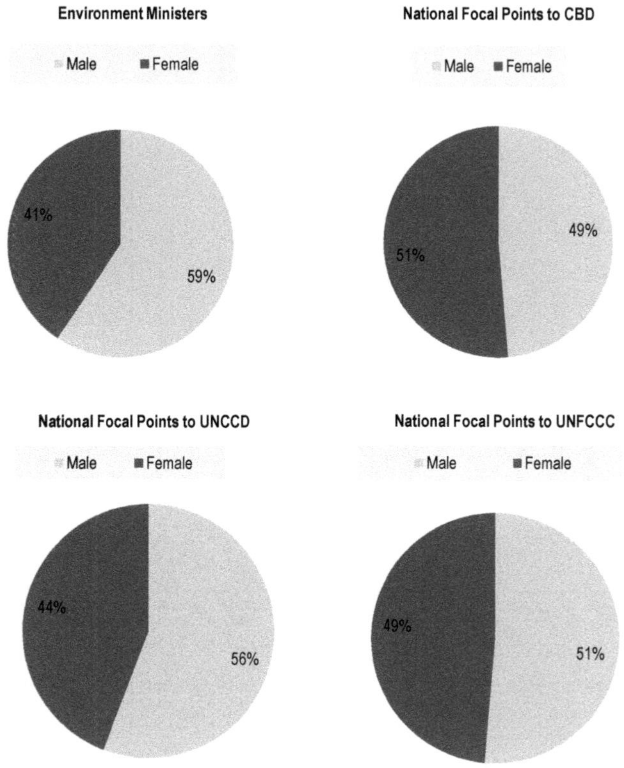

Note: Where more than one Focal Points are appointed per country, the gender of the most senior is taken into consideration. Information is not available for National Focal Points to UNCCD for Canada, Luxembourg and New Zealand.
Source: Authors research for Environment Ministers; for CBD: https://www.cbd.int/doc/lists/nfp-cbd.pdf; for UNCCD: https://knowledge.unccd.int/home/country-information/overview-countries-unccd-annex; for UNFCCC: https://unfccc.int/process/parties-non-party-stakeholders/parties/national-focal-point (accessed 24 May 2020).

Women's participation in national representations of OECD countries to Conferences of the Parties to the UNFCCC (COP) meetings between 2008 and 2019 also showed an upward trend (Figure 2.3). Australia, Colombia, Estonia, Finland, Latvia, Lithuania, Spain, Sweden and the United Kingdom surpassed, on average, 50% representation of women over that period. Latvia, Lithuania and Spain maintained a female participation level of over 40%. Chile's delegation was led by a woman at nine COP meetings, followed by Sweden's eight times. In contrast, Austria, Ireland, Japan, Slovak Republic and Turkey did not appoint a woman to lead their COP delegation between 2008 and 2019.

Figure 2.3. Women's participation in COP as country representatives for OECD countries

Percentage of women per national delegation

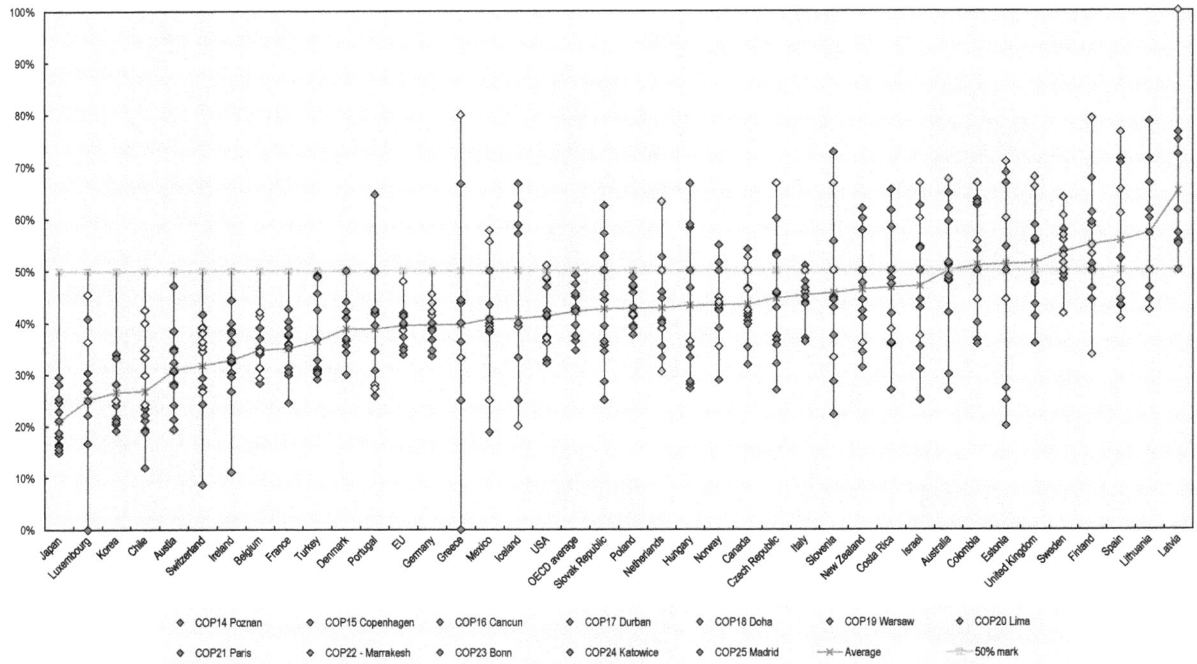

Note: Women's participation to the annual Conference of the Parties to the UN Framework Convention on Climate Change (COP) for the period 2008-2019.Yellow diamonds indicate a woman was heading the delegation. Red line projects average value per country. OECD average includes all OECD Members at the time of writing, for all years. Costa Rica and EU not included in OECD average calculations.
Source: Gender Climate Tracker, Women's Environment and Development Organization, accessed 5 June 2020.

Despite relatively good levels of women in environmental and environment-related positions, women are largely under-represented in high-level public positions of finance and infrastructure planning. In June 2020, only 4 out of 37 OECD Member countries had women heading their government's finance portfolio (less than 11%). As such, national agenda setting, finance and budget allocation, as well as land-use and construction prioritisation, still remain largely in the hands of men.

Gender-balanced representation is equally important for achieving parity in the decision-making bodies of climate mechanisms and funds. Guaranteeing women's equal representation in these bodies may lead to more gender-responsive selection and financing of projects. Despite the fact that women are the majority of the world's poor and are highly affected by climate change, parity has not yet been achieved in some of these mechanisms and funds (Figure 2.4).

Figure 2.4. Percentage of women's participation in climate mechanisms and funds

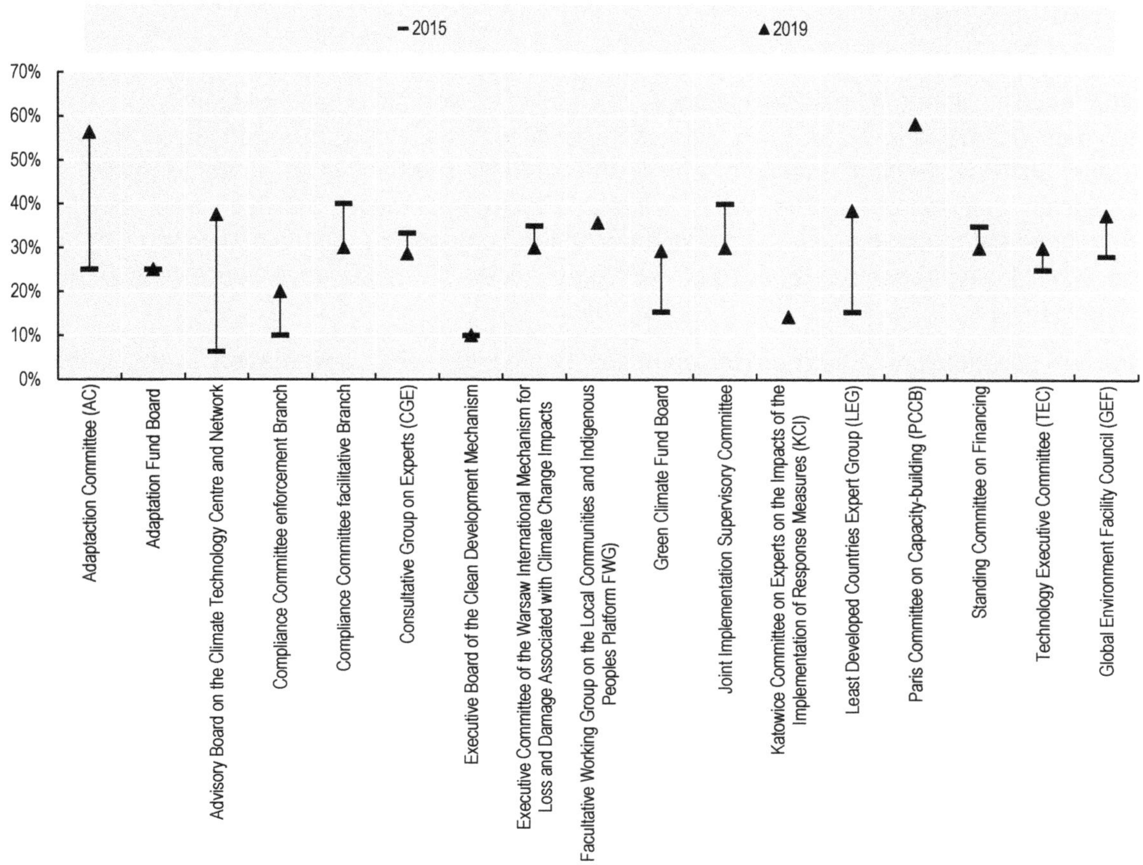

Source: Gender Climate Tracker, Women's Environment and Development Organization; GEF data analysed by authors (accessed 5 June 2020)

Women and men often have different policy priorities. In an attempt to capture gender differences on national budget issues addressed by parliamentary bodies, a 2018 study by 50:50 Parliament reviewed 1.2 million interventions in the UK House of Commons and 500 000 interventions in the US House of Representatives. The results demonstrated that women of all political parties spent more time than their male counterparts addressing environment-related topics (D'souza, 2018[36]).

Studies show that countries with higher proportions of women in parliament are more likely to endorse environmental treaties and policies. Women were found to be more environmentally risk-averse than men, to have a more negative perception of nuclear power and waste, and to represent the vast majority (60% to 80%) of membership in mainstream environmental organisations (Norgaard and York, 2005[37]).

2.3.2. Women as brokers of environmental sustainability in private sector leadership

Promoting gender balance in corporate boards and senior management positions not only supports good corporate governance, but also helps business to grow, to perform better and to improve its environmental outcomes. Companies with at least one female director generate on average 3.5% higher returns on equity than those with no female directors (Kersley et al., 2019[38]). Companies with more than 20% of woman senior managers perform better by 3.6% when compared to companies with less than 15% woman managers (Kersley et al., 2019[38]). Increasing women's participation in upper-level management positions results in better performance even when compared to women's participation in boards (supervisory roles) (Kersley et al., 2019[38]).

Gender diversity can improve a company's reputation and employee retention. Improving a company's gender equality sends a positive message internally, to workforce, and externally, to investors and consumers (Kamalnath, 2015[39]). It also represents legitimacy and trustworthiness for stakeholders (Perrault, 2015[40]), as the presence of women in leadership positions is positively correlated with ethical and social compliance (Isidro and Sobral, 2015[41]). Gender balance also helps minimise governance-related controversies: in a study of 2 400 companies monitored between 2012 and 2015, those with at least three female board members experienced 24% fewer governance-related controversies than the average.

Increased participation of women on company boards can shift governance styles, enhancing the collective, collaborative decision making usually required from boards of directors (Kamalnath, 2015[39]). Yet, women's participation in boards remains below 30% in OECD countries (median) (Figure 2.5). According to the OECD Analytical Database on Individual Multinationals and their Affiliates (ADIMA), women make up only 16% of board members in the top 500 multinational companies (see also Chapter 9).

Figure 2.5. Women's participation in boards remains below 30% in OECD countries (median)

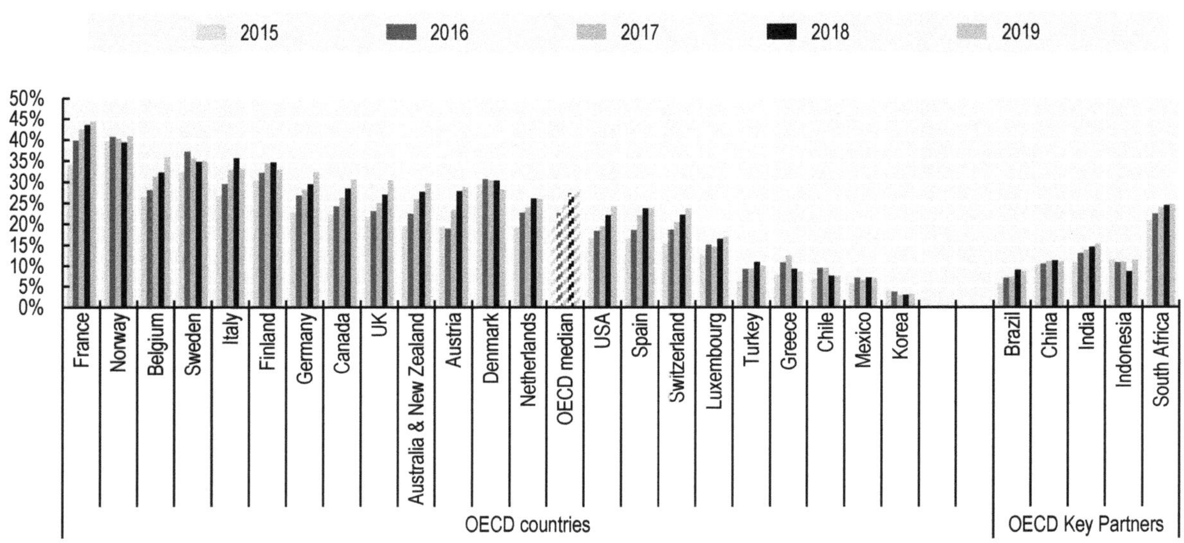

Note: Information available for 23 OECD member countries. OECD median calculated based on data available.
Source: Authors calculations based on data available at (Kersley et al., 2019[42])

Achieving greater gender diversity on company boards and in senior management positions could bring about an acceleration towards the green transition, as it would allow for more effective integration of environmental and gender goals. Analysis shows that decision makers are highly influenced not only by their education and background, but also by their experiences and social considerations. Increasing the number of board members with experience in environmental sustainability would increase the probability that related issues will be introduced in the agenda (Walls and Hoffman, 2013[43]).

Firms with three or more female members in their board of directors show more environmental corporate social responsibility in issues such as pollution prevention, emissions reduction, use of recycled materials in production, use of clean energy, commitment to energy efficiency measures, and environment-related reporting, as women are overall more attentive towards environment-related issues (Post, Rahman and

Rubow, 2011[44]). There is evidence that the higher the number of female directors in a company's board, the more carbon-related information may be disclosed (Hossain et al., 2017[45]).

According to the OECD's ADIMA database, the percentage of female board members in the energy sector is low (14%). 2019 data from Credit Suisse on 30 000 executive positions in 3 000 companies across 56 countries shows that only about 2% of companies in the energy sector have a female Chief Executive Officer (CEO) and just over 9% have a female Chief Financial Officer (CFO) (Figure 2.6). In 2010, in Germany, Spain and Sweden, 64% of energy companies had no women in their senior management or board of directors (Carlsson-Kanyama, Lindén and Thelander, 1999[46]). Equal by 30, an initiative of the Clean Energy Ministerial, examined 68 energy companies in 2018 and found that on average only 18% of management positions were held by women. Equal by 30 member countries are introducing mentorship programmes where female senior managers can help newcomers in the clean energy sector advance in their careers (C3E International, 2019[47]).

Figure 2.6. Women in management by economic sector

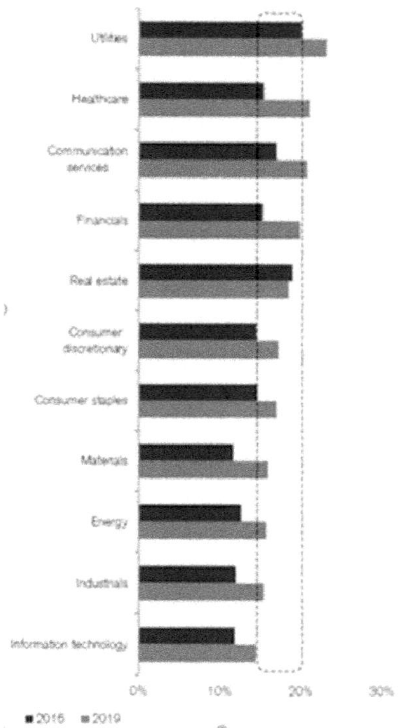

Source: (Kersley et al., 2019[42])

The G20/OECD Principles on Corporate Governance, endorsed by G20 leaders in 2015, propose the introduction of targets to further increase gender diversity on boards and senior management, and many OECD countries have already introduced relevant provisions (OECD, 2019[25]). The EU has also introduced new guidelines for disclosure of information on the presence of women in senior management and boards of directors. Considering the interlinkages between gender diversity and climate-related disclosure of information, it would be appropriate to consider an integrated gender-responsive policy framework that could support the private sector transition to lower-carbon economy practices. More research on environment-related sectors, and female participation in the workforce and senior management positions, as well as how this links to companies' transitions to lower-carbon solutions, would assist policy makers in better defining future possible initiatives and measures in integrating gender considerations in environmental policies.

2.4. Advances on environmental goals and the SDGs

With less than ten years left before the 2030 deadline to achieve the SDGs, countries around the world are developing national frameworks based on the UN's global indicator framework, which measures progress on reaching the 169 targets (United Nations, n.d.[48]). The framework currently comprises 247 indicators, 231 of which are unique (United Nations, n.d.[49]).[2]

A recent UNEP report analysing 93 environment-related indicators across all SDGs found that progress has been made in only in 23% of them. For the majority of indicators examined (68%), there is insufficient data to evaluate progress on biodiversity, ecosystems, water efficiency, pollution reduction and waste management. For the remaining 9%, there appears to be negative trends in progress made on forest areas, sustainable fisheries, endangered species, sustainable consumption, and material footprint (UNEP, 2019[50]).

Despite an improvement in access to electricity (indicator for Target 7.1), there are still 860 million people around the world without access, 80% of whom live in sub-Saharan Africa (IEA, 2020[51]). Total global GHG emissions (indicator for Target 13.2) reached an all-time annual high in 2018 (UNEP, 2019[52]). Based on the latest FAO data, the global proportion of fish stocks respecting biologically sustainable levels (indicator for Target 14.4) continues to diminish (FAO, 2020[53]). In 2018, 16.1 million people were displaced due to storms, floods, droughts, wildfires, landslides and extreme temperatures (IDMC, 2019[54]). The Intergovernmental Science-Policy Platform on Biodiversity and Ecosystem Services marks negative trends in biodiversity and ecosystems, which are expected to limit progress to 80% of the targets related to poverty, health, hunger, water, climate, oceans and land (IPBES, 2019[55]). The COVID-19 pandemic and recent findings on the correlation between increasing air pollution exposure and vulnerability to infectious virus may further derail progress on air quality and environmental health (Chapter 3).

OECD analysis of Member countries' distance to achieving the SDGs shows that the gender equality targets under SDG 5 are the farthest from being reached. Distances are shorter for the targets of the nine environment-related goals, but lack of data for many indicators implies high uncertainty about countries' performance levels, especially on goals for sustainable production, oceans and cities (Figure 2.7) (OECD, 2019[56]). Moreover, like the SDG targets and indicators themselves, the reporting exercise does not capture non-linearities in environmental damage timelines such as feedback loops in climate change. In other words, the indicators do not account for cascading impacts of climate change that can lead to additional effects, for example when extra water vapour in the air amplifies the initial warming (WRI, 2018[57]). Therefore, though distances to targets may seem small, real achievement of environmental sustainability may be further away than calculated.

Figure 2.7. OECD countries' average distance to targets by SDG

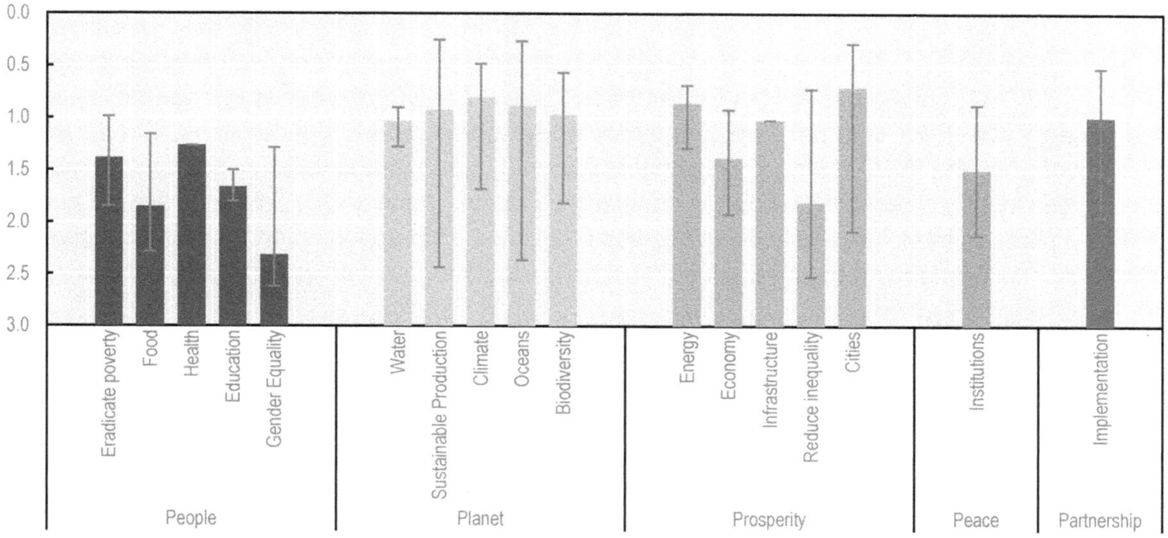

Note: This figure shows the average distance OECD countries need to travel to reach each SDG. Distances are measured in standardised units, from 0 indicating that the 2030 level has already been attained, to 3 as most OECD countries have already reached this distance. Bars show OECD countries' average performance against all targets under the relevant Goal for which data are available. Whiskers show uncertainties due to missing data, based on the alternative assumptions that either missing indicators are 3 standardised distances away from the 2030 target or that they are all already at the target level. Longer whiskers indicate larger data gaps.
Source: (OECD, 2019[56]).

2.5. The large data deficit on the gender-environment nexus

A basic challenge for addressing and leveraging the gender-environment nexus is gathering the necessary evidence for informed policy decisions. While there is a large body of evidence on the gender-environment nexus in developing countries from case studies and project reports by UN bodies, other international organisations and NGOs, systematic data collection is in short supply. With few exceptions, the nexus is largely absent from domestic policy debates on gender equality and environmental sustainability in OECD countries, and data collection initiatives are scant.

2.5.1. The gender- environment nexus is largely missing in the nine environment-related SDGs and current indicators framework

The gender dimension is largely missing from the nine environment-related SDGs and the existing indicators framework. While data availability is a major limitation, the framework itself does not adequately capture the interlinkages between environmental and gender goals. Hence, the agreed SDG indicators fall short in capturing the extent to which SDG targets are gender-responsive or could be linked to women's and girls' empowerment. A stronger focus on the gender-environment nexus in the SDG framework, and possible development of additional indicators that encapsulate it, would strengthen focus amongst policy makers and other stakeholders (Box 2.2).

Time frame may play a role in the gender-environment nexus being under-recognised. Some of the SDG indicators have no direct link to environmental policies or environment-related effects on women and men in the short term, though such links could emerge from a longer-term perspective. Further methodological work in this area could therefore include an indirect mapping approach and a gender-environment assessment of other indicators beyond those already identified under the gender-environment nexus.

Box 2.2. Gender-disaggregation for the SDGs under the United Nations system

The Global Gender Statistics Programme, supported by the Inter-Agency and Expert Group on Gender Statistics (IAEG-GS) of the United Nations Statistics Division (UNSD), examines key gender issues that have arisen since 2006, and develops proposals to overcome related gender gaps. Gender-related topics covered by the IAEG-GS encompass statistics on (i) birth and death; (ii) migration; (iii) marriage and divorce; (iv) population registers; (v) population size and density; (vi) time use series; and (vii) violence against women. The IAEG-GS is developing guidance to support countries' statistics gathering on time-use, acknowledging the difficulties and peculiarities that may be faced by different countries.

Since the adoption of the 2030 Agenda in 2016, the United Nations Department of Economic and Social Affairs (UNDESA) has maintained a data hub, Women and Sustainable Development: Building a Better Future for All, supported by countries such as Ireland, UNDESA provides insights based on national and subnational data provided under three categories: (i) women's economic empowerment, focusing mainly on women's labour force participation and breaking poverty chains; (ii) women's voice, focusing on women's participation in government and public office positions; and (iii) women's safety and human rights, providing data on SDG indicators 5.2.1 (Proportion of ever-partnered women and girls subjected to physical and sexual violence by a current or former intimate partner in the previous 12 months), 5.3.1 (Proportion of women aged 20-24 years who were married or in a union before age 18), and 5.3.2 (Proportion of girls and women aged 15-49 years who have undergone female genital mutilation/cutting, by age). In fact, Ireland recognises all SDG indicator sets (UN, EU, OECD and ILO) and strives to keep up to date with all developments in this complex space.

Moreover, the Inter-Agency and Expert Group on the SDGs (IAEG-SDG) has developed a dedicated work stream striving for data disaggregation for all SDG indicators. Sex is defined as a disaggregation dimension for all SDGs, except for SDG 6 (Clean water and sanitation), SDG 14 (Life below water) and SDG 15 (Life on land). It should be noted, however, that SDG Target 6.2 (By 2030, achieve access to adequate and equitable sanitation and hygiene for all and end open defecation, paying special attention to the needs of women and girls and those in vulnerable situations) already references the needs of women and girls. In total, the IAEG-SDG proposes a minimum set of gender-disaggregation even for several SDG indicators with no specific reference to gender, sex or women, and identifies future additional disaggregation countries should aim for. Still, only eight SDG environment-related indicators have been identified where data is expected to be produced; and five for possible future additional disaggregation.

Source: (UNDESA, n.d.[58]); (UNSD, n.d.[59]); (UNSD, n.d.[60])

A UNEP analysis of the 2019 list of SDG indicators identified at least 93 environment-related indicators across all SDGs. It did not, however, include all indicators that may refer to environment-related sectors such as agriculture, tourism, manufacturing, innovation, and decent work (part of which could cover green jobs and a just transition) (UNEP, 2019[50]).

UN Women identified 54 gender-related indicators in the 2018 list, defining them as those that specifically address women and girls, or where gender-disaggregated data is required. But this approach left out SDG indicators that could cover economic benefits for environment and gender, such as for access to electricity (SDG indicator 7.1.1), clean fuels and technology (SDG indicator 7.1.2), and adequate housing (SDG indicator 11.1.1) (UNWomen, 2018[61]).

Of the 93 environment-related indicators identified by UNEP, only 7 overlap with UN Women's list, as shown in Table 2.2 below. In other words, under the (UNEP, 2019[50]) and (UNWomen, 2018[61]) indicator groupings, the environment-related indicators which specifically address women and girls or require gender disaggregation represent only 3% of the 231 unique SDG indicators.

Table 2.2. SDG indicators identified under the gender-environment nexus (based on UNEP and UN Women)

Indicator	Indicator Label
1.4.2	Proportion of total adult population with secure tenure rights to land, with legally recognized documentation and who perceive their rights to land as secure, by sex and by type of tenure
4.7.1	Extent to which (i) global citizenship education and (ii) education for sustainable development, including gender equality and human rights, are mainstreamed at all levels in: (a) national education policies, (b) curricula, (c) teacher education and (d) student assessment
5.a.1	(a) Proportion of total agricultural population with ownership or secure rights over agricultural land, by sex; and (b) share of women among owners or rights-bearers of agricultural land, by type of tenure
8.9.2	Number of jobs in tourism industries as a proportion of total jobs and growth rate of jobs, by sex
11.2.1	Proportion of population that has convenient access to public transport, by sex, age and persons with disabilities;
11.7.1	Average share of the built-up area of cities that is open space for public use for all, by sex, age and persons with disabilities
13.b.1	Number of least developed countries and small island developing States that are receiving specialized support, and amount of support, including finance, technology and capacity-building, for mechanisms for raising capacities for effective climate change-related planning and management, including focusing on women, youth and local and marginalized communities

Note: The UNEP report and UN Women report on which this analysis is based do not cover the latest 2020 Comprehensive Review changes made by IAEG-SDG on the global indicator framework for the SDGs. Since these reports were issued, SDG indicator 8.9.2 has been deleted from the framework; and SDG indicator 13.b.1 has been revised.

Source: Authors computations based on (UNEP, 2019[50]) and (UNWomen, 2018[61]).

By applying a gender lens to the methodology used in *Measuring the Distance to SDG Targets* (OECD, 2019[56]), the OECD assessed the distances to SDG targets for women and girls. The working paper "How far are OECD countries from achieving SDG targets for women and girls?" includes several approaches for identifying gender-related indicators, following the UN's global SDG indicator framework as closely as possible and adding OECD data when relevant (Box 2.3). Based on preliminary analysis, 102 of the 247 indicators in the SDG indicator framework are identified as gender-relevant. That is equivalent to 41% and almost double the amount identified in the UN Women analysis (Cohen and Shinwell, 2020[62]).

Box 2.3. Identifying gender-related indicators under the Measuring the Distance to SDG Targets methodology

The OECD working paper "How far are OECD countries from achieving SDG targets for women and girls?: Applying a gender lens to measuring distance to SDG targets" bases its analysis on a dual approach, using both a text analysis of the indicators, as well as an indicator classification. An indicator is deemed to be gender-related if the indicator's name includes gender-related terms (e.g. men, women, boy, girl, gender, etc.). In addition, as some gender-relevant indicators do not refer explicitly to gender, the indicators were also classified manually according to individual-level disaggregation and gender-relevance. It should, however, be noted that there are inconsistencies between the indicator text and the disaggregation, most notably on Health (SDG 3), where most indicators are measured at the individual-level and could thus be measured for women and men (or for women only), but are not identified as gender-relevant according to the text analysis, i.e. do not have gender relevant wording. It should also be clarified that, even if the relevant SDG target is gender-relevant but the indicators are not, then these indicators are excluded from the analysis.

Source: (Cohen and Shinwell, 2020[62])

Figure 2.8 shows that these gender-relevant indicators are unevenly spread across the 17 SDGs. Most gender-relevant indicators are identified for Goals on Eradicating Poverty, Health, Education, Gender Equality, Economy, and Institutions (SDGs 1, 3, 4, 5, 8 and 16). The share of gender-relevant indicators varies widely across Goals. Unsurprisingly, all indicators are gender-relevant within Gender Equality (SDG 5), 82% within Health (SDG 3), 75% within Education (SDG 4), a mere 4% within Partnerships (SDG 17), and none within 3 Planet Goals (SDGs 12, 14 and 15).

Figure 2.8. Number of gender-related indicators in the UN global SDG indicator framework by Goal

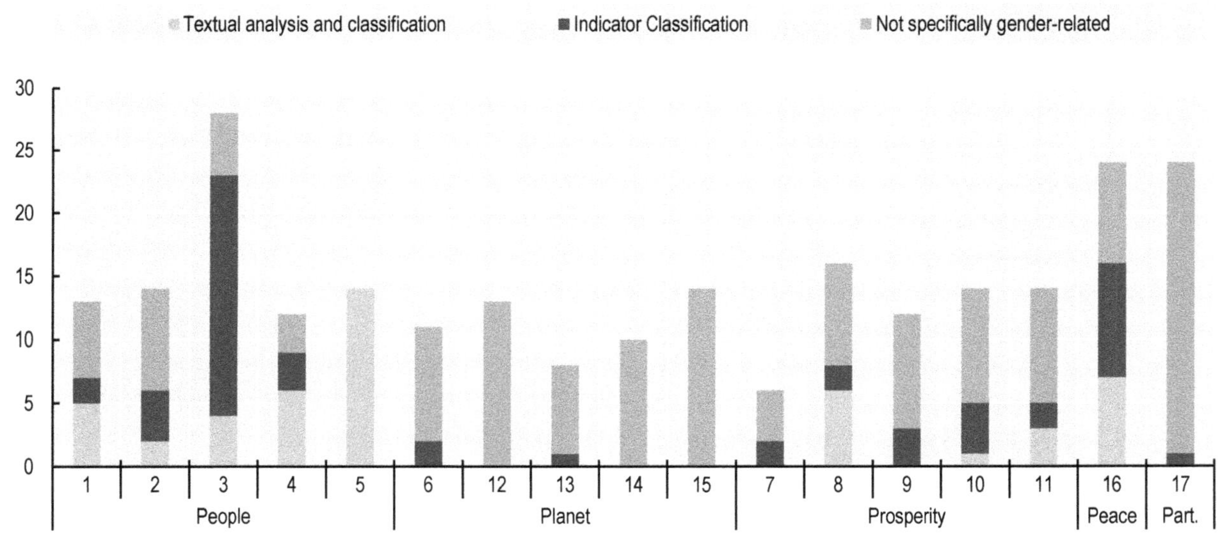

Note: The figure shows the indicators in the UN Global Indicator Framework which are identified as gender relevant in the analysis in (Cohen and Shinwell, 2020[62]). Each bar represents one of the Goals in order from 1 to 16. Light green bars represent indicators identified by both indicator classification and textual analysis, dark red bars represent indicators identified by the indicator classification only. Light blue bars represent indicators identified as not specifically gender related.

Source: UN Global Indicator Framework for the SDGs as presented in (Cohen and Shinwell, 2020[62])

The SDG framework's environment-related indicators go well beyond the Planet goals and other environment-related SDGs. To determine the environment-related indicators the following criteria were set: (i) indicator to include a textual reference to the environment, sustainability, nature, natural resources, biodiversity, conservation, ecosystems, disasters, pollution, water and sanitation, climate adaptation, waste and material management; (ii) indicator to be classified under sustainable resource management, climate change, circular economy, environmental health, natural disaster prevention, sustainable production and consumption, sustainable infrastructure, and green finance and investment. Following this strict methodology, 97 environment-related indicators were identified, much in line with the UNEP methodology.

Alternatively, when the methodology is broadened to include indicators: (i) which cover economic or other activities where sustainability could be envisaged (agriculture, energy, infrastructure, tourism, manufacturing); and (ii) for which data could be extracted, if available, for environment-related fields (such as eco-innovation) or the transition to a low carbon economy (green jobs), a total of 112 environment-related indicators were identified. That is 45% of the 247 indicators under the UN Global indicator framework for the SDGs, and 19 more than found using the UNEP methodology. The OECD methodology's broader categorisation of SDG indicators as gender- or environment-related has to do with the interconnectedness and spillover effects between the social, environmental and economic dimensions of the SDG Framework.

A cross-examination of the 102 gender-related and 112 environment-related indicators to identify the gender-environment intersections produces a shortlist of only 22 SDG indicators, which cover the gender-environment nexus (Table 2.3). That is just below 9% of the full set of 247 SDG indicators (more in Annex A). Differently phrased, only 20 of the 231 (8.7%) unique environment-related indicators in the SDG Framework can be disaggregated by gender or categorised as environmental indicators relevant to gender policies according to the SDG Framework (because their texts address gender).

Table 2.3. SDG indicators identified under the gender-environment nexus

Based on OECD analysis

1.4.2	Proportion of total adult population with secure tenure rights to land, (a) with legally recognized documentation, and (b) who perceive their rights to land as secure, by sex and type of tenure
1.5.1, 11.5.1, 13.1.1	Number of deaths, missing persons and directly affected persons attributed to disasters per 100,000 population
2.3.2	Average income of small-scale food producers, by sex and indigenous status
3.9.1	Mortality rate attributed to household and ambient air pollution
3.9.2	Mortality rate attributed to unsafe water, unsafe sanitation and lack of hygiene (exposure to unsafe Water, Sanitation and Hygiene for All (WASH) services)
3.9.3	Mortality rate attributed to unintentional poisoning
5.a.1	(a) Proportion of total agricultural population with ownership or secure rights over agricultural land, by sex; and (b) share of women among owners or rights-bearers of agricultural land, by type of tenure
5.a.2	Proportion of countries where the legal framework (including customary law) guarantees women's equal rights to land ownership and/or control
6.1.1	Proportion of population using safely managed drinking water services
6.2.1	Proportion of population using (a) safely managed sanitation services and (b) a hand-washing facility with soap and water
7.1.1	Proportion of population with access to electricity
7.1.2	Proportion of population with primary reliance on clean fuels and technology
8.3.1	Proportion of informal employment in total employment, by sector and sex
9.1.1	Proportion of the rural population who live within 2 km of an all-season road
9.5.2	Researchers (in full-time equivalent) per million inhabitants
9.c.1	Proportion of population covered by a mobile network, by technology
11.1.1	Proportion of urban population living in slums, informal settlements or inadequate housing

11.2.1	Proportion of population that has convenient access to public transport, by sex, age and persons with disabilities
11.7.1	Average share of the built-up area of cities that is open space for public use for all, by sex, age and persons with disabilities
11.7.2	Proportion of persons victim of physical or sexual harassment, by sex, age, disability status and place of occurrence, in the previous 12 months

Note: In total, 22 indicators were identified under the gender-environment nexus. However, three indicators are identical (1.5.1, 11.5.1 and 13.1.1), so they appear together in the table. Analysis based on UN Global Indicator Framework for the SDGs as stands based on 2020 Comprehensive Review changes.
Source: Authors' own computations based on UN Global Indicator Framework for the SDGs for determining the environment-related indicators; (Cohen and Shinwell, 2020[62]) analysis provided for gender-related indicators. More analytical information provided in Annex A.

Furthermore, 9 of the 22 SDG indicators on the gender-environment nexus are related to either environmental health and access to water and sanitation (SDGs 3 and 6) or natural disasters and land tenure (SDGs 1 and 5).

Figure 2.9. Only 14 gender-relevant indicators under the environment-related SDGs

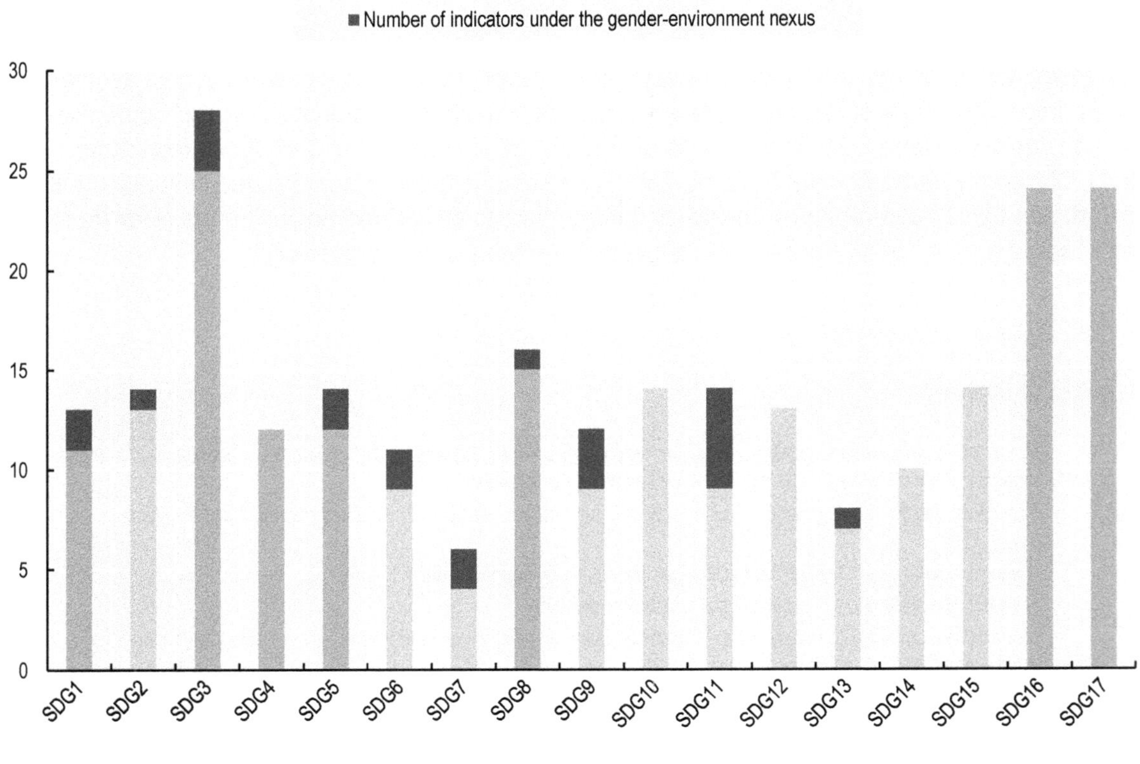

Note: In red the SDG indicators identified under the gender-environment nexus. In green the indicators for the environment-related SDGs. In blue the remaining SDG indicators.
Source: Authors' own computations based on UN Global Indicator Framework for the SDGs for determining the environment-related indicators; (Cohen and Shinwell, 2020[62]) analysis provided for gender-related indicators. More analytical information provided in Annex A.

Within the 9 environment-related goals (SDGs 2, 6, 7, 9, 11, 12, 13, 14, and 15) there are only 14 gender-relevant indicators (Figure 2.9). Within the Planet Goals (SDGs 6, 12, 13, 14, 15), only 3 indicators out of the total 56 are identified as gender relevant, that is over 5%. For the environment-related Prosperity Goals (SDGs 7, 9, 11) the equivalent is 10 indicators out of 32 (about 31%). For SDG 2, and only in relation to sustainable agriculture, 1 out of 14 indicators, just over 7%, is gender-relevant. No indicators from the gender-environment nexus are found in four "environmental" SDGs; three of the four fall under the Planet category, namely SDG 12 on sustainable production and consumption, SDG 14 on oceans, and SDG 15 on biodiversity.

Many of the SDG indicators focusing on gender equality and empowering women and girls[3] - such as ending discrimination, equal access to education and health, ensuring equal rights to property and voice and representation in decision-making - are key to allow women to engage in economic activities that protect the environment and promote sustainable development. They also serve to mitigate the negative impact of environmental damage on women. In this regard, the SDG Framework effectively addresses the causality between gender equality and environmental sustainability.

The SDG framework also effectively tackles environmental sustainability Goals. Environment-related targets are identified in all SDGs, with 112 indicators having an environmental angle. In short, the SDG Framework addresses stand-alone gender equality issues well and stand-alone environmental Goals well. But it clearly falls short in embedding a gender equality perspective in the nine key environment-related SDGs. Examples of such embedding could be to analyse i) the specific impact of climate change, environmental damage and biodiversity loss on women or ii) the role of women in sustainable production and consumption.

2.5.2. Data on SDG gender-environment nexus indicators is scant

In practice, there is little data on the very small set of gender-relevant environmental SDG indicators. Based on UNEP (2019) and UN Women (2018) analysis, data availability is scant for many developing countries (UNEP, 2019[50]); (UNWomen, 2018[61]). Even though commitments have been made and actions have been taken to mainstream the SDGs into national development strategies and priorities, in most cases data is not available to measure any progress made. Where data do exists, the changes in the indicators, even when positive, do not reflect the achievement of the relevant SDG target. Developing countries face data limitations, lack or regular credible surveys to measure changes, and often than not a question of credibility of statistical data generated. Further strengthening of their statistical systems is necessary. This would require, among other actions, technical and other support to generate much needed data, as, for example, geospatial data that provide a basis for analysis interlinkages of environment and human behaviour (UNEP, 2019[50]).

PARIS 21 and UN Women collaborate since 2018 to assess the state of gender statistics in developing countries and to mainstream gender statistics in national statistical systems of developing countries (PARIS21, n.d.[63]). This technical support provided to countries helps them identify data gaps and statistical capacity areas that are lagging behind. This relates to the production, dissemination and use of gender statistics in the country. In a forthcoming report by PARIS 21, it is observed that, while countries consider the gender dimension across sectoral statistical strategies, this often fails to be done in environmental statistics. The gender-environment nexus is a good distillation of issues affecting statistics in general: national statistical agencies do not cater to users' needs, there is a lack of gender (and environmental) -sensitivity when designing data collections, lack of basic data disaggregation, lack of prioritisation of such data collections and inability to communicate the findings to policymakers, among other concerns (PARIS21, n.d.[64]).

In OECD countries, data are systematically available[4] for only 35 indicators (34%) of the 102 gender-related indicators (Cohen and Shinwell, 2020[62]). Most gender data is available for Goals on Health, Education, Economy and Gender Equality (SDGs 3, 4, 8 and 5); but even in these cases significant data gaps exist, especially for Institutions, Health and Gender Equality (respectively, SDGs 16, 3 and 5). No gender data are available for the indicators under eight out of the nine environment-related SDGs; either because no indicator has been identified as gender-related – as in the case for sustainable production and consumption (SDG 12), oceans (SDG 14) and biodiversity (SDG 15) – or because there are no data available for at least 10 OECD Member countries - as for water, climate, energy and cities). When examining the 20 unique gender-environment nexus indicators identified in Table 2.3, only 2 sets of gender-disaggregated data are available from OECD sources, both under SDG indicator 9.5.2, on the share of women inventors, and on researchers per million inhabitants (Cohen and Shinwell, 2020[62]).

The OECD has identified environment-related indicators where the gender dimension could be further developed. These include: (i) exposure to environmental risks, differentiated by risk type (air pollutant and natural hazards), by sex, age and sociodemographic attributes, (ii) mortality rates from air pollution, differentiated by pollutant, sex, age, country and year; and (iii) development of 'green' technologies, based on patenting activity, differentiated by domain, country, year and sex of the inventor (OECD, 2020[65]). These indicators are in alignment, or can provide additional information under SDG indicators 1.5.1, 3.9.1, 3.9.2 and 9.5.2, respectively. Alternatively, other data available under the OECD Statistical Database could complement data available under the UN Global Database, to support OECD Members in determining their actions under the gender-environment nexus.

At the country reporting level, it would appear that data are more available, mainly on other indicators not included in the SDG Framework. In 2013, a report of the Statistical Commission of the United Nations Economic and Social Council (ECOSOC) on the state of gender statistics collected by national governments around the world revealed that sex-disaggregated agriculture and water statistics are amongst the least available (Figure 2.10) (ECOSOC, 2013[66]). Overall, more than half of countries do not produce any gender statistics related to these two environment-related sectors.

Figure 2.10. Percentage of countries "regularly" producing sex-disaggregated statistics on specific issues (%)

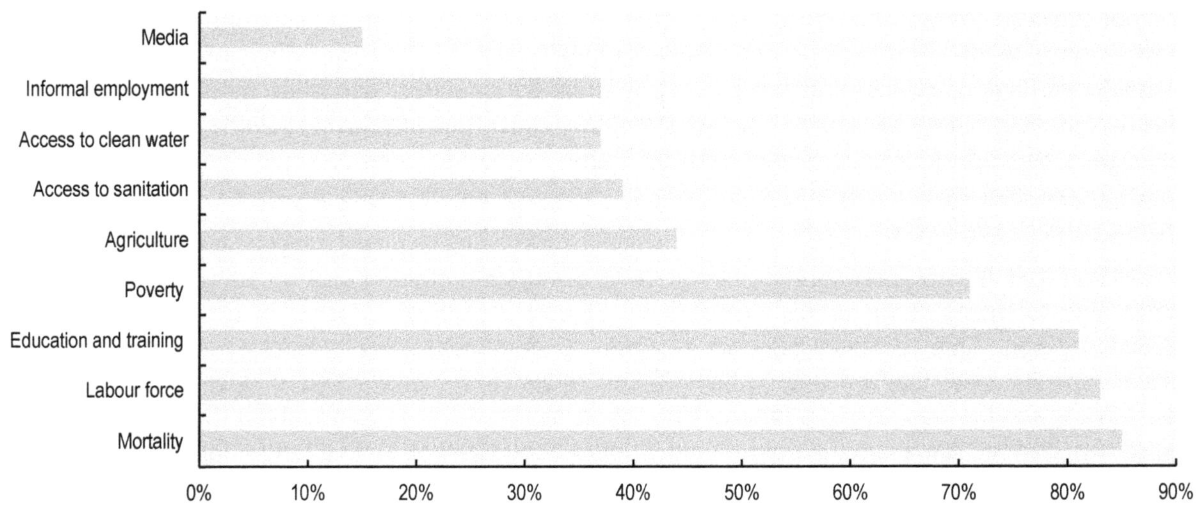

Source: (Seager, 2015[67])

2.5.3. Ongoing efforts to collect gender-disaggregated environmental data

There are a number of international initiatives to further develop gender-disaggregation of environmental data, especially since the lack of gender-disaggregated data has been reflected under the UN (Box 2.2), as in the case of the Gender Action Plan adopted by UNFCCC COP 25 in 2019. UN Women and the UN Statistics Division, along with other organisations, have developed new gender-related indicators, but few are linked to the environment (UNSD, 2019[68]). In March 2019, the International Union for Conservation of Nature (IUCN) and the United Nations Environment Programme (UNEP) published a report "Gender and Environment Statistics: Unlocking information for action and measuring the SDGs", which proposes 18 gender-environment indicators, across four priority areas: the right to land, natural resources and biodiversity; access to food, energy, water and sanitation; climate change, sustainable production and consumption, and health; and women in environmental decision-making at all levels (UNEP and IUCN, 2019[69]) . Some of these indicators are more relevant for developing countries. There are also specific efforts under way to improve gender-disaggregated environmental data for specific SDGs, such as by the Convention on Biological Diversity (CBD) in relation to SDG 15, nevertheless, there is room for improvement.

A number of regional level UN initiatives have also been launched. For instance, UN ESCAP analysis led by (Serrao et al., 2019[70]) takes stock of related data and capacity gaps in the Asia-Pacific region and puts forward a proposal for a Gender-Environment Indicator Set, which includes indicators from the UN Global Indicator Framework for the SDGs and beyond, capturing issues of particular relevance for the gender-environment nexus in the region. Specifically, (Serrao et al., 2019[70]) identify 19 gender-environment indicators, 2 of which are directly from the 93 environment SDG indicator framework (identical to SDG indicators 1.4.2 and 5.a.1), 7 are modified by extending or merging SDG indicators (similar to SDG indicators) and 10 are from outside the SDG Framework (non-SDG indicators).

Even beyond the SDG Framework, data are available under the gender-environment nexus, such as national and regional administrative records, or population-based surveys; which can provide for rich information if collected in an effective manner. Administrative data collection is not, however, evident in developing countries, especially in Africa (UNWomen, 2019[71]). The National Statistical Organisations can play a primary role in developing the instruments for collecting basic information under the gender-environment nexus. Increasing the use of Administrative Registers, with a systematic compilation, identifying and characterising them for their use could lead to more statistics that contribute to the updating, and creation of public policies, as well as evidence-based decision-making.

Given the horizontal nature of its work, the OECD could contribute to the recognition of the gender – environment nexus as a useful dimension for the development of high quality environmental data and statistics, in a manner that is internationally harmonised and applicable to all countries.

While the OECD and its Member countries have been active in strengthening data gathering on gender aspects of economic and social policies, this has not been the case for the environment and environmental policies. The OECD has done some work on the collection and comparability of data related to the gender-environment nexus among its Members. For example, the 2008 and 2011 Surveys on Environmental Policy and Individual Behaviour Change (EPIC), contained questions pertaining to the collection of some gender-disaggregated data on sociodemographic characteristics, waste, transport, energy, food and water consumption and preference patterns at the household level (OECD, 2011[72]). Extensive work on the gendered effects of chemical exposure has been produced through the OECD Standardised Test Guidelines Evaluating Chemicals, especially on endocrine disruptors (OECD, 2013[73]). However, more work is needed to fully integrate gender equality into environmental policies and to adequately measure the interlinkages of the two.

A 2017 Survey on gender-disaggregated data collection in OECD countries showed that about half of the respondents stated that they do not collect such data related to environmental policies, nor do they plan to do so. Less than 10% of the respondents stated that they collect such data on a regular basis (Figure 2.11).

Figure 2.11. Collection of Gender-Disaggregated data across sectors

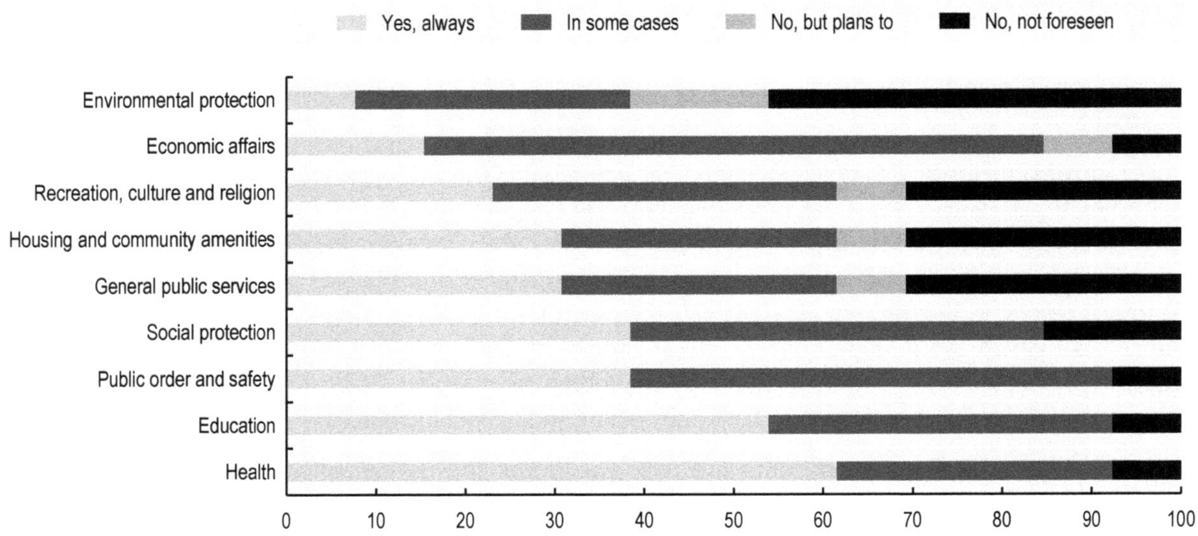

Source: (OECD, 2017[74]), "OECD Survey on National Gender Equality Frameworks and Public Policies".

In an effort to accelerate gender-responsive policies, the OECD launched a Gender Mainstreaming Policy Platform in 2019. Among other objectives, the Platform aims to advance evidence gathering on systemic inequalities issues beyond social aspects, and in particular related to the gender-environment nexus. A survey on "Integrating Gender in Environmental Policies" was circulated to its Member countries in 2019 to gather information on how countries consider gender in environment-related policy-making, budgeting, and governance. The survey addressed both national strategies, actions or mechanisms to mainstream gender into environmental policy and decision-making, as well as some thematic questions: labour implications of greener economies for men and women, gender and infrastructure, sustainable consumption patterns by gender, and different health impacts on men and women based on exposure to environmental toxins.

Thirty-one out of the 37 Member countries, as well as Costa Rica, responded to the questionnaire, and 2 Members provided information without replying to the questions. The results to the survey are mixed, and the scope and detail provided by countries varies. Several countries did not fully complete the questionnaire, which may indicate a lack of attention paid to the gender-environment nexus, and/or that gender-environment action is based on a more piecemeal approach, whereby policy or data centres around one or two chosen subjects.

Figure 2.12. OECD Member countries responses to the Survey on integrating gender equality in environment-related data collection and policy-making

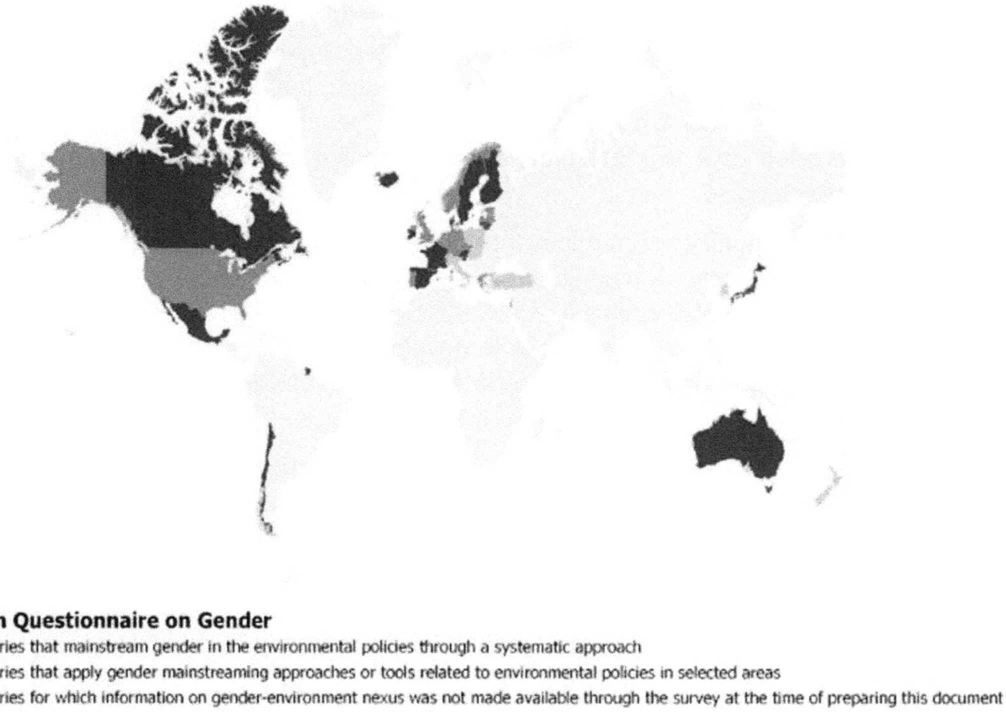

Note: Map depicting OECD Member countries' responses to the survey on integrating gender in environmental policies. Costa Rica, an OECD accession country at the time the Survey was conducted, falls under category 1 "OECD Countries that mainstream gender in the environmental policies through a systematic approach".
Source (OECD, 2020[75]): OECD Survey on integrating gender in environmental policies.

Figure 2.12 presents the OECD countries under three distinct groupings, based on the approach and level of mainstreaming gender in environmental policies. Seventeen OECD countries mainstream gender in their environmental policies through a systematic approach; this covers countries that have both gender equality and environmental national strategies (including action plans or principles), and have in place policy tools to integrate them (fully or partially) on a regular basis[5]. Examples range from Iceland's Deployment Plan on Gender Responsive Budgeting; to data evaluation practices such as Sweden's gender statistics on the environmental goods and services sector and on bio-economy; and to environment-related education as in the case of Chile. Twelve countries apply gender mainstreaming approaches or tools related to environmental policies in selected areas. Countries in this category stated that they do not apply a comprehensive, integrated approach. However, they provided information on sectorial approaches that they follow (regularly or occasionally). Examples include applying a gender lens in some environment-related sectors or collecting gender-disaggregated data through selected initiatives. Examples of policies in this group include Israel's gender considerations in household surveys.

On data collection, only ten OECD Member countries and Costa Rica replied affirmatively to whether they collect gender-disaggregated data related to the environment and/or environmental policy-making. The United Kingdom, for example, has been collecting gender-disaggregated data through the "Monitor of Engagement with the Natural Environment" survey, which was recently replaced by the "People and Nature Survey" and the "Survey on Attitudes to the Environment". These surveys provide relevant findings by gender, including on people's use of the natural environment, and attitudinal and behavioural data. The Census in the United Kingdom asks about transport use, such as how many cars are available for use by members of the household – which could be relevant to accessing green space, and may be linked to wider environmental attitudes and behaviours. Yet, from the individual replies and information provided by countries, it appears that more data are being collected, albeit in specific sectors or around specific policies that could be categorised under the gender-environment nexus. The data are also collected via different sources, including perception and attitude surveys, national statistics or research. From the 21 countries that replied they do consider gender aspects in environmental policy-making, only 8 affirmed the collection of relevant data, pointing towards the conclusion that integrating the gender equality and environmental agendas is far from complete in some countries. It is also less clear whether OECD Members are providing such gender-disaggregated data to other international organisations and databases, or whether they simply do not recognise doing so.

The survey also identified a number of countries that are launching data collection exercises on the nexus. For instance, Finland is introducing a module on gender-environment interlinkages for its annual Gender Equality in Finland report. The 2020 edition is to include a gender breakdown on issues such as recycling and transport modes (time use statistics). Chile is developing an Atlas of Information on Gender and Climate Change and sectoral gender indicators to identify gender gaps and climate change risks in climate-sensitive sectors (OECD, 2020[75]) .

Two thirds of the responding countries also identified areas of interest within the gender-environment nexus for the OECD Secretariat to explore further. These include the economic implications of the green transition for men and women, climate change implications particularly to women, sustainable consumption and production patterns by gender, greening infrastructure and its implications on men and women as well as environmental effects on health by gender (Figure 2.13).

Figure 2.13. OECD Members' indication of interest for future work on the gender-environment nexus

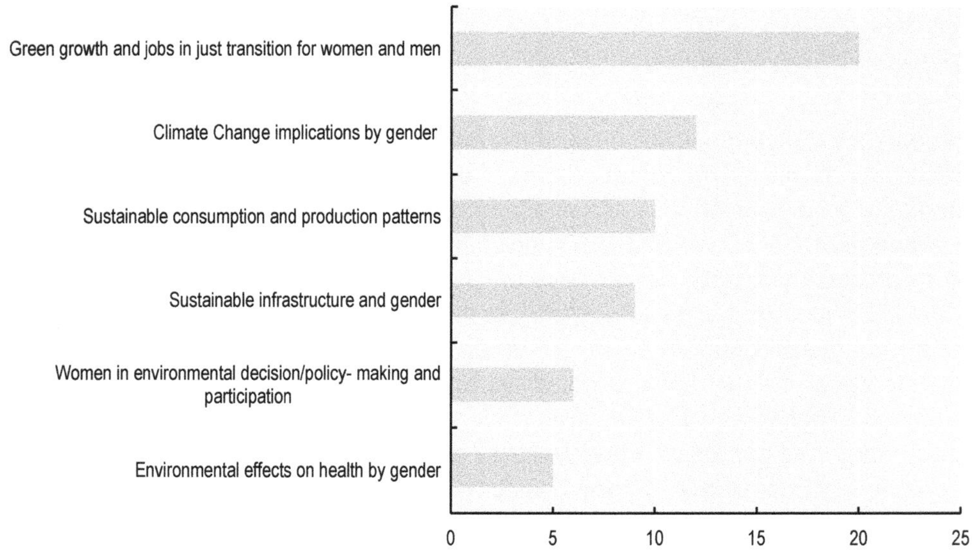

Note: Ranking according to the number of OECD countries that indicated an interest in each topic. Open-ended responses provided. No prioritisation or ranking of selection of options. No ceiling on possible listing of interest. Survey was initiated before the outbreak of COVID-19 and therefore any COVID-related issues were not raised
Source: (OECD, 2020[75]), OECD Survey on integrating gender in environmental policies

2.5.4. Supporting data collection efforts through development co-operation

Gender-disaggregated data is key to strengthening the gender-environment nexus in development co-operation. The OECD is able to track Official Development Assistance (ODA) for the environment and for climate change adaptation and mitigation, focused on gender equality and empowering women and girls. The most recently published analysis of ODA figures shows a continuing increase in bilateral allocable aid focusing on gender equality and women's empowerment, which reached 45% for 2018-19, the highest figure yet (GENDERNET, 2021[76]). The figures, notwithstanding the increase, indicate more than half of bilateral allocable aid still remains broadly gender-blind.

When looking more closely into the sectoral distribution of total gender equality focused ODA, it is clear that some of the sectors identified have an environmental link, and could support or hamper environmental outcomes. For example, the agricultural sector, where women constitute the majority (East Asia and Southeast Asia) or a growing number of the agricultural workforce, is an evident case for introducing a gender- and environment-responsive perspective. This is also apparent by the focus towards water supply and sanitation, and general environmental protection; two areas which could be strongly linked with progress in achieving SDG 6 and SDG 15, respectively. Other areas, such as access to sustainable and affordable energy for all (SDG 7) would also require further support. Unfortunately, gender equality-focused bilateral ODA in these sectors remains limited (Figure 2.14).

Figure 2.14. Bilateral ODA for Gender Equality by Sector (share)

Average per year 2018-19

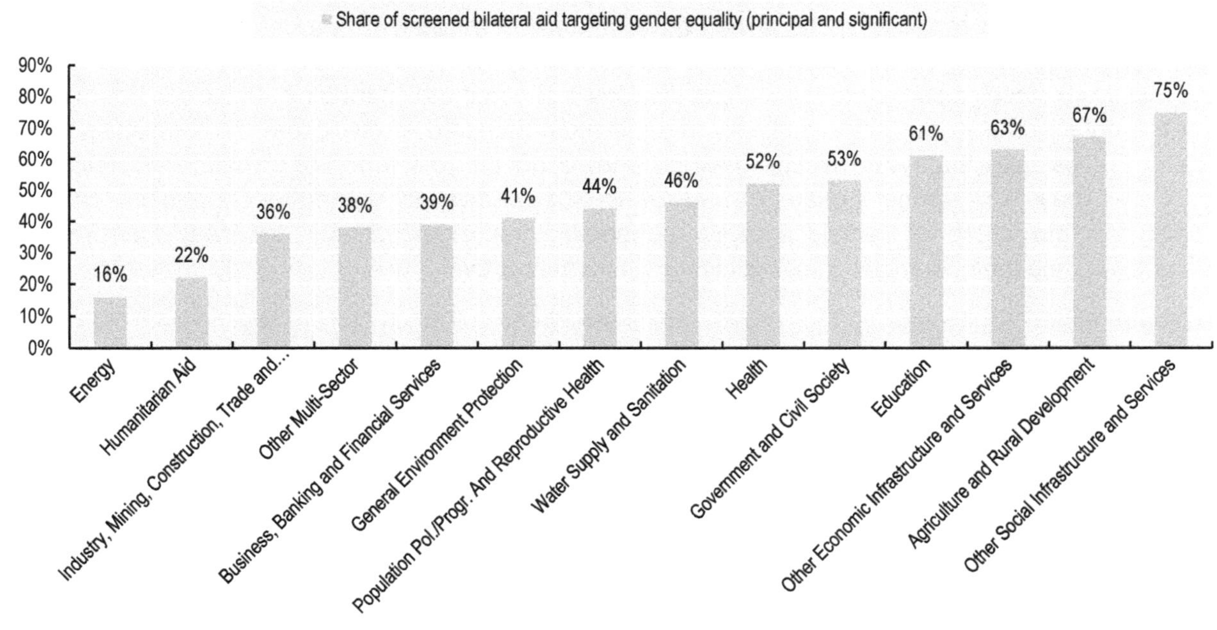

Source: (GENDERNET, 2021[76])

Furthermore, in a 2019 report highlighted the need to align development co-operation support to the Paris Agreement objectives (OECD, 2019[77]). The report noted that even though 75% of developing countries have been identifying sectors such as agriculture, forestry, biodiversity and ecosystems, health and water as priority for adaptation-related action, development financing had not necessarily followed the same track. Considering that some of these sectors have a strong gender component, it would be a good opportunity to work on an integrated approach.

2.5.5. Non-governmental data collection initiatives on the gender-environment nexus

Beyond the limited gender-disaggregated data available from governmental sources, data is being generated by other stakeholders. The universal nature of the SDGs has led not only international organisations and governments, but also the private sector and civil society into generating their own gender- or environment- related data (see below) or acknowledging the existing data gap in the gender-environment nexus [as for example in the case of Data2X, an NGO working on mobilising action for gender-sensitive data collection (Grantham, 2020[78])]. Citizen-generated data (CGD) could play an important role in monitoring and driving progress on sustainable development, having the potential to fill in data gaps in official reporting, and flag topics that matter to citizens most [see case of CGD in Philippines (PARIS21, 2020[79])]. Digitalisation and new technologies are facilitating such data collection. Even though such a plethora of information should be welcome, it also needs to be checked for quality and consistency across countries. The OECD, together with other international organisations, could play a valuable role in reviewing and filtering such 'big data', allowing policy-makers to use it in a systematic way for policy decisions.

Equal Measures 2030 uses a scoring system to mark countries' advancement towards achieving gender equality (Equal Measures 2030, 2019[80]). By examining different indicators set under the SDG Gender Index, covering 14 out of 17 SDGs, the Index compares countries' performance to others for each indicator identified. It does not, however, mark each country's progress towards achieving the SDGs. Some of the indicators cover also issues linked to environment, namely water and sanitation (SDG 6), and climate (SDG 13). It covers also environment-related SDGs on energy (SDG 7), infrastructure (SDG 9), and cities (SDG 11). Other tools, i.e. evidence gathering and case studies, which seem to support the analysis based on the scoring system, support the Index.

The Global Reporting Initiative (GRI), a non-governmental organisation, has developed Sustainability Reporting Standards, which are globally embraced by a large number of large corporations. Standards focus mainly on sustainability performance and disclosure of corporate information. Initiatives like the GRI go in the right direction, but set a relatively low minimum standard of disclosure on companies (GRI, 2020[81]). For instance, there is no specific gender standard, nor any joint reporting on gender-sustainability impact. The main GRI standard relating women, GRI 405 on diversity and equal opportunity, calls for reporting on the share of female workers performing the organisation's activities, their relative remuneration, and their participation at the highest governance level.

On climate-related disclosures, various organisations have been collecting and processing such data. CDP Global runs a global disclosure system, where companies, investors, as well as cities and regions, voluntarily disclose information relating to their activity and the effect on climate, water and forestry (CPD, 2020[82]). The Task Force on Climate-related Financial Disclosures (TCFD), an industry-led initiative established by the Financial Stability Board, has developed voluntary recommendations on how to better align existing disclosure regimes and enhance climate-related reporting. The level of engagement in the implementation of the Task Force on Climate-related Financial Disclosures (TCFD) Recommendation and gender equality targets vary between companies, but they are becoming increasingly common practice (OECD, 2018[83]). In the 2019 TCFD report on the implementation progress, the number of companies that are now implementing (partly) the Recommendations, is constantly increasing (Quarles, 2019[84]). However, there is no specific link made to the gender-specific impact of climate change.

Some reporting initiatives (e.g. taking the GRI example again) seemingly encourage greater economic opportunities for women in the form of higher labour force participation. However, an economic empowerment-related approach that does not take into account the potential challenges that women may face when they lack the necessary physical and social infrastructure and support from their family, may actually be damaging to women's well-being. For instance, working women are more often than men in charge of child and elderly care, and the household and they often have different mobility patterns from working men. To give women and men an equal footing to participate in the labour force, for example, their specific needs regarding the frequency of public transport off-peak hours need to be addressed.

A better understanding of the factors that influence individual travel behaviour can reveal preferences and attitudes, provide insights to existing travel patterns, improve transport planning, prepare for future infrastructure needs and services, and help better design and implement sustainable and inclusive transport policies that will meet different environmental goals. Sex disaggregated data on the labour force in male dominated sectors would also need to be collected and better understood, in order to increase gender equality and to ensure adequate representation of women's needs.

2.6. Limited integration of the gender-environment nexus in policy decisions

Before delving into each of the nine "environmental" SDGs (Chapters 6-14), this section reviews the extent to which current environmental policies and regulations, whole-of-government policies, including taxation and budgeting, and transboundary policies (development cooperation, trade and investment) integrate a gender equality dimension. The analysis focuses mainly on OECD countries and refers to existing literature on developing countries. It is worth noting that, beyond introducing gender-sensitive or gender-responsive policies, there is also a need to follow up on implementation and effectiveness. Considering the multi-faceted issues that would entail a gendered approach – including women's and girls' empowerment – measuring the effectiveness of the policy measures introduced is essential.

2.6.1. Environmental policies

Globally, efforts vary in the extent to which a gender equality dimension is integrated into environmental strategies and policies. Since the UN Conference on Environment and Development (UNCED) in 1992 in Rio de Janeiro, gender aspects have received more attention in international environmental fora. Gender issues are now firmly established in several platforms, such as the UN Convention on Biological Diversity (CBD), the UN Convention to Combat Desertification (UNCCD), and the UN Framework Convention on Climate Change (UNFCCC). Many national-level environmental strategies and climate action plans promote the integration of a gender equality dimension. UNEP highlights in particular the cases of Cambodia and Rwanda (UN Environment, 2016[85]). One of the guiding principles of the Cambodia Climate Change Strategic Plan (2014-23) refers to "reducing [...] gender vulnerability". In Rwanda, poverty, gender equality, environment and climate change issues were successfully integrated into the national economic development and poverty reduction strategy, aligning these objectives in its budgeting cycle. As a result of these efforts and external financial support, Rwanda's agricultural budget jumped by 26.3% from 2009 to 2011, while its average expenditure on environment and climate change rose from 0.4% of GDP in 2005-2008 to 2.8% in 2008-2012 (UN Environment, 2016[85]).

The OECD survey on "Integrating Gender in Environmental Policies" from 2019 found that the majority of OECD countries have a national gender strategy, action plan or set of principles that apply horizontally and require for gender mainstreaming in all policies. In at least 18 OECD countries, the national environmental authority contributes to the gender strategy's implementation. This is usually done by engaging in disaggregated data collection, gender-based analysis, and participation in the governance structures for gender mainstreaming in the public administration. Nineteen OECD countries claim to consider gender aspects in environmental policy-making, either systematically or occasionally. Gender equality and women's empowerment considerations are mostly integrated into policies relating to climate change; green entrepreneurship and green jobs, including in agricultural and forestry sectors; as well as women's participation and leadership in environment-related decision-making (Figure 2.15) (OECD, 2020[75]).

Figure 2.15. Mapping of OECD countries' environmental or environment-related policies with integrated gender equality considerations

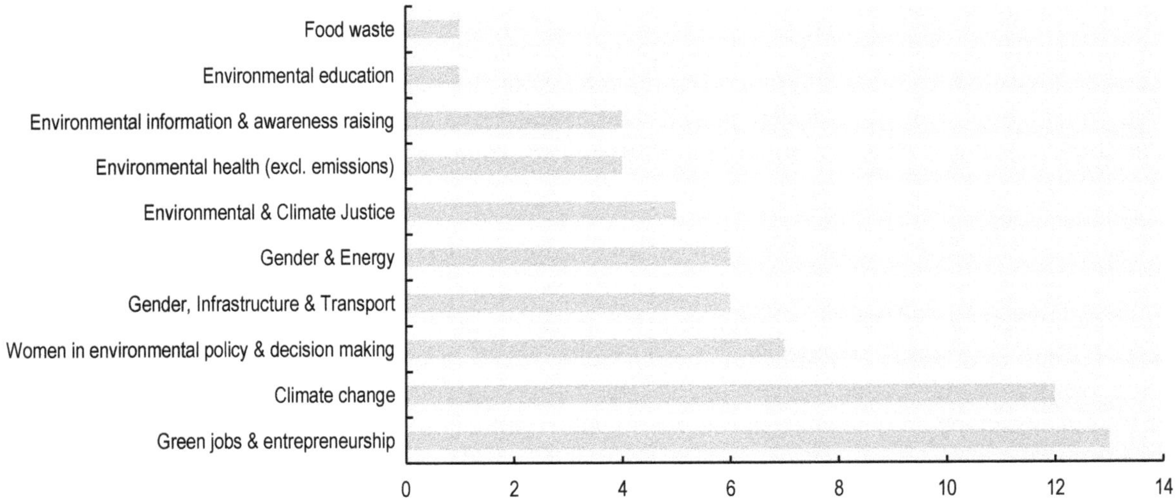

Source: Authors own research based on replies to (OECD, 2020[75]) Survey on integrating environmental policies

In Spain, gender mainstreaming and women's empowerment considerations are taken into account in policies and measures adopted by the Ministry for Ecological Transition and Demographic Challenge. In particular, as part of the Strategic Framework on Energy and Climate, Spain is progressing with the implementation of a Just Transition Strategy, aiming at maximising employment opportunities within the transition to a low carbon and sustainable economy. Guaranteeing equal use of opportunities through gender equality measures in green jobs is part of the Strategy's strategic objectives (OECD, 2020[75]). In Mexico, the Ministry of Environment and Natural Resources (SEMARNAT) following the National Development Plan 2019-2024 promotes sustainability programmes within the framework of human rights and gender equality, both at the national and international levels. High priority is particularly given to women's leadership in community revitalisation and in natural resources management. In parallel, Mexico's "National Program for Equality between Women and Men" focuses on substantive actions to mainstream gender into public policy instruments on climate change, as well as to meet the needs of women and strengthen their leadership and negotiation capacity (OECD, 2020[75]). Sweden's Environmental Protection Agency introduced a gender lens when supporting unemployed people as well as newcomers to Sweden (former refugees) to work in forestry in 2018 (OECD, 2020[75]).

2.6.2. Regulatory impact assessments

A growing number of OECD countries integrate the impact of proposed policies on gender equality, when conducting regulatory impact assessments (Deighton-Smith, Erbacci and Kauffmann, 2016[86]). In parallel, many more have already been integrating environmental considerations in their regulatory impact assessments, including impact assessments covering climate change concerns (Jacob et al., 2011[87]). Different tools are being developed to guarantee non-market or subjective well-being valuation (OECD, 2018[88]).

Environmental Impact Assessments are also already widespread in OECD countries, mainstreaming the environment in project decision-making. In some cases, their input may also be used as part of the regulatory impact assessments. The OECD adopted a 1979 *Recommendation on the Assessment of Projects with Significant Impact on the Environment*. The Recommendation was amended in November

2019, to also integrate environmental assessment into the drawing and development of plans and programmes [OECD/LEGAL/0172].

The 2012 *Recommendation on Regulatory Policy and Governance* highlights the need to "adopt ex ante impact assessment practices that are proportional to the significance of the regulation, and include benefit cost analyses that consider the welfare impacts of regulation taking into account economic, social and environmental impacts including the distributional effects over time, identifying who is likely to benefit and who is likely to bear costs" (OECD, 2012[89]). An integrated impact assessment framework, encompassing both gender/youth, as well as indigenous or other groups, and environmental considerations in the different stages of policy development and implementation, as well as at the programme and project level, would help both overcome adverse socioeconomic and environmental effects at the implementation phase, and empower women and youth who would not be excluded from the process. Analysis on a sustainability impact assessment model was conducted in the past in the OECD, encompassing both gender and social, and environmental considerations (OECD, 2010[90]). Such model could be complemented to guarantee a holistic and integrated approach.

In practice, few countries integrate the nexus into regulatory impact assessments. Belgium is using ex-ante regulatory impact assessments with a sustainability angle. Their assessments are composed of over 20 themes, with the 4 most prominent ones being gender, small and medium-sized enterprises, administrative burden and policy coherence for development. Since 2013, regulatory impact assessments provide screening through a sustainable development lens, which integrate gender equality, SME and policy coherence for sustainable development considerations. Regulatory impact assessments are obligatory for all legislation, including environmental.

2.6.3. Taxation and budgeting policies

To ensure that women's and girls' needs and interests are better addressed in future policies, the OECD has been arguing for gender- sensitive and gender- responsive resource allocation and budgeting (Downes and Nicol, 2020[91]); (Downes, von Trapp and Nicol, 2017[92]). Moreover, considering the government-wide nature of the budgetary process, introducing gender equality as part of the process would help influence policy-making horizontally (Downes and Nicol, 2020[91]). The same could apply to "green budgeting". The Paris Collaborative on Green Budgeting, launched at the One Planet Summit in 2017, assesses the alignment of national expenditure and revenue processes with international environmental goals.

Negative environmental impact and gender inequalities of tax and public expenditure often go hand in hand. For instance, subsidies to fossil fuel-based energy and other industries with a heavy environmental impact, such as mining and chemical manufacturing, may deepen gender inequalities, because the majority of the workforce in those sectors is male (OECD.Stat, n.d.[93]). Similarly, men are more exposed to the hazardous and toxic substances used in such sectors.

OECD governments transfer hundreds of billions in subsidies to different sectors, and much of this support is potentially environmentally harmful. Despite the downward trend from 2013, 2019 was the first year to mark an increase in support for fossil fuels among OECD and G20 economies, reaching USD 178 billion, while the combined estimate of government support for fossil fuels measured by the International Energy Agency (IEA) and the OECD was USD 478 billion (OECD, 2020[94]). COVID-19 and fuel prices may lead to more state subsidies for fossil fuels and fossil-dependent industries (OECD, 2020[94]). In addition, to better assess the effects of harmful subsidies on the environment (OECD, 2005[95]), governments need to consider the distributional aspects, including the impact by gender (Section 11.6).

More recent OECD analysis shows that energy-use taxation has different distributional effects on households depending on their socio-demographic characteristics such as income, size, age, location etc. (Flues and Thomas, 2015[96]). Energy affordability risk also depends on household income level and consumption, and varies according to the tax system implemented (Flues and van Dender, 2017[97]). Such considerations should be analysed on a more granular basis to include gender, then used to set up national redistribution mechanisms.

Gender budgeting is an increasingly common practice countries apply at both national and sub-national levels, to ensure that women's and girls' concerns are addressed in policy-making and resource allocation. About half of OECD countries report that they have introduced, plan to introduce, or are actively considering introducing gender budgeting (Downes, von Trapp and Nicol, 2017[92]). Gender considerations are included mostly during budget preparation; through impact assessments, resource allocation and performance setting (OECD, 2018[98]).

Governments are also applying environmentally responsive or "green budgeting" which is a way to record and communicate policy progress on environmental objectives through budgeting processes. This is a crucial step in achieving a common objective of several key international agreements – such as the Paris Agreement, the Aichi Biodiversity Targets, and the SDGs – to align national policy frameworks and financial flows with a pathway towards low greenhouse gas emissions and environmentally sustainable development.

Gender budgeting and green budgeting could be brought together in a "SDG-budgeting" or "well-being budgeting" process. Such an approach could ensure the integration of the gender-environment nexus into the budgeting process. It would also pave the way for embedding all the SDGs into the budget process. New Zealand and some European countries are making major advances in this direction (Box 2.4). There has also been good progress on this in some African countries such as Uganda and Rwanda (Stotsky et al., 2016[99]). The way governments choose to spend their money will be decisive to achieve these commitments. The opportunity for progress is enormous, especially given the existing misalignment between the SDGs and current public expenditure and taxation practices.

Box 2.4. Aligning Budgeting Practices with the SDGs

OECD countries are increasingly applying gender budgeting and green budgeting principles. As the name indicates, gender budgeting aims to promote gender equality and empowering women and girls throughout all categories of public expenditure, guided by a whole of government strategy or policy. More than half of OECD Members have introduced gender budgeting.

Green budgeting involves the integration of climate and broader environmental goals within the budget process. Like gender budgeting, it requires a whole of government approach, engaging the different ministries that oversee expenditure affecting the environment. While both gender and green budgeting are gaining popularity, few countries have aimed to integrate these two approaches effectively. The examples below show efforts being made to integrate the gender-environment nexus into budgeting practices.

New Zealand's Well-Being Budget

New Zealand is the first country worldwide to set a well-being budget. Since 2019, it uses well-being evidence, and has integrated well-being considerations into the Treasury's cost-benefit analysis tool, to help with setting budgetary priorities. National authorities are encouraged to submit quantifiable proposals for initiatives developed via a collaborative process. These initiatives are assessed by New Zealand's Living Standards Framework, and the LSF Dashboard, which provides a range of well-being indicators and analysis under three sections – country, people and future – and around enhance the country's natural, human, social, and financial and physical capital. The distribution of well-being is grouped under 12 well-being categories, examining for different population groups of citizens, with characteristics such as sex, age, ethnicity, family type, region, hours worked and neighbourhood deprivation). Gender-disaggregated data are collected where available. Moreover, the LSF is in line with the SDGs, even though the two frameworks serve different purposes. The LSF approach allows for better understanding the interactions between potential policy choices, and assessing well-being benefits the same way as assessing fiscal costs.

New Zealand's LSF Dashboard was recently updated and now includes more or revised environmental indicators. New Zealand's Well-being budget for 2020 is prioritising the transition to a low carbon emissions economy.

Ireland's Equality Budgeting

Ireland has been piloting since 2017 equality budgeting, building on the existing performance budgeting framework. Different departments are subscribing to an equality lens in their performance budgeting, setting specific targets and improving performance data collection. The equality budgeting covers issues beyond gender, spreading the focus too thinly, raising difficulties at the implementation and monitoring phase of the budget's performance. Ireland is also undergoing other budgeting reforms, and is moving towards green and SDG budgeting, by tagging and tracking expenditures for better environmental outcomes or for supporting SDGs implementation. A coherent and integrated approach between the equality, green and SDG budgeting should be considered, as it could advance better policy-making in Ireland.

Source: (OECD, 2019[100]); (New Zealand. Treasury, 2019[101]); (Pinar, n.d.[102])

Canada is also in the process of integrating the gender-environment nexus into budgetary policies, by applying a Gender-Based Analysis Plus (GBA+) lens to all government decisions relating to taxation, budgeting and expenditures, domestically and internationally, in all policy sectors, including infrastructure

(Government of Canada, 2020[103]). Through this inclusive analytical tool, Canada is assessing how different groups (based on gender, race, ethnicity, age, disability etc.) can maximise positive benefits and address identified challenges. The GBA+ lens is being integrated into climate change policies, and Canada's International Climate Change Action Programme is considering gender in the design, decision-making, and implementation of projects (Government of Canada, 2019[104]).

2.6.4. Development co-operation policies

Development co-operation Agencies in DAC Member countries have long been focusing on integrating environment and climate change, and gender considerations in development cooperation and programmes. Although the interlinkages between gender and environment are being recognised to some extent, such as the one between the effects of climate change on women and gender equality in the developing countries, only a few DAC Members, namely Sweden and Ireland, seem to have considered gender and environment holistically in their policies and programming.

SIDA, the Swedish Development Agency, has been following a gender analysis in all of its environmental programming and projects in developing countries. Areas covered are exposure to chemicals and pollution, participation in waste management, access and management of water and energy resources, participation in agriculture and fishing, and engaging in forestry management. Through applying SIDA's Gender Toolbox in environmental work, development experts map opportunities and challenges, and the gender-differentiated impact of their approach. They also collect the gender-disaggregated data, which enables them to measure policy impact. Finally, they engage locally with women and girls, financially supporting women entrepreneurs and workers in environment-related sectors (SIDA, 2016[105]).

2.6.5. Trade and investment policies

International trade policies are slowly integrating gender equality considerations, not only from the perspective of women participating in Global Value Chains or consuming imported end-products, but also by embedding gender equality considerations in Trade Agreements (Monteiro, 2018[106]); (Korinek, Moïsé and Tange, 2021[107]). Recent OECD analysis points out that gender considerations are being raised in Trade Agreements, either through aspirational provisions reaffirming parties' commitments to gender equality; or through gender-responsive provisions, such as positive discrimination measures despite restrictive effects on trade (Korinek, Moïsé and Tange, 2021[107]). Where safeguards exist, these tend to link to existing labour standards, or implementing gender-positive policies and practices, such as the OECD Guidelines for Multinational Enterprises. Nevertheless, in all cases, such provisions have limited enforceability, as they are rarely subject to Dispute Settlement Mechanisms.

Environment-related clauses are being gradually integrated into Trade Agreements at a greater pace than gender clauses. In fact the upward trend of references to environmental provisions has been remarkable, with such references in Regional Trade Agreements increasing on average from 30% in 2007 to 70% in 2012 (George, 2014[108]). Following a different typology on environmental provisions, (WTO, 2016[109]) identifies an even larger percentage of RTAs with environmental provisions, which reach up to 97% in year 2015 (WTO, 2016[109]). In both analyses, environmental co-operation scores high as a substantive environmental provision.

In only a few cases are gender considerations integrated into environmental agreements. As analysed by (Monteiro, 2018[106]), 34 trade agreements covering the broad area of sustainable development (not limited to environmental issues) contain references to gender equality and women's empowerment. The number of environmental agreements with such references are even fewer (Monteiro, 2018[106]).

International efforts to promote gender equality and environmental goals in investment policies – and more generally in private sector codes of conduct – also tend to apply the two criteria separately, without systematically looking at possible interactions. Such is the case for the OECD Guidelines for Multinational Enterprises, which do not specifically address the gender-environment nexus in their framework (Box 2.5).

Box 2.5. Promoting responsible business conduct along supply chains

The OECD Guidelines for Multinational Enterprises (the Guidelines) call on companies to avoid causing or contributing to adverse impacts through their own activities and to seek to prevent and mitigate adverse impacts in their supply chains. The Guidelines have various Chapters, including one on human rights and another one on employment and industrial relations where issues related to gender equality and women's empowerment are considered. There is also a separate Chapter on the Environment. The Guidelines do not specifically consider the interactions between gender and environmental criteria.

As part of its work to promote the Guidelines, the OECD has developed guidance for supply chain due diligence across a number of sectors, including specific recommendations that promote the well-being of women. In particular, the guidance for the garment and footwear sector addresses sexual harassment and sexual and gender-based violence in the workplace and includes recommendations on mainstreaming gender equality into company due diligence approaches. The guidance on mineral supply chains addresses widespread sexual violence and child labour. In this regard, while men hold most jobs in the large mining companies, approximately 30% of the world's artisanal miners are women. Agriculture also has a large percentage of female labour; the guidance for agricultural supply chains calls on companies to end discrimination against women and enhance their participation in decision-making and access and control over natural resources.

Under the Guidelines, Adherents (48) are required to establish National Contact Points (NCPs) whose role is to promote the Guidelines and provide implementation (including for environmental, labour and human rights standards).

Some countries have also introduced legislation to ensure that companies control their supply chains more closely. The UK Modern Slavery Act, Section 3017 of the United States Tariff Act and the California Transparency in Supply Chains Act all include expectations related to supply chain transparency. France mandates supply chain due diligence in accordance with the OECDMNE Guidelines and requires large companies to publish due diligence plans for human rights and environmental and social risks. In 2014, the EU passed a directive on disclosure of non-financial and diversity information for listed companies over a certain size. None of these national and regional initiatives addresses directly the gender-environment nexus.

References

Azcona, G. et al. (2020), *From Insights to Action - Gender Equality in the Wake of COVID-19*, UN Women, https://www.unwomen.org/-/media/headquarters/attachments/sections/library/publications/2020/gender-equality-in-the-wake-of-covid-19-en.pdf?la=en&vs=5142 (accessed on 5 April 2021). [8]

Bonewit, A. and R. Shreeves (2015), *The Gender Dimension of Climate Justice In-Depth Analysis*, http://www.europarl.europa.eu/supporting-analyses. [34]

Breschi, S., J. Lassébie and C. Menon (2018), "A portrait of innovative start-ups across countries", *OECD Science, Technology and Industry Working Papers*, No. 2018/2, OECD Publishing, Paris, https://dx.doi.org/10.1787/f9ff02f4-en. [28]

C3E International (2019), *STATUS REPORT ON GENDER EQUALITY IN THE ENERGY SECTOR MAPPING GENDER DIVERSITY IN THE ENERGY SECTOR*. [47]

Carlsson-Kanyama, A., A. Lindén and Å. Thelander (1999), "Insights and applications gender differences in environmental impacts from patterns of transportation - A case study from Sweden", *Society and Natural Resources*, Vol. 12/4, pp. 355-369, http://dx.doi.org/10.1080/089419299279641. [46]

Chamberlain, G. (2017), "Why climate change is creating a new generation of child brides", *The Guardian*. [6]

Cohen, G. and M. Shinwell (2020), "How far are OECD countries from achieving SDG targets for women and girls? : Applying a gender lens to measuring distance to SDG targets", *OECD Statistics Working Papers*, No. 2020/02, OECD Publishing, Paris, https://dx.doi.org/10.1787/17a25070-en. [62]

CPD (2020), *CPD.net*, https://www.cdp.net/en (accessed on 25 May 2020). [82]

Deighton-Smith, R., A. Erbacci and C. Kauffmann (2016), "Promoting inclusive growth through better regulation: The role of regulatory impact assessment", *OECD Regulatory Policy Working Papers*, No. 3, OECD Publishing, Paris, https://dx.doi.org/10.1787/5jm3tqwqp1vj-en. [86]

Downes, R. and S. Nicol (2020), "Designing and implementing gender budgeting – a path to action", *OECD Journal on Budgeting*, https://dx.doi.org/10.1787/689198fa-en. [91]

Downes, R., L. von Trapp and S. Nicol (2017), "Gender budgeting in OECD countries", *OECD Journal on Budgeting*, https://dx.doi.org/10.1787/budget-16-5jfq80dq1zbn. [92]

D'souza, D. (2018), *100 Years of Women in the House of Commons*, https://pudding.cool/2018/07/women-in-parliament/. [36]

ECOSOC (2013), *Gender statistics Report of the Secretary-General*, Statistical Commission of the United Nations Economic and Social Council. [66]

Equal Measures 2030 (2019), *Harnessing the Power of Data for Gender Equality: Introducing the 2019 EM2030 SDG Gender Index*, https://data.em2030.org/2019-sdg-gender-index/key-findings/. [80]

FAO (2020), *Global proportion of fish stocks within biologically sustainable levels*, http://www.fao.org/sustainable-development-goals/indicators/1441/en/ (accessed on 27 May 2020). [53]

Ferrant, G. and A. Thim (2019), "Measuring women's economic empowerment: Time use data and gender inequality", *OECD Development Policy Papers*, No. 16, OECD Publishing, Paris, https://dx.doi.org/10.1787/02e538fc-en. [26]

Flues, F. and A. Thomas (2015), "The distributional effects of energy taxes", *OECD Taxation Working Papers*, No. 23, OECD Publishing, Paris, https://dx.doi.org/10.1787/5js1qwkqqrbv-en. [96]

Flues, F. and K. van Dender (2017), "The impact of energy taxes on the affordability of domestic energy", *OECD Taxation Working Papers*, No. 30, OECD Publishing, Paris, https://dx.doi.org/10.1787/08705547-en. [97]

GENDERNET (2021), *Development Finance for Gender Equality and Women's Empowerment: A 2021 Snapshot*, OECD DAC Network on Gender Equality, https://www.oecd.org/development/gender-development/Development-finance-for-gender-equality-2021.pdf (accessed on 6 April 2021). [76]

George, C. (2014), "Environment and Regional Trade Agreements: Emerging Trends and Policy Drivers", *OECD Trade and Environment Working Papers*, No. 2014/2, OECD Publishing, Paris, https://dx.doi.org/10.1787/5jz0v4q45g6h-en. [108]

Government of Canada (2020), *Gender-Based Analysis Plus*, https://cfc-swc.gc.ca/gba-acs/index-en.html#what (accessed on 11 February 2020). [103]

Government of Canada (2019), *Departmental Plan 2019 to 2020, supplementary tables, Environment and Climate Change Canada, Chapter 4*, http://Departmental Plan 2019 to 2020, supplementary tables, Environment and Climate Change Canada, chapter 4. [104]

Grantham, K. (2020), *Mapping Gender Data Gaps: An SDG Era Update*, https://data2x.org/resource-center/mappinggenderdatagaps/. [78]

GRI (2020), *Global Reporting Initiative. GRI Sustainability Reporting Standards*, https://www.globalreporting.org/Pages/default.aspx (accessed on 2 June 2020). [81]

Halabisky, D. (2018), "Policy Brief on Women's Entrepreneurship", *OECD SME and Entrepreneurship Papers*, No. 8, OECD Publishing, Paris, https://dx.doi.org/10.1787/dd2d79e7-en. [27]

Hossain, M. et al. (2017), "Women in the boardroom and their impact on climate change related disclosure", *Social Responsibility Journal*, Vol. 13/4, pp. 828-855, http://dx.doi.org/10.1108/SRJ-11-2016-0208. [45]

IDMC (2019), *2019 Global Report on International Displacement*, International Displacement Monitoring Centre. [54]

IEA (2020), *Universal Access to Electricity*, https://www.iea.org/reports/sdg7-data-and-projections/access-to-electricity#abstract (accessed on 27 May 2020). [51]

ILO (2020), *COVID-19 and the world of work: Impact and policy responses*, International Labour Organisation, https://gisanddata.maps.arcgis.com/apps/opsdashboard/index.html#/bda7594740fd40299423467b48e9ecf6.CEPR.https://voxeu.org/content/economics-time-covid-193SeeforexampleUNCTAD,https://unctad.org/en/pages/PressRelease.aspx?OriginalVersionID=548. [15]

ILO (2020), *World Employment and Social Outlook EXECUTIVE SUMMARY*, International Labor Organization, https://www.ilo.org/wcmsp5/groups/public/---dgreports/---dcomm/---publ/documents/publication/wcms_734479.pdf. [11]

ILO (2018), *ILO Labour Force Estimates and Projections 2018- Key Trends*, International Labor Organization, https://www.ilo.org/ilostat-files/Documents/LFEPbrief.pdf. [12]

ILO and OECD (2020), *Women at Work in G20 countries: Progress and Policy Action since 2019*, Paper prepared for the G20 Employment Working Group. Saudi Arabia's G20 Presidency 2020. [16]

IPBES (2019), *The Global Assessment Report on Biodiversity and Ecosystem Services. Summary for Policymakers of the IPBES Global Assessment Report on Biodiversity and Ecosystem Services*, Intergovernmental Science-Policy Platform on Biodiversity and Ecosystem Services (IPBES), Bonn, https://ipbes.net/sites/default/files/inline/files/ipbes_global_assessment_report_summary_for_policymakers.pdf. [55]

Isidro, H. and M. Sobral (2015), "The Effects of Women on Corporate Boards on Firm Value, Financial Performance, and Ethical and Social Compliance", *Journal of Business Ethics*, Vol. 132/1, pp. 1-19, http://dx.doi.org/10.1007/s10551-014-2302-9. [41]

IUCN (2020), *GENDER-BASED VIOLENCE AND ENVIRONMENT LINKAGES DURING COVID-19: INFORMATION NOTE*. [4]

Jacob, K. et al. (2011), *Integrating the Environment in Regulatory Impact Assessments*, OECD, http://www.oecd.org/regreform. [87]

Kamalnath, A. (2015), "The Value of Board Gender Diversity vis-a-vis the Role of the Board in the Modern Company", *SSRN Electronic Journal*, http://dx.doi.org/10.2139/ssrn.2608301. [39]

Kersley, R. et al. (2019), *The CS Gender 3000 in 2019: The changing face of companies*. [38]

Kersley, R. et al. (2019), *The CS Gender 3000 in 2019: The changing face of companies*, Credit Suisse Research Institute, http://credit-suisse.com/researchinstitute (accessed on 25 November 2020). [42]

Korinek, J., E. Moïsé and J. Tange (2021), "Trade and gender: A Framework of analysis", *OECD Trade Policy Papers*, No. 246, OECD Publishing, Paris, https://dx.doi.org/10.1787/6db59d80-en. [107]

Monteiro, J. (2018), "Gender-Related Provisions in Regional Trade Agreements", No. ERSD-2018-15, World Trade Organization, Economic Research and Statitistics Division. [106]

New Zealand. Treasury (2019), *The Living Standards Framework : Dashboard Update, 12 December 2019*. [101]

Norgaard, K. and R. York (2005), *Gender equality and state environmentalists*, http://dx.doi.org/10.1177/0891243204273612. [37]

OECD (2020), "Aid Focussed on Gender Equality and Women's Empowerment: A Snapshot of Current Funding and Trends Over Time in Support of the Implementation of the Beijing Declaration and Platform for Action", Vol. OECD DAC Network on Gender Equality (GENDERNET), https://www.oecd.org/development/gender-development/Aid-Focussed-on-Gender-Equality-and-Women-s-Empowerment-2020.pdf. [1]

OECD (2020), *Fossil Fuel Support Data and Country Notes*, https://www.oecd.org/fossil-fuels/data/ (accessed on 15 June 2020). [94]

OECD (2020), *Gender and Environmental Statistics - Exploring available Data and Developing New Evidence Contents*, https://www.oecd.org/environment/brochure-gender-and-environmental-statistics.pdf. [65]

OECD (2020), *Gender wage gap* (indicator), https://dx.doi.org/10.1787/7cee77aa-en (accessed on 20 May 2020). [21]

OECD (2020), *How's Life? 2020: Measuring Well-being*, OECD Publishing, Paris, https://dx.doi.org/10.1787/9870c393-en. [14]

OECD (2020), *Social Institutions and Gender Index (SIGI)*, https://www.genderindex.org/ (accessed on 23 May 2020). [30]

OECD (2020), *Survey on integrating gender in environmental policies - Reporting on key findings*, https://one.oecd.org/document/ENV/EPOC(2020)9/en/pdf. [75]

OECD (2020), "Women at the core of the fight against COVID-19", https://read.oecd-ilibrary.org/view/?ref=127_127000-awfnqj80me&title=Women-at-the-core-of-the-fight-against-COVID-19-crisis. [3]

OECD (2019), *Aligning Development Co-operation and Climate Action: The Only Way Forward*, The Development Dimension, OECD Publishing, Paris, https://dx.doi.org/10.1787/5099ad91-en. [77]

OECD (2019), *Gender, Institutions and Development Database*, https://oe.cd/ds/GIDDB2019. [10]

OECD (2019), *Government at a Glance 2019*, OECD Publishing, Paris, https://dx.doi.org/10.1787/8ccf5c38-en. [23]

OECD (2019), *Measuring Distance to the SDG Targets 2019: An Assessment of Where OECD Countries Stand*, OECD Publishing, Paris, https://dx.doi.org/10.1787/a8caf3fa-en. [56]

OECD (2019), *OECD Corporate Governance Factbook 2019*, http://www.oecd.org/corporate/corporate-governance-factbook.htm. [25]

OECD (2019), *OECD Economic Surveys: New Zealand 2019*, OECD Publishing, Paris, https://dx.doi.org/10.1787/b0b94dbd-en. [100]

OECD (2019), "The gender pension gap is large", in *Pensions at a Glance 2019: OECD and G20 Indicators*, OECD Publishing, Paris, https://dx.doi.org/10.1787/b6d3dcfc-en. [22]

OECD (2019), *Risks that Matter: Main Findings from the 2018 OECD Risks that Matter Survey*, http://www oecd org/social/risks-that-matter htm. [29]

OECD (2019), *SIGI 2019 Global Report: Transforming Challenges into Opportunities*, Social Institutions and Gender Index, OECD Publishing, Paris, https://dx.doi.org/10.1787/bc56d212-en. [31]

OECD (2018), *2018 International Budget Practices and Procedures Database*, https://qdd.oecd.org/subject.aspx?Subject=BPP_2018 (accessed on 17 June 2020). [98]

OECD (2018), *Bridging the Digital Gender Divide*, http://www.oecd.org/internet/bridging-the-digital-gender-divide.pdf. [17]

OECD (2018), *Climate-Related Financial Disclosures and Corporate Board Practices Taking Stock of the TCFD Recommendations*, 2018 OECD-ASIAN ROUNDTABLE ON CORPORATE GOVERNANCE. [83]

OECD (2018), *Cost-Benefit Analysis and the Environment: Further Developments and Policy Use*, OECD Publishing, Paris, https://dx.doi.org/10.1787/9789264085169-en. [88]

OECD (2017), *2013 OECD Recommendation of the Council on Gender Equality in Education, Employment and Entrepreneurship*, OECD Publishing, Paris, https://dx.doi.org/10.1787/9789264279391-en. [18]

OECD (2017), *Meeting of the OECD Council at Ministerial Level - Report on the implementation of the OECD gender recommendations*, http://www.oecd.org/mcm-2018/documents/C-MIN-2017-7-EN.pdf. [20]

OECD (2017), *OECD Champion Mayors: Gender inequality in numbers*, http://www.oecd-inclusive.com/wp-content/uploads/2020/03/OECD-Champion-Mayors-March-on-Gender-flyer.pdf. [24]

OECD (2017), *OECD Survey on National Gender Equality Frameworks and Public Policies*. [74]

OECD (2017), *The Pursuit of Gender Equality: An Uphill Battle*, OECD Publishing, Paris, https://dx.doi.org/10.1787/9789264281318-en. [2]

OECD (2016), *2015 OECD Recommendation of the Council on Gender Equality in Public Life*, OECD Publishing, Paris, https://dx.doi.org/10.1787/9789264252820-en. [19]

OECD (2013), *Introduction to OECD Test Guidelines on Pesticide Residues Chemistry - Section 5 Part A*, OECD Guidelines for the Testing of Chemicals, Section 5, OECD Publishing, Paris, https://dx.doi.org/10.1787/9789264203761-en. [73]

OECD (2012), *Recommendation of the Council on Regulatory Policy and Governance*, OECD Publishing, Paris, https://dx.doi.org/10.1787/9789264209022-en. [89]

OECD (2011), *Greening Household Behaviour: The Role of Public Policy*, OECD Studies on Environmental Policy and Household Behaviour, OECD Publishing, Paris, https://dx.doi.org/10.1787/9789264096875-en. [72]

OECD (2010), *Guidance on Sustainability Impact Assessment*, OECD Publishing, Paris, https://dx.doi.org/10.1787/9789264086913-en. [90]

OECD (2005), *Environmentally Harmful Subsidies: Challenges for Reform*, OECD Publishing, Paris, https://dx.doi.org/10.1787/9789264012059-en. [95]

OECD Publishing, P. (ed.) (2019), *Social Institutions and Gender Index*, https://doi.org/10.1787/bc56d212-en. [32]

OECD.Stat (n.d.), *Employment by activities and status (ALFS)*, https://stats.oecd.org/Index.aspx?DataSetCode=ALFS_EMP#. [93]

OECD/CAWTAR (2014), *Women in Public Life: Gender, Law and Policy in the Middle East and North Africa*, OECD Publishing, Paris, https://dx.doi.org/10.1787/9789264224636-en. [35]

Offermann, L. and K. Foley (2020), "Is There a Female Leadership Advantage?", in *Oxford Research Encyclopedia of Business and Management*, Oxford University Press, http://dx.doi.org/10.1093/acrefore/9780190224851.013.61. [33]

PARIS21 (2020), *Use of Citizen-Generated Data for SDG Reporting in the Philippines: A Case Study*, https://paris21.org/sites/default/files/inline-files/PSA-report-FINAL.pdf (accessed on 19 October 2020). [79]

PARIS21 (n.d.), *PARIS21 and Women Count - Synthesis Report (forthcoming)*. [64]

PARIS21 (n.d.), *Supporting Gender Statistics*, https://paris21.org/supporting-gender-statistics (accessed on 9 September 2020). [63]

Perrault, E. (2015), "Why Does Board Gender Diversity Matter and How Do We Get There? The Role of Shareholder Activism in Deinstitutionalizing Old Boys' Networks", *Journal of Business Ethics*, Vol. 128/1, pp. 149-165, http://dx.doi.org/10.1007/s10551-014-2092-0. [40]

Pinar, G. (n.d.), *Public Governance Directorate Senior Budget Officials Working Party on Gender Mainstreaming and Governance OECD Scan: Equality Budgeting in Ireland*. [102]

Post, C., N. Rahman and E. Rubow (2011), "Green governance: Boards of directors' composition and environmental corporate social responsibility", *Business and Society*, Vol. 50/1, pp. 189-223, http://dx.doi.org/10.1177/0007650310394642. [44]

Quarles, M. (2019), *The Task Force on Climate-related Financial Disclosures i Letter from Michael R. Bloomberg*. [84]

Seager, J. (2015), *Sex-disaggregated indicators for water assessment, monitoring and reporting United Nations World Water Assessment Programme*, UNESCO, https://unesdoc.unesco.org/ark:/48223/pf0000234082. [67]

Serrao, S. et al. (2019), *Mainstreaming gender in environment statistics for the SDGs and beyond: Identifying priorities in Asia and the Pacific*, http://www.unescap.org/resource-series/sd-working-papers. [70]

SIDA (2016), *Gender and the Environment Brief. Gender Tool Box*, https://www.sida.se/contentassets/0b57532e484543199b0485c0984d731a/gender_and_environment.pdf. [105]

Stotsky, J. et al. (2016), *Sub-Saharan Africa: A Survey of Gender Budgeting Efforts*. [99]

UN Environment (2016), *Global Gender and Environment Outlook 2016*, United Nations, New York, https://dx.doi.org/10.18356/0b979453-en. [85]

UNDESA (n.d.), *Women and Sustainable Development: Building a Better Future for All...*, https://maps4stats.maps.arcgis.com/apps/MapSeries/index.html?appid=6bf7ee97799846ec950b6ef5c521503d (accessed on 29 November 2020). [58]

UNEP (2019), *Measuring Progress towards Achieving the Environmental Dimension of the SDGs*, United Nations Environment Programme, Nairobi, http://www.unenvironment.org. [50]

UNEP (2019), *The Emissions Gap Report 2019*, United Nations Environment Programme, Nairobi. [52]

UNEP and IUCN (2019), *Gender and environment statistics: Unlocking information for action and measuring the SDGs*, http://www.un.org/Depts/Cartographic/english/htmain.htm. [69]

United Nations (n.d.), *Global indicator framework for the Sustainable Development Goals and targets of the 2030 Agenda for Sustainable Development*, https://unstats.un.org/sdgs/indicators/indicators-list/ (accessed on 19 June 2020). [48]

United Nations (n.d.), *Inter-agency and Expert Group on SDG Indicators*, https://unstats.un.org/sdgs/iaeg-sdgs/ (accessed on 8 September 2020). [49]

UNSD (2019), *The United Nations Minimum Set of Gender Indicators. A Product of the Inter-Agency and Expert Group on Gender Statistics*, http://genderstats.un.org. [68]

UNSD (n.d.), *Global Gender Statistics Programme*, https://unstats.un.org/unsd/demographic-social/gender/#home (accessed on 29 November 2020). [59]

UNSD (n.d.), "IAEG-SDGs - Data Disaggregation for the SDG Indicators", https://unstats.un.org/sdgs/iaeg-sdgs/disaggregation/ (accessed on 29 November 2020). [60]

UNWomen (2020), *Gender Equality: Women's Rights in Review 25 Years after Beijing*, United Nations, http://unwo.men/eDNK50yyBhA. [7]

UNWomen (2019), *Advancing administrative sources of data for monitoring gender-specific Sustainable Development Goals in Africa*, http://africa.unwomen.org/en/digital-library/publications. [71]

UNWomen (2018), *Turning promises into Action : Gender Equality in the 2030 Agenda for Sustainable Development*, https://www.unwomen.org/en/digital-library/publications. [61]

UNWomen and UNDESA (2019), *Progress on the Sustainable Development Goals -The Gender Snapshot 2019*, https://unstats.un.org/sdgs/report/2019/gender-snapshot.pdf (accessed on 17 September 2020). [9]

USAID (2020), "RISE Challenge Winners". [5]

Walls, J. and A. Hoffman (2013), "Exceptional boards: Environmental experience and positive deviance from institutional norms", *Journal of Organizational Behavior*, Vol. 34/2, pp. 253-271, http://dx.doi.org/10.1002/job.1813. [43]

WHO (2019), *Delivered by women, led by men: A gender and equity analysis of the global health and social workforce. Human Resources for Health Observer Series No. 24*, World Health Organisation. [13]

WRI (2018), *Why Positive Climate Feedbacks Are So Bad*, https://www.wri.org/blog/2018/08/why-positive-climate-feedbacks-are-so-bad. [57]

WTO (2016), "Typology of Environment-Related Provisions in Regional Trade Agreements", *WTO Working Papers*, No. 2016/13, World Trade Organization, Geneva, https://dx.doi.org/10.30875/2963576b-en. [109]

Notes

[1] This issue has been recognised, among others, in UN HABITAT's Policy and Plan for Gender Equality and the Empowerment of Women for 2014-19.

[2] From the 247 indicators of the UN Global Indicator Framework for the SDGs, 231 are unique, meaning they are only used once to measure one specific target. The remaining 12 indicators are used to measure 2 or 3 different targets under different SDGs. The following indicators are those repeated: (i) 7.b.1 and 12.a.1; (ii) 8.4.1 and 12.2.1; (iii) 8.4.2 and 12.2.2; (iv) 10.3.1 and 16.b.1; (v) 10.6.1 and 16.8.1; (vi) 13.2.1 and 13.b.1 (not identical); (vii) 15.7.1 and 15.c.1; (viii) 15.a.1 and 5.b.1; (ix) 1.5.1, 11.5.1 and 13.1.1; (x) 1.5.3, 11.b.1 and 13.1.2; (xi) 1.5.4, 11.b.2, and 13.1.3; and (xii) 4.7.1, 12.8.1 and 13.3.1.

[3] These indicators fall mainly under the "People", "Prosperity", and "Peace" Goals: SDG 1, SDG 3, SDG 4, SDG 5, SDG 16 and SDG 17.

[4] Data is considered to be available for a specific indicator when it is reported for a minimum of 10 OECD countries.

[5] Countries included in this category responded yes to questions 1 and 2 AND Always, Often, Sometimes to Question 3a of the Gender-Environment Survey ENV/EPOC(2020)9. Austria is an outlier, as they do not acknowledge their principles as strategy. Costa Rica does not appear in the Map as it is still not included in the OECD database of Member countries.

3 Economic and well-being benefits of better integrating gender equality and environmental goals

Existing evidence shows that environmental factors have differentiated impact by gender, making women in some cases more impacted by certain environmental and occupational risks. Climate change and extreme weather events also affect men and women differently, with women often suffering most due to traditional gender roles. Developing quality infrastructure, which takes into account different needs by gender, and accelerating the transition to a low carbon economy could further women's participation in the labour market. The effects of the current COVID-19 crisis should also be taken into account when developing policies to close gender gaps.

3.1. Key findings

Drawing on the OECD's Well-being framework, this chapter reviews the existing evidence on the differentiated impact of environmental factors by gender and the benefits of better tailoring environmental policies to women's and men's needs and risk factors. While in OECD countries men suffer more premature deaths than women due to environmental and occupational risks, there are many non-fatal impacts that can reduce women's well-being more significantly than men's. Globally, more women than men die prematurely due to second-hand smoke, unsafe water sources, indoor air pollution, unsafe sanitation, and lack of access to handwashing facilities. Hazardous chemicals have also been found to have differentiated impacts on men and women.

Climate change also has a gender dimension. An increasing incidence and intensity of natural hazards such as droughts, landslides, floods and hurricanes tend to affect women more due to their greater economic vulnerability. In 2018 women accounted for more than 75% of displaced persons from such hazards (UNHCR, 2019[1]) Furthermore, traditional gender roles dictate that women become the primary caregivers for those affected by disasters – such as children, the injured, sick, and elderly – substantially increasing their emotional and material workload.

Addressing the specific environmental impacts on women and men can therefore save lives, reduce healthcare costs, improve well-being and reduce inequalities. In addition, incorporating a gender lens in policies that have an impact on the environment can generate numerous and broad economic benefits. There are three main areas of greatest relevance for OECD countries:

- Ensuring a "just transition" to low carbon economies for men and women can increase productivity and lead to better economic outcomes and more resilient societies. Enhancing the participation of women in green innovation can be a source of high-skilled jobs for women and boost overall productivity;
- Access to sustainable infrastructure (transport, energy, water, etc.) which meets women's needs is a key requirement to enhance women's economic empowerment and labour force participation. Designing such environmentally friendly infrastructure with a gender lens would provide win-win outcomes for all and improve well-being across the population.
- Incorporating a gender lens into public policies such as product labelling, public information campaigns and targeted education programmes can help accelerate women's contribution towards more sustainable consumption patterns and boost the overall sustainability of production and consumption.

The COVID crisis has also exposed many systemic weaknesses in societies, including women's greater vulnerability to such crises. A "gendered" approach to the recovery can put economies on a greener and more sustainable path, by building better healthcare systems, increasing food security, developing more sustainable work and travel practices as well as more sustainable production and consumption patterns.

3.2. The environment's impact on women's health

The synergies between gender equality and environmental goals translate into positive economic and well-being outcomes across a number of dimensions. In particular, by advancing towards the nine environment-related SDGs, the benefits for women are observed in other SDGs such as SDG 1 (no poverty), SDG 3 (good health and well-being), SDG 4 (quality education), SDG 8 (decent work and economic growth) and SDG 10 (reduced inequalities). Similarly, improving gender equality and women's economic empowerment can bring about both positive environmental impacts and improved economic prospects for all. This depends to a large extent on whether women are provided with the necessary education and awareness of environmental sustainability.

The OECD has developed a Well-being Framework that incorporates 11 dimensions of well-being. The environmental quality dimension addresses indicators such as exposure to outdoor air pollution and access to urban green spaces (OECD, 2020[2]). The framework has many parallels with the SDG indicators, but includes some dimensions not featured in the SDGs (e.g. relational aspects, or subjective well-being). It also has a more targeted number of indicators and methodically incorporates distributional measures (averages, inequalities across groups in the population – including gender – inequalities between top and bottom performers, and deprivations). Furthermore, the 11 dimensions of current well-being are complemented by four key resources for future well-being: economic, social, human and natural capital. They are measured in terms of stocks, flows, risk factors and resilience. Incorporating such a well-being framework in policy-making would go a long way to addressing and leveraging the gender-environment nexus.

Environmental and climate-related effects on human health – both physical and mental – exist all around the world. The environmental impacts on health outcomes depend not only on differences in *exposure* to environmental risks (e.g. arising from occupational exposures or differences in how domestic tasks like the cooking and cleaning are shared) but also on differences in *vulnerability* (e.g. baseline health, access to healthcare, knowledge of risks, biological differences etc.). These inequalities and inequities[1] by gender exist both in developing and developed countries, albeit with different intensities and natures. Overcoming them is a global challenge often requiring customised, local solutions. This is often the case in gender inequalities overall, even though the degree varies depending on the country, the income level, the geographical location etc. Even though the level of inequalities may be reducing in developed countries, when comparing with the rest of the world, this should not be interpreted as achievement of gender equality. Contrary, it may be an issue of inequalities existing under different issues (for example, women's role in fetching fuel and water is mainly a developing economy issue, however, women facing more frequently energy poverty is a developed and emerging economies' issue).

Throughout this chapter, data presented on mortality estimates are from the Global Burden of Disease project (GBD) (GBD, 2019[3]). GBD is a systematic, scientific effort to quantify the comparative magnitude of health loss due to diseases, injuries, and risk factors by age, sex, and geographic regions over time. Environmental and occupational risks accounted for 14% of premature deaths in 2019 in OECD countries, while the global average was at 36% (Figure 3.1.). Though the percentage is relatively small compared to other contributors to mortality in OECD countries, such as unhealthy lifestyles and the development of metabolic disease, environmental and occupational risks remain very important because they help interpret the linkages between human activity and environmental effects. They also provide background for estimating and mitigating exposure to harmful environmental and other agents that affect both the environment and public health.

Figure 3.1. Share of total premature deaths attributable to environmental and occupational risks in percentage

2019 data

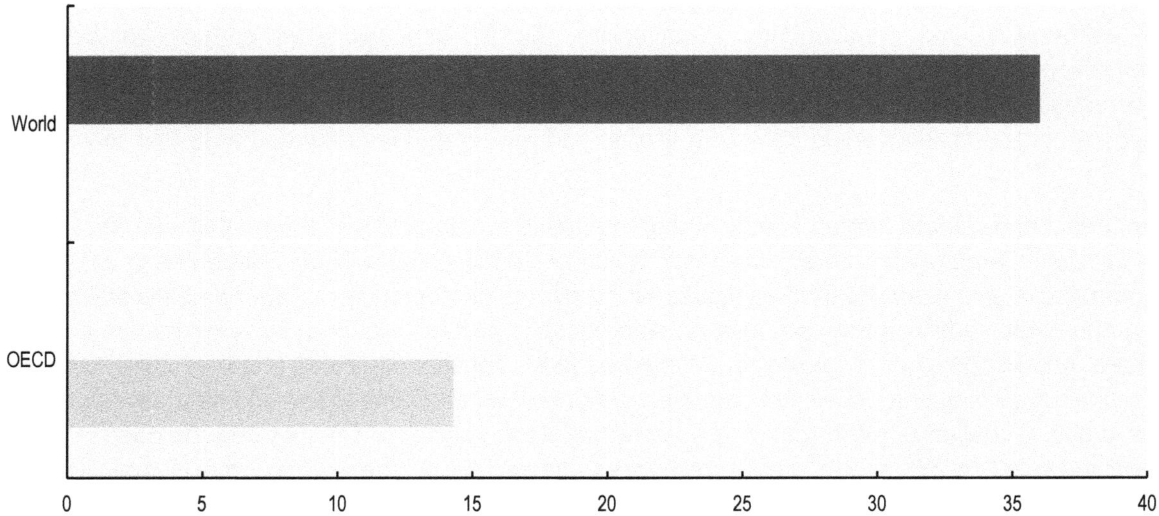

Note: Share of premature deaths attributable to environmental and occupational risks (GBD classification), 2019
Source: Institute for Health Metrics and Evaluation (IHME), GBD Compare, as presented in (OECD, 2021[4]).

In OECD countries and globally, poor air quality --specifically ambient particulate matter (PM) -- constitutes the main contributor to premature deaths attributed to environmental and occupational risks, accounting respectively for 5.5% and 11.8% of total premature deaths , in 2019 (Roy and Braathen, 2017[5]) (Figure 3.2). For OECD countries, the other main environmental and occupational contributors to premature deaths are occupational carcinogens (2.9%) and second-hand smoke (2.3%). At a global level, the other main contributors are indoor air pollution (residential PM) (6.6%) and unsafe water sources (3.5%) (OECD, 2021[4])

As seen in Figure 3.2, 44% of premature deaths attributed to environmental and occupational risks are linked to air pollution in OECD countries. Globally, air pollution is linked to 54% of premature deaths. For OECD countries, about 26% of premature deaths derive from environment-related occupational risks, while globally this risk factor accounts for 7%. Such stark difference can be explained mainly by the share of deaths attributed to occupational carcinogens, which in OECD countries almost triples the world average. Occupation carcinogens include a series of agents to which the population is exposed through different economic activities (arsenic, benzene, beryllium, cadmium, chromium, diesel engine exhaust, formaldehyde, nickel, polycyclic aromatic hydrocarbons, silica, sulphuric acid, and trichloroethylene). These cause a wide range of cancers; cancers of the lung and other respiratory sites, followed by skin, account for the largest proportion (OECD, 2020[6]). The dominant routes of exposure are inhalation and dermal contact. Globally, almost 21% of premature deaths are attributed to unsafe water, sanitation and handwashing.

Figure 3.2. Risk factors contributing to environmental and occupation-related premature deaths by share of deaths attributed in percentage

2019 data

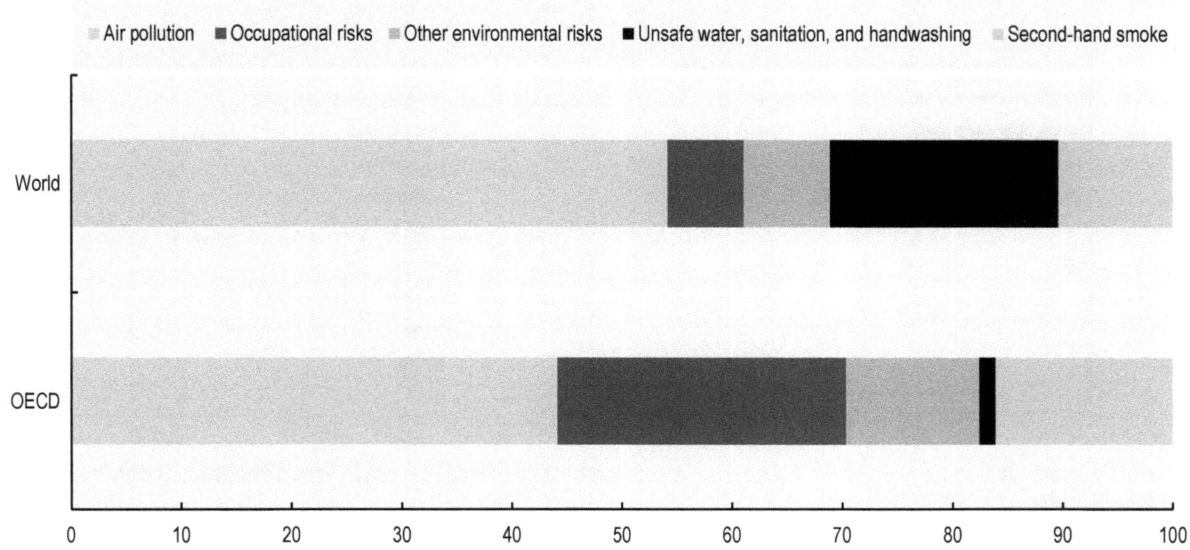

Note: Risk factors contributing to environmental and occupational related premature deaths expressed in percentages.
Source: Institute for Health Metrics and Evaluation (IHME), GBD Compare, as presented in (OECD, 2021[4]).

Environmental and occupational risk factors have differentiated effects on men and women. Men seem to be more vulnerable than women, accounting in general for more premature deaths due to environmental and occupational risks in 2009 both in OECD and non-OECD countries (Figure 3.3). But some exceptions exist. For OECD countries, women show higher levels than men of premature death due to household air pollution from solid fuels. This is estimated based on the proportion of households using solid cooking fuels including coal, wood, charcoal, dung, and agricultural residues (OECD, 2020[6]). Globally, more women than men die prematurely due to second-hand smoke, unsafe water sources, unsafe sanitation, and no access to handwashing facilities according to the model developed with the data from GBD (Figure 3.3). It is worth noting that elderly women are disproportionately impacted by these risks. This could be attributed to differences in life expectancy.

Figure 3.3. Premature deaths attributed to environmental and certain occupational risks by gender per million inhabitants

2019 data

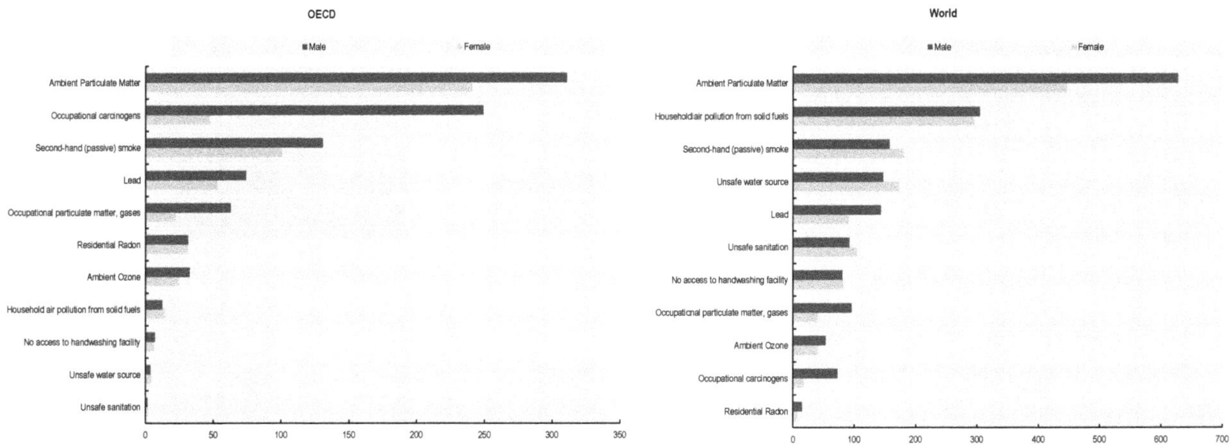

Note: Premature deaths attributed to environmental and certain occupational risks by gender, per million female inhabitants and per million male inhabitants respectively.
Source: Institute for Health Metrics and Evaluation (IHME), GBD Compare, as presented in (OECD, 2021[4]).

Examining the trends over the past 30 years is encouraging. Deaths caused by environmental and occupational risks have been decreasing globally and in OECD countries. This drop in OECD countries, for both men and women, can be attributed mainly to improvements in ambient particulate matter (PM). Since 1990, an 18% decrease in environment-related premature deaths has been observed in OECD countries. However, not all risks in Figure 3.3 have been decreasing over that period (OECD, 2021[4]).

Despite the drop in premature deaths from environment-related risks, the welfare costs of these deaths remain considerable. The costs for all OECD countries amount to approximately 6.8% of GDP, equivalent to about USD 4 trillion for 2019 (Figure 3.4). Welfare costs are estimated to be less than 5% of GDP in only ten OECD countries (Iceland, Sweden, Ireland, Norway, Finland, New Zealand, Australia, Luxembourg, Canada and Israel), while Hungary's welfare cost reaches almost 17%. Expressed per capita, this is equivalent to around USD 1 000 to 5 000 per capita per year among OECD countries. Globally, welfare costs surpassed 17% of global GDP in 2017, mainly due to excess costs for India and China.

Figure 3.4. Welfare cost of premature deaths attributed to environmental and occupational risks

Percentage GDP equivalent, 2019 data

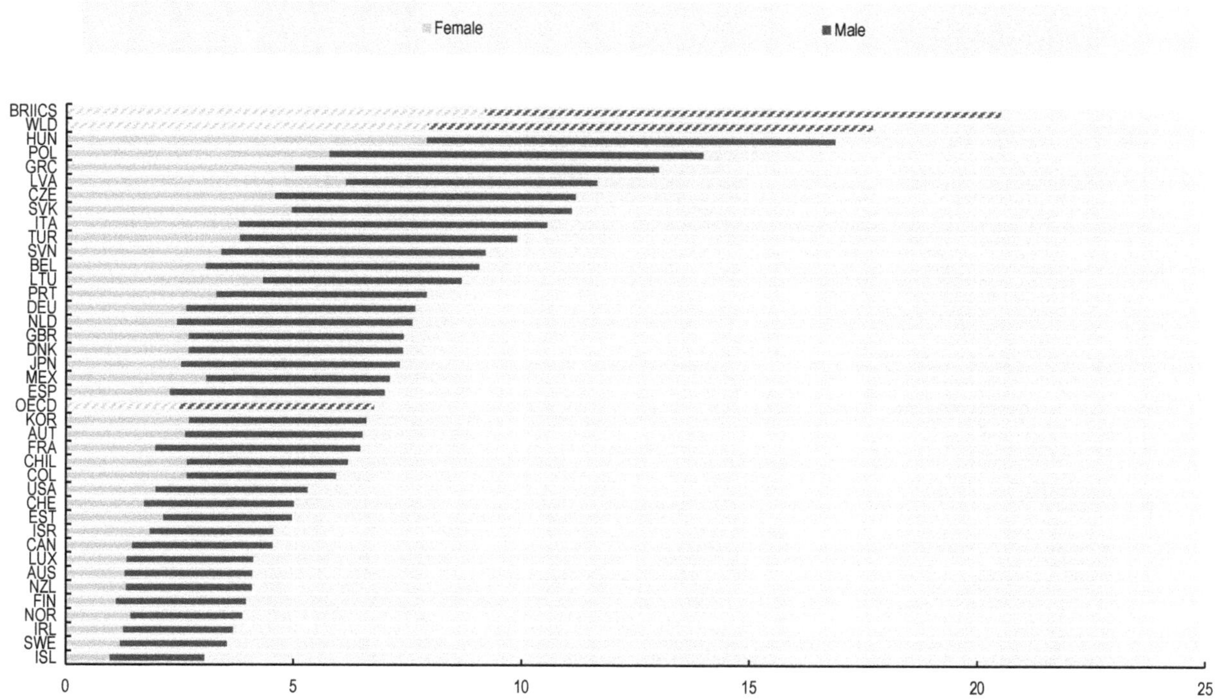

Note: Welfare cost of premature deaths attributed to environmental and occupational risks, in percentage of GDP equivalent. Data on mortality and DALYs from exposure to environmental risks are taken from (GBD, 2019[3]), Global Burden of Disease Study 2019 Results. Welfare costs are calculated using a methodology adapted from the OECD, (Roy and Braathen, 2017[5]) 'Rising Cost of Ambient Air Pollution thus far in the 21st Century: Results from the BRIICS and the OECD Countries'.
Source: Institute for Health Metrics and Evaluation (IHME), GBD Compare, as presented in (OECD, 2021[4]).

3.2.1. Cost of air pollution

Concentration of and exposure to certain pollutants has increased over the last decades (Manisalidis et al., 2020[7]). With 91% of the world's population living in places where air pollution exceeds WHO guideline limits, poor air quality poses the single biggest threat to human health, accounting for 3 to 4 million premature deaths per year (Roy and Braathen, 2017[5]), and shortening life expectancy by 1.8 years globally (Prüss-Üstün, Corvalán and WHO, 2006[8]). Furthermore, increasing global temperatures often exacerbate the effects of pollution on human health with urban areas being most affected (OECD, 2016[9]). Only 2% of the global urban population lives today under what is identified as acceptable PM_{10} concentration levels (per WHO Air Quality Guidelines) (OECD, 2012[10]). Different studies show particularly negative correlations between high concentrations of air pollutants and health of humans, with women, the elderly and children displaying greater vulnerability (Balestra and Sultan, 2013[11]); (Inyinbor et al., 2018[12]).

Figure 3.5 shows the welfare cost of premature deaths from outdoor air pollution associated with $PM_{2.5}$ and ozone concentrations. The OECD average is 2.7% of its GDP while for BRIICS is triple the percentage. Welfare cost for men is higher than for women, as a percentage to the GDP, for all countries. Figure 3.6 on the other hand shows the development of averages in the World, OECD countries and BRIICS countries from 2008 to 2019; BRIICS countries have been on the rise, whereas the World and OECD averages plateau.

Figure 3.5. Welfare cost of premature deaths from outdoor pollution by gender

Percentage by GDP equivalent, 2019 data

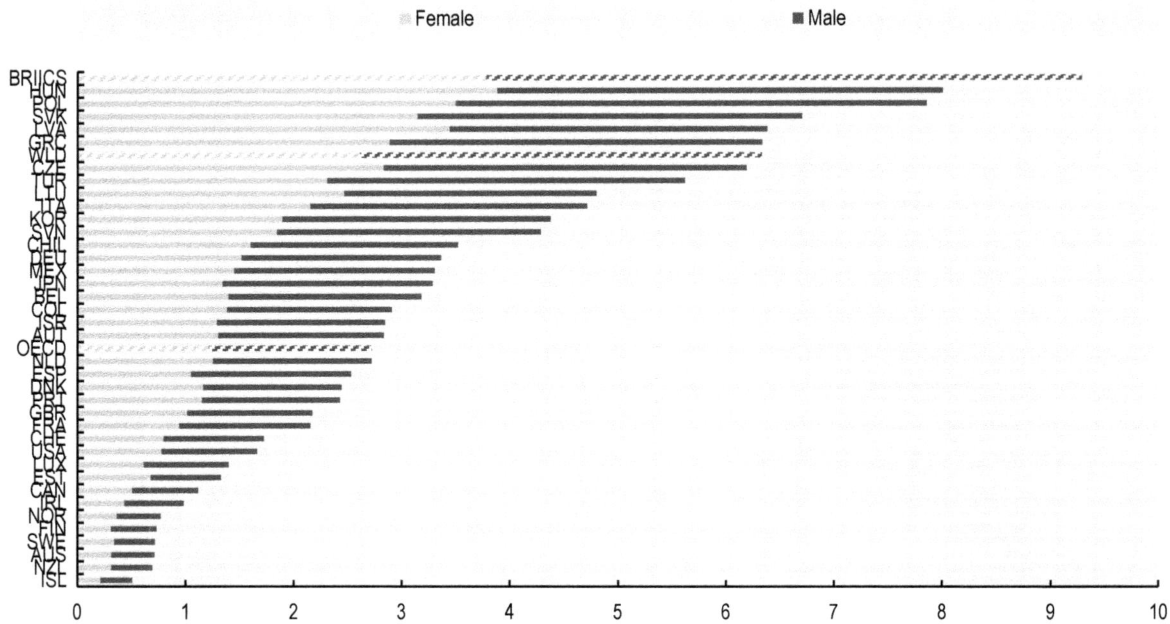

Note: Outdoor air pollution includes Ambient Particulate Matter (PM2.5) and Ambient Ozone. Data on mortality and DALYs from exposure to environmental risks are taken from (GBD, 2019[3]), Global Burden of Disease Study 2019 Results. Welfare costs are calculated using a methodology adapted from the OECD, (Roy and Braathen, 2017[5]) 'Rising Cost of Ambient Air Pollution thus far in the 21st Century: Results from the BRIICS and the OECD Countries'.
Source: Institute for Health Metrics and Evaluation (IHME), GBD Compare, as presented in (OECD, 2021[4]).

Figure 3.6. Welfare cost of premature deaths attributed to outdoor air pollution

In millions based on 2015 USD PPP, 2019 data

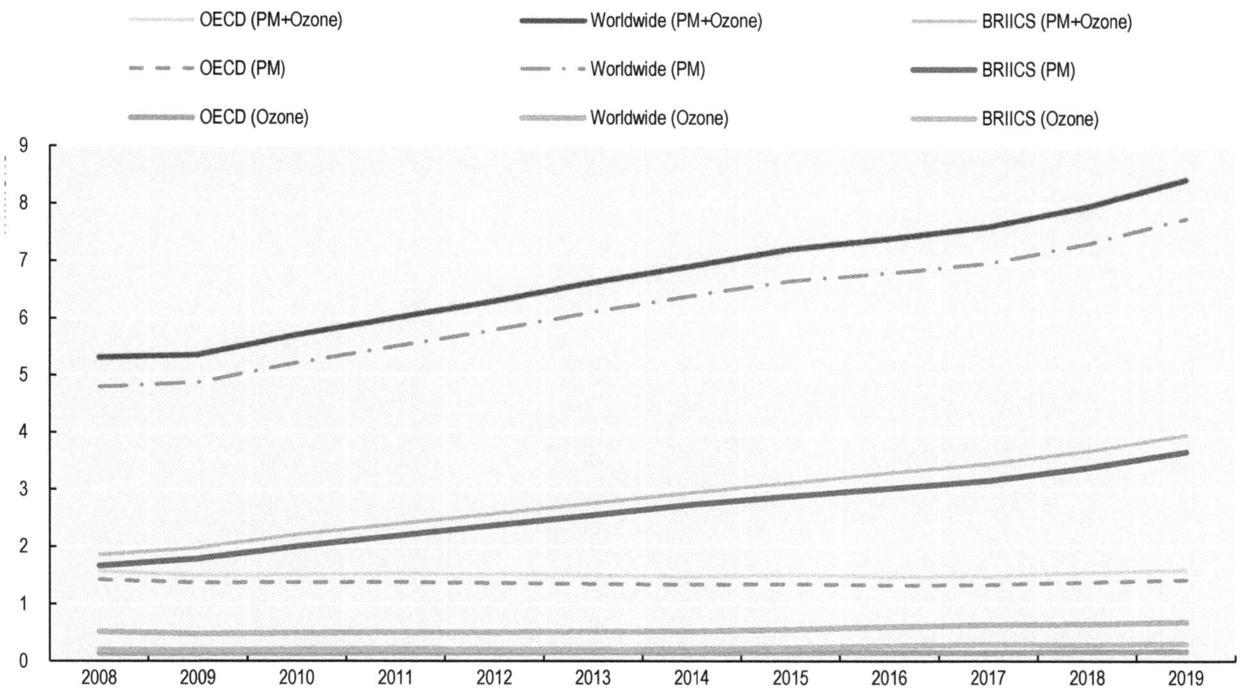

Note: Outdoor air pollution includes Ambient Particulate Matter (PM2.5) and Ambient Ozone. Welfare cost of premature deaths attributed to outdoor air pollution in millions (2015 USD PPP). Data on mortality and DALYs from exposure to environmental risks are taken from (GBD, 2019[3]), Global Burden of Disease Study 2019 Results. Welfare costs are calculated using a methodology adapted from the OECD, (Roy and Braathen, 2017[5]) 'Rising Cost of Ambient Air Pollution thus far in the 21st Century: Results from the BRIICS and the OECD Countries'.
Source: Institute for Health Metrics and Evaluation (IHME), GBD Compare, as presented in (OECD, 2021[4]).

Indoor air pollution can also pose a serious threat to human health, mainly affecting women and children in developing countries (WHO, 2016[13]), (Okello, Devereux and Semple, 2018[14]). According to GBD, in 2019 over 2 million people died prematurely in the world due to household air pollution from solid fuels and over 18 000 in OECD countries (GBD, 2019[3]). Although indoor air pollution constitutes for a greater threat to developing countries and emerging economies, it also remains important for OECD countries. Beyond the death toll, household pollution is linked to a non-negligible welfare cost for some OECD members (Figure 3.7). For OECD countries, the 2019 welfare cost of premature deaths attributed to indoor pollution was 0.075% of GDP equivalent. While this might be a small percentage, a closer look to the data shows stark differences between OECD countries, ranging from 0.001% welfare cost in Switzerland to 2.8% in Hungary. It is also worth noting that the welfare cost from indoor air pollution is higher for women, whereas the welfare cost from outdoor air pollution is higher for men, in both OECD and non-OECD countries. This result is consistent with the findings that men spend more time outdoors, such as for traveling to work, and that women spend more time cooking and heating the house (WHO, 2016[15]).

Figure 3.7. Welfare cost of premature deaths attributable to indoor air pollution

Percentage of GDP equivalent, 2019 data

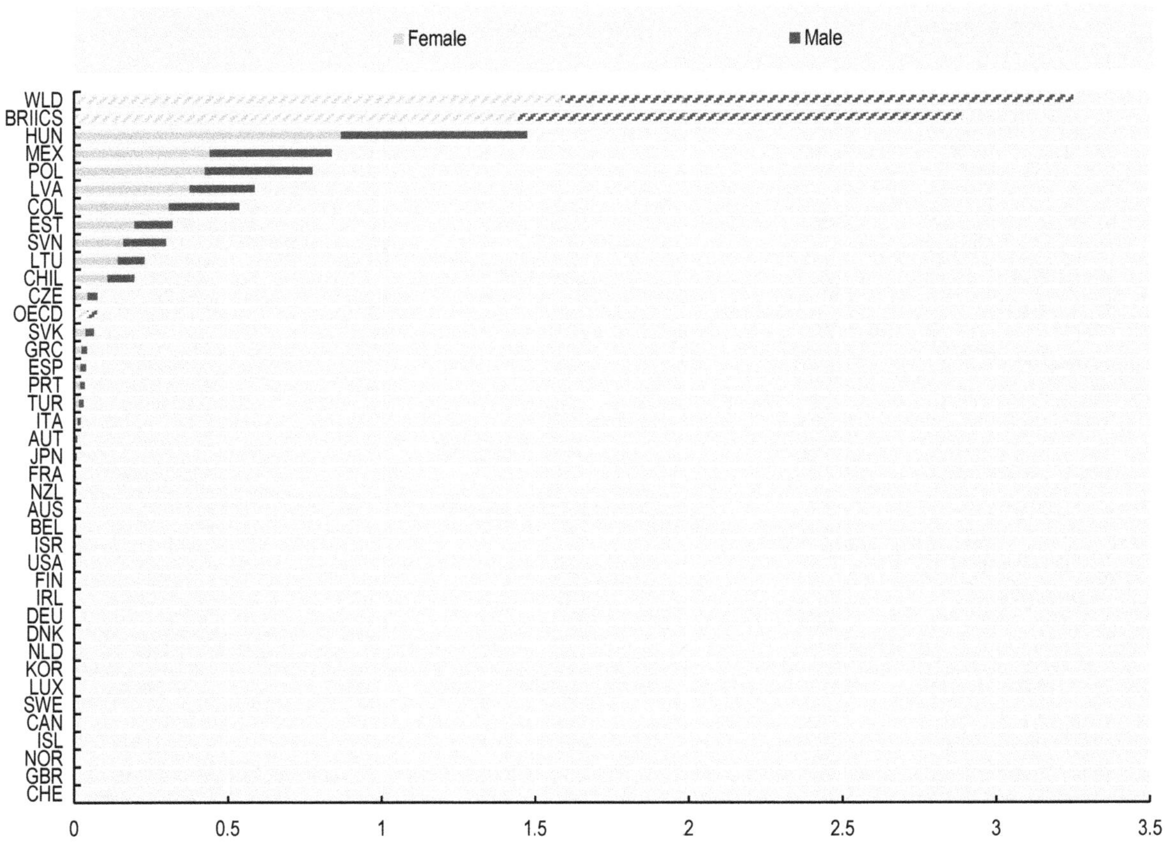

Note: Indoor air pollution refers to household air pollution from fossil fuels. Data on mortality and DALYs from exposure to environmental risks are taken from GBD (2019), Global Burden of Disease Study 2019 Results. Welfare costs are calculated using a methodology adapted from the OECD, (Roy and Braathen, 2017[5]) 'The Rising Cost of Ambient Air Pollution thus far in the 21st Century: Results from the BRIICS and the OECD Countries.'
Source: Institute for Health Metrics and Evaluation (IHME), GBD Compare, as presented in (OECD, 2021[4]).

SDG 3 on ensuring healthy lives and promoting well-being for all and at all ages, includes a specific target focusing on substantially reducing the number of deaths and illnesses from hazardous chemicals and air, water and soil pollution and contamination. All three indicators identified under the gender-environment nexus fall under the specific SDG 3 target (Table 2.2). Data availability allows for measuring mortality rates attributed to household and ambient air pollution (SDG indicator 3.9.1).

Increased air pollution exposure causes a variety of health problems, including decreased lung function, aggravated asthma, chronic bronchitis, diabetes, irregular heartbeat, nonfatal heart attacks, and contribute to premature death in people with heart and lung disease (OECD, 2012[16]); (OECD, 2014[17]). Research links increased levels of PM in the air with respiratory and cardiovascular diseases, noting that the effects are more negative for children and the elderly compared to adults (Aragón, Miranda and Oliva, 2017[18]).

Ambient air pollution influences levels of infant mortality and morbidity, especially in the first weeks of a child's life, while there are also indications linking pregnant women's exposure to air pollutants with negative effects on the foetus (Bové et al., 2019[19]); (Currie and Neidell, 2004[20]). Increased levels of NO_2, produced usually by fuel combustion in diesel vehicles, by 10-ppb per week, have been associated with a

16% rise in the probability of pregnancy loss. This can have the same harmful effect on the foetus as tobacco smoking during the first trimester of pregnancy (Carrington, 2019[21]); (Saha et al., 2007[22]).

Low-income households located close to freeway traffic are among the most affected, with children's health suffering most; (Suissa and Edwardes, 1997[23]) (Gauderman et al., 2007[24]). The 2019 OECD study "The Economic Cost of Air Pollution: Evidence From Europe" shows that exposure to air pollution correlates with education and income levels in European member countries (Dechezleprêtre, Rivers and Stadler, 2019[25]). As a result, air pollution can exacerbate socio-economic gaps and further contribute to the intergenerational transmission of poverty. Compared to rural dwellers, urban dwellers in OECD countries are less satisfied with their local environmental quality. (Balestra and Sultan, 2013[11]). As women spend more time walking than men (who spend more time driving individual cars), they are exposed to different sources of urban air pollution that could potentially lead to differentiated effects on their health (ITF, 2018[26]). Even in cases where both men and women use private cars for work, there may be differences in levels of exposure, depending on location, geography and different daily patterns between men and women (Setton et al., 2010[27]). Research shows that because of biological factors, women are more vulnerable to environmental pollution (Butter, 2006[28]). In developing countries, charcoal production by main roads is also a major source of pollutants affecting the health of those who spend long periods walking along them (Girard, 2002[29]).

The aforementioned OECD study on the economic cost of air pollution in Europe finds also a correlation between increased air pollution and productivity levels and economic activity (Dechezleprêtre, Rivers and Stadler, 2019[25]). The results show that increasing average annual concentration of $PM_{2.5}$ by 1µg/m³ reduces total GDP by 0.83% and decreases output by 0.80% per worker. These reductions could result from changes in work productivity (reduced work attendance and absenteeism) as well as the direct effect of pollution on some sectors. When focusing particularly in the agricultural sector, evidence in Europe shows that a 1 µg/m³ increase in $PM_{2.5}$ concentration in air can reduce agricultural gross value added by 4.6%, both due to the environmental effects and shifts in workers' productivity (Dechezleprêtre, Rivers and Stadler, 2019[25]). This economic analysis supports existing literature on the detrimental effect of air pollution to human health and agricultural yields (Agrawal et al., 2003[30]); (Chay and Greenstone, 2003[31]). A gender dimension is particularly relevant in countries where women represent more than half the rural population, e.g. Central and Eastern Europe (non-EU) (Kovačićek and R. Franić, 2019[32]), or in areas where women are in charge of sustenance agriculture.

Numerous other studies confirm the negative social and economic impact of air pollution. A survey in Lima, Peru, shows that households with dependent members (i.e. children, elderly) are more severely affected during days with higher levels of air pollution, than those without. A 10 µg/m³ increase in $PM_{2.5}$ levels leads to a reduction of two working hours per week per household, as care responsibilities increase (Aragón, Miranda and Oliva, 2017[18]). This could imply that women, responsible for the caregiving tasks in the household, are the ones most affected by high pollution days. In Santiago, Chile, where extremely high pollution days – of over 100 µg/m³ of PM_{10} – are common, women are more likely to stay at home with their children or elderly family members (Montt, 2018[33]). This doubles the gender gap in working hours between men and women, as women tend to reduce their hours worked in weeks of high pollution and men compensate by increasing theirs (Montt, 2018[33]).

In the context of COVID-19, growing evidence finds a clear link between exposure to air pollution and increase in susceptibility to viral infection (Abdo et al., 2011[34]). A recent study by the University of Harvard shows that an increase of 1µg/m3 in $PM_{2.5}$ is associated with an 8% increase in the COVID-19 death rate in the United States, adding to existing knowledge on increased risk for patients with cardiovascular and lung disease (Wu et al., 2020[35]). In supporting this statement, emerging evidence suggests that PM pollution has increased the transmission rate of COVID-19 in Italian towns and cities (Setti et al., 2020[36]). Additional work identifies PM itself as a vector for the transmission of viruses and a cause for the increased vulnerability to diseases due to air pollution exposure (Setti et al., 2020[37]). Furthermore, in previous coronavirus outbreaks in China, such as the one in 2002, analysis showed that patients from regions with high air pollution levels had twice the mortality risk of patients from regions with low pollution levels (Cui et al., 2003[38]).

Although men appear to be more likely to die from the current virus, this pandemic illustrates that its impact is not limited to biological determinants but is influenced by social norms as well (Zhonghua, Xing and Z, 2020[39]). These in turn differentially affect health behaviour of women and men. For instance, the European Institute for Gender Equality calls for clinical trials for a COVID-19 vaccine to include a gender-balanced representation of women, to prevent a differentiated gendered effect (EIGE, 2020[40]). Minimising individual vulnerability to infection should be a top priority for countries, as should consideration of the gender dimension and its differentiated impact.

Analysis also highlights that there is an increasing link on the economic consequences of air pollution and climate change, with the negative effects visible in many Asian and African economies. Outdoor air pollution is an emerging problem in Africa, driven by increased traffic, power generation and industries. Roy (2016) estimates that dirty air could be killing 712,000 people a year prematurely, compared to approximately 542,000 deaths from unsafe water and 391,000 from unsafe sanitation (Roy, 2016[41]).

Other emerging evidence attempts to provide a link between air pollution and mental and physical health, cognitive performance, and even violent behaviour. Kioumourtzoglou et al. (2017) show that long-term exposure to elevated levels of $PM_{2.5}$ and ozone in the United States increases the risk of depression in middle-aged and older women (Kioumourtzoglou et al., 2017[42]), while others show links between depression and air pollution (Xin, Xiaobo and Xi, 2015[43]). On the other hand, contemporaneous and cumulative exposure to air pollution appears to affect men's cognitive performance more negatively than women's (Chen, Zhang and Zhang, 2017[44]).

Recent studies have also linked increased exposure to $PM_{2.5}$ and ozone to aggressive behaviour and increased domestic violence (Nickerson, 2019[45]); (Burkhardt et al., 2019[46]). Experimental behavioural analysis of people living in the United States and Indian cities showed that air pollution elevates anxiety, triggering unethical behaviour among adults (Lu et al., 2018[47]). Further recent findings in the United States by Burkhardt et al (2019) suggest a link between air pollution and violent behaviour (Burkhardt et al., 2019[46]). More specifically, they calculate that – for the period between 2006 and 2013 – a 10% increase in $PM_{2.5}$ and a 10% increase in ozone were associated with 0.14% and 0.3% increases in violent crimes and assault, respectively (Burkhardt et al., 2019[46]). These correlations are valid both for assaults in and out of the house, linking especially changes in outdoor $PM_{2.5}$ with domestic violence.

Women were statistically the main victims of domestic violence between 2003 and 2012 in the United States (76% female victims vs. 24% male) (Truman and Morgan, 2014[48]). Burkhardt et al. (2019) also calculate the financial benefits from decreased violence as a result of a reduction in air pollution (Burkhardt et al., 2019[46]). According to their calculations, a 10% reduction of $PM_{2.5}$ concentrations could reduce crime costs by more than USD 400 million, and a 10% reduction of ozone concentrations by USD 1 billion per year. Similar findings in London link increased crime activity to ambient air pollution (Bondy, Roth and Sager, 2018[49]).

3.2.2. Water and soil contamination

Water contamination is a growing problem, affecting women in particular. In the context of COVID-19, water access points can become clusters of infection, which mainly affect women. Therefore, ensuring safe access to clean water is key to mitigating infection. Up to 80% of illnesses in the developing world are linked to inadequate water quality and poor sanitation (Fauconnier, Jenniskens and Perry, 2018[50]). Every year, unsafe water sickens about 1 billion people. Water pollution caused 1.8 million deaths in 2015, according to The Lancet (Landrigan et al., 2018[51]). It is estimated that over 800 000 people die each year from diarrhoea as a result of unsafe drinking water and poor sanitation and hand hygiene (WHO, 2014[52]). In low-income countries, women are more exposed to the transmission of diseases because they are often in charge of disposing of dirty water and human waste and they rarely have access to safe or private sanitation facilities (WHO and UNICEF, 2017[53]). Even in developed countries, polluted water is a major concern influencing women's health foremost (Landrigan et al., 2018[51]) (Watts et al., 2019[54]) (Woodcock et al., 2009[55]).

SDG 3 has one indicator on the health impact of water contamination, which also falls under the gender-environment nexus. This underscores the importance of safe water for women and the environment. Indicator 3.9.2 on mortality rate attributed to unsafe water, unsafe sanitation and lack of hygiene provides further insight on how women are more influenced than men from exposure to unsafe water, and from a lack of sanitation and handwashing facilities. Whereas in OECD countries, the number of premature deaths from unsafe water, sanitation and lack of hygiene is limited, and the welfare cost is minimum barely reaching 1% in GDP equivalent, this is not the case at the global level (Figure 3.8). Globally, women are clearly more affected, and female premature deaths' welfare cost as percentage to GDP at 2% is higher than for men. The main contributor to these deaths is the lack of access to safe water.

Figure 3.8. Welfare cost of premature deaths related to unsafe water, sanitation and handwashing

Percentage of GDP equivalent, 2019 data

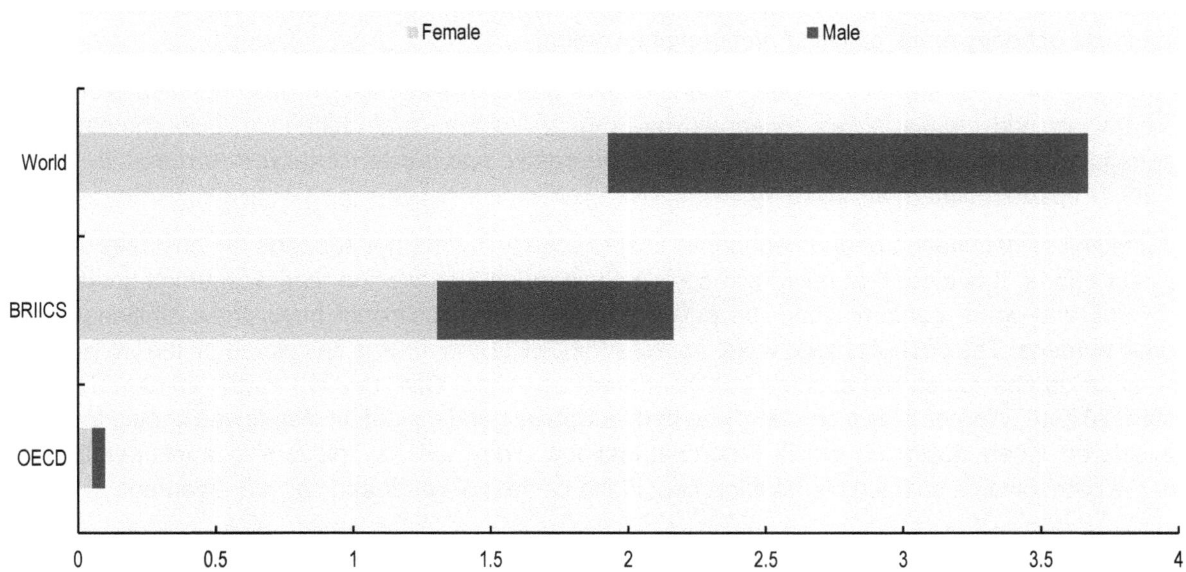

Note: Welfare cost of premature deaths related to unsafe water, sanitation and handwashing in percentage of GDP equivalent. Data on mortality and DALYs from exposure to environmental risks are taken from GBD (2019), Global Burden of Disease Study 2019 Results. Welfare costs are calculated using a methodology adapted from the OECD, (Roy and Braathen, 2017[5]), The Rising Cost of Ambient Air Pollution thus far in the 21st Century: Results from the BRIICS and the OECD Countries.
Source: Institute for Health Metrics and Evaluation (IHME), GBD Compare, as presented in (OECD, 2021[4]).

Despite limited premature deaths due to unsafe water, sanitation and hygiene (WASH) in OECD countries, water and soil contamination remains a concern. A recent OECD study indicates that there are increasing environmental concerns from active pharmaceutical residues in freshwater (OECD, 2019[56]). As the consumption of such products increases, better monitoring and assessment of the effects of such ingredients on the environment is needed, as are improvements to the treatment of water resources. The study also points out the need to more thoroughly examine the effect of such pharmaceutical ingredients and mixtures on human health, especially the most sensitive groups of the population, such as pregnant women, foetuses and children (OECD, 2019[56]).

Water and soil contamination have a greater impact on women from minority groups and lower income levels. This is because they face greater difficulties avoiding pollution by moving to cleaner locations, for instance. In a study on the state of New Jersey, United States, Currie et al. (2013) find a correlation between women's level of education and the probability of a household moving as a result of contaminated water. This indicates a clear effort by women to protect themselves and their families from environmental harm (Currie et al., 2013[57]).

There are many examples of excessive use of toxic chemicals (e.g. pesticides) in agriculture, where women in many developing countries represent about 70% of the labour force. In Tanzania, for example, women do the planting and harvesting, and even the mining, whereas men do the more "mainstream" dangerous jobs (Mrema et al., 2017[58]); (Roser and Ritchie, 2020[59]); (Lal, 2020[60]). The United Nations Development Programme (UNDP) has been working extensively on identifying guidelines for the sound management of chemicals in developing countries. As part of this work, it has been strengthening the gender dimensions (UNDP, 2011[61]).

The extensive use of hazardous chemicals can potentially affect women more than men, especially in rural areas of developing countries where women are highly dependent on natural resources (UNEP, 2013[62]). The impacts of plastic litter, air pollution, mercury and other pollutants on animal and plant biodiversity have been widely documented (Lovett et al., 2009[63]); (IPBES, 2019[64]) and tend to have a greater impact on traditional and indigenous populations, with a specific incidence on women [see (Inyinbor et al., 2018[12]) for the effects of heavy metal pollution on pregnant women].

A recent study on a number of European countries has provided evidence of the continuing problem of toxic chemicals and metals in fish consumed by pregnant women and children. It also compares the concentrations of hazardous compounds contained in organic and conventionally grown produce due to pesticides (Papadopoulou et al., 2019[65]).

Water and soil contamination bear an economic cost to society that further supports the business case for abatement efforts. It is clear that mitigation costs bear a much higher price than adaptation costs in the case of soil and water contamination, as purifying these resources could pose great challenges and economic burdens. The cost of unsafe water sources for OECD countries is calculated by the welfare cost of premature deaths, which represented 0.03% of member states' GDP in 2019 (GBD, 2019[3]) (Roy and Braathen, 2017[5]). Women play a crucial role in both adaptation and mitigation stages and should therefore be considered when designing policy recommendations. They are key players in implementing and securing a path towards sustainable development in the context of water and soil management.

3.2.3. Other exposure to hazardous chemicals

The burden of disease from exposure to hazardous chemicals is significant worldwide and falls more heavily in non-OECD countries where good chemical safety measures are not always in place (OECD, 2018[66]). Men and women are exposed to chemicals on a daily basis, both at home and at work. The level of exposure, however, may differ depending on the length of exposure and be exacerbated by additional stressors such as heat waves [see the example of Paris (Lemonsu et al., 2015[67]) and (McGregor, 2015[68]). In addition, there are gender-differentiated impacts based on women and men's physiological, hormonal, and enzyme differences, potentially posing differentiated risks related to absorption, distribution, metabolism, storage and excretion.

Chemical substances such as Persistent Organic Pollutants (POPs), heavy metals and Endocrine Disrupting Chemicals (EDCs), have been widely identified as having differentiated impacts on men and women (Street et al., 2018[69]); (WHO, 2016[70]). In a recent study on pregnant women, EDC mixtures were found to have adverse health effects on new-born babies' and children's neurodevelopment, metabolism and growth, among others, and hence affecting mental and physical health of their mothers (Bergman, Rüegg and Drakvik, 2019[71]).

As the non-OECD countries' share of the world's chemical production increases, the burden of diseases attributed to hazardous chemicals exposures is expected to grow. According to OECD calculations, a six-fold increase in chemical production in non-OECD countries is expected by 2050, mainly in the major emerging economies, such as Brazil, Russian Federation, India, Indonesia, China and South Africa (BRIICS) (OECD, 2012[10]). This would also increase the risk of exposure, especially for the most vulnerable populations.

Figure 3.9. SDG indicator 3.9.3 - Mortality rate attributed to unintentional poisonings, by sex

Deaths per 100 000 population

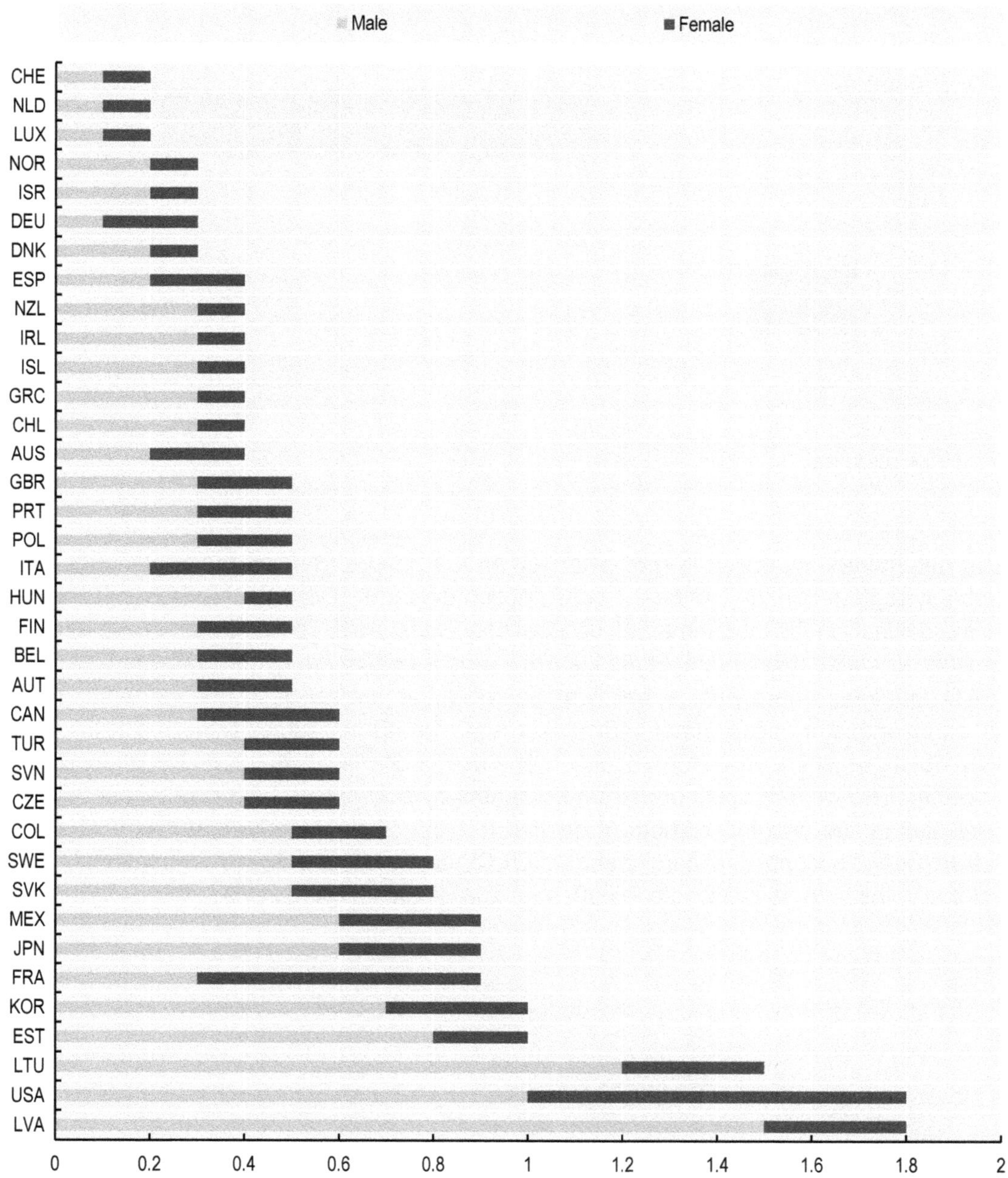

Source: (UNSD, n.d.[72])

Within the SDG Framework, the indicator for measuring the decreased number of deaths and illnesses from hazardous chemicals only measures the mortality rate from unintentional poisoning (SDG indicator 3.9.3). According to data available for OECD countries, men are more often the victims of unintentional poisoning than women in most countries (Figure 3.9). However, further data disaggregation would be necessary to detect the differentiated impacts of poison sources by gender. Although in OECD countries on average, men's deaths attributed to unintentional poisoning were almost double that of women, the global scale on average shows a marginal difference between the two sexes (Figure 3.10).

Figure 3.10. Mortality rate attributed to unintentional poisonings, by gender

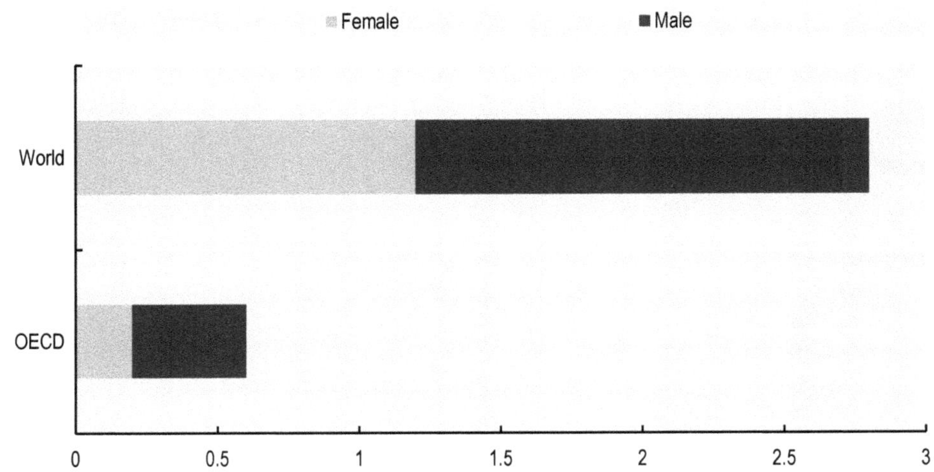

Note: Deaths per 100 000 population
Source: (UNSD, n.d.[72])

Social factors determine differences in men and women's exposure to hazardous chemicals based on traditional labour segregation and different consumption patterns. Despite the fact that women are participating increasingly in the labour market, occupational exposure to certain carcinogenic agents is still monitored mainly on males (Hohenadel et al., 2015[73]). This is confirmed by the available data for OECD and non-OECD countries, where what is mainly measured is the number of premature deaths caused by occupational carcinogens or occupational particulate matter, gases and fumes (Figure 3.11). This can be interpreted as job segregation, whereby production and use of chemicals is more characteristic of male-dominated sectors. The welfare costs of premature deaths by occupational risks as percentage of GDP equivalent are also in line with the number of deaths. It is interesting to note that the most substantial welfare costs are due to occupational carcinogens in OECD countries, and due to occupational PM, gases and fumes globally; the latter is applicable to both men and women (Figure 3.11).

Figure 3.11. Welfare cost of premature deaths attributed to environmental and occupational risks by gender

Percentage of GDP equivalent, 2019 data

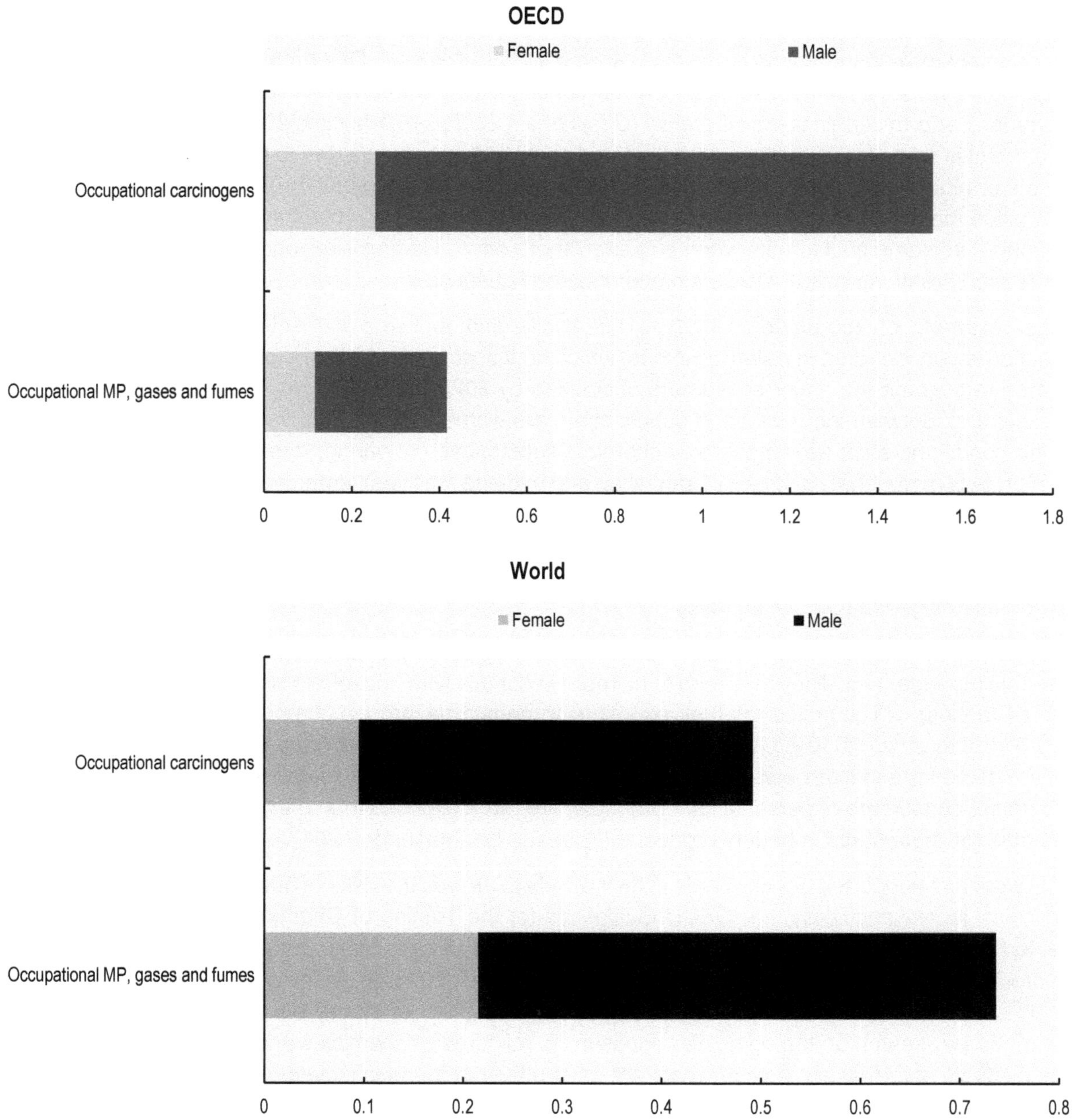

Note: Welfare cost of premature deaths attributed to environmental and occupational risks by gender in percentage of GDP equivalent (2019 data). Data on mortality and DALYs from exposure to environmental risks are taken from (GBD, 2019[3]), Global Burden of Disease Study 2019 Results. Welfare costs are calculated using a methodology adapted from the OECD, (Roy and Braathen, 2017[5]) 'Rising Cost of Ambient Air Pollution thus far in the 21st Century: Results from the BRIICS and the OECD Countries'.
Source: Institute for Health Metrics and Evaluation (IHME), GBD Compare, as presented in (OECD, 2021[4]).

However, studies on occupational exposure identify differences in exposure levels to various chemicals between male and female workers. A study in Italy has identified higher levels of exposure to certain chemicals for men or women related to task segregation in the wood industry and in furniture manufacturing

(Scarselli et al., 2018[74]). It is clearly necessary to take into account women's and men's differing occupational roles and exposure in order to conduct meaningful research and monitor the effects of chemicals on human health.

Research also shows differences in chemical exposure even when men and women have the same occupation (based on job titles). The aforementioned Italian study identified higher levels of exposure to nickel and chromium VI compounds for women working as machine operators, when compared to the predominately-male workforce in the sector (Scarselli et al., 2018[74]). Other research, trying to identify the non-biological reasons for these differences, has linked them to differences in cognitive skills and how men and women perform certain tasks differently (Czaja et al., 2006[75]); (Arbuckle, 2006[76]). Moreover, the work environment in some traditionally male-dominated sectors is usually adapted to men's needs, so protective uniforms or gloves may not be adequately sized for women (Arbuckle, 2006[76]). There is room for further examination on the ergonomic nature of jobs (i.e. handling heavy machinery, or repetitive aerobic movement), as some could make women to exert more effort, leading – beyond other health impacts – to an increased breathing rate and thus a higher intake of chemicals.

Another example of segregated labour is the textile and footwear industries. Since the mid-2000s, production is concentrated in Asian countries, which now account for 62% of global exports, and which are expected to become the major consumers of clothing by 2025 (ILO, 2019[77]). The majority of workers in the textile and footwear industries and supply chain are women (80%). This sector's workers face unsafe working conditions such as exposure to chemical substances (colouring, dyes, adhesives and primers, lack of protective materials and lack of sanitation and hygiene facilities), among other factors (Ahmed et al., 2004[78]). The OECD's Due Diligence Guidance for Responsible Supply Chain in the Garment and Footwear Sector provides a list of recommendations and a toolkit that helps companies assess their environmental and social performance, and to integrate gender equality, health and environmental issues into their due diligence (OECD, 2018[79]).

Due to social norms, socio-economic status and demographic trends, women are often in charge of household management. They thus tend to be more in contact with household cleaning products and waste (such as faeces), which increases their exposure to certain hazardous chemicals and toxic substances (Hertz-Picciotto et al., 2010[80]). Women are also more exposed to chemicals in personal care products, such as cosmetics and even jewellery (UNDP, 2011[61]). Recent US data, for example, showed that women, as the major consumers of personal care products, are more exposed than men to mercury, parabens and phthalates (all ingredients in beauty products) (Zota and Shamasunder, 2017[81]).

OECD work has supported governments in their efforts to assess the risks of human exposure to individual chemicals[2]. More specifically, the OECD Guidelines for the Testing of Chemicals provide internationally accepted standard methods to assess the potential effects of chemicals (industrial, pesticides, personal care products, etc.) on humans and the environment (OECD, 2013[82]). Many of these tests evaluate sex-specific effects, which is particularly relevant for the evaluation of chemicals that disrupt the endocrine system. More research on the combined exposure to mixtures of chemicals and potential male- / female-specific effects is necessary, as chemicals are most often not found in isolation.

While the OECD has also been working on identifying the environmental impacts of plastics and plastic waste, more work could be carried out on their human health impacts. In a recent research paper, Ten Brink et al. refer to the potential hazardous effect on human health of various chemicals added to plastics (Ten Brink et al., 2016[83]). They refer especially to the potentially problematic use of plastic packaging for food and children's toys; plastic sewage and water pipes and how chemical additives limit the recycling of plastic (OECD, 2018[84]). Such analysis should have a gender aspect, since women are most likely to be in contact with such products (e.g. plastic packaging for food) and are the decision-makers about waste management in the household (Lynn, Mantingh and Rech, 2017[85]).

The OECD is currently carrying out a project on the willingness-to-pay (WTP) to avoid chemicals-related negative health impacts (OECD, 2018[86]). In a first phase, surveys will be implemented in selected countries to estimate the WTP to avoid asthma, IQ loss in children, low birthweight, kidney failure and fertility loss (Alberini et al., 2010[87]). As in most stated-preference surveys, gender is one of the socio-economic variables respondents are asked to answer. This could serve as an example for future studies (Cascajo, Garcia-Martinez and Monzon, 2017[88]).

3.2.4. Climate change

Women's health is also affected differently by climate change and increased temperatures, both in OECD and non-OECD countries. For example, the 2003 heat wave in France led to the premature death of 15 000 people; the mortality rate for women was 75% higher than for men (Fouillet et al., 2006[89]). [3] A 2019 study focusing on Spain showed that women of all ages are more susceptible to die of cardiovascular disease than men. Cardiovascular disease may be caused by exposure to high temperatures (Achebak, Devolder and Ballester, 2019[90]); (Yin et al., 2019[91]). Considering Spain has a mortality rate of 2,683 deaths per year from airbound pollution, and temperatures are rising, effects on women could be disproportionate (Ortiz et al., 2017[92]).

Climate change brings about a higher incidence and intensity of natural hazards such as droughts, landslides, floods and hurricanes. These hazards have a greater impact on more vulnerable populations because of their greater dependence on natural resources for their livelihoods, a lower capacity to adapt, lower quality dwellings and more exposed locations. Women, in particular, are disproportionately likely to lose their livelihoods, especially in developing regions, from the increased occurrence of hazardous events (UNEP, 2011[93]). As they account for the majority of the world's poor, women often face higher risk and greater burdens from the impacts of climate change such as uncertainty of sustenance, health risks, etc. Extreme events such as droughts coupled with gender inequities lead to women having to bear disaster effects disproportionally (UN Women, 2018[94]).

Women also appear to be less able to adapt to climate change, as such adaptation is influenced by social and economic status as well as access to resources. An example of work leading global adaptation efforts is the G20 Climate Sustainability Working Group's Adaptation Programme. It strives to ensure the inclusion of women in adaptation planning. Especially in non-OECD countries, women are essential in developing adaptation mechanisms due to their key role managing resources to sustain their households (UNEP, 2011[93]).

Lack of equal access to formal education, gender-based discrimination and social exclusion reduce women's ability to cope effectively with the demands of climate change adaptation. In addition, climate change forces households to migrate, worsening both the gender gap and mitigation efforts (Fauconnier, Jenniskens and Perry, 2018[50]). A 2016 study of Nepalese households with members that have migrated shows that women and girls in the families decrease their weekly hours in less productive activities by 7.8% and 4.1% respectively, and increase more than proportionally the time they spend on productive activities (8.2% and 5.5% respectively), when compared to men and boys. It also showed that women tend to shift from wage-employment to sustenance farming and work in family farms (Phadera, 2016[95]).

The effects of climate change could lead, in the long and short-term, not only to unbearable economic costs but to increased gender disparity. Tackling these issues concurrently, by aligning SDGs, could result in a more effective, inclusive economic solution to climate change and other environmental issues.

3.3. Access to sustainable and quality infrastructure and economic opportunities for women

A particularly important economic channel of the gender-environment nexus is how better access to sustainable infrastructure for women (water, energy, transport, housing and social infrastructure, communications, etc.)[4] can boost their labour market participation and productivity, while reducing environmental externalities. While in developing countries a gender gap exists across all types of infrastructure, in OECD countries the main concern is the inadequacies of transport and social infrastructure.[5]

To improve women's access to and use of transport and social infrastructure, a number of factors must be taken into account. First, women's specific travel patterns: they tend to be more irregular and varied than men's, as women more often combine household, family and work duties. Studies have found a stronger negative correlation between commuting time and participation in the labour force for women than for men and women's higher preference for flexible modes of transport as well as for public transport. EIGE's Gender Equality Index shows that 24.5% of women use public transport, compared with 18% of men; 25% of them cycle or walk, compared to 20.25% of men. On the contrary, 57.5% of men use their car as the preferred mode of transport, compared to 48.75% of women. Eighteen per cent of single parents rely exclusively on public transport (EIGE, 2020[96]). Secondly, women's greater exposure to harassment and physical violence reduces the attractiveness of public transport for them and their ability to work in certain neighbourhoods (ITF, 2018[97]). Cases show that women all around the globe restrict their use of public transport because they fear harassment or other forms of violence, sometimes due to past experiences (see more on this topic under Part II of this report, forthcoming). Measuring accessibility provided by sustainable transport, and adapting policy measures to the findings and needs, could help better serve women and men, while minimising environmental impact (OECD, 2019[98]).

The COVID-19 pandemic has upended travel patterns throughout the world, and affected public transport most. Even as mobility restrictions have been lifted in many countries, the attractiveness of public transport has declined compared to the pre-crisis situation because of the chances of contagion from close physical contact. Given their greater preference for public transport, women's mobility has been particularly affected by the pandemic and its aftermath (EIGE, 2020[96]). People have been opting for alternative travelling modes, such as walking and cycling, especially since in many cases there were limitations placed on travel distances (ITF, 2020[99]). Women's mobility patterns were, in a way, generalised during the COVID-19 crisis, and magnified on top by the physical distances rules, bringing to the forefront the need to adapt urban infrastructure to more gender-responsive requirements (ITF, 2020[99]). Mainstreaming gender could thus eventually lead to increasing urban resilience to shocks such as COVID-19.

In rural areas, where women's livelihoods would improve drastically by sustainable infrastructure development (food, health, energy, water and sanitation, transport); the COVID-19 crisis seem to disproportionately affect women and girls the most. In these difficult times, rural women – both in developed and developing countries - seem to experience more challenges, due to unpaid care work, their employment informality, and their dependence on natural resources (Salcedo-La Viña, Singh and Elwell, 2020[100]) (EmPower, 2020[101]), as well as more gender-based violence in the household (Moffitt et al., 2020[102]). Sustainable transport infrastructure would provide easier access to women for their daily activities, and also a safer environment outside the house.

In parallel, the COVID-19 crisis has boosted remote working, shopping, financing and other activities, bringing to the forefront the need for resilient digital infrastructure. The existing gender digital divide, both in OECD and non-OECD countries, whereby women face more digital exclusion, needs to be overcome to guarantee women are not left behind (OECD, 2018[103]), especially considering women's vulnerability to health crises from an employment perspective (OECD, 2020[104]). Analysis from the United Kingdom and the United States indicates that women were more likely to lose their jobs during the COVID-19 crisis, spend more time at home and take on more caring duties than usual (Adams-Prassl et al., 2020[105]). At the same time, the COVID-19 crisis may offer greater flexibility to digitally-savvy women to better combine work and home responsibilities, if a change in social and cultural norms leads more men to participate in the unpaid care work (Alon et al., 2020[106]). Irrespective of COVID-19, OECD analysis showed that digital technologies and improving access to digital infrastructure can increase women's labour market participation and women's economic empowerment (OECD, 2018[103]).

There are few studies on the economic benefits of improving women's access to infrastructure. Initial analysis focuses on women's role in unpaid care and household work, and how improving (sustainable) infrastructure can benefit women as end-users (Clancy, Skutsch and Batchelor, 2003[107]). Agénor and Agénor (2014) produced a framework applicable to low income countries, based on which access to infrastructure services improves women's time allocated to market production and household activities, providing women with an income, improving children's health and education and eventually contributing to economic growth (Agénor and Agénor, 2014[108]). Other analysis presents cases where better road, electricity and digital infrastructure led to an increase in women's labour participation (Kabeer, 2012[109]). OECD estimates show that improvements in access to social infrastructure could increase (primarily) women labour market participation by around 3%, which would add 2.5% to the GDP per capita globally (Figure 3.12).

Figure 3.12. Impact of improved access to social infrastructure on GDP per capita

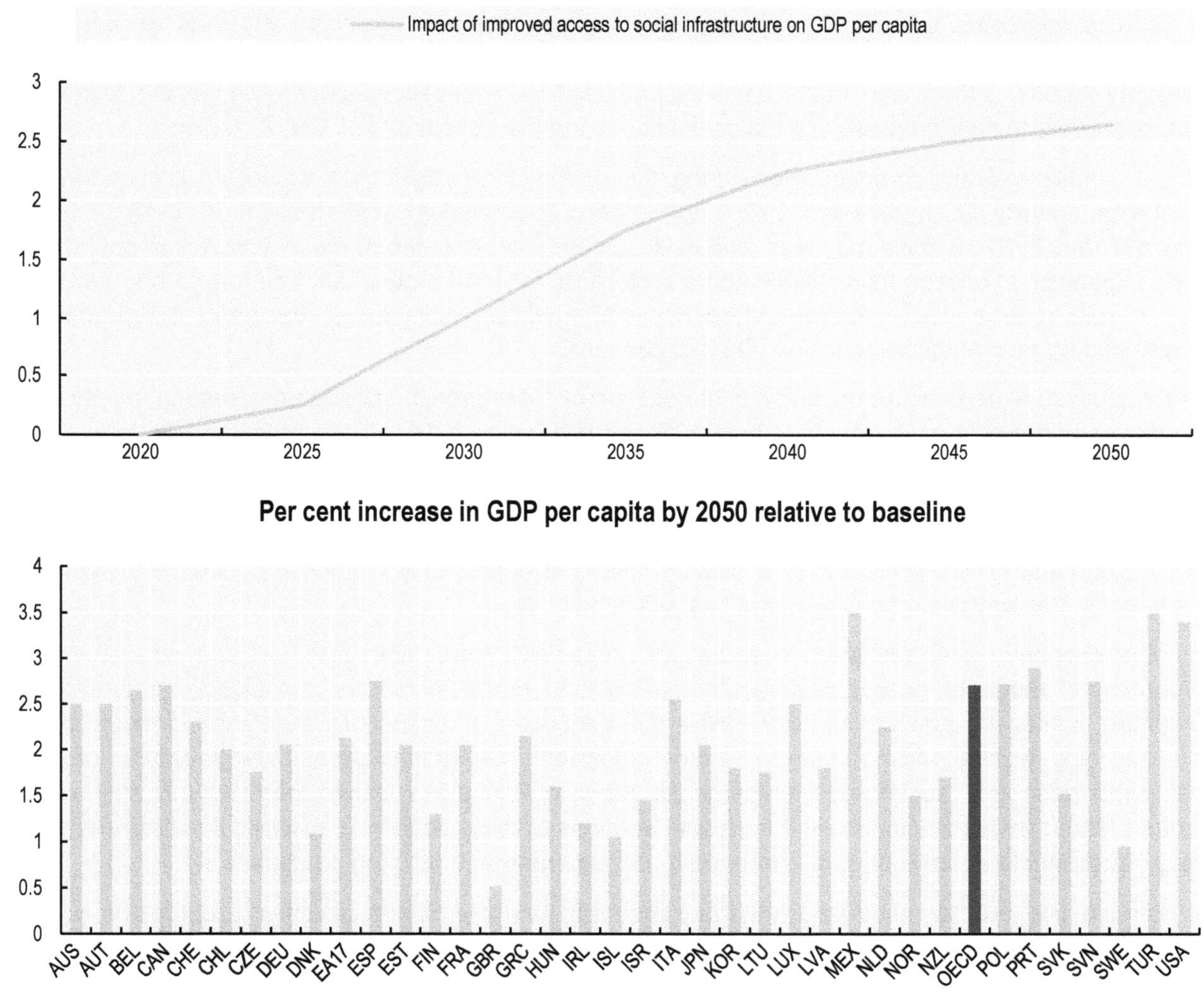

Note: The calculation models OECD countries closing half of the gap in access to social infrastructure with best practices (average for the top-5 countries). This leads to an increase of the OECD female employment rate by about 3 percentage points by 2050 relative to baseline. This translates into a gain in GDP per capita of over 2½ per cent by 2050 relative to baseline. It takes some time for the full effect of the policy shock to be phased in so the gains would continue to accrue for some time and would eventually reach about 3%. The impact varies country by country, depending on how far a country starts from best practices (chart below). The weakest impacts are in GBR and SWE because they already score well on these policy indicators. The largest gains are in MEX and TUR but also USA where social policy is less developed.
Source: OECD ECO's estimation

3.4. Women in green jobs and green innovation in the post-COVID 19 low-carbon transition

Increasing women's participation in the labour force is both a gender equality and an economic imperative. OECD estimates made before the COVID-19 crisis suggest that, on average across OECD countries, halving the gender gap in labour force participation rates by 2040 could boost annual average GDP per capita growth rates by 0.04 percentage points, relative to the baseline. Going further and eliminating the gender participation gap could boost average annual GDP per capita growth by roughly 0.15 percentage points (OECD, 2018[110]). Ostry et al. (2018) argue that narrowing gender gaps in labour participation will bring even larger than expected economic gains, due to the production growth brought by gender diversity, and the welfare gains from removing social and other barriers. More specifically, they show that men and women complement each other at work, especially when women are scarce in a sector, leading to increased productivity and economic growth. Gender considerations can thus influence the benefits from labour re-allocation to sectors were women are not present (Ostry et al., 2018[111]). They finally indicate the need to overcome barriers for women's labour participation, in line with what has already been presented by the OECD on supporting women's economic empowerment through putting in place the necessary conditions (from legal rights to assets, participation in relevant education and training, to tackling informal barriers to their progress and discrimination in the market place) (OECD, 2012[112]).

With the climate and environmental crises luring, the urgency for a transition to a low carbon economy has grown exponentially. Such transition is expected to bring about major transformations in whole economic sectors. The COVID-19 crisis may also lead to an acceleration of some of these transformations, driven by the expansion in telecommunications and a preference for local production. The low carbon transition can also help reduce existing social and economic inequalities, including gender gaps, if it guarantees fairness and enhanced social cohesion (OECD, 2020[113])

The transition to a green economy and the introduction of green growth policies are foreseen to only bring marginal aggregate effects on labour (Chateau, Bibas and Lanzi, 2018[114]). According to (Chateau, Bibas and Lanzi, 2018[114]), the labour implications of climate and energy policies in OECD members are expected to be higher in sectors that rely mostly on labour, such as mining and quarrying, electricity, chemicals and food products. They conclude that the sectors where most low-skilled jobs will be lost are in mining and quarrying and electricity (especially fossil-fuel dependent). Conversely, jobs are expected to be created in transportation services and construction sectors.

Six main economic activities are the source of most GHG emissions, pollution and other forms of environmental damage: energy generation, mineral and metal extraction, manufacturing processes, agriculture, transport, and construction. With the exception of agriculture and some manufacturing processes (e.g. textiles), women tend to be most underrepresented in these sectors globally. In order to meet jointly economic, social and environmental goals, policymakers should therefore aim to increase women's labour force participation in the greener versions of these economic activities such as renewable energy, sustainable agriculture, public transport, and cleaner manufacturing processes.

For instance, the FAO has estimated that equal access to land and other productive resources for women and men could increase total agricultural output in developing countries by 2.5% to 4% (FAO, 2011[115]). But it is equally important to consider that better access to land, credit, and technology for women could also improve the sustainability of agricultural practices, considering that women – especially in developing countries - are mostly small-scale holders that often follow traditional knowledge practices in their agricultural methods (see more under Chapter 6).

In OECD countries, women are not particularly present in the GHG emissions and energy intensive sectors (Figure 3.13). While on average around half of women in OECD countries were employed in 2018 (compared to over 65% of men), they are overwhelmingly concentrated in the services sector. The manufacturing, mining, energy, transport and construction sectors tend to be male-dominated. Based on

ILO 2017 data for OECD countries, women occupy on average less than 10% of jobs in construction; just over 14% of mining and quarrying (including extraction of crude petroleum and natural gas); and almost 19% of manufacturing of coke and refined petroleum products. In transport, women occupy almost 22% of jobs. They are better represented in air transport (47%), and postal and courier activities (35%), but occupy only 22% and 12% of positions in water and land transport, respectively. Women also account for only 28% of the agricultural labour force (crop, animal production, hunting), about 20% of fishing and aquaculture labour force, and 17% of forestry jobs in OECD countries. These figures can be contrasted with the health and social sector, where around 70% of the workforce is female. Women even more heavily dominate the long-term care sector, holding, on average, about 90% of jobs (OECD, 2020[116]).

Figure 3.13. Labour by gender in specific economic activities in OECD countries

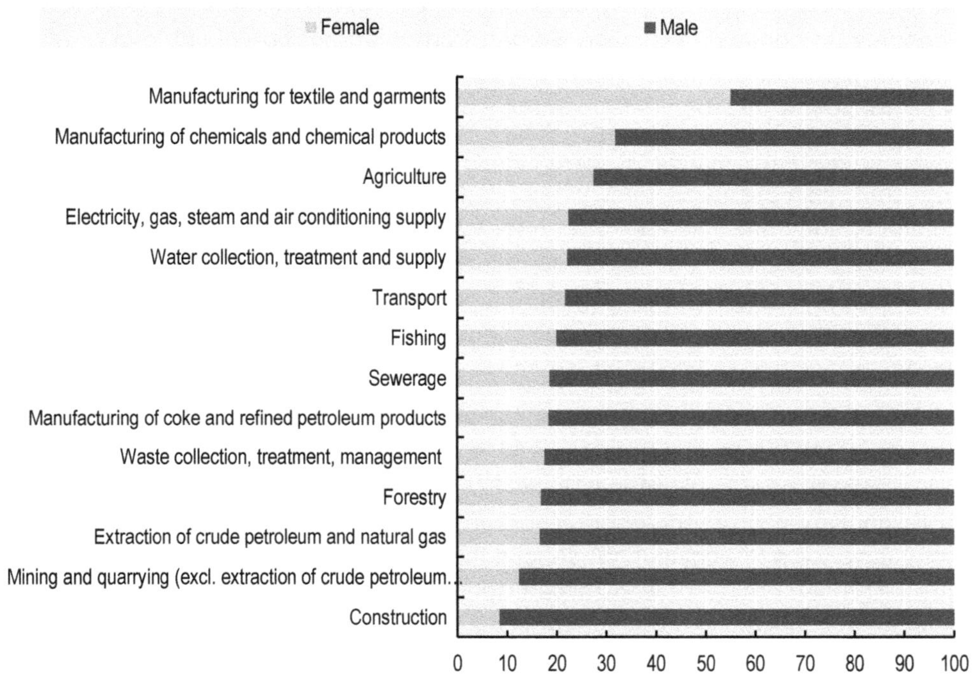

Note: 2017 data. Average for OECD does not include data for Australia, Canada, Japan, Korea and New Zealand. Data used under economic activity classification ISIC-Rev.4 (2-digit level); except for Chile and Colombia where data under ISIC-Rev-3.1 were used.
Source: ILOSTAT

There are also important differences in female participation across manufacturing sectors. Women are mainly occupied in sectors linked to the manufacturing of household and personal use products, or to service provision. Examples are textile and garment manufacturing, the chemical product manufacturing (such as fertilisers, plastics and cleaning products) and with agricultural product manufacturing. In OECD countries, women occupy 55% of jobs in and around fashion manufacturing, and 32% of jobs in chemicals manufacturing.

The transition to a green economy and technological advancements are expected to shift jobs within these sectors and establish new, greener sectors of growth. The ILO provides the following definition of green jobs: "Green jobs are decent jobs that contribute to preserve or restore the environment, be they in traditional sectors such as manufacturing and construction, or in new, emerging green sectors such as renewable energy and energy efficiency. Green jobs help improve energy and raw materials efficiency, limit greenhouse gas emissions; minimize waste and pollution, protect and restore ecosystems, and support adaptation to the effects of climate change" (ILO, 2016[117])

Empirical evidence shows that women have a greater presence in the greener parts of these economic sectors, for instance renewable energy. A global survey conducted in 2018 by the International Renewable Energy Agency (IRENA) shows that women account for 32% of the workforce in the renewable energy sector, compared to 22% in the oil and gas industry sector. Yet most occupy administrative or non-STEM (Science, Technology, Engineering and Mathematics) technical positions (IRENA, 2019[118]).

Furthermore, a recent OECD report on the labour implications of the transition to a resource efficient and circular economy, calculates that green jobs, such as those in secondary-based metal production and recycling sectors are expected to increase by 27% and 48% respectively by 2040 (Chateau and Mavroeidi, 2020[119]). These are partly due to labour shifts from other sectors such as chemicals or textiles' manufacturing. Moreover, these green jobs are expected to require medium and high skills.

Considering the benefits from women's labour participation to economic growth, guaranteeing women's engagement in green jobs could potentially be beneficial for the transition to a green, resource efficient and circular economy. In contrast, excluding women from this transition could lead to an even greater gender gap of labour participation in the "greener" sectors and economic activities of the future. Achieving a shift in today's paradigm would require fundamental changes in women's position in the labour market.

Existing obstacles to women's economic advancement limit their participation in the green economy. Addressing them could shift this trend. First, women today are less likely to occupy full-time positions and open-ended contracts; they are paid less than men for the same job; and they face greater barriers to getting promoted due to discrimination social norms (e.g. childcare, household upkeep), and conscious and unconscious biases (OECD, 2017[120]). In many countries, women also have greater difficulty accessing finance, thereby reducing their chances of becoming entrepreneurs or developing their business (OECD, 2016[121]).

A second factor relates to women's and girls' education and skills. Green economy jobs tend to be high-skilled jobs and are expected to be even more so in the future, requiring specific technical expertise (OECD, 2012[112]). Educational backgrounds in STEM subjects and natural sciences are priced in the innovative and technology-rich green sector. Yet, from an early age, it is mostly boys who more often choose a career in science and engineering, despite the fact that girls also score highly in the PISA tests (OECD, 2020[122]). The percentage of women participating (working as professionals and technicians) in technology development (inventive activity) remains low, reaching only 15% on average across all countries and all technology domains (OECD, 2017[123]). There is a relatively higher participation observed for chemistry and health-related technologies (20% and 24% respectively), while environment-related technologies are just below the average participation, and the rate is even lower for power generation and general engineering technologies (10% and 8% respectively (OECD, 2021[124]).Addressing education gaps of girls studying STEM subjects should therefore be a key part of any strategy to boost female employment and prevent their being left out of the green, low carbon transition.

3.5. Women's role in accelerating the shift towards sustainable consumption patterns

The transition to a low carbon, green economy requires not only a shift towards sustainable production but also a change in consumption patterns, both for end-consumers and for small and medium sized enterprises (SMEs). Indisputably, consumption patterns are highly dependent on socio-economic factors, income level, race, geography, behaviour etc. They are often dependent on sustainable and social infrastructure (as in the case of transport, education and health expenses for the household); or on policy measures such as pricing, environmental taxation and subsidies, which all influence end-consumers' preferences (Sharma, Nguyen and Grote, 2018[125]); (Noël, 2018[126]).

Gender appears to be an important factor, which influences consumption behaviour and patterns at the individual level. Several studies mark the social and/or behavioural reasoning behind such attitudes (Bharti and Faust, 2020[127]); (Mirosa, 2014[128]). The 2011 OECD household survey indicated differences between the consumption preferences of men and women, based on participants own responses. These differences occur in terms of the importance given to pressing environmental issues and in terms of consumption preferences, such as energy saving (OECD, 2011[129]) (see more on this topic under Chapter 11).

Toro, Serrano and Guillen (2019) estimated the gendered environmental footprints generated from private consumption (Toro, Serrano and Guillen, 2019[130]). Using single-person households in Spain for their research, they calculated that, for the period 2008-2013, male households generated more GHG emissions than female ones, despite the fact that in total, there is a decrease in the GHG emissions produced by Spanish single-person households. Women's carbon footprints come from consuming "food and non-alcoholic beverages", "clothing and footwear" and "rentals and supplies". Conversely, men's carbon footprints are higher, coming from the purchase and use of personal vehicles. When considering age, men under 50 seem to generate more GHG emissions than women of the same age group. The consumption ratio is inversed for men and women over 50. If expenditure level is another variable besides GHG footprint, then women appear to generate more GHG emissions than men.

3.6. The gender-environment nexus in economic accounting and well-being frameworks

For some time, economists and statisticians have been working to develop integrated economic measurement and analytical frameworks that incorporate economic, social and environmental considerations. Currently the UN is leading work on the so-called System of Environmental-Economic Accounting (SEEA), which aims to integrate economic, environmental and social data into a single, coherent framework for holistic decision-making (UN, n.d.[131]). The SEEA framework follows a similar accounting structure to the System of National Accounts (SNA) (UN, n.d.[132]). The SEEA Central Framework was adopted by the UN Statistical Commission as the first international standard for environmental-economic accounting in 2012.

Such initiatives on national statistics should eventually allow the development of new composite macro indicators that would complement the GDP as a measure of economic development with information on net environmental value created. As such, it presents an opportunity to incorporate the role of non-market transactions, including the contribution of women to sustainable development through non-remunerated household and community work.

A second important strand of the measurement agenda relates to non-material measures of well-being; which are already integrated into the OECD Well-being Framework. These have also been applied to a recent OECD report where climate change mitigation policies in specific sectors are viewed under a well-being lens (OECD, 2019[98]). Such measures, which cover quality of life aspects (e.g. health, knowledge and skills, safety) and relational aspects (e.g. social connections, work-life balance, civic engagement) complement the material aspects (also essential to people's well-being). All these aspects constitute the ingredients for a good life and show what people themselves value the most.

References

Abdo, M. et al. (2011), “Impact of Urban Air Pollution on Acute Upper Respiratory Tract Infections”, in *Advanced Topics in Environmental Health and Air Pollution Case Studies*, InTech, http://dx.doi.org/10.5772/17085. [34]

Achebak, H., D. Devolder and J. Ballester (2019), “Trends in temperature-related age-specific and sex-specific mortality from cardiovascular diseases in Spain: a national time-series analysis”, *The Lancet Planetary Health*, Vol. 3/7, pp. e297-e306, http://dx.doi.org/10.1016/s2542-5196(19)30090-7. [90]

Adams-Prassl, A. et al. (2020), *Inequality in the Impact of the Coronavirus Shock: Evidence from Real Time Surveys*, http://ftp.iza.org/dp13183.pdf. [105]

Agénor, P. and M. Agénor (2014), “Infrastructure, women’s time allocation, and economic development”, *Journal of Economics/ Zeitschrift fur Nationalokonomie*, Vol. 113/1, pp. 1-30, http://dx.doi.org/10.1007/s00712-013-0358-0. [108]

Agrawal, M. et al. (2003), “Effect of air pollution on peri-urban agriculture: a case study”, *Environmental Pollution*, Vol. 126/3, pp. 323-329, http://dx.doi.org/10.1016/s0269-7491(03)00245-8. [30]

Ahmed, S. et al. (2004), *Health and Safety in the Textile Dyeing Industry*, https://assets.publishing.service.gov.uk/media/57a08cc9e5274a27b2001415/R8161-Safety.pdf. [78]

Alberini, A. et al. (2010), *Valuation of Environment-Related Health Risks for Children*, OECD, http://dx.doi.org/10.1787/9789264038042-en. [87]

Alon, T. et al. (2020), *The Impact of COVID-19 on Gender Equality*, National Bureau of Economic Research, Cambridge, MA, http://dx.doi.org/10.3386/w26947. [106]

Aragón, F., J. Miranda and P. Oliva (2017), “Particulate matter and labor supply: The role of caregiving and non-linearities”, *Journal of Environmental Economics and Management*, Vol. 86, pp. 295-309, http://dx.doi.org/10.1016/j.jeem.2017.02.008. [18]

Arbuckle, T. (2006), “Are there sex and gender differences in acute exposure to chemicals in the same setting?”, *Environmental Research*, Vol. 101/2, pp. 195-204, http://dx.doi.org/10.1016/j.envres.2005.08.015. [76]

Balestra, C. and J. Sultan (2013), “Home Sweet Home: The Determinants of Residential Satisfaction and its Relation with Well-being”, *OECD Statistics Working Papers*, No. 2013/5, OECD Publishing, Paris, https://dx.doi.org/10.1787/5jzbcx0czc0x-en. [11]

Bergman, A., J. Rüegg and E. Drakvik (2019), *Integrating Epidemiology and Experimental Biology to Improve Risk Assessment of Exposure to Mixtures of Endocrine Disruptive Compounds*, ECD-MixRisk, https://edcmixrisk.ki.se/wp-content/uploads/sites/34/2019/09/EDC-MixRisk_Final-technical-report_f20190629.pdf. [71]

Bharti, M. and N. Faust (2020), *The Impact of Gender and Culture in Consumer Behavior*, Cambridge University Press., https://www.cambridge.org/core/books/cambridge-handbook-of-the-international-psychology-of-women/impact-of-gender-and-culture-in-consumer-behavior/CD2E91FC3CF739FB5D7EBBF1E8A6DEEA. [127]

Bondy, M., S. Roth and L. Sager (2018), "Crime is in the Air: The Contemporaneous Relationship between Air Pollution and Crime", *Institute of Labor Economics*, http://ftp.iza.org/dp11492.pdf. [49]

Bové, H. et al. (2019), "Ambient black carbon particles reach the fetal side of human placenta", *Nature Communications*, Vol. 10/1, http://dx.doi.org/10.1038/s41467-019-11654-3. [19]

Burkhardt, J. et al. (2019), "The effect of pollution on crime: Evidence from data on particulate matter and ozone", *Journal of Environmental Economics and Management*, Vol. 98, p. 102267, http://dx.doi.org/10.1016/j.jeem.2019.102267. [46]

Butter, M. (2006), "Are Women More Vulnerable to Environmental Pollution?", *Journal of Human Ecology*, Vol. 20/3, pp. 221-226, http://dx.doi.org/10.1080/09709274.2006.11905931. [28]

Carrington, D. (2019), *Air Pollution 'As Bad as Smoking in Increasing Risk of Miscarriage'"*,, https://www.theguardian.com/environment/2019/jan/11/air-pollution-as-bad-as-smoking-in-increasing-risk-of-miscarriage. [21]

Cascajo, R., A. Garcia-Martinez and A. Monzon (2017), "Stated preference survey for estimating passenger transfer penalties: design and application to Madrid", *European Transport Research Review*, Vol. 9/3, http://dx.doi.org/10.1007/s12544-017-0260-x. [88]

Chateau, J., R. Bibas and E. Lanzi (2018), "Impacts of Green Growth Policies on Labour Markets and Wage Income Distribution: A General Equilibrium Application to Climate and Energy Policies", *OECD Environment Working Papers*, No. 137, OECD Publishing, Paris, https://dx.doi.org/10.1787/ea3696f4-en. [114]

Chateau, J. and E. Mavroeidi (2020), "The jobs potential of a transition towards a resource efficient and circular economy", *OECD Environment Working Papers*, No. 167, OECD Publishing, Paris, https://dx.doi.org/10.1787/28e768df-en. [119]

Chay, K. and M. Greenstone (2003), "The Impact of Air Pollution on Infant Mortality: Evidence from Geographic Variation in Pollution Shocks Induced by a Recession", *The Quarterly Journal of Economics*, Vol. 118/3, pp. 1121-1167, http://dx.doi.org/10.1162/00335530360698513. [31]

Chen, X., X. Zhang and X. Zhang (2017), "Smog in Our Brains: Gender Differences in the Impact of Exposure to Air Pollution on Cognitive Performance", *IZA Institute of Labour Economics* 10628, http://ftp.iza.org/dp10628.pdf. [44]

Clancy, J., M. Skutsch and S. Batchelor (2003), *The Gender-Energy-Poverty Nexus: Finding the Energy to Address Gender Concerns in Development*, https://www.researchgate.net/publication/237232946_The_Gender-Energy-Poverty_Nexus_Finding_the_Energy_to_Address_Gender_Concerns_in_Development. [107]

Cui, Y. et al. (2003), "Air pollution and case fatality of SARS in the People's Republic of China: an ecologic study", *Environmental Health*, Vol. 2/1, http://dx.doi.org/10.1186/1476-069x-2-15. [38]

Currie, J. et al. (2013), "Something in the water: contaminated drinking water and infant health", *Canadian Journal of Economics/Revue canadienne d'économique*, Vol. 46/3, pp. 791-810, http://dx.doi.org/10.1111/caje.12039. [57]

Currie, J. and M. Neidell (2004), *Air Pollution and Infant Health: What Can We Learn From California's Recent Experience*, National Bureau of Economic Research, Cambridge, MA, http://dx.doi.org/10.3386/w10251. [20]

Czaja, S. et al. (2006), "Factors predicting the use of technology: Findings from the center for research and education on aging and technology enhancement (create).", *Psychology and Aging*, Vol. 21/2, pp. 333-352, http://dx.doi.org/10.1037/0882-7974.21.2.333. [75]

Dechezleprêtre, A., N. Rivers and B. Stadler (2019), "The economic cost of air pollution: Evidence from Europe", *OECD Economics Department Working Papers*, No. 1584, OECD Publishing, Paris, https://dx.doi.org/10.1787/56119490-en. [25]

EIGE (2020), "Beijing +25: the fifth review of the implementation of the Beijing Platform for Action in the EU Member States", https://eige.europa.eu/publications/beijing-25-fifth-review-implementation-beijing-platform-action-eu-member-states. [40]

EIGE (2020), *Gender Equality index 2019 Work-Life Balance*, http://dx.doi.org/10.2839/852588. [96]

EmPower (2020), *The Impact of COVID-19 on Rural Women and Enterprises: A Rapid Socio-Economic Assessment in Viet Nam by the EmPower Project*, Sida, UN Enviornment Programme, UN Women, https://reliefweb.int/sites/reliefweb.int/files/resources/The%20impact%20of%20COVID-19%20on%20rural%20women%20and%20enterprises%20-%20A%20rapid%20socio-economic%20assessment%20in%20Viet%20Nam%20by%20the%20empower%20project.pdf (accessed on 30 November 2020). [101]

FAO (2011), *The State of Food and Agriculture. Women in Agriculture: Closing the Gender Gap for Development*, Food and Agriculture Organization of the United Nations, Rome, http://www.fao.org/publications/sofa/2010-11/en/. [115]

Fauconnier, I., A. Jenniskens and P. Perry (2018), *Women as change-makers in the governance of shared waters*, IUCN, International Union for Conservation of Nature, http://dx.doi.org/10.2305/iucn.ch.2018.22.en. [50]

Fouillet, A. et al. (2006), "Excess mortality related to the August 2003 heat wave in France", *International Archives of Occupational and Environmental Health*, Vol. 80/1, pp. 16-24, http://dx.doi.org/10.1007/s00420-006-0089-4. [89]

Gauderman, W. et al. (2007), "Effect of exposure to traffic on lung development from 10 to 18 years of age: a cohort study", *The Lancet*, Vol. 369/9561, pp. 571-577, http://dx.doi.org/10.1016/s0140-6736(07)60037-3. [24]

GBD (2019), *Global Burden of Disease Study 2019 Results*, Institute for Health Metrics and Evaluation, Seattle, http://ghdx.healthdata.org/gbd-results-tool. [3]

Girard, P. (2002), *Xharcoal Production and Use in Africa: What Future?*, https://www.researchgate.net/publication/283832140_Charcoal_production_and_use_in_Africa_What_future. [29]

Hertz-Picciotto, I. et al. (2010), "Blood Mercury Concentrations in CHARGE Study Children with and without Autism", *Environmental Health Perspectives*, Vol. 118/1, pp. 161-166, http://dx.doi.org/10.1289/ehp.0900736. [80]

Hohenadel, K. et al. (2015), "The Inclusion of Women in Studies of Occupational Cancer: A Review of the Epidemiologic Literature From 1991-2009", *American Journal of Industrial Medicine*, Vol. 58/3, pp. 276-281, http://dx.doi.org/10.1002/ajim.22424. [73]

ILO (2019), *The Future of Work in Textiles , Clothing, Leather and Footwear*, ILO, https://www.ilo.org/sector/Resources/publications/WCMS_669355/lang--en/index.htm. [77]

ILO (2016), "What is a Green Job?", https://www.ilo.org/global/topics/green-jobs/news/WCMS_220248/lang--en/index.htm. [117]

ILO (2000), *ABC for Women Workers' Rights and Gender Equality*, International Labour Office, Geneva, https://www.ilo.org/wcmsp5/groups/public/---dgreports/---gender/documents/publication/wcms_087314.pdf (accessed on 20 October 2020). [133]

Inyinbor, A. et al. (2018), "Water Pollution: Effects, Prevention, and Climatic Impact", in *Water Challenges of an Urbanizing World*, InTech, http://dx.doi.org/10.5772/intechopen.72018. [12]

IPBES (2019), *Global assessment report on biodiversity and ecosystem services of the Intergovernmental Science-Policy Platform on Biodiversity and Ecosystem Services*, https://ipbes.net/global-assessment. [64]

IRENA (2019), *Renewable Energy: A Gender Perspective*, IRENA, https://www.irena.org/publications/2019/Jan/Renewable-Energy-A-Gender-Perspective. [118]

ITF (2020), *Re-spacing Our Cities for Resilience: Covid-19 Transport Brief*, OECD/ITF, https://www.itf-oecd.org/sites/default/files/respacing-cities-resilience-covid-19.pdf. [99]

ITF (2018), *Understanding Urban Travel Behaviour by Gender for Efficient and Equitable Transport Policies*, OECD Publishing, Paris, https://doi.org/10.1787/eaf64f94-en. [26]

ITF (2018), *Women's Safety and Security*, OECD/ITF, https://www.itf-oecd.org/womens-safety-security. [97]

Kabeer, N. (2012), *Women's Economic Empowerment and Inclusive Growth: Labour Markets and Enterprise Development*, https://www.lse.ac.uk/gender/assets/documents/research/choice-constraints-and-the-gender-dynamics-of-lab/Women%27s-economic-empowerment-and-inclusive-growth.pdf. [109]

Kioumourtzoglou, M. et al. (2017), "The Association Between Air Pollution and Onset of Depression Among Middle-Aged and Older Women", *American Journal of Epidemiology*, Vol. 185/9, pp. 801-809, http://dx.doi.org/10.1093/aje/kww163. [42]

Kovačićek, T. and R. R. Franić (2019), "The Professional Status of Rural Women in the EU", *European Parliament*, https://www.europarl.europa.eu/RegData/etudes/STUD/2019/608868/IPOL_STU(2019)608868_EN.pdf. [32]

Lal, R. (ed.) (2020), *Soil and Fertilizers*, CRC Press, http://dx.doi.org/10.1201/9780429471049. [60]

Landrigan, P. et al. (2018), "The Lancet Commission on pollution and health", *The Lancet*, Vol. 391/10119, pp. 462-512, http://dx.doi.org/10.1016/s0140-6736(17)32345-0. [51]

Lemonsu, A. et al. (2015), "Vulnerability to heat waves: Impact of urban expansion scenarios on urban heat island and heat stress in Paris (France)", *Urban Climate*, Vol. 14, pp. 586-605, http://dx.doi.org/10.1016/j.uclim.2015.10.007. [67]

Lovett, G. et al. (2009), "Effects of Air Pollution on Ecosystems and Biological Diversity in the Eastern United States", *Annals of the New York Academy of Sciences*, Vol. 1162/1, pp. 99-135, http://dx.doi.org/10.1111/j.1749-6632.2009.04153.x. [63]

Lu, J. et al. (2018), "Polluted Morality: Air Pollution Predicts Criminal Activity and Unethical Behavior", *Psychological Science*, Vol. 29/3, pp. 340-355, http://dx.doi.org/10.1177/0956797617735807. [47]

Lynn, H., M. Mantingh and S. Rech (2017), *Plastic, Gender and the Environment. Findings of a Literature Study on the Lifecycle of Plastics and its Impacts on Women and Men, from Production to Litter*, http://dx.doi.org/DOI:10.13140/RG.2.2.33644.26242. [85]

Manisalidis, I. et al. (2020), "Environmental and Health Impacts of Air Pollution: A Review", *Frontiers in Public Health*, Vol. 8, http://dx.doi.org/10.3389/fpubh.2020.00014. [7]

McGregor, G. (2015), *Heatwaves and Health:: Guidance on Warning-System Development*, World Health Organization (WHO), https://www.who.int/globalchange/publications/WMO_WHO_Heat_Health_Guidance_2015.pdf. [68]

Mirosa, M. (2014), "Sustainable Consumption and Gender", in *Encyclopedia of Food and Agricultural Ethics*, Springer Netherlands, Dordrecht, http://dx.doi.org/10.1007/978-94-007-0929-4_461. [128]

Moffitt, P. et al. (2020), "Intimate Partner Violence and COVID-19 in Rural, Remote, and Northern Canada: Relationship, Vulnerability and Risk", *Journal of Family Violence*, http://dx.doi.org/10.1007/s10896-020-00212-x. [102]

Montt, G. (2018), "Too polluted to work? The gendered correlates of air pollution on hours worked", *IZA Journal of Labor Economics*, Vol. 7/1, http://dx.doi.org/10.1186/s40172-018-0067-6. [33]

Mrema, E. et al. (2017), "Pesticide Exposure and Health Problems Among Female Horticulture Workers in Tanzania", *Environmental Health Insights*, Vol. 11, p. 117863021771523, http://dx.doi.org/10.1177/1178630217715237. [58]

Nickerson, S. (2019), "Air Pollution Exposure Is Linked to Increased Violent Crime, Domestic Violence", *EcoWatch*, https://www.ecowatch.com/air-pollution-violent-crime-domestic-2640927925.html?rebelltitem=1#rebelltitem1. [45]

Noël, R. (2018), *Race, Economics, and Social Status*, U.S. Bureau Labour Statistics, https://www.bls.gov/spotlight/2018/race-economics-and-social-status/pdf/race-economics-and-social-status.pdf. [126]

OECD (2021), *Mortality, Morbidity and Welfare Cost from Exposure to Environment-related Risks*, OECD, Paris, https://stats.oecd.org/Index.aspx?QueryId=90835#. [4]

OECD (2021), *OECD Environment Statistics*, https://www.oecd-ilibrary.org/environment/data/oecd-environment-statistics_env-data-en#:~:text=relevant%20environmental%20statistics.-,The%20OECD%20Environmental%20Statistics%20database%20provide%20a,of%20policy%2Drelevant%20environmental%20statistics.&te. [124]

OECD (2020), *COVID-19 and the Low-carbon Transition: Impacts and Possible Policy Responses*, OECD Publishing, Paris, https://www.oecd.org/coronavirus/policy-responses/covid-19-and-the-low-carbon-transition-impacts-and-possible-policy-responses-749738fc/. [113]

OECD (2020), *Dream Jobs? Teenagers' Career Aspirations and the Future of Work*, OECD Publishing, Paris, https://www.oecd.org/berlin/publikationen/Dream-Jobs.pdf. [122]

OECD (2020), *How's Life? 2020: Measuring Well-being*, OECD Publishing, Paris, https://dx.doi.org/10.1787/9870c393-en. [2]

OECD (2020), *Mortality, Morbidity and Welfare Cost From Exposure to Environment-Related Risks*, OECD, Paris, https://stats.oecd.org/FileView2.aspx?IDFile=1356df09-6bd4-4b0b-9a95-d56e145769ad. [6]

OECD (2020), *Who Cares? Attracting and Retaining Elderly Care Workers*, OECD, http://dx.doi.org/10.1787/92c0ef68-en. [116]

OECD (2020), *Women at the Core of the Fight against COVID-19 Crisis*, OECD Publishing, Paris, https://read.oecd-ilibrary.org/view/?ref=127_127000-awfnqj80me&title=Women-at-the-core-of-the-fight-against-COVID-19-crisis. [104]

OECD (2019), *Accelerating Climate Action*, OECD, http://dx.doi.org/10.1787/2f4c8c9a-en. [98]

OECD (2019), *Pharmaceutical Residues in Freshwater: Hazards and Policy Responses*, OECD Publishing, Paris. [56]

OECD (2018), *Bridging the digital Gender Divide: Include, Upskill Innovate*, OECD Publishing, Paris, https://www.oecd.org/going-digital/bridging-the-digital-gender-divide-key-messages.pdf. [103]

OECD (2018), *Considerations for Assesing the Risks of Combined Exposure to Multiple Chemicals*, https://www.oecd.org/chemicalsafety/risk-assessment/considerations-for-assessing-the-risks-of-combined-exposure-to-multiple-chemicals.pdf. [66]

OECD (2018), *Improving Plastics Management: Trends, Policy Responses, and the Role of International Co-operation and Trade*, OECD Publishing, Paris, https://www.oecd.org/environment/waste/policy-highlights-improving-plastics-management.pdf. [84]

OECD (2018), *Is the Last Mile the Longest? Economic Gains from Gender Equality in Nordic Countries*, OECD, http://dx.doi.org/10.1787/9789264300040-en. [110]

OECD (2018), *OECD Due Diligence Guidance for Responsible Supply Chains in the Garment and Footwear Sector*, OECD Publishing, Paris, https://dx.doi.org/10.1787/9789264290587-en. [79]

OECD (2018), *Presentations from OECD Workshop on the Best Practices in Assessing the Soical Costs of Selected Chemicals*, https://www.oecd.org/officialdocuments/publicdisplaydocumentpdf/?cote=env/jm/mono(2018)22/ann1&doclanguage=en. [86]

OECD (2017), *Going Digital: The Future of Work for Women*, https://www.oecd.org/employment/Going-Digital-the-Future-of-Work-for-Women.pdf. [123]

OECD (2017), *Meeting of the OECD Council at Ministerial Level - Report on the Implementation of the OECD Gender Recommendations*, http://www.oecd.org/mcm-2018/documents/C-MIN-2017-7-EN.pdf. [120]

OECD (2016), *Entrepreneurship at a Glance 2016*, OECD, http://dx.doi.org/10.1787/entrepreneur_aag-2016-en. [121]

OECD (2016), *The Economic Consequences of Outdoor Air Pollution*, OECD Publishing, Paris, https://dx.doi.org/10.1787/9789264257474-en. [9]

OECD (2014), *The Cost of Air Pollution*, OECD, http://dx.doi.org/10.1787/9789264210448-en. [17]

OECD (2013), *OECD Guidelines for the Testig of Chemicals*, OECD Publishing, Paris, https://www.oecd-ilibrary.org/environment/oecd-guidelines-for-the-testing-of-chemicals_72d77764-en. [82]

OECD (2012), *Environmental Quality and Life Satisfaction: Evidence on Microdata*, OECD Publishing, Paris, https://doi.org/10.1787/19970900. [16]

OECD (2012), *OECD Environmental Outlook to 2050: The Consequences of Inaction*, OECD Publishing, Paris, https://dx.doi.org/10.1787/9789264122246-en. [10]

OECD (2012), "The Jobs Potential of a Shift Towards a Low-Carbon Economy", *OECD Green Growth Papers*, No. 2012/1, OECD Publishing, Paris, https://dx.doi.org/10.1787/5k9h3630320v-en. [112]

OECD (2011), *Greening Household Behaviour*, OECD, http://dx.doi.org/10.1787/9789264096875-en. [129]

Okello, G., G. Devereux and S. Semple (2018), "Women and girls in resource poor countries experience much greater exposure to household air pollutants than men: Results from Uganda and Ethiopia", *Environment International*, Vol. 119, pp. 429-437, http://dx.doi.org/10.1016/j.envint.2018.07.002. [14]

Ortiz, C. et al. (2017), "Evaluation of short-term mortality attributable to particulate matter pollution in Spain", *Environmental Pollution*, Vol. 224, pp. 541-551, http://dx.doi.org/10.1016/j.envpol.2017.02.037. [92]

Ostry, J. et al. (2018), *Economic Gains From Gender Inclusion : New Mechanisms, New Evidence*, IMF, https://www.imf.org/en/Publications/Staff-Discussion-Notes/Issues/2018/10/09/Economic-Gains-From-Gender-Inclusion-New-Mechanisms-New-Evidence-45543. [111]

Papadopoulou, M. et al. (2019), "TCR Sequencing Reveals the Distinct Development of Fetal and Adult Human Vγ9Vδ2 T Cells", *The Journal of Immunology*, Vol. 203/6, pp. 1468-1479, http://dx.doi.org/10.4049/jimmunol.1900592. [65]

Phadera, L. (2016), *International Migration and its Effect on Labor Supply of the Left-Behind Household Members: Evidence from Nepal*, Agricultural and Applied Economics Association, http://dx.doi.org/DOI: 10.22004/ag.econ.235968. [95]

Prüss-Üstün, A., C. Corvalán and WHO (2006), *Preventing Disease Through Healthy Environments : Towards an Estimate of the Environmental Burden of Disease*, https://apps.who.int/iris/handle/10665/43457. [8]

Roser, M. and H. Ritchie (2020), *Fertilizers*, Our World in Data, https://ourworldindata.org/fertilizers. [59]

Roy, R. (2016), "The cost of air pollution in Africa", *OECD Development Centre Working Papers*, No. 333, OECD Publishing, Paris, https://dx.doi.org/10.1787/5jlqzq77x6f8-en. [41]

Roy, R. and N. Braathen (2017), "The Rising Cost of Ambient Air Pollution thus far in the 21st Century: Results from the BRIICS and the OECD Countries", *OECD Environment Working Papers*, No. 124, OECD Publishing, Paris, https://dx.doi.org/10.1787/d1b2b844-en. [5]

Saha, S. et al. (2007), "Cigarette smoke and adverse health effects: An overview of research trends and future needs", *International Journal of Angiology*, Vol. 16/03, pp. 77-83, http://dx.doi.org/10.1055/s-0031-1278254. [22]

Salcedo-La Viña, C., R. Singh and N. Elwell (2020), *Rural Women Must Be at the Heart of COVID-19 Response and Recovery*, World Resources Institute, https://www.wri.org/blog/2020/09/rural-women-must-be-heart-covid-19-response-and-recovery (accessed on 30 November 2020). [100]

Scarselli, A. et al. (2018), "Gender differences in occupational exposure to carcinogens among Italian workers", *BMC Public Health*, Vol. 18/1, http://dx.doi.org/10.1186/s12889-018-5332-x. [74]

Setti, L. et al. (2020), *SARS-Cov-2 RNA Found on Particulate Matter of Bergamo in Northern Italy: First Preliminary Evidence*, Cold Spring Harbor Laboratory, http://dx.doi.org/10.1101/2020.04.15.20065995. [37]

Setti, L. et al. (2020), *The Potential role of Particulate Matter in the Spreading of COVID-19 in Northern Italy: First Evidence-based Research Hypotheses*, Cold Spring Harbor Laboratory, http://dx.doi.org/10.1101/2020.04.11.20061713. [36]

Setton, E. et al. (2010), "Gender Differences in Chronic Exposure to Traffic-Related Air Pollution—A Simulation Study of Working Females and Males", *The Professional Geographer*, Vol. 62/1, pp. 66-83, http://dx.doi.org/10.1080/00330120903404728. [27]

Sharma, R., T. Nguyen and U. Grote (2018), "Changing Consumption Patterns—Drivers and the Environmental Impact", *Sustainability*, Vol. 10/11, p. 4190, http://dx.doi.org/10.3390/su10114190. [125]

Street, M. et al. (2018), "Current Knowledge on Endocrine Disrupting Chemicals (EDCs) from Animal Biology to Humans, from Pregnancy to Adulthood: Highlights from a National Italian Meeting", *International Journal of Molecular Sciences*, Vol. 19/6, p. 1647, http://dx.doi.org/10.3390/ijms19061647. [69]

Suissa, S. and M. Edwardes (1997), "Adjusted Odds Ratios for Case-Control Studies with Missing Confounder Data in Controls", *Epidemiology*, Vol. 8/3, p. 275, http://dx.doi.org/10.1097/00001648-199705000-00008. [23]

Ten Brink, P. et al. (2016), *Plastics Marine Litter and the Circular Economy*, IEEP. [83]

Toro, F., M. Serrano and M. Guillen (2019), *"Who pollutes more? Gender Differences in Consumption Patterns*, Research Institute of Applied Economics, https://www.ub.edu/irea/working_papers/2019/201906.pdf. [130]

Truman, J. and R. Morgan (2014), "Nonfatal Domestic Violence, 2003-2012", *Bureau of Justice Statistics*, https://www.bjs.gov/content/pub/pdf/ndv0312.pdf. [48]

UN (n.d.), *System of Environmental-Economic Accounting (SEEA)*, United Nations (UN), https://seea.un.org/. [131]

UN (n.d.), *System of National Accounts (SNA)*, United Nations (UN), https://unstats.un.org/unsd/nationalaccount/sna.asp. [132]

UN Women (2018), *Turning promises into action: Gender equality in the 2030 Agenda for Sustainable Development*, https://www.unwomen.org/en/digital-library/publications/2018/2/gender-equality-in-the-2030-agenda-for-sustainable-development-2018. [94]

UNDP (2011), *Chemicals and Gender Energy Map: Environment Practice Gender Mainstreaming Guidance Series Chemicals Management.*, https://www.undp.org/content/dam/aplaws/publication/en/publications/environment-energy/www-ee-library/chemicals-management/chemicals-and-gender/2011%20Chemical&Gender.pdf. [61]

UNEP (2013), *Women and Natural Resources : Unlocking the Peacebuilding Potential...* [62]

UNEP (2011), *Women at the Frontline of Climate Change: Gender Risks and Hopes*, http://hdl.handle.net/20.500.11822/7985. [93]

UNHCR (2019), *Global Trends: Forced Displacement in 2018*, UN High Commissioner for Refugees (UNHCR), https://www.unhcr.org/statistics/unhcrstats/5d08d7ee7/unhcr-global-trends-2018.html. [1]

UNSD (n.d.), *SDG Indicators. United Nations Global SDG Database*, https://unstats.un.org/sdgs/indicators/database/ (accessed on 20 October 2020). [72]

Watts, N. et al. (2019), "The 2019 report of The Lancet Countdown on health and climate change: ensuring that the health of a child born today is not defined by a changing climate", *The Lancet*, Vol. 394/10211, pp. 1836-1878, http://dx.doi.org/10.1016/s0140-6736(19)32596-6. [54]

WHO (2016), "Preventing Disease Through Healthy Environments: A global Assessment of the Burden of Disease from Environmental Risks", https://www.who.int/quantifying_ehimpacts/publications/preventing-disease/en/. [13]

WHO (2016), *The Public Health Impact of Chemicals: Knowns and Unknowns*, World Health Organization (WHO), https://apps.who.int/iris/handle/10665/206553. [70]

WHO (2014), "Preventing Diarrhoea Through Better Water, Sanitation and Hygiene: Exposures and impacts in low=and middle-income countries", *World Health Organization*. [52]

WHO and UNICEF (2017), "Progress on Drinking Water, Sanitation and Hygiene: Joint Monitoring Programme 2017 update and SDG baselines", https://www.who.int/water_sanitation_health/publications/jmp-2017/en/. [53]

Woodcock, J. et al. (2009), "Public health benefits of strategies to reduce greenhouse-gas emissions: urban land transport", *The Lancet*, Vol. 374/9705, pp. 1930-1943, http://dx.doi.org/10.1016/s0140-6736(09)61714-1. [55]

World Health Organisation (ed.) (2016), *Burning Opportunity: Clean Household Energy for Health, Sustainable Development, and Wellbeing of Women and Children*, https://www.who.int/airpollution/publications/burning-opportunities/en/. [15]

Wu, X. et al. (2020), "Exposure to air pollution and COVID-19 mortality in the United States", http://dx.doi.org/10.1101/2020.04.05.20054502. [35]

Xin, Z., Z. Xiaobo and C. Xi (2015), "Happines in the Air: How Does a Dirty Sky Affect Subjective Well-Being?", *ZA – Institute of Labor Economics*, https://www.econstor.eu/bitstream/10419/120969/1/dp9312.pdf. [43]

Yin, Q. et al. (2019), "Mapping the increased minimum mortality temperatures in the context of global climate change", *Nature Communications*, Vol. 10/1, http://dx.doi.org/10.1038/s41467-019-12663-y. [91]

Zhonghua, L., B. Xing and X. Z (2020), "The epidemiological characteristics of an outbreak of 2019 novel coronavirus diseases (COVID-19) in China", *Epidemiology Working Group for NCIP Epidemic Response, Chinese Center for Disease Control and Prevention.*, http://dx.doi.org/10.3760/cma.j.issn.0254-6450.2020.02.003. [39]

Zota, A. and B. Shamasunder (2017), "The environmental injustice of beauty: framing chemical exposures from beauty products as a health disparities concern", *American Journal of Obstetrics and Gynecology*, Vol. 217/4, pp. 418.e1-418.e6, http://dx.doi.org/10.1016/j.ajog.2017.07.020. [81]

Notes

[1] Gender equality and gender equity are two related yet distinct concepts. Based on ILO definitions, "gender equity means fairness of treatment for women and men, according to their respective needs and interests. This may include equal treatment or treatment that is different but considered equivalent in terms of rights, benefits, obligations and opportunities"; "Gender equality refers to the enjoyment of equal rights, opportunities and treatment by men and women and by boys and girls in all spheres of life. It asserts that people's rights, responsibilities, social status and access to resources do not depend on whether they are born male or female" (ILO, 2000[133]). Although there is a distinction between equality and equity, for ease of reference and simplicity's sake, this report uses only the term "inequalities".

[2]See REACH – Eliminating Toxic chemicals in the EU (https://www.wecf.eu/english/campaigns/2004/reach.php)

[3] Worth noting that life expectancy for women is larger than for men and that vulnerability to heatwaves increases with age.

[4] OECD's statistical definition of infrastructure refers to "the system of public works in a country, state or region, including roads, utility lines and public buildings". However, the term infrastructure from a policy perspective covers a wider set of systems and services, including infrastructure investment, planning and management; and eventually usage and economic spillovers.

[5] Social infrastructure refers to infrastructure that supports the development of the human resource potential and ameliorates living conditions. It includes, but is not limited to, infrastructure relating to education; health; and water supply, sanitation and sewerage.

4 Women and the Environmental Action Movement

Environmental justice refers to a fair and inclusive engagement in the development, implementation and enforcement of environmental legislation at national and international levels. Girls and boys, youth (civil society organisations as well as young professionals), indigenous peoples (including differences between men and women) and women are often not fairly represented or lack a voice in decision-making processes and in environmental policy-making. As a result, their environment-related needs and preferences may be disregarded. Developing countries, Small Island Developing States (SIDS) and indigenous communities are particularly vulnerable to environmental threats; women in those countries and groups often bear a heavy burden for environmental damage and natural disasters. In addition to governments and the international community, businesses and philanthropy are also playing an increasingly important role in promoting environmental and climate justice and supporting women's economic empowerment and environmental leadership. The COVID-19 pandemic has also created a unique momentum for unprecedented change, as new policies and investments are needed at a large scale to tackle the health, economic, climate and biodiversity crises concurrently.

4.1. Key findings

Environmental justice broadly refers to fair and inclusive engagement in the development, implementation and enforcement of environmental legislation at national and international levels. The last few decades have seen a flurry of action on environmental justice at both levels. Some countries have made important strides towards environmental justice by including the right to a healthy environment in their constitutions. The global community also recognised environmental justice as a basic right in the 1992 Rio Declaration on Environment and Development, and in the 1998 UNECE Convention on Access to Information, Public Participation in Decision-Making and Access to Justice in Environmental Matters (the Aarhus Convention). Yet many countries, including some OECD countries, have yet to ratify the Aarhus Convention. Among those who have, the degree of implementation varies.

Children, youth, and women often lack a voice and representation in decision-making processes. This is especially the case for those belonging to vulnerable and disadvantaged societal groups. Environmental justice is a major concern in developing countries, given that large agricultural, industrial and infrastructure projects are not always subject to environmental and social impact controls. Environmental human rights defenders – often women – continue to be persecuted and harassed in many countries.

Women and youth are prominent among the leading global campaigners against climate change and to ensure effective environmental protection, across both developed and developing countries. The growth of social media has allowed local communities, grassroots movements, and civil society organisations to magnify their voice and impact. Indigenous communities have also become more assertive in protecting their right to ancestral lands and nature-based services. Women are active in the environmental justice action movement in Small Island Developing States (SIDS), which are the most vulnerable to climate change and natural hazards. Some philanthropic organisations are also very active in the gender equality and environmental justice agenda in both developed and developing countries.

Ultimately, however, the onus mainly falls on business to comply with environmental legislation and respect environmental rights and on governments to ensure that the legal and governance frameworks in the country allow for effective environmental justice, including by:

- clearly outlining citizens' environmental rights in relevant legislation;
- ensuring transparency on the state of environment and the impact on human health and protecting the right to obtain information on environmental matters;
- carrying out social impact assessments of projects that may have an impact on the environment, and including a gender dimension;
- organising public consultations for environment-related decision-making and projects with an environmental impact, and ensuring access to o groups to such consultations;
- facilitating both formal legal action and information mediation and redress mechanisms to protect environmental rights and compensate those affected by environmental harm.

4.2. Environmental justice: from a fringe to world-wide phenomenon

Even though there is no internationally accepted definition, environmental justice broadly covers fair and inclusive engagement in the development, implementation and enforcement of environmental legislation.[1] It implies access to environment-related goods such as clean water and energy, or safe urban areas, and protection from negative environmental pressures such as air and water pollution or deforestation (distributional justice). It also translates into equal access to the decision-making process of environmental policies (procedural justice) (Brulle and Pellow, 2006[1]). It has been argued that environmental justice should also achieve a healthy environment for all (substantive justice) (Bell, 2016[2]).

The grassroots environmental justice movement started in the United States in the 1970s, when indigenous people and local communities of different racial backgrounds and of poorer socio-economic status (a majority of them women) sounded the alarm over the impact of environmental degradation on their communities. The movement was very successful in advocating for environmental protection and in engaging with the US Environmental Protection Agency and state governments to address environmental degradation at the local level (OECD, 2017[3]). Environmental justice has only recently gained ground as an issue in Europe (EEA, 2018[4]); (Lakes, Brückner and Krämer, 2014[5]), while in other parts of the developed world the movement is still in its initial stages (OECD, 2017[3]).[2]

Even more importantly, a 2019 Report by Front Line Defenders – an international non-governmental organisation protecting human rights defenders at risk - reported that from the 321 human rights defenders who were killed in 2018 (an increase of 67% from 2017), 77% were working on land, indigenous peoples and environmental rights. Women are very much at the forefront of the human rights' movement worldwide (Front Line Defenders, 2019[6]). Front Line Defenders (2019) have developed special considerations for tackling gender inequality from a human rights perspective specifically as over 1 in 10 environmental defenders killed were women with two-thirds of killings taking place in Latin America (Global Witness, 2020[7]). The 2019 United Nations High Human Rights Council Resolution "[recognises] the contribution of environmental human rights defenders to the enjoyment of human rights, environmental protection and sustainable development" (UN, 2019[8]).

A 2019 Austrian study acknowledged that issues of environmental justice exist in Europe and deserve the attention of policy makers. It found that environmental inequalities mainly affected immigrants from former Yugoslavia, Turkey, and other European countries that were not EU member states prior to 2004; people with no tertiary education; and people forced to live in restricted spaces (Glatter-Götz et al., 2019[9]).

Environmental justice is a major concern in developing countries, given that large industrial and infrastructure projects are not always subject to strict environmental and social impact controls. Well-known eco-feminists, such as Vandana Shiva and the late Wangari Maathai, have been vocal on the role of women as agents of change for environmental protection. Vandana Shiva, a leader in the eco-feminist movement (Mies and Shiva, 1993[10]), a long-time advocate for the role of women in biodiversity conservation and in sustainable management of natural resources, established Navdanya, a community seed bank that provides local farmers resources, training, and other tools to advance their business and at the same time protect biological and cultural diversity (Navdanya International, 2020[11]). Wangari Maathai initiated the Green Belt Movement in Africa, linking environmental conservation to democracy and peace. Women held decision-making roles within the movement, as they were the ones holding the knowledge on local natural resources (Sandra et al., 2007[12]).

The Paris Agreement notes the importance of "climate justice", while also hinting towards its limited ownership. Article 7.5 states that "adaptation action should follow a country-driven, gender-responsive, participatory and fully transparent approach, taking into consideration vulnerable groups, communities and ecosystems, and should be based on and guided by the best available science and, as appropriate, traditional knowledge, knowledge of indigenous peoples and local knowledge systems, with a view to integrating adaptation into relevant socioeconomic and environmental policies and actions, where appropriate" (UN, 2015[13]).

Environmental human rights defenders – often women – continue to be persecuted and harassed in many countries (Front Line Defenders, 2019[14]). In developing countries, women's rights defenders and environmentalists belonging to racialised, ethnicised and indigenous people and communities often experience sexual violence and harassment. In Russia, for instance, human rights defenders have long faced harassment, intimidation, physical attacks and arbitrary arrests because of their work (Amnesty International, 2019[15]). Some countries (e.g. Costa Rica) (OHCHR, 2013[16]) have made important strides towards environmental justice by including a right to a healthy environment in their constitutions.

The global community has recognised environmental justice as a basic right. The 1992 Rio Declaration on Environment and Development called for citizens' access to information, public participation and access to justice. The 1998 UNECE Convention on Access to Information, Public Participation in Decision-Making and Access to Justice in Environmental Matters (Aarhus Convention) (UNECE, 1998[17]) set the ground for civil society and citizens' engagement to: (i) request information on the state of the environment and the impact on human heath, (ii) participate in public consultations for environment-related decision-making, and (iii) proceed to legal action when their environmental rights are at stake. In 1998, OECD Member countries adopted in the Recommendation on Environmental Information [OECD/LEGAL/0296], which recommends promoting the dissemination of information to allow citizens to assess the environmental consequences of business and other activities. References to both the Rio Declaration and the Aarhus Convention are also included in the OECD Guidelines for Multinational Enterprises [OECD/LEGAL/0144], which set the framework for business conduct relating to environmental matters (OECD, 2012[18]).

In the years following, much action has taken place in the international arena. The European Union translated the Aarhus Convention into EU legislation (European Parliament and Council of the European Union, 2006[19]). In 2010 UNEP developed the Bali Guidelines to support countries in developing national legislation on these issues (UNEP, 2015[20]), and has since presented its own Environmental Rights Initiative. This Initiative brings together country representatives and other stakeholders; with a rights-based approach it enhances access to environmental information, promotes environmental justice and assists in developing a compliance culture (UNEP, 2020[21]). Further engagement on the topic has been spreading in other organisations, such as the World Bank and the UNDP (UNDP, 2014[22]), as well as at regional level, for example, through the recently agreed Escazú Agreement on Access to Information, Public Participation and Justice in Environmental Matters in Latin America and the Caribbean (UN, 2018[23]). The Escazú Agreement is entering into force on 22nd April 2021, after being ratified by 11 out of the 33 countries on Latin America and the Caribbean. At the same time, only 46 out of 57 states and the EU have so far ratified the Aarhus Convention (UNECE, 2020[24]), and among those, there are different levels of commitment to the principles set.[3] The European Commission recently proposed amending EU legislation, to facilitate access to information not only by individuals but also NGOs, as well as to provide ample time to review the information provided (EC, 2020[25]).

4.3. Women and environmental justice

As women account for a larger share of the world's poor and 80% of people displaced by the impacts of climate change and environmental degradation,[4] and because of their traditional roles related to household and community responsibilities in many societies, they are more likely to be negatively affected by environmental degradation (for more information see Chapters 6 to 14). In developing countries, women and children are often the most affected by the erosion of ecosystems and climate change because of their greater dependence on traditional household and community life and small-scale farming, (wetlands dependency) as well as the unsustainable use of natural resources and the effects of climate change, such as increased frequency and intensity of droughts and floods. They are also most likely to be excluded from the decision-making process with regards to such issues.

Children, youth, and women often lack a voice and representation in decision-making processes. This is especially the case for those belonging to vulnerable and disadvantaged societal in society. As evidenced in the OECD Development Centre Social Institution and Gender Index (SIGI), women in many countries are still the subject of discriminatory laws, social norms and practices. These have implications for women's right to own their own land and therefore to obtain, or not (ground) water concessions, and therefore to manage natural resources, but also to seek redress for environmental damage brought upon them (OECD, 2019[26]).

Women – especially of colour and from indigenous communities - have been the majority of those engaged in the environmental justice movement in the United States, among other countries, as they are more likely to experience the impact of local environmental degradation in their day-to-day individual and family lives (Unger, 2008[27]). In developing countries, women are usually most affected by the unsustainable use of natural resources and the effects of climate change, such as increased frequency and intensity of pollution (e.g. because of larger scale agricultural and mining activities), droughts and floods. They are also most likely to be excluded from the decision making process with regards to such issues.

Women in developed countries are increasingly concerned about residue of hormones, pesticides and microbiotics and plastics in the water (and agriculture products) and the impact this may have on their health. An example on endocrine disruptors shows implications for pregnancy and fertility and further reinforces the urgency of this issue (van Duursen et al., 2020[28]).

Youth and children also have limited opportunities to raise awareness on their case, as they hardly participate in decision-making processes. Beyond the formality of not being able to vote under a certain age, the OECD Youth Stocktaking Report demonstrates that young people continue to be significantly underrepresented in decision-making positions and engage less in institutionalised forms of participation such as voting and party membership, undermining their ability to shape environmental policy decisions and outcomes. While expressing lower levels of trust in governments, young people demonstrate strong awareness for inequalities and climate change. In particular, younger generations of men and women are showing growing awareness and agency to drive change towards more sustainable consumption, travel, and overall lifestyles (OECD, 2018[29]).

An intergenerational equity perspective on environmental policy is key to ensuring that benefits and costs are distributed in a fair way across generations, even among generations that are yet to be born as today's actions affect the present and they also affect the future. Businesses and civil society, including women and youth groups, could also have an important role to play in ensuring environmental justice. There is a growing number of grassroots initiatives worldwide that seek to incorporate women and youth considerations into environment-related policies (Allen, Lyons and Stephens, 2019[30]).

In particular, women and youth are prominent among the leading global campaigners against climate change. The climate justice movement has rapidly expanded in reach and impact in recent years, as people have raised their voice to call for action against phenomena that are becoming more and more visible. Women have been calling for climate justice since the 1990s,[5] and they are continuing to do so, raising awareness and campaigning for a gender-just transition.[6] The growth of social media has allowed local communities, grassroots movements, and civil society organisations to magnify their voice and impact. Women are raising their own voice in the debate on climate change adaptation, not only because they are more vulnerable to climate change to a greater extent (due to the gender inequalities), but also because they may have a different sense of what constitutes a bigger climate risk than men (Terry, 2009[31]). The 1992 Beijing Platform for action contains a specific chapter on environment but it has only been debated once at the Commission on the status of Women (CSW) and falls short when it comes to implementation. Explicit recommendations from the Commission on Sustainable Development have been accepted but are largely ignored (CSD 2004, CSD 17, CSD 19, etc.).

Concerns about intergenerational fairness are also mobilising thousands of young people around the globe to call for bold government action against climate change, as exemplified by the #FridaysforFuture movement. This youth movement against climate change can be traced back to 2015, when students from around the world decided to act by skipping school to protest against adults who are shirking their responsibility for "avoiding dangerous climate change" (Climate Strike, n.d.[32]). A student climate strike was organised around COP21. In 2018, Greta Thunberg camped outside the Swedish Parliament requesting action against climate change. Ever since, students strike every Friday around the world. The student movement started with scattered youth initiatives and has now grown into a global one. The 3rd global climate strike, which took place on the 20-27 September 2019, saw – according to the movement's own estimates - 7.6 million people in 185 different countries taking action demanding "an end to the age of fossil fuels" (Global Climate Strike, n.d.[33]); (Fridays For Future, n.d.[34]). The strike was organised through social media – with banners, widgets and push notifications – and received support from more than 10,000 companies, non-governmental organisations and on-line platforms.

The 2018 OECD Youth Stocktaking Report shows that, even though young people engage less in institutionalised forms of participation such as voting and party membership, they are using digital technologies to discuss social and political issues and to mobilise others. Twenty-seven out of 35 OECD countries have, at some point, drafted a multi-year youth strategy; however, in 2018, only 14 of these countries had an operational strategy. It is worth noting that, from the 27 national youth strategies, 89% set gender-specific objectives, and 52% provide gender-disaggregated data. Even though in 67% of the strategies there is a reference to monitoring and evaluating their implementation, only a few have enacted such mechanisms, engaging with youth representatives (OECD, 2018[29]) .

A noteworthy example is Denmark, where in 2019, the Ministry of Energy, Utilities and Climate set up Ungeklimarådet, the Youth Climate Council. The Council has an advisory role to the government, submitting concrete recommendations towards adapting society to a more sustainable lifestyle, raising awareness among youth on the imminent need for action, and empowering youth by providing a way for direct participation. The Youth Climate Council has already set ambitious targets. It proposed for Denmark to become carbon neutral by 2040, it requested the integration of climate considerations in all policy spheres by moving towards sustainable production and consumption patterns; it called for a tripartite dialogue to be established between government, business and youth; and it requested for green budgeting and the integration of negative environmental, economic and social externalities based on the cost of climate-damaging behaviour (Energi-, Forsynings- og Klimaministeriet, 2019[35]).

In 2018, the Supreme Court of Colombia issued a decision in the favour of young Colombians, who sued public authorities asking the state to take immediate action to reduce deforestation rates in the Colombian Amazon to zero by 2020 (Corte Suprema de Justicia, 2018[36]). The youth claimed that increasing deforestation in Colombia is affecting the ecosystems, and therefore negatively influences their lives and futures. The legal argumentation for the case was built on the right to a healthy environment, which is provided for in the Colombian Constitution.

4.4. Women in indigenous communities and the fight for conservation

According to the United Nations, indigenous people constitute around 5% of the world's population, and 15% of the world's poor (UNDESA, 2020[37]). Based on a recent OECD Report on Linking Indigenous Communities with Regional Development, indigenous populations are mainly concentrated in rural areas, compared to non-indigenous populations, making them more susceptible to changes in the local environment (OECD, 2019[38]).

For indigenous communities, the unsustainable use of natural resources, along with clarification of property rights over land and water, is not just a question of human rights, but also of survival. Where local populations are dependent on local natural resources, climate change and economic activity are damaging existing community-based natural resources management patterns. A pointed example of this is the Arctic (Larsen and Fondahl, 2014[39]), where women have been traditionally active in ecosystem preservation and maintenance of traditional knowledge and in playing a fundamental role in environmental protection and conservation. However, changes related to increased interaction with other communities, have marginalised women's role in natural resource management (Section 14.5.2).

Safeguarding indigenous land and water rights is also important for these communities, both to protect their cultural and language diversity, and to mitigate the effects of climate change (indigenous peoples manage forests, which act as carbon sinks) (OECD, 2019[38]). Indigenous women have been strongly advocating for sustainable and environmental issues,[7] and have been active in claiming land rights. In Sri Lanka, for example, they actively requested, and managed to get most of their land back, changing initial plans for a tourist resort project. Such achievements depend critically on guaranteeing equal access to the decision-making and to land rights (Oxfam, International Land Coalition and Rights and Resources Initiative, 2016[40]).

The Native Women's Association of Canada, an umbrella organisation for 12 indigenous women's organisations, has argued that indigenous women are more "likely to suffer disproportionate negative environmental effects from mining activities locally" (Bond and Quinlan, 2018[41]). According to their analysis, despite the existing companies-communities agreements in place, indigenous women face a greater risk of exposure to mining-related toxic substances and climate change. Contributing factors include physiological and socioeconomic vulnerabilities, including their role in managing local land and water sources. They have also argued that the positive economic effects of the mining activities may not counterbalance the negative ones. They call for greater support for women's engagement in the decision-making processes, by providing more vocational education and training aligned to the cultural characteristics of the peoples and of women, and by taking action against discrimination and violence against women. Indigenous women generally also have less access to education and therefore do not have equal opportunities to work in the mining sector; they are most often the victims of sexual and other types of violence and abuse from people outside their communities; and they experience some of the negative effects from substance abuse from the men occupied in the sector (Bond and Quinlan, 2018[41]).

4.5. Women's role in environmental action in Small Island Developing States

Small Island Developing States (SIDS), which include some of the smallest and most remote countries in the world, do not constitute a homogenous group; they are at different levels of economic development, their demographics and social fabric vary. They have, however, been facing similar challenges that jeopardise their future development. The fight for climate justice has also been raised by these countries as they are influenced the most by climate change. Based on a recent OECD report, when compared with upper middle-income countries in the same income group, SIDS are 73% more vulnerable to climate change and natural hazards (OECD, 2018[42]). Combined with a lack of economic diversification and volatile growth, this vulnerability makes most SIDS highly dependent on development aid (of which 79% comes from bilateral providers and 21% from multilateral ones) and fragmented concessional finance.

Supporting the transition to low-carbon and climate-resilient choices will require access to more innovative climate finance instruments, greening fiscal reforms, and adequate debt relief mechanisms for these countries (OECD, 2018[42]). To date, gender equality and women's empowerment has been prioritised as a component of such concessional finance; 24% of concessional finance allocated to SIDS in the period 2012-2015 had a gender component, which shows a step in the right direction. However according to the latest OECD 2017 figures, only 1.9% of all ODA actually reaches women's organisations.

Women are among those most affected by climate change in SIDS, as they are often tasked with gathering water, fishing, or farming – all of which are highly affected by flooding and other natural hazards. Women in SIDS have been advocating for better representation in all future discussions on the future of their countries (Women's Major Group, 2014[43]). The SAMOA Pathway agreed during the 2014 International Year for Small Island Development States, acknowledged women's role as agents of change for sustainable development (UN, 2014[44]). The Pathway set up a Partnership Framework that enables durable partnerships for the sustainable development of SIDS. Environmental protection and climate change, and gender equality play a prominent role in the priorities set. However, in the recently released SAMOA Pathway mid-term review, even though climate and environment-related global partnerships are well underway, gender remains under-represented as a priority (Goransson, Vierros and Borrevik, 2019[45]).

4.6. The private sector and philanthropy as actors in the gender equality and environmental justice debate

Businesses have an important role to play in ensuring environmental and climate justice. For instance, the United States Environment Protection Agency (EPA) has encouraged businesses in local communities to take voluntary action based on environmental justice, examples of which include the setting up a local health clinic, public disclosure of post compliance monitoring information, and the signing of "good neighbour agreements" between local communities and business to facilitate licensing issues not covered by legislation (US Environmental Protection Agency, 2011[46]). The World Economic Forum is also engaging with businesses to realign their priorities and look beyond the bottom line and shareholder value to support profitable, sustainable growth. However, as economies continue to rely on natural resource-intensive activities, a more systematic approach is necessary.

Global Witness has reported on gender inequality in mining towns, whereby environmental resources become degraded, such as depletion of water resources, due to economic activity and which have a great effect on women's well-being (Global Witness, 2017[47]). In the cases they looked at in Afghanistan and D.R. Congo, conflict and corruption exacerbated unequal opportunities, so women had less access to the benefits associated with the extraction of minerals, while their vulnerability increased (Global Witness, 2017[47]). A recent IUCN report supports that large-scale agricultural and extractive industries are linked to increased human rights violations which disproportionately affect women and therefore a gender-inclusive plan needs to be developed in order to tackle both the environmental and human rights issue (Castañeda Carney et al., 2020[48]).

The OECD Guidelines for Multinational Enterprises [OECD/LEGAL/0144] and related Due Diligence guidance call on the private sector to avoid contributing to adverse impacts through their own activities or to mitigate such impacts in their supply chains (see also Section 2.3.4). A gender-perspective is applied to risk-based due diligence in order to allow for reflexion over how real or potential adverse impacts may differ for, or may be specific to, women. The OECD Due Diligence Guidance for Responsible Business Conduct recommends that in assessing adverse impacts, businesses pay special attention "to populations that may have a heightened risk of vulnerability or marginalisation, and to different risks that may be faced by women and men" (OECD, 2018[49]). In particular, businesses should be aware of gender issues and women's human rights in situations where women may be disproportionately impacted. The Guidelines also include specific recommendations that promote the well-being of women. National Contact Points set up in 48 Adherents under the Decision on the MNE Guidelines [OECD/LEGAL/0307] are a non-judicial mechanism providing access to remedy for stakeholders (including civil society) for bad business practices and harms committed (e.g. relating to environmental, labour or human rights standards) (OECD, 2016[50]). National regulators and businesses are increasingly making use of the MNE Guidelines and the Due Diligence guidelines. Business-led efforts include the Coalition of Business for Inclusive Growth established during the French Presidency of the G7 in 2019 (B4IG, 2020[51]).

Philanthropic institutions are also engaged in women's empowerment and climate justice. In the context of COVID-19 and its disproportionate effect on women, foundations should reorient their priorities towards the urgent needs generated by the pandemic (Azcona et al., 2020[52]). An OECD survey on private philanthropy for development showed that only 1% of philanthropic flows for environmental protection and only 3% of flows for agriculture were gender-relate (OECD netFWD, 2019[53]) d . Examples include the Ford Foundation, which has been supporting initiatives through grants and fellowships in areas that are challenging multiple drivers of inequality. The Foundation identifies the following five drivers of inequality: (1) entrenched cultural narratives that undermine fairness, tolerance and inclusion; (2) failure to invest in and protect vital public goods, such as education and natural resources; (3) unfair rules of the economy that magnify unequal opportunity and outcomes; (4) unequal access to government decision-making and resources; and (5) persistent prejudice and discrimination against women, people with disabilities and racial, ethnic, and caste minorities. Within this framework, the Ford Foundation supports efforts across the globe to strengthen civil society, to enhance fair and inclusive political participation, to empower women and girls, and to reduce environmental crimes associated with the natural resource sector (Davies, 2018[54]). Although philanthropic institutions seem to be more active in supporting women's issues and organisations, here, only 2,5% of all financial support reaches women's organisations directly (OECD netFWD, 2019[53]).

References

Allen, E., H. Lyons and J. Stephens (2019), "Women's leadership in renewable transformation, energy justice and energy democracy: Redistributing power", *Energy Research and Social Science*, Vol. 57, http://dx.doi.org/10.1016/j.erss.2019.101233. [30]

Amnesty International (2019), *Unfair Game: Persecution of Human Rights Defenders in Russia Intensifies*, http://www.amnesty.org. [15]

Azcona, G. et al. (2020), *From Insights to Action - Gender Equality in the Wake of COVID-19*, UN Women, https://www.unwomen.org/-/media/headquarters/attachments/sections/library/publications/2020/gender-equality-in-the-wake-of-covid-19-en.pdf?la=en&vs=5142 (accessed on 5 April 2021). [52]

B4IG (2020), "The B4IG international coalition united against the inequalities deepened by the COVID-19 pandemic", *OECD*. [51]

Bell, K. (2016), "Bread and roses: A gender perspective on environmental justice and public health", *International Journal of Environmental Research and Public Health*, Vol. 13/10, http://dx.doi.org/10.3390/ijerph13101005. [2]

Bioneers (n.d.), *As Long as Grass Grows: The Indigenous Fight for Environmental Justice*, https://bioneers.org/the-indigenous-fight-for-environmental-justice-ze0z1906/ (accessed on 11 February 2020). [59]

Bond, A. and L. Quinlan (2018), *Indigenous Gender-based Analysis for Informing the Canadian Minerals and Metals Plan - Policy Paper*, Native Women's Association of Canada. [41]

Brulle, R. and D. Pellow (2006), "Environmental Justice: Human Health and Environmental Inequalities", *Annual Review of Public Health*, Vol. 27/1, pp. 103-124, http://dx.doi.org/10.1146/annurev.publhealth.27.021405.102124. [1]

Castañeda Carney, I. et al. (2020), *Gender-based violence and environment linkages: The violence of inequality*, IUCN, International Union for Conservation of Nature, http://dx.doi.org/10.2305/IUCN.CH.2020.03.en. [48]

Climate Strike (n.d.), *It's Time for a Climate Strike*, https://www.climatestrike.net (accessed on 11 February 2020). [32]

Corte Suprema de Justicia (2018), *Radicación n. 11001-22-03-000-2018-00319-01*, http://www.cortesuprema.gov.co/corte/wp-content/uploads/2018/04/STC4360-2018-2018-00319-011.pdf. [36]

Davies, P. (2018), *Off the Beaten Track, Women Leaders are on the Rise*, https://www.fordfoundation.org/ideas/equals-change-blog/posts/off-the-beaten-track-women-leaders-are-on-the-rise/ (accessed on 11 February 2020). [54]

EC (2020), *Proposal for a Regulation of the European Parliament and of the Council on amending Regulation (EC) No 1367/2006 of the European Parliament and of the Council of 6 September 2006 on the application of the provisions of the Aarhus Convention on Access to Information, Public Participation in Decision-making and Access to Justice in Environmental Matters to Community institutions and bodies*, European Commission, Brussels. [25]

EEA (2018), *Unequal Exposure and Unequal Impacts: Social Vulnerability to Air Pollution, Noise and Extreme Temperatures in Europe*, http://dx.doi.org/10.2800/324183. [4]

Energi-, Forsynings- og Klimaministeriet (2019), *Ungeklimarådets overordnede målsætninger 2019*, https://kefm.dk/media/12724/anbefalinger-fra-ungeklimaraadet_overordnet-maalsaetningspapir.pdf. [35]

European Parliament and Council of the European Union (2006), “Regulation (EC) No 1367/2006 6 September 2006 on the Application of the Provisions of the Aarhus Convention on Access to Information, Public Participation in Decision-Making and Access to Justice in Environments”, https://eur-lex.europa.eu/legal-content/EN/TXT/PDF/?uri=CELEX:32006R1367&from=EN. [19]

Fridays For Future (n.d.), *Fridays For Future*, http://Fridays For Future (accessed on 11 February 2020). [34]

Front Line Defenders (2019), *Font Line Defenders Global Analysis 2018*, https://www.frontlinedefenders.org/sites/default/files/global_analysis_2018.pdf. [14]

Front Line Defenders (2019), *Global Analysis 2019*, https://www.frontlinedefenders.org/en/resource-publication/global-analysis-2019 (accessed on 3 December 2020). [6]

Glatter-Götz, H. et al. (2019), “Environmental inequality in Austria: Do inhabitants' socioeconomic characteristics differ depending on their proximity to industrial polluters?”, *Environmental Research Letters*, Vol. 14/7, http://dx.doi.org/10.1088/1748-9326/ab1611. [9]

Global Climate Strike (n.d.), *Join Us in Fighting For Our Future*, https://globalclimatestrike.net/ (accessed on 11 February 2020). [33]

Global Witness (2020), *Defending Tomorrow. The Climate Crisis and Threats Against Land and Environmental Defenders*, Global Witness. [7]

Global Witness (2017), “Sharing the spoils: gender and the mining industry”. [47]

Goransson, O., M. Vierros and C. Borrevik (2019), *Partnerships for Small Island Developing States*, United Nations, https://sustainabledevelopment.un.org/content/documents/24591SIDS_Partnerships_May_2019_web.pdf. [45]

Herrera, C. (2017), *Indigenous Women: Defending the Environment in Latin America*, https://www.nrdc.org/experts/carolina-herrera/indigenous-women-defending-environment-latin-america (accessed on 12 February 2020). [58]

Lakes, T., M. Brückner and A. Krämer (2014), “Development of an environmental justice index to determine socio-economic disparities of noise pollution and green space in residential areas in Berlin”, *Journal of Environmental Planning and Management*, Vol. 57/4, pp. 538-556, http://dx.doi.org/10.1080/09640568.2012.755461. [5]

Larsen, J. and G. Fondahl (2014), *Arctic Human Development Report. Regional Processes and Global Linkages*, Norden, http://dx.doi.org/10.6027/TN2014-567. [39]

Mies, M. and V. Shiva (1993), *Ecofeminism*, Zed Books, London. [10]

Milieu Consulting Sprl (2019), *Study on EU implementation of the Aarhus Convention in the area of access to justice in environmental matters*, European Commission, https://ec.europa.eu/environment/aarhus/pdf/Final_study_EU_implemention_environmental_matters_2019.pdf. [56]

Navdanya International (2020), *Navdanya International*, https://navdanyainternational.org/what-we-do/navdanya-community-seed-banks/ (accessed on 11 February 2020). [11]

OECD (2019), *Linking Indigenous Communities with Regional Development*, OECD Rural Policy Reviews, OECD Publishing, Paris, https://dx.doi.org/10.1787/3203c082-en. [38]

OECD (2019), *SIGI 2019 Global Report: Transforming Challenges into Opportunities*, Social Institutions and Gender Index, OECD Publishing, Paris, https://dx.doi.org/10.1787/bc56d212-en. [26]

OECD (2018), *Making Development Co-operation Work for Small Island Developing States*, OECD Publishing, Paris, https://dx.doi.org/10.1787/9789264287648-en. [42]

OECD (2018), *OECD Due Diligence Guidance for Responsible Business Conduct*. [49]

OECD (2018), *Youth Stocktaking Report*, https://www.oecd.org/gov/youth-stocktaking-report.pdf. [29]

OECD (2017), *OECD Environmental Performance Reviews: Korea 2017*, OECD Environmental Performance Reviews, OECD Publishing, Paris, https://dx.doi.org/10.1787/9789264268265-en. [3]

OECD (2016), *Implementing the OECD Guidelines for Multinational Enterprises: The National Contact Points from 2000 to 2015*, https://mneguidelines.oecd.org/oecd-report-15-years-national-contact-points.pdf. [50]

OECD (2012), "Declaration on International Investment and Multinational Enterprises", in *Annual Report on the OECD Guidelines for Multinational Enterprises 2011: A New Agenda for the Future*, OECD Publishing, Paris, https://dx.doi.org/10.1787/mne-2011-14-en. [18]

OECD netFWD (2019), *Philanthropy and Gender Equality - Insights on Philanthropy for Gender Equality*, OECD Development Centre. [53]

OHCHR (2013), *Independent Expert Concludes Visit to Costa Rica Mission*, https://newsarchive.ohchr.org/EN/NewsEvents/Pages/DisplayNews.aspx?NewsID=13609&LangID=E (accessed on 11 February 2020). [16]

Oxfam, International Land Coalition and Rights and Resources Initiative (2016), *Common Ground: Securing Land Rights and Safeguarding the Earth*, Oxfam. [40]

Sandra, M. et al. (2007), *Women As Green Agents of Change (A Study of Wangari Maathai As An Environmentalist)*, http://www.ijesi.org. [12]

Terry, G. (2009), "No climate justice without gender justice: an overview of the issues", *Gender and Development*, Vol. 17/1, pp. 5-18. [31]

UN (2019), *Recognizing the contribution of environmental human rights*, United Nations, New York., https://undocs.org/A/74/53. [8]

UN (2018), *Regional Agreement on Access to Information, Public Participation and Justice in Environmental Matters in Latin America and the Caribbean*, http://www.cepal.org/es/suscripciones. [23]

UN (2015), *Paris Agreement*, https://unfccc.int/files/essential_background/convention/application/pdf/english_paris_agreement.pdf. [13]

UN (2014), *SIDS Accelerated Modalities of Action (SAMOA) Pathway*, https://www.un.org/ga/search/view_doc.asp?symbol=A/RES/69/15&Lang=E. [44]

UNDESA (2020), *Indigenous Peoples, Economic and Social Development*, https://www.un.org/development/desa/indigenouspeoples/mandated-areas1/economic-and-social-development.html (accessed on 11 February 2020). [37]

UNDP (2014), *Environmental Justice: Comparative Experiences in Legal Empowerment*, United Nations Development Programme. [22]

UNECE (2020), *Environmental Policy - Status of Ratification*, https://www.unece.org/env/pp/ratification.html (accessed on 15 February 2020). [24]

UNECE (1998), *Convention on Access to Information, Public Participation in Decision-Making and Access to Justice in Environmental Matters*, https://www.unece.org/fileadmin/DAM/env/pp/documents/cep43e.pdf. [17]

UNEP (2020), *What is the Environmental Rights Initiative?*, https://www.unenvironment.org/explore-topics/environmental-rights-and-governance/what-we-do/advancing-environmental-rights/what-1 (accessed on 11 February 2020). [21]

UNEP (2015), *Putting Rion Principle 10 into Action. An Implementation Guide*, http://www.unep.org/civil_society. [20]

Unger, N. (2008), "The Role of Gender in Environmental Justice", *Environmental Justice*, Vol. 1/3, pp. 115-120, http://dx.doi.org/10.1089/env.2008.0523. [27]

US Environmental Protection Agency (2011), *Plan EJ 2014*. [46]

US Environmental Protection Agency (n.d.), *Environmental Justice*, https://www.epa.gov/environmentaljustice (accessed on 15 February 2020). [55]

van Duursen, M. et al. (2020), "Safeguarding Female Reproductive Health Against Endocrine Disrupting Chemicals—The FREIA Project", *International Journal of Molecular Sciences*, Vol. 21/9, http://dx.doi.org/10.3390/ijms21093215. [28]

VERVE (2019), *When We Protect Indigenous Women We Are Protecting The Environment*, https://medium.com/verve-up/when-we-protect-indigenous-women-we-are-protecting-the-environment-c0e66b9f6764 (accessed on 11 February 2020). [60]

Women's Environmental Network (2010), *The impacts of climate change on women and public policy. Gender And The Climate Change Agenda*. [57]

Women's Major Group (2014), *Envisioning Just, Sustainable Futures for SIDS Women and Girls*, http://www.sids2014.org/content/documents/7080women.pdf. [43]

Notes

[1] The definition provided by the US Environmental Protection Agency is the following: "Environmental justice (EJ) is the fair treatment and meaningful involvement of all people regardless of race, colour, national origin, or income with respect to the development, implementation and enforcement of environmental laws, regulations and policies" (US Environmental Protection Agency, n.d.[55]).

[2] Although some projects are still at early stages, there are some success stories. See for instance the work of Waterlex in sustainable water use and support in improving access to safe water for all (https://www.waterlex.org/).

[3] For example, EU member states' approaches on granting legal standing vary (Milieu Consulting Sprl, 2019[56]). In Latin America and the Caribbean progress is noted, but not in a linear way (UN, 2018[23]) .

[4] Studies done in 2009 report that women comprise 20 million of the 26 million people estimated to have been displaced by climate change (Women's Environmental Network, 2010[57])

[5] WEDO, the Women's Environment and Development Organisation, a non-governmental organisation, was founded in 1991, and has successfully put women's rights at the forefront of international conferences and actions (https://wedo.org/about-us-2/).

[6] See the work of WEDO. For example: https://wedo.org/what-we-do/our-programs/mobilizing-womenfor-climate-justice/; http://www.wecf.eu/english/campaigns/2018/WECF-at-COP24.php.

[7] There are myriads examples of indigenous women's environmental activist groups, both in countries with and without a framework linked to environmental justice, see (Herrera, 2017[58]); (Bioneers, n.d.[59]); (VERVE, 2019[60]). There are also more women getting engaged in representing their indigenous communities (Davies, 2018[54]) .

5 Towards a joint gender and environment agenda

Integrating gender equality and environmental considerations in policy decisions can deliver greater well-being for all and accelerate the achievement of all SDGs. Key prerequisites include taking into account the specific needs, preferences and well-being of women and ensuring their involvement in decision-making. Yet, the gender-environment nexus is largely missing in existing global standards. An integrated policy framework is necessary, bringing together gender and sustainability goals, and considering the trade-offs and complementarities at the local, national and international levels.

5.1. Key findings

Leveraging the gender-environment nexus requires the design and implementation of policies along three vectors: (i) gender equality and women's empowerment, (ii) environment-related domestic policies, and (iii) transboundary policies. Implementation could use a number of available OECD standards, and assessment and evaluation mechanisms. However, some adjustments and revisions to the existing tools may be necessary to leverage the nexus effectively. The key actions include:

- Advancing gender equality policies with environmental goals in mind, taking into consideration that gender equality and women's empowerment can help mitigate the negative impact of environmental degradation; empowering women in environment-related sectors including equal access to quality education, health and other social services and ending legal barriers to gender equality and discrimination against women; gender equality in employment policies and practices; gender parity in decision-making bodies in the public and private spheres;
- Integrating a gender angle into environmental strategies and policies, by collecting gender-disaggregated evidence and applying a gender lens in the design of national environmental policies and specific plans on climate change, biodiversity, oceans, and circular economy; establishing environmental standards that take into consideration the differential impacts of environmental hazards and risks for men and women; adapting environmental taxes, subsidies and budgetary tools to consider gender segregation, addressing stereotypes and cultural differences; "genderising" such sectors as energy, transport and farming policies; providing access to finance and technology for green initiatives driven by women and for women's empowerment;
- Mainstreaming a gender angle into the environmental aspects of transboundary policies such as trade, foreign direct investments, responsible business conduct, and development co-operation.

This transformative action needs to take place also at the international level. Initiatives and partnerships are currently being set up, addressing among other issues the gender-environment nexus. However, a holistic approach is essential to ensure that crucial evidence collection and analysis takes place.

5.2. The need for an integrated approach to gender equality and environmental sustainability

As this report shows, the relationship between gender equality and environmental sustainability is still an emerging area of research that lacks systematic collection of data and monitoring of initiatives. Despite the international commitments and drive, it is often overlooked by policy makers, businesses and sometimes women themselves. Yet, the existing evidence shows that - in both advanced and developing countries - women are generally more vulnerable to the effects of environmental degradation, are more conscious about environmental risks and more sensitive to a sustainable management of natural resources. Integrating gender equality and environmental considerations in policy decisions can therefore deliver greater well-being for all and accelerate the achievement of all SDGs. It is also clearly beneficial from an economic perspective, as it can boost female employment, promote research and innovation in new technologies and thereby raise productivity.

As highlighted in the report, the intersection between gender equality and environmental sustainability lies ultimately in the fact that discrimination and biases against women, biological and behavioural factors and their role in societies, make women disproportionally vulnerable to and affected by unequal access to assets, energy poverty, unsustainable production, inadequate access to water and sanitation, climate change, in-door air pollution, biodiversity loss, and other forms of environmental degradation. Women are also systematically on the front line of natural hazards and suffer most from crime and chronic stress related to inadequate infrastructure and urban development. At the same time, as users of energy and sustainable consumers, women tend to be more sensitive to ecological, environmental and health concerns.

These differential gender effects and needs are particularly evident in low-income countries, where discriminatory legislation and social norms severely curtail economic opportunities and further expose women to the ongoing degradation of the environment and climate hazards. In advanced countries, there are also various aspects of the gender-environment nexus that need to be tackled, from the impact of air pollution on pregnant women, exposure to chemicals in household products and access to adequate infrastructure, to the role of women in sustainable consumption and the promotion of economic opportunities for women in the green sector. On the other hand, because of their larger presence in manufacturing sectors, men are more exposed to occupational health hazards overall, including exposure to toxic substances.

The main conclusion from the analysis on the gender-environment nexus is the need for an integrated approach to gender equality and sustainability that, on the one hand, takes into account the specific needs, preferences and well-being of women and, on the other hand, ensures their involvement in decision-making. Both are mutually reinforcing: the more women are consulted regarding projects that have an environmental impact and the more positions of responsibility they take up, the more likely will policies and investment projects take into account both gender and environmental considerations. A key policy implication from this analysis is that women must be empowered in a fundamental way to achieve the 2030 Agenda.

The report has highlighted two main challenges to accelerating action to leverage the gender-environment nexus. First, the lack of systematic evidence gathering on gender-differentiated environmental impacts and actions. Second, the absence of a truly integrated, general policy framework addressing economic, social and environmental goals that could be transposed to address the nexus and guide policy choices.

5.2.1. Lack of systematic data collection on the gender-environment nexus

When making economic policies, designing cities, housing, infrastructure, making trade agreements, or using natural resources, the differential impact on women should be reported and collected. The evidence gathered in this paper is based largely on case studies across sectors and countries. In general, there is no systematic data collection that would allow governments and private companies to define their strategies and projects in a more gender-conscious way. Similarly, there is very limited information on transboundary gender and environmental effects.

Agenda 2030 itself is relatively comprehensive in addressing basic gender equality and women's and girls' empowerment goals, which are critical to strengthen their positive contribution to environmental goals. However, it falls short in embedding a gender equality perspective in the nine "environmental" SDGs, with six having few gender-specific targets and indicators (SDG 2, 6, 7, 9, 11, 12 and 13) and two (SDG 14 and 15) having none at all (see Table 5.1and Annex A).

Efforts are under way to improve gender-disaggregated environmental data at the global level, coordinated by the UN Statistical Commission, and with contributions by different United Nations agencies in particular UN Women and the UN Environmental Programme, and by the Convention on Biological Diversity (CBD) in relation to SDG 15. Various UN reports have also recently addressed the data gap and identified a way forward, including UN Environment Programme (UNEP, 2019[1]), UN Women (UN Women, 2018[2]), and UN Women (UN Women, 2018[3]). The OECD has also recently started addressing the data gap on the gender-environment nexus as part of the Gender Mainstreaming Platform and the work of the OECD Environmental Policy Committee. While all these efforts are welcome and necessary, there is still a long way to go.

5.2.2. The gender-environment nexus is largely missing in existing global standards

While the SDG framework clearly sets out a broad set of targets and indicators regarding gender equality and environmental sustainability goals, it only addresses some aspects of the nexus related to gender discrimination, education and air pollution. It is largely silent on other gender-differentiated environmental impacts, women's role in environmental protection and sustainable consumption, and access to sustainable infrastructure.

The OECD has developed two Gender Recommendations. The 2013 Recommendation of the Council on Gender Equality in Education, Employment, and Entrepreneurship sets out a number of policy measures and actions to address gender inequalities in education, employment and entrepreneurship (OECD, 2017[4]). Beyond initiatives to provide equal access to education (including measures to make STEM inclusive and attractive for both boys and girls), and put an end to discrimination and sexual harassment in the workplace, it sets out actions to better enable female labour force participation, such as promoting family-friendly policies and working conditions, and fostering greater male uptake of unpaid work. It also calls on governments and business to work toward a better gender balance in positions of public and private sector leadership, and promote entrepreneurship among women.

The 2013 Recommendation provides clear guidance on the different aspects of gender equality from a labour market, education policy and entrepreneurship policy angle. All these elements are important ingredients to leverage the gender-environment nexus, in particular in relation to the role of women as economic actors in the transition to a low-carbon and sustainable economy, as leaders, employees and entrepreneurs.

The 2015 Recommendation of the Council on Gender Equality in Public Life identifies the need to "mainstream gender equality in the design, development, implementation and evaluation of relevant public policies and budgets" (OECD, 2016[5]). This requires the development and implementation of a whole-of government strategy for effective gender equality and mainstreaming, the integration of evidence-based assessments of gender impacts and considerations into various dimensions of public governance, measures to achieve gender-balanced representation in decision-making at all levels of government. In addition, the evidence base for measuring progress towards gender equality – across all policy dimensions – needs to be systematically strengthened.

The 2015 Recommendation, therefore, clearly sets out the general goal of gender mainstreaming, systematic evidence gathering and impact assessment. Yet, it does not provide specific guidance by policy area, nor does it develop an integrated framework for policy analysis.

The OECD Framework for Policy Action on Inclusive Growth (IG) is designed to help countries achieve economic growth on a sustainable basis that raises living standards while also respecting environmental boundaries and providing equal opportunities to all by distributing the benefits from economic growth. The Framework is supported by a dashboard of indicators and consolidates key OECD policy recommendations into three areas of action: (i) investment in people and places left behind (for example, through optimal resource management for sustainable growth), (ii) supporting business dynamism and inclusive labour markets (through access to good quality jobs, especially for women and under-represented groups), and (iii) building efficient and responsive government (including the integration of distributional aspects upfront in policy design). It helps countries to consider ex-ante equity issues in policy design (OECD, 2018[6]).

The OECD is currently working on deepening the linkages between the Green Growth Strategy and the Inclusive Growth Framework. The first deliverable is a report that analyses the environment-inequality nexus and outlines policy actions for a just, green transition that fairly redistributes the cost of action and inaction in well-coordinated policy packages It considers the differential impact by gender of air pollution and climate change on vulnerable groups, workers, and regions, across 4 of the 11 well-being dimensions i.e. income and wealth, health, work and job quality, and safety (OECD, 2021[7]).

Neither women nor men are a uniform group, hence a basic condition for better policies is obtaining more granularity on women's and men's needs and preferences and better understanding their local conditions, including how environmental changes affect them. There is also a need to map policies to different indicators of women's and men's well-being, including health, personal safety and ability to deliver childcare and elderly care. Finally, the interaction between goals and policies should be addressed, so that governments can take actions that ensure policy coherence, address trade-offs and complementarities.

Given all these considerations, a new policy instrument could be developed specifically addressing the gender-environment nexus, or integrating other policy domains where gender mainstreaming is necessary, such as trade, investment and development co-operation.

5.3. Closing the data gap on the gender-environment nexus

Following the analysis of gender-environment interlinkages in each of the nine "environmental" SDGs, Table 5.1 shows the various targets that the SDG framework currently "tags" as gender-specific, as well as those for which gender-disaggregation would be relevant.

Table 5.1. Most targets under the "environmental" SDGs are potentially gender-related

SDG	Explicit links between gender equality and environment in SDG Targets	Other possible gender-environment entry points to SDG targets	Description of interlinkages between gender equality and environmental sustainability
SDG 2. End hunger, achieve food security and improved nutrition and promote sustainable agriculture	2.2: By 2030, end all forms of malnutrition, including achieving, by 2025, the internationally agreed targets on stunting and wasting in children under 5 years of age, and address the nutritional needs of adolescent girls, pregnant and lactating women and older persons. 2.3: By 2030, double the agricultural productivity and incomes of small-scale food producers, in particular women, indigenous peoples, family farmers, pastoralists and fishers, including through secure and equal access to land, other productive resources and inputs, knowledge, financial services, markets and opportunities for value addition and non-farm employment.	2.1. By 2030, end hunger and ensure access by all people, in particular the poor and people in vulnerable situations, including infants, to safe, nutritious and sufficient food all year round. 2.4. By 2030, ensure sustainable food production systems and implement resilient agricultural practices that increase productivity and production, that help maintain ecosystems, that strengthen capacity for adaptation to climate change, extreme weather, drought, flooding and other disasters and that progressively improve land and soil quality. 2.5. By 2020, maintain the genetic diversity of seeds, cultivated plants and farmed and domesticated animals and their related wild species, including through soundly managed and diversified seed and plant banks at the national, regional and international levels, and promote access to and fair and equitable sharing of benefits arising from the utilization of genetic resources and associated traditional knowledge, as internationally agreed. 2.a. Increase investment, including through enhanced international co-operation, in rural infrastructure, agricultural research and extension services, technology development and plant and livestock gene banks in order to enhance agricultural productive capacity in developing countries, in particular least developed countries. 2.b. Correct and prevent trade restrictions and distortions in world agricultural markets, including through the parallel	Agriculture is strongly linked to education and accessing new skills and knowledge, which can support a transition to sustainability. It is also a key component for income generation and economic growth, which can empower women. There is a strong gender component in ending hunger (2.1), as women are greatly affected by food shortages. At the same time, women empowerment would allow them for a more active role in managing food resources at the household level. Mainstreaming lessons learnt from women's traditional knowledge (2.5) and engagement with sustenance farming could advance more sustainable and resilient agricultural practices (2.4). At the same time, eliminating barriers, such as those on women's access to assets, could support an increase in productivity and production. Introducing gender sensitive and gender inclusive aspects in agricultural investment, trade and value chains, and rural infrastructure policies could further enhance women's empowerment and strengthen their position as small-scale farmers (2.a). In addition, moving away from agricultural export subsidies that have an adverse impact on sustainable agriculture, and by supporting non-traditional agricultural exports, could empower women in the agricultural sector (2.b, 2.c).

SDG	Explicit links between gender equality and environment in SDG Targets	Other possible gender-environment entry points to SDG targets	Description of interlinkages between gender equality and environmental sustainability
		elimination of all forms of agricultural export subsidies and all export measures with equivalent effect, in accordance with the mandate of the Doha Development Round. 2.c. Adopt measures to ensure the proper functioning of food commodity markets and theirderivatives and facilitate t mely access to market information, including on food reserves, in order to help limit extreme food price volatility.	
SDG 6. Ensure availability and sustainable management of water and sanitation for all	6.1: By 2030, achieve universal and equitable access to safe and affordable drinking water for all. 6.2. By 2030, achieve access to adequate and equitable sanitation and hygiene for all and end open defecation, paying special attention to the needs of women and girls and those in vulnerable situations.	All targets under SDG 6 are potentially gender-related	Guaranteeing access to safe and affordable water releases women from traditional roles in water collection, especially in developing countries (6.1 and 6.2). Women in poor environments may be more at risk from low water quality and inadequate sanitation facilities (6.3). Gender-sensitive water management - international, national, local - may guarantee water-use efficiency for all, taking into consideration the vulnerabilities of certain population groups (6.4, 6.5, 6.b). Women's role in water management, due to their local natural resources knowledge and skills from household water management (plastics and medicine residue presence in water affects pregnant women in both developing and developed), could result in better functioning and more sustainable water systems, and eventually in restoring water-related ecosystems (6.6). Integrating gender considerations in all development co-operation and financing for water-related programmes, would enhance better and more sustainable water- and sanitation-related management mechanisms (6.a).
SDG 7. Ensure access to affordable, reliable, sustainable and modern energy for all	7.1: By 2030, ensure universal access to affordable, reliable and modern energy services.	All targets under SDG 7 are potentially gender-related	Women's empowerment and leadership in the energy sector may play a catalytic role in promoting clean energy and more efficient energy use, as well as in helping to tackle energy poverty (7.1, 7.2, 7.3). To achieve a "just transition" as part of the transition to a low carbon economy, it is necessary to guarantee equal opportunities for both men and women in the workforce. This requires gender equality in STEM education, and in research and technology, by shifting international co-operation and investments in this direction (7.a). Finally, accessible clean energy, through sustainable infrastructure, can support women's empowerment, especially in local communities that are most left behind or are often marginalised (7.b).
SDG 9. Build resilient infrastructure, promote inclusive and sustainable industrialisation	9.1. Develop quality, reliable, sustainable and resilient infrastructure, including regional and transborder infrastructure, to support economic development and human well-being, with a focus on affordable and	All targets under SDG 9 are potentially gender-related	Achieving SDG 9 would require a transformation in production processes, especially for energy- intensive industries and economic activities. Such transformation is rarely gender neutral, due to existing gender divide in the labour force in these sectors, e.g. manufacturing and transport. Moreover, often lack of sustainable infrastructure, especially in

SDG	Explicit links between gender equality and environment in SDG Targets	Other possible gender-environment entry points to SDG targets	Description of interlinkages between gender equality and environmental sustainability
and foster innovation	equitable access for all. 9.5. Enhance scientific research, upgrade the technological capabilities of industrial sectors in all countries, in particular developing countries, including, by 2030, encouraging innovation and substantially increasing the number of research and development workers per 1 million people and public and private research and development spending. 9.c. Significantly increase access to information and communications technology and strive to provide universal and affordable access to the Internet in least developed countries by 2020.		rural areas, affects women the most, as they have less access to resources that can support their well-being (9.1). Promoting inclusive and sustainable industrialisation with a gender perspective (9.2) and supporting women entrepreneurs who are more often than not excluded from access to credit (9.3) could set the ground for a truly sustainable growth path. Encouraging women's further participation in eco-innovation (9.5) and in high-tech industries (9.b) by tackling barriers to their participation in STEM subjects, or in senior management positions, could lead to better diversity, wider technological breadth and more economically valuable research results. More sustainable infrastructure to support such efforts could enhance women's further participation to economic and other activities, without negatively affecting their local environment, on which, especially in developing countries, they are often depended to (9.4, 9.a, 9.c).
SDG 11. Make cities and human settlements inclusive, safe, resilient and sustainable	11.1. By 2030, ensure access for all to adequate, safe and affordable housing and basic services and upgrade slums. 11.2. By 2030, provide access to safe, affordable, accessible and sustainable transport systems for all, improving road safety, notably by expanding public transport, with special attention to the needs of those in vulnerable situations, women, children, persons with disabilities and older persons. 11.5. By 2030, significantly reduce the number of deaths and the number of people affected and substantially decrease the direct economic losses relative to global gross domestic product caused by disasters, including water-related disasters, with a focus on protecting the poor and people in vulnerable situations. 11.7. By 2030, provide universal access to safe, inclusive and accessible, green and public spaces, in particular for women and children, older persons and persons with disabilities.	11.3 By 2030, enhance inclusive and sustainable urbanization and capacity for participatory, integrated and sustainable human settlement planning and management in all countries. 11.6. By 2030, reduce the adverse per capita environmental impact of cities, including by paying special attention to air quality and municipal and other waste management. 11.a. Support positive economic, social and environmental links between urban, peri-urban and rural areas by strengthening national and regional development planning. 11.b. By 2020, substantially increase the number of cities and human settlements adopting and implementing integrated policies and plans towards inclusion, resource efficiency, mitigation and adaptation to climate change, resilience to disasters, and develop and implement, in line with the Sendai Framework for Disaster Risk Reduction 2015–2030, holistic disaster risk management at all levels.	Women and men relate to urban and settlement design and transport infrastructure differently due to different social roles, occupational patterns and preferences. Urban and settlement planning and transport infrastructure that do not take into account the needs of different users, can significantly reduce their economic opportunities and well-being. Any sustainable housing, transport and urbanisation policy should therefore include a gender perspective, to guarantee the benefits are distributed to all (11.1, 11.2, 11.3, 11.7). Moreover, women's greater involvement in decision-making in these sectors could help reduce the overall environmental footprint of infrastructure. Women are, in addition, greatly affected by indoor air pollution and could play a major role in recycling waste due to their sustainable behaviour and preferences (11.6 and SDG12).

SDG	Explicit links between gender equality and environment in SDG Targets	Other possible gender-environment entry points to SDG targets	Description of interlinkages between gender equality and environmental sustainability
SDG 12. Ensure sustainable consumption and production patterns	No SDG 12 targets specifically address gender	12.3 By 2030, halve per capita global food waste at the retail and consumer levels and reduce food losses along production and supply chains, including post-harvest losses. 12.5 By 2030, substantially reduce waste generation through prevention, reduction, recycling and reuse. 12.6. Encourage companies, especially large and transnational companies, to adopt sustainable practices and to integrate sustainability information into their reporting cycle. 12.7. Promote public procurement practices that are sustainable, in accordance with national policies and priorities. 12.8 By 2030, ensure that people everywhere have the relevant information and awareness for sustainable development and lifestyles in harmony with nature. 12.b Develop and implement tools to monitor sustainable development impacts for sustainable tourism that creates jobs and promotes local culture and products.	Women make more purchasing decisions on household perishables but have less of a say in production chains. At the same time, unsustainable production, waste generation and pollution often have distinct harmful impacts on women, in particular on those from socially disadvantaged layers. Acknowledging differentiated consumption patterns between men and women; and women's more "green" behaviour in the household could help reduce food waste (12.3) and cut down waste generation (12.5). Empowering women and engaging them more in circular economy and in senior management could help companies move towards more sustainable practices (12.6, 12.7). Engaging more with women to mainstream their sustainable behaviour consumer patterns could help ensure a swift towards more 'sustainable lifestyles' (12.8). Guaranteeing just, safe, and equal labour opportunities for women in sectors such as tourism, could help introduce and implement monitoring standards to measure sustainability (12.b).
SDG 13. Take urgent action to combat climate change and its impacts	13.1. Strengthen resilience and adaptive capacity to climate-related hazards and natural disasters in all countries. 13.b*: Promote mechanisms for raising capacity for effective climate change-related planning and management in least developed countries and small island developing States, including focusing on women, youth and local and marginalized communities.	13.2. Integrate climate change measures into national policies, strategies and planning. 13.3 Improve education, awareness-raising and human and institutional capacity on climate change mitigation, adaptation, impact reduction and early warning. 13.a. Implement the commitment undertaken by developed country parties to the United Nations Framework Convention on Climate Change to a goal of mobilizing jointly $100 billion annually by 2020 from all sources to address the needs of developing countries in the context of meaningful mitigation actions and transparency on implementation and fully operationalize the Green Climate Fund through its capitalization as soon as possible.	Tackling climate change is intrinsically linked to gender equality. In developing countries, the disproportionate impact climate change has on women is well-documented. Physiological and other differences between genders may also explain why climate-related hazards and natural disasters could affect women more (13.1). A gender-sensitive approach to national climate change policies would acknowledge women's role in resource management, in adaptation and in mitigation (13.2), and how this could be strengthened via education and awareness-raising (13.3). Mobilising finance for climate change should specifically support initiatives which have at their core gender equality and women's empowerment (13.a), and which can engage more prominently women in national strategies and adaptation plans (13.b).
SDG 14. Conserve and sustainability use the oceans, seas and marine resources for sustainable development	No SDG 14 targets specifically address gender	14.1. By 2025, prevent and significantly reduce marine pollution of all kinds, in particular from land-based activities, including marine debris and nutrient pollution. 14.2 By 2020, sustainably manage and protect marine and coastal ecosystems to avoid significant adverse impacts, including by strengthening their resilience, and take action for their restoration in order to achieve healthy and productive oceans. 14.4. By 2020, effectively regulate harvesting and end overfishing, illegal, unreported and unregulated fishing and destructive fishing practices and implement science-based management plans, in order to restore fish	Women have a special sensitivity to the health of the oceans. They can also contribute to more sustainable management of maritime ecosystems. Yet, none of the SDG 14 targets address gender equality or the relation of marine resources to the livelihoods of women and men, including the role they can play in food security, employment and poverty reduction. Considering gender differences in consumption, production and waste management, women could help reduce marine pollution (14.1), and protect and restore ecosystems (14.2). As they constitute the majority of workers in secondary marine-related activities, they could also support increasing the economic benefits from sustainable use of marine resources (14.7) and sustainable fishing

SDG	Explicit links between gender equality and environment in SDG Targets	Other possible gender-environment entry points to SDG targets	Description of interlinkages between gender equality and environmental sustainability
		stocks in the shortest time feasible, at least to levels that can produce maximum sustainable yield as determined by their biological characteristics. 14.6. By 2020, prohibit certain forms of fisheries subsidies which contribute to overcapacity and overfishing, eliminate subsidies that contribute to illegal, unreported and unregulated fishing and refrain from introducing new such subsidies, recognizing that appropriate and effective special and differential treatment for developing and least developed countries should be an integral part of the World Trade Organization fisheries subsidies negotiation. 14.7. By 2030, increase the economic benefits to small island developing States and least developed countries from the sustainable use of marine resources, including through sustainable management of fisheries, aquaculture and tourism. 14.b Provide access for small-scale artisanal fishers to marine resources and markets.	(14.4). A gender-sensitive approach to supporting small-scale fishers could particularly benefit women (14.b); as would any fisheries subsidies that could negatively affect the transition to responsible and sustainable fisheries (14.6).
SDG 15. Protect, restore and promote sustainable use of terrestrial ecosystems, sustainably manage forests, combat desertification, and halt and reverse land degradation and halt biodiversity loss	No SDG 15 targets specifically address gender	15.1. By 2020, ensure the conservation, restoration and sustainable use of terrestrial and inland freshwater ecosystems and their services, in particular forests, wetlands, mountains and drylands, in line with obligations under international agreements. 15.2. By 2020, promote the implementation of sustainable management of all types of forests, halt deforestation, restore degraded forests and substantially increase afforestation and reforestation globally. 15.3. By 2030, combat desertification, restore degraded land and soil, including land affected by desertification, drought and floods, and strive to achieve a land degradation neutral world. 15.4. By 2030, ensure the conservation of mountain ecosystems, including their biodiversity, in order to enhance their capacity to provide benefits that are essential for sustainable development. 15.5. Take urgent and significant action to reduce the degradation of natural habitats, halt the loss of biodiversity and, by 2020, protect and prevent the extinction of threatened species. 15.6. Promote fair and equitable sharing of the benefits arising from the utilisation of genetic resources and promote appropriate access to such resources, as internationally agreed" could specifically address the benefits to women. 15.a. Mobilize and significantly increase financial resources from all sources to	Women, especially in traditional societies are especially affected by biodiversity loss. Lack of women's rights and access to resources intensifies these negative effects. At the same time, women can be agents for change, leading biodiversity protection, conservation and sustainable farming efforts. Such leadership role - at the international, national and local levels - could help ensure conservation, restoration and sustainable use of ecosystems (15.1, 15.4); and promote the implementation of sustainable management (15.2). Women's access to land assets could also help combat desertification and biodiversity loss, considering women's sustainable use of natural resources and traditional knowledge (15.3, 15.5, 15.6). As in other SDGs, guaranteeing sufficient financing for the sustainable use of biodiversity and ecosystems would only benefit from a gender-perspective, for more sustainable management of natural resources (15.a, 15.b).

SDG	Explicit links between gender equality and environment in SDG Targets	Other possible gender-environment entry points to SDG targets	Description of interlinkages between gender equality and environmental sustainability
		conserve and sustainably use biodiversity and ecosystems. 15.b. Mobilize significant resources from all sources and at all levels to finance sustainable forest management and provide adequate incentives to developing countries to advance such management, including for conservation and reforestation.	

Note: Even though SDG Target 13.b explicitly refers to women, the indicator used to measure this target's achievement does not, hence the inconsistency when comparing with Annex A.

It is also important to go beyond gender-disaggregated data, and account for the interaction with other related sources inequalities and discrimination that women face, based on ethnicity, faith, socio-economic status and age, among others.

In many countries, mainly non-OECD, capacity development is essential in guaranteeing that statistical authorities will be able to construct and monitor gender-disaggregated indicators and collect data. Capacity development is also necessary to facilitate better statistical co-ordination between countries, spreading methodological good practices for quality statistics, and promoting comparability and benchmarking.

PARIS 21[1], based at the OECD, works closely with low and middle-income countries to strengthen the capacity of their national statistical systems. In a 2017-2018 survey addressed to 195 states, of which 47% replied, the environmental sector was the one identified as requiring immediate capacity development efforts for statistical data collection (see Figure 5.1) (PARIS 21, 2018[8]). Over the past 10 years, environment-related statistics have been getting less support, compared to economic and demographic statistics, despite the latter being already more developed (PARIS 21, 2018[8]).The aforementioned survey also identified gender-disaggregated data collection as requiring capacity development, even though not at the top of priorities (PARIS 21, 2018[8]).

Figure 5.1. Priority areas for 87 countries requiring immediate capacity development in sectoral statistics

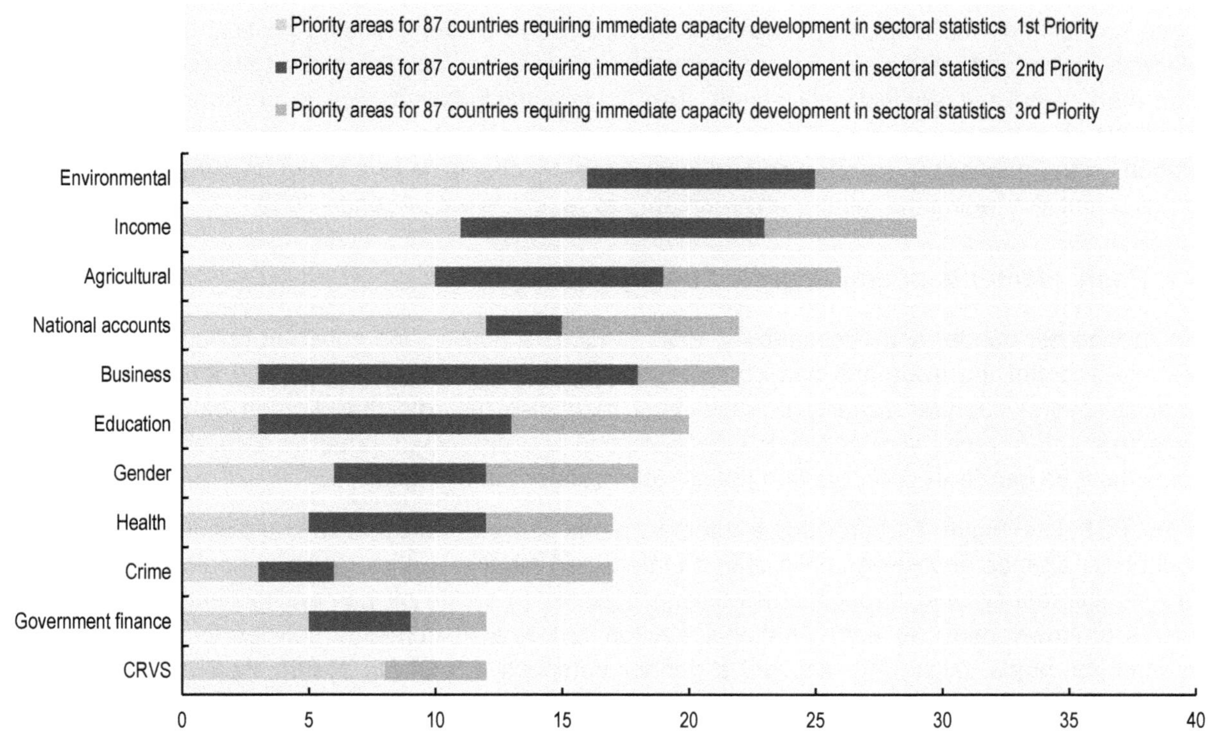

Source: (PARIS 21, 2018[8]), Joint survey on New approaches to Capacity Development and Future

Both PARIS 21 and the OECD have identified capacity development for the national statistical authorities as one of the points needing further attention (PARIS 21, 2018[8]); (OECD, 2019[9]). As gender-disaggregated data is scarce, more capacity development for new instruments, methodologies, and standards to facilitate gender-responsive data collection is needed. To support truly gender-sensitive policy-making, such data collection would need to take place in both the monitoring and evaluation phases, as well as at the diagnostic and design phases of environmental and climate-related policies.

A new PARIS 21 project, supported under the framework of UN Women's flagship programme "Making every woman and girl count", is currently under way, aiming at mainstreaming gender in the national statistical system in Cambodia, Dominican Republic, Egypt, El Salvador, Jordan, Kyrgyzstan, Lesotho, Maldives, and Senegal. The main objective of this project is to ensure that national statistical systems are equipped to produce, disseminate and use high quality and timely gender statistics to inform policy-making and support gender equality. The first step of this process is to assess the current state of gender statistics in the country and integrate gender equality into the National Strategies for Development of Statistics (5-10 year strategic plans, prioritising data collection for the national statistical system) (UN Women, 2019[10]).

5.4. Developing a whole-of-government vision, action plan and an integrated policy framework to leverage the gender-environment nexus

In order to bring about lasting and impactful change that tackles the environmental concerns affecting women, there is a need for a whole-of-government approach that brings together these goals at the core of the 2030 Agenda. The adoption of joint gender-sustainability mainstreaming mechanisms and tools, including infrastructure and fiscal policies, is crucial to ensure that administrations build the culture and the capacity to identify differentiated gender needs within their population in relation to the management of natural resources and environmental risks, and to respond to them with gender sensitive policies, services and budgets.

Various institutional and political mechanisms need to be in place, including political commitment and leadership, policy and institutional co-ordination (led either by, or with the explicit support of, Centres of Government), local and regional involvement, stakeholder participation as well as monitoring and reporting. The OECD Recommendation on Policy Coherence for Sustainable Development provides additional guidance on the necessary governance and institutional mechanisms to achieve an integrated approach to tackling and leveraging the gender-environment nexus, in line with Agenda 2030.

5.4.1. Basic elements of an integrated policy framework

Bringing together gender and sustainability goals requires a holistic and coherent policy framework that takes into account the trade-offs and complementarities at the local, national and international levels (global spillovers). Gender equality policies must recognise the role that women play in maintaining ecosystems and in promoting responsible consumption and production patterns. Similarly, sustainability policies must be gender-responsive and mainstream gender equality goals.

The picture below (Figure 5.2) provides a summary of the policy vectors that can help align the gender and sustainability agenda and design policies in an integrated manner. Policy makers should act on all three pillars simultaneously and through cross-cutting policies: (i) tackle all barriers to gender equality and women's empowerment, (ii) adjust national environment-related domestic policies to align them with environmental goals, taking into account a gender perspective, and (iii) systematically include gender equality and environmental considerations into transboundary policies, that directly affect the operation of local firms abroad (trade and foreign investment) as well as development co-operation.

Figure 5.2. Main policy vectors to leverage the gender-environment nexus

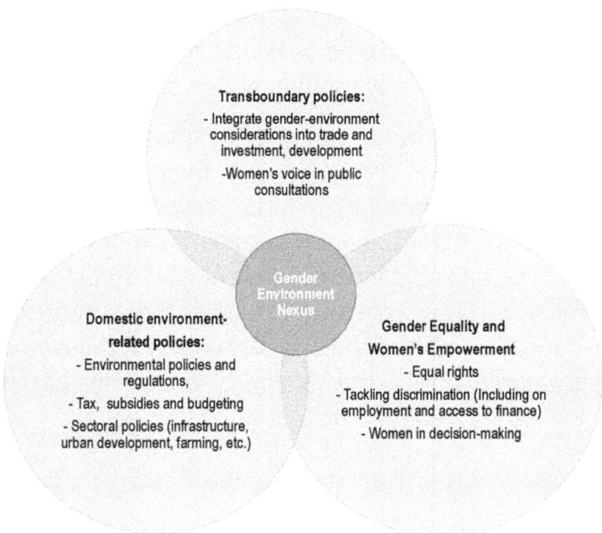

5.4.2. Applying the principles of Policy Coherence for Sustainable Development to the gender-environment nexus

An integrated policy framework should consider these three pillars systematically, addressing both domestic and transboundary impacts and applying an intergenerational timeframe, in accordance with the Recommendation on Policy Coherence for Sustainable Development.

Transboundary policies are of particular importance in tackling gender inequality and sustainability. In particular, gender and sustainability should be mainstreamed into trade, investment, migration and development co-operation policies.

Stronger monitoring of the activities of companies in developing (and to some extent developed) countries is essential to ensure that corporations promote labour practices that are respectful of women's rights and the environment. Ensuring decent work and social security to migrant workers in developed countries should be accompanied by efforts to improve companies' awareness about environmental footprints. A gender and sustainability lens should also be applied to imports, requiring importers to carry out due diligence on their supply chains. The effective implementation of existing international standards, such the OECD Guidelines on Responsible Business Conduct, requires a stronger sanctioning mechanism than is currently in place.

Analysis of the gender-environment nexus also requires a time dimension, as the causal relationships between gender equality, women's well-being and the environment might only manifest over long time periods. In particular, intergenerational effects are also inherent to both gender and sustainability goals. Gender inequalities tend to be 'sticky' and perpetuate themselves across generations, e.g. in environments where women's empowerment is restrained such as low income households priority tends to be given to boys over girls, be it in education, health or inheritance. This is of particular concern as generational social mobility has been decreasing in OECD countries over recent decades (OECD, 2017[11]). Environmental damage is also by nature an intergenerational process that can take many years to reveal its true cost.

5.5. Policy recommendations to jointly advance gender equality and environmental sustainability

Leveraging the gender-environment nexus requires the design and implementation of policies in the three vectors mentioned above: gender equality and women's empowerment, environment-related domestic policies, and transboundary policies.

When implementing an agenda for gender equality and sustainability based on these policy vectors, governments can rely on a number of OECD standards as well as assessment and evaluation mechanisms. The following (Sections 5.5.1, 5.5.2and 5.5.3) is a non-exhaustive list of such standards/tools currently available and which can be used in the deployment of a gender and sustainability strategy. In some cases, some adjustments and revisions to the existing toolkit will be necessary to leverage the nexus effectively.

5.5.1. Advancing gender equality policies with environmental goals in mind

Creating policies to advance gender equality and women's empowerment are the first and probably most important actions to leverage the gender-environment nexus for environmental sustainability and tackling climate change. All aspects of gender equality and women's empowerment can contribute to reducing the negative impact of environmental degradation on women and advancing their role in protecting the planet. Some of the most relevant aspects of gender equality legislation, policies and practices for environmental sustainability include the following:

- Equal access to quality education, health and other social services and ending discrimination against women in environmental research and innovation;
- Investing in girls' and women's education and training with a specific focus on sustainable development and STEM subjects, including vocational training and life-long-learning;
- Equality in land tenure, inheritance rights, and access to commons such as forests, rivers and marine resources, not only from a legal standpoint but also via effective implementation and enforcement measures;
- Gender equality in employment policies and practices, with a specific focus on environment-sensitive sectors (mining, transport, water, energy, chemicals, and other heavy manufacturing industries) and ending discriminatory employment practices;
- Gender parity in decision-making bodies, in both the public and private sector. A greater presence and the meaningful engagement of women, in all their diversity, is needed in environmental decision-making at all levels, including environmental planning, financing, budgeting, and policy-making, from international environmental negotiations to local environmental decision-making;
- Within the private sector, there is a need for greater female representation in company boards and executive positions, in particular in environment-sensitive sectors that are traditionally male-dominated;
- Representation of women's voices in public consultations regarding environment-sensitive projects, in particular, major urban and transport projects, energy, water and other infrastructure development;
- Equal access to environmental justice for women while further supporting women's environmentalist movements and amplifying them through community engagement.

5.5.2. Mainstreaming gender equality in environmental strategies/policies

Using a gender lens in the design of environmental policies is not only necessary to address the specific environment-related challenges and impacts faced by women, but it also makes these policies more effective. In turn, if gender is not mainstreamed into environment policies, there is a risk of aggravating existing gender inequalities.

National environmental strategies and specific plans on climate change, biodiversity, oceans, and circular economy

National sustainable development strategies, environmental action plans and other economic planning documents need to integrate the gender-environment nexus by including a gender equality dimension to environmental goals and actions. This should include the application of gender impact assessments (GIAs) to different environmental policies under consideration.

A gender lens also needs to be applied to broad-ranging environmental issues, such as climate change, as well as specific environmental policies and tools.

Effective climate change action requires for better gender-responsive national action plans. In turn, this requires bringing a gender lens into sustainability policies targeting the main sectors accounting for GHG emissions: energy, transport and farming (see below). Both the impact of climate change on women and their role in addressing climate change need to be considered.

The twenty-third session of the Conference of Parties to the United Nations Framework Convention on Climate Change (UNFCCC), COP 23, in 2017 fully recognised the link between gender and climate change. Parties adopted the Gender Action Plan to support the implementation of gender-related decisions and mandates under the UNFCCC process (UNFCCC, 2019[12]). The aim of the Gender Action Plan is to accelerate the implementation of the existing more than 60 decisions with gender-related mandates adopted by Parties between 2007 and 2017. Moreover, Basel, Rotterdam and Stockholm Conventions (BSR) have developed a Gender Action Plan (GAP) in order to implement the BRS-GAP's vision aims to ensure that the principles of gender equality are firmly embedded in the activities undertaken by the BRS Secretariat (BRS, 2019[13]). Additionally, conventions like CBD, Ramsar and World Heritage have initiated similar projects.

A second area of environmental policy that requires greater consideration of gender equality and women's issues is the protection of biodiversity and ecosystems. Policies regarding the management of forests, natural reserves, parks and wildlife should incorporate a gender equality dimension to ensure that the specific role of women in the sustainable management of and their dependence on consumption from these resources is well accounted for. This includes understanding the specific status of women in forest-dependent communities, among whom are indigenous groups. In many developing countries, a root problem to address is the gender gap in access to forest resources, due to customary laws and social norms that discriminate against women. Growing over-exploitation of forests for commercial purposes, which in some cases involves land grabbing, illegal logging and wildlife trade has made this problem worse.

Governments should also continue efforts to incorporate a gender equality perspective into National Biodiversity Strategies and Action Plans (NBSAPs), the key mechanism through which signatories to CBD implement their goals. NBSAPs provide a major opportunity to integrate women's empowerment and gender equality considerations into biodiversity management across the agriculture, forestry and fisheries sectors.

Governments also need to design policy solutions to better conserve the oceans with a gender-lens, addressing the specific concerns of degrading oceans for women, including the impact of coastal storms, the depletion of fish stocks and the increase of marine litter. Women also need to be better empowered to contribute to preserve marine ecosystems and sustainably use marine resources and protect coastal areas (in particular mangrove swamps and coral reefs). Their role in developing small-scale, sustainable fishing and their contribution to the livelihood of local communities should also be considered.

A fourth area of environmental policy, which would benefit from stronger integration of gender equality is promoting a circular economy. Despite the large evidence reported on gender differences regarding attitudes among consumers to ecolabels and purchase patterns (e.g. fashion, cosmetics), circular economy strategies rarely include a gender angle. For instance, the EU Circular Economy Action Plan does not report any differentiated gender actions (EC, 2020[14]).

Promoting green energy in the context of energy frameworks, women need to be considered as agents of change and not just stakeholders thus expanding the role women play in the energy transition (Prebble et al., 2017[15]). Energy frameworks from developed countries tend to put forward a gender-responsive approach through designing opportunities for women in energy technology and innovation while developing countries tend to reflect more diverse opportunities to advance a gender-responsive approach, including by addressing time poverty, energy poverty in rural and urban areas and women's health and well-being (Prebble et al., 2017[15]).

Environmental standards

While over time environmental standards have been raised in most countries, there is still insufficient attention being paid to the differential impact of environmental hazards by gender. One of the few areas where there is a consistent gender-based approach is the testing of chemicals. The OECD Guidelines for the Testing of Chemicals specifically require the evaluation of sex-specific effects for many of the tests covered, particularly those of chemicals that disrupt the endocrine system (OECD, n.d.[16]).

Air pollution and water contamination are other environmental hazards that require a gender lens, both because of the specific exposure of women in some contexts (in particular in-door air pollution in developing countries), and the specific biological effects on women. Policymakers should also specifically consider the dangers of high pollution exposure for pregnant women and infants and take the necessary preventive measures.

Environmental taxes and subsidies and budgetary tools

Environmental taxes and subsidies and other environmental policy instruments can also have a differential effect by gender that needs to be considered as part of policy evaluation. In general, women tend to be more present in green sectors than in polluting industries. Women also tend to be more present in small-scale, artisanal fishing and agriculture, while men dominate large-scale farming and industrial fishing (FAO, 2015[17]) Hence, environmentally centred policy efforts together with a well-structured approach to gender equality can have a positive net effect on female employment in addition to protecting the planet.

Understanding the differentiated impact of public policies, programmes and budgets on the economy, society and the environment is crucial for advancing equitable and inclusive outcomes across all policy sectors. One way to integrate the gender-environment nexus into budgeting is via a "well-being-budgeting" or "SDG-budgeting" approach.

Environment-sensitive sectors: "genderising" energy, transport, and farming policies

Among all the different sectors concerned by the gender-sustainability agenda, infrastructure (in particular energy and transport) and farming stand out for their potential to accelerate the transition towards achieving the SDGs (OECD, 2017[11]); (OECD/FAO, 2019[18]).

Moving towards a low-carbon infrastructure development model, while tackling gender gaps in infrastructure access and employment, requires mainstreaming gender and environmental considerations throughout the governance cycle and financing, including strategic planning, consultations process, co-ordination across levels and entities of government, adequate use of data and operational quality (Box 5.1).

Box 5.1. Integrating a gender-environment lens into the OECD Framework for Better Governance of Infrastructure

All five elements of the OECD Framework for Better Governance of Infrastructure could be enhanced with a gender-environment lens: (i) a strategic vision for infrastructure; (ii) integrate a consultation process; (iii) co-ordinate infrastructure policy across levels and entities of government; (iv) generate, analyse and disclose useful data; and (v) asset perform throughout its life cycle (OECD, 2017[11]).

When designing the vision for infrastructure, setting out infrastructure development plans, and identifying specific projects, an integrated gender-environment lens should be applied. Women should participate directly in local, national and international decision-making bodies and at all stages of policy-making. Consultation processes with stakeholders should include women's groups. Data should involve gender-disaggregation. In addition, when assessing performance, the specific impact on women of infrastructure projects should be considered.

More effective gender mainstreaming is key for sustainable economic and social outcomes of these projects via improved access to and use of infrastructure, which in turn enhances their economic opportunities and labour market participation of women, including in decision-making positions. Applying a gender lens is also necessary to mitigate negative spillovers on women and other vulnerable groups from project construction and operation, and provides for greater environmental protection, leading to increased well-being for all.

A key policy tool for all infrastructure projects are impact assessments. Such assessments must be comprehensive and be carried out by institutions independent of the project contractors. They must include environmental and inclusiveness considerations in an integrated manner.

Infrastructure also tends to be a male-dominated industry, in part because of the still heavy manual input involved. An added advantage of women's involvement in the governance of infrastructure is their greater sensitivity to environmental risks.

Farming policies also need to integrate the gender-environment nexus. Tackling gender discrimination and women's empowerment needs to go beyond private land titles and agricultural production and address the need for women to access shared resources from forests, mountains, rivers, and other commons. This is especially important for indigenous communities given their dependence on shared, ancestral lands.

Policymakers should also consider the specific role of women in traditional and self-sufficient farming and small fisheries and ensure that they consider the gender dimension of the impact of farming and fisheries policies on small landowners. This is highly relevant considering the crucial role women play in the fishing sector, where according to FAO, women account for 50% of fisheries workforces (14-15% in harvesting and up to 90% in post-harvest value chain roles) (FAO, 2015[19]).

There is also a need to better integrate gender equality considerations into National Biodiversity Strategies and Action Plans (NBSAPs). In particular, there is a need to ensure gender balanced decision-making and access to technology and finance for women-led projects.

Access to finance and technology for green ventures

Policies to facilitate access to finance and technology require a specific focus on the gender-environment nexus. Because of explicit or implicit discrimination and biases, women may be at disadvantage from accessing adequate finance for green innovation and start-ups. Beyond legislative reform to correct discrimination, positive action to overcome social norms, practices and cultural barriers may include the development of special programmes targeting women green entrepreneurs and small forms run by women.

5.5.3. Integrating a gender angle into the environmental aspects of transboundary policies

Trade policies

While there is a growing recognition of the importance of including a gender lens in trade policies, there has been little progress in applying a gender perspective in trade agreements. It is important for such agreements and trade policies in general to prioritise the different needs and rights of disadvantaged groups, in particular (poor) women.

Trade agreements and trade policies should also consider specific aspects of the gender-environment nexus. For instance, trade facilitation initiatives can be particularly beneficial for SMEs, where women's economic activity tends to be concentrated. Access to trade can particularly benefit small-scale women producers and female cooperatives in the agricultural sector.

In 2017, World Trade Organisation (WTO) members agreed to a Joint Declaration on Trade and Women's Economic Empowerment, which aims to increase women's participation in trade (WTO, 2017[20]). A number of recent bilateral and regional trade agreements also include chapters on trade and gender, as well as chapters on trade and environment. There is a need, not only to expand such chapters in trade agreements, but also to ensure an effective implementation of the gender and environmental dimensions.

Foreign investment and RBC

Businesses investing abroad should be required to integrate the gender-environment nexus into their investment decisions. The OECD Guidelines for Multinational Enterprises [OECD/LEGAL/0144] provides a framework for integrating human rights, environmental and social considerations in business strategies and operations. This framework, together with the accompanying Due Diligence Guidance on Responsible Business Conduct [OECD/LEGAL/0443], should be applied to foreign investment decisions and operations and ensure that it incorporates gender equality and environmental goals in an integrated manner.

The OECD has also developed a Foreign Direct Investment (FDI) Qualities framework that addresses both gender equality and environmental objectives. However, the framework tackles these issues separately, and does not refer to the nexus.

In particular, when assessing potential and actual environmental impacts of their operations, companies should evaluate specific gender-based effects. Furthermore, companies should ensure adequate representation of women's groups when carrying out stakeholder consultations on foreign investments.

Development co-operation

While development co-operation efforts are increasingly SDG-aligned, there is still much work to do, as highlighted in the recent G20 Contribution to the 2030 Agenda report (OECD, 2019[21]). Sectors such as agriculture, forestry, biodiversity and ecosystems, health and water, which are a priority for adaptation-related action, would deserve receiving a larger share development financing. They are also sectors with differentiated gender impacts and where women can play a central role in advancing more sustainable solutions. Hence, an integrated gender-environment approach to development co-operation is key.

Critically, a better integration of gender equality considerations is needed in mitigation-oriented climate finance, in particular for economic infrastructure, including transport and energy. In particular, more support is needed to improve opportunities for women in developing countries to participate in the green economy. The Green Climate Fund has adopted a dedicated Gender Policy, updated in 2019, which both promotes gender equality in a project's management, and ensures gender-sensitive financing through gender- and environment- assessments at the preparation and implementation stages of the project (GCF, 2019[22]).

5.6. Working in partnerships to deliver transformative change

Neither gender equality nor environmental sustainability will be achieved "automatically". Clear progress can only be achieved by a transformative vision and determined policy action, leadership, commitment, resources and engagement of all stakeholders. Tools for monitoring also need to be further developed, including more disaggregated data on the determinants and the impacts of women's contribution to SDGs, including with specific evidence on policies that enable women to be full actors of sustainable development.

UN agencies such as UN Women and UNEP, and the UNFCCC have launched a number of partnerships, which address more specifically the gender-sustainability nexus than older initiatives such as the UN Global Compact or the Global Reporting Initiative (UN Global Compact, 2003[23]). However, none of these initiatives provide the necessary integrated, holistic approach to the nexus, nor do they ensure effective evidence gathering, which is the basis for decision-making.

Together with a number of partners, the OECD has set up the "Gender Policy Platform: Accelerating Gender Mainstreaming through the SDGs" to bring together stakeholders from the public and private sector and civil society to deliver on gender equality, inclusiveness and sustainability agendas in an integrated manner. Initially building on existing work on gender and SDGs as part of the gender initiative and the OECD Action Plan on the SDGs, the Platform is engaging stakeholders in a dialogue to advance evidence gathering and policy analysis, and identify actions and measures that can be taken at global, regional, national and community levels to:

- Fully integrate gender equality, inclusiveness and sustainability dimensions into policy-making in a holistic and coherent manner, while taking into account transboundary and intergenerational effects;
- Enhance the role of women in promoting sustainable development via women's full participation in political, social and economic life, while also ensuring the achievement of inclusiveness and sustainability goals;
- Engage the private sector in advancing gender equality and sustainability objectives.

The Platform aims to expand its research on the gender-sustainability nexus and develop further the methodology proposed in this report. As one of its outputs, the study "Measuring Distance to SDG Targets" (OECD, 2019[9])has been already extended to outline the statistical agenda ahead for greater granularity in the measurement of the SDGs as well as to provide an overview of key strengths and challenges faced in meeting the SDG targets for women.

The Platform is also building up its awareness-raising activities and engage in partnerships with other international organisations, business and civil society to support a better understanding, evidence gathering and effective reporting on the gender-sustainability nexus.

References

BRS (2019), *Gender Action Plan of the Secretariat of the Basel, Rotterdam and Stockholm Conventions (BRS-GAP)*, http://www.basel.int/Portals/4/Basel%20Convention/docs/meetings/cop/cop9/bali-declaration/BaliDeclaration.pdf;. [13]

EC (2020), *A new Circular Economy Action Plan for a Cleaner and More Competitive Europe*, https://ec.europa.eu/environment/circular-economy. [14]

FAO (2015), *A Review of Women's access to Fish in Small Scale Fisheries*, Food and Agriculture Organization (FAO), Rome, https://www.google.com/url?sa=t&rct=j&q=&esrc=s&source=web&cd=&cad=rja&uact=8&ved=2ahUKEwidtaXL44zwAhWrxIUKHTRTAG0QFjAAegQIBRAD&url=http%3A%2F%2Fwww.fao.org%2Ffamily-farming%2Fdetail%2Fen%2Fc%2F385279%2F&usg=AOvVaw0JqLezmjdY-ltoCTzPAkbA. [17]

FAO (2015), *The role of women in the seafood industry*, http://www.globefish.org. [19]

GCF (2019), *Gender Policy*, Green Climate Fund, https://www.greenclimate.fund/sites/default/files/document/gcf-gender-policy.pdf (accessed on 7 April 2021). [22]

OECD (2021), "The inequalities-environment nexus: Towards a people-centred green transition", *OECD Green Growth Papers*, No. 2021/01, OECD Publishing, Paris, https://dx.doi.org/10.1787/ca9d8479-en. [7]

OECD (2019), *Measuring Distance to the SDG Targets 2019*, OECD, http://dx.doi.org/10.1787/a8caf3fa-en. [9]

OECD (2018), *Opportunities for All*, OECD, http://dx.doi.org/10.1787/9789264301665-en. [6]

OECD (2017), *Getting Infrastructure Right*, OECD, http://dx.doi.org/10.1787/9789264272453-en. [11]

OECD (2017), *Meeting of the OECD Council at Ministerial Level - Report on the implementation of the OECD gender recommendations*, https://www.oecd.org/els/2013-oecd-recommendation-of-the-council-on-gender-equality-in-education-employment-and-entrepreneurship-9789264279391-en.htm. [4]

OECD (2016), *2015 OECD Recommendation of the Council on Gender Equality in Public Life*, OECD Publishing, Paris, https://www.oecd.org/gov/2015-oecd-recommendation-of-the-council-on-gender-equality-in-public-life-9789264252820-en.htm#:~:text=The%202015%20OECD%20Recommendation%20of,to%20inform%20inclusive%20policy%20decisions. [5]

OECD (n.d.), *OECD Guidelines for the Testing of Chemicals*, https://www.oecd.org/chemicalsafety/testing/oecd-guidelines-testing-chemicals-related-documents.htm#:~:text=The%20OECD%20Guidelines%20for%20the,assess%20the%20safety%20of%20chemicals. [16]

OECD/FAO (2019), *OECD-FAO Agricultural Outlook 2019-2028*, OECD Publishing, Paris/Food and Agriculture Organization of the United Nations, Rome, https://dx.doi.org/10.1787/agr_outlook-2019-en. [18]

OECD, U. (2019), *G20 Contribution to the 2030 Agenda: Progress and Way Forward*, OECD/UNDP, https://www.undp.org/content/dam/undp/library/bpps-spu/OECD-UNDP_G20_Contribution_to_2030_Agenda.pdf. [21]

PARIS 21 (2018), *Survey Results - New Approaches to Capacity Development and Future Priorities,*, https://paris21.org/capacity-development-40/cd40-survey. [8]

Prebble, M. et al. (2017), *Energizing Equality: The importance of integrating gender equality principles in national energy policies and frameworks SEPTEMBER 2017 AUTHORS GRAPHIC DESIGN*, http://www.estudiorelativo.com. [15]

UN Global Compact (2003), *Global Reporting Initiative*, https://www.unglobalcompact.org/what-is-gc/participants/4378-Global-Reporting-Initiative. [23]

UN Women (2019), *Making Every Woman and Girl Count: Mid Term Review*, https://data.unwomen.org/sites/default/files/documents/Publications/AR2019Annex/Women-Count-Annual-Report-2019_WEB_FINAL.pdf. [10]

UN Women (2018), *Gender Equality and Big Data. Making Gender Data Visible..*, https://www.unwomen.org/en/digital-library/publications/2018/1/gender-equality-and-big-data. [2]

UN Women (2018), *Turning promises into action : Gender Equality in the 2030 Agenda for Sustainable Development*, https://www.unwomen.org/en/digital-library/publications/2018/2/gender-equality-in-the-2030-agenda-for-sustainable-development-2018. [3]

UNEP (2019), *The Emissions Gap Report 2019,*, United Nations Environment Programme, Nairobi, https://www.unep.org/resources/emissions-gap-report-2019. [1]

UNFCCC (2019), *Gender Action Plan*, UN Climate Change Conference, https://unfccc.int/documents/204536. [12]

WTO (2017), *Joint Declaration on Trade and Women's Economic Empowerment on the Occasion of the WTO Ministerial Conference in Buenos Aires*, https://www.wto.org/english/thewto_e/minist_e/mc11_e/genderdeclarationmc11_e.pdf. [20]

Notes

[1] The Partnership in Statistics for Development in the 21st Century (PARIS 21) was established in 1999 to support developing countries in better using and producing statistics. The PARIS 21 Secretariat is hosted within the OECD's Statistics and Data Directorate. For more information: https://paris21.org/about-paris21

6 Women and SDG 2 – Promoting sustainable agriculture

While women account for a growing share of agricultural workers, gender discrimination means that in much of the developing world, women are more vulnerable than men to hunger and the negative effects of environmental damage caused by unsustainable agricultural practices. Tackling discrimination in access to land and natural resources, and addressing gender gaps in education, training and finance are essential to allow women to increase agricultural productivity and promote more sustainable farming practices. Some of these challenges – in particular in relation to skills gaps and representation in decision-making - also persist in advanced countries.

6.1. Key findings

This chapter provides a description of the links between gender equality and sustainable agriculture. Lack of gender-disaggregated data is a major challenge to advance the necessary analysis, but existing evidence shows some links between gender discrimination, undernourishment, and unsustainable farming practices. Tackling this vicious circle requires urgent action, given women's growing role in agriculture production:

- Environmental damage and climate change are important stressors on food systems, notably by impacting agricultural production and by affecting crucial ecosystems. In turn, agricultural production is an important stressor to the environment, with agriculture, forestry and other land use accounting for around 23% of greenhouse gas emissions.
- In Africa and Asia, women already constitute between 43-50% of all farmworkers. About 80% of farmland is managed by small-scale farmers, who in turn also provide around 80% of the food supply. Among 70% of small-scale African farmers are women (FAO, 2016[1]).
- The majority of agricultural workers everywhere are informal (98% in developing countries, 93% in emerging and 59% in developed countries). Female agricultural workers, who make up about 43% of the agricultural labour force in developing countries, are over-represented in unpaid and low-paid seasonal or part-time jobs and thus likely to be left out of social protection systems (Rapsomanikis, 2015[2]).
- In much of the developing world, the largest barrier for women farmers is their limited rights to inherit, access and use land and other productive resources than men, leading to smaller production by 20-30% when compared to that of men (FAO, 2020[3]).
- Breaking legal and cultural barriers to women's full engagement in agriculture is key. In developing countries, for which data are available, on average 16% of all landholders are women in comparison to 21% in developed economies (UN Women, 2019[4]).
- Trade and investment policies, international agreements and development co-operation should incorporate and intensify mechanisms to integrate gender equality and sustainability in relation to the agricultural sector, as well as to provide more equal access to markets and market information.
- There is a need to strengthen sex- and gender-disaggregated data collection and mixing of existing data on the impact of unsustainable farming practices (e.g. pesticides exposure and impact), and on women's contribution to advance sustainable agricultural methods, including technologies that reduce pesticides, such as precision agriculture or biotech.
- Supporting women-led sustainable agriculture activities requires a more thorough gender-sensitive, place-based approach. In addition, women and indigenous communities, due to their traditional knowledge, may help identify issues and difficulties the local population is confronted with, and may also provide alternatives in providing solutions.

6.2. Key interlinkages between gender equality, the promotion of sustainable agriculture and other SDGs

Agriculture development is key to human well-being and has major implications for the environment. As the world's population continues to grow, the need for more and better quality food will be imperative, especially considering the various health and environmental challenges around the globe (from COVID-19 to other infectious diseases which affect livestock production). The COVID-19 pandemic has revealed that vulnerabilities and inadequacies of global food systems still persist and under pressure, impacts on production, distribution and consumption can affect livelihoods considerably (FAO et al., 2020[5]). Recent OECD-FAO projections estimate that global agricultural production will continue to increase in the next decade, resulting in growing demand due to population growth. Food is also expected to be more affordable for households as income increases, albeit with variations between countries of different income levels. Yet, vulnerable groups and groups with the lowest income, often women, remain more at risk from changes in production and food prices (OECD/FAO, 2020[6]).

However, agricultural and food production increase (agricultural commercialisation) can also create significant pressure on the environment. The Agriculture, Forestry and other Land Use (AFOLU) sector accounts for 23.1% of global greenhouse gas emissions (IPCC, 2019[7]). Further intensification of certain agricultural activities may have further negative effects on the environment, reducing biodiversity, worsening water scarcity and causing soil degradation (FAO, 2011[8]). The economic costs of the negative externalities associated with certain agricultural practices are enormous, and include – among others - the loss of free products and services provided by nature to humanity, climate change, and the increased incidence and impact of zoonosis, which often originate in unsustainable human farming and eating habits (OECD, 2020[9]); (OECD, 2020[10]). Run-offs from the excessive use of fertilisers and pesticides can also heighten risks to human health.

Environmental damage and climate change are also important stressors on food systems, notably by impacting agricultural production and by affecting crucial ecosystems through systematic and industrial hunting and fishing. This is especially true in Canada's Northern region, where climate change is significantly impacting First Nations and causing food insecurity up to 50% in these communities (Human Rights Watch, 2020[11]). Food poverty will worsen as climate change impacts intensify and accelerate, further undermining these communities' access to food, worsening health outcomes and reinforcing inequalities. Overall, women, children, the elderly, indigenous and disabled people face the highest levels of vulnerability to severe food insecurity and malnutrition, which are further worsened by climate change (FAO, 2019[12]).

The 'triple challenge' of providing food security and nutrition; ensuring livelihoods; and using natural resources sustainably and mitigating climate change is pressing. Efficiency gains and innovation are crucial to improve productivity, which could reduce land use change (LUC) and the resulting greenhouse gas emissions (OECD, 2021[13]). Technological uptake, such as new plant breeding techniques, could be particularly important for increasing yields in regions where the agricultural expansion involves the conversion of carbon rich and biodiverse landscapes (IPCC, 2019[7]). However, as many farmers continue to rely on informal markets for buying their products, their access to new technologies is often limited.

SDG 2, in line with the 2012 Rio+20 United Nations Conference on Sustainable Development, sets the ground for promoting sustainable agriculture and transitioning to more sustainable agricultural production methods. Advancing towards sustainable agriculture is not only key to achieving zero hunger (SDG 2), but also to promoting better health; and reducing mortality rates due to chemicals use, unsafe water and soil pollution and contamination (SDG 3). Sustainable agriculture is linked directly to the use of natural resources, and as such goes hand in hand with sustainable management of water (SDG 6); responsible production and consumption patterns (SDG 12); climate change (SDG 13); sustainable use of ecosystems and forests, and land and biodiversity preservation (SDG 15). It is also influenced by urbanisation, especially when this occurs in former agricultural lands (SDG 11). In addition, part of agricultural production is used as biofuel, influencing fossil fuel and renewable energy use, as well as land use, income and food generation (SDG 7). Agriculture, finally, is strongly linked to education and accessing new skills and knowledge which can support a transition to sustainability (SDG 4); while it is a key component for income generation and economic growth (SDG 8).

Gender equality (SDG 5) is strongly linked to achieving SDG 2 on sustainable agriculture. The SDG framework refers to women's (and other groups') role as small-scale farmers, acknowledges traditional knowledge and maintaining the genetic diversity of seeds, plants and animals (Target 2.5), and supports equal ownership of and access to agricultural land (Target 5.a). Providing equal access to productive resources for both men and women is expected to increase agricultural output. Delivering on SDG 5, hence, stands as an essential milestone to realise SDG 2.

6.3. Gender gaps in agriculture, food security and health impacts of unsustainable agriculture

6.3.1. Women in agriculture

In some countries, the female share of the agricultural labour force is increasing, a trend that is particularly noticeable in small-scale farming. Female employment in agriculture worldwide was at 25.3% of total female employment in 2019, while respective male employment was 27.7% (ILOSTAT, 2021[14]).

Figure 6.1. Distribution of total employment by gender and by sector

Percentage, 2019 data

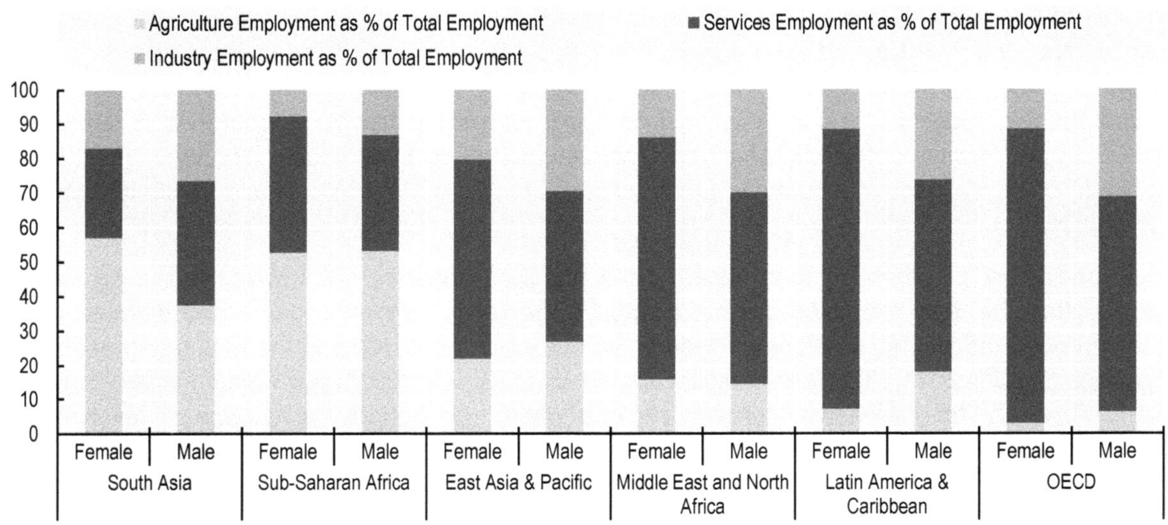

Note: The International Labour Organization (ILO) classifies economic activity using the International Standard Industrial Classification (ISIC) of All Economic Activities, revision 2 (1968), revision 3 (1990), and revision 4 (2008). Classification is based on industry, not type of work performed (trade or occupation). Categories should sum to 100%. Where they do not, the differences are due to workers who are not classified by economic activity. The series is part of the ILO estimates and is harmonized to ensure comparability across countries and over time by accounting for differences in data source, scope of coverage, methodology, and other country-specific factors. The estimates are based mainly on nationally representative labour force surveys, with other sources (population censuses and nationally reported estimates) used only when no survey data are available.

Source: International Labour Organization, ILOSTAT database (ILOSTAT, 2021[14]). ILO Estimates as presented in the World Development Indicators (WDI, 2021[15]).

Figure 6.1shows the distribution of total employment between men and women across the agriculture, industry and services sectors in 2019. It covers the regions of Sub-Saharan Africa, Latin America and the Caribbean, East Asia and Pacific, Middle East and North Africa and South Asia and the OECD. We observe that the agricultural sector is the major employer in Sub-Saharan Africa and South Asia for both men and women. In these regions female employment in agriculture exceeds 50% of total female employment. This stands in contrast with the agricultural female workforce of OECD countries that is below 5%.The largest gender disparity in the agriculture sector can be observed in South Asia where almost 20% more of the total female workforce works in agriculture compared to the male workforce. The region that shows the most gender equality in labour participation in the agricultural sector is Sub-Saharan Africa.

Figure 6.2. Distribution of employment by gender in agricultural sector (OECD countries)

Percentage, 2019 data

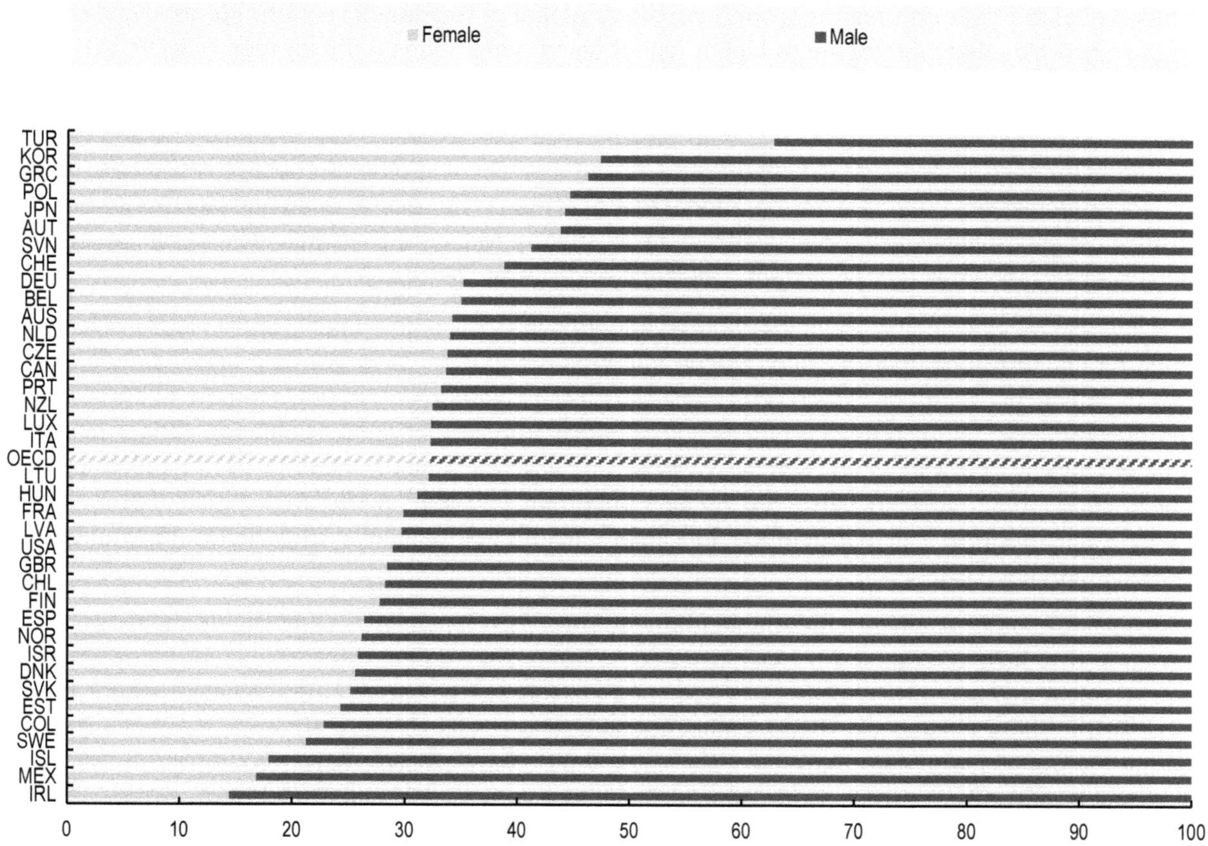

Note: Presented data has been calculated using the ILO indicators of 'Employment to population ratio by gender, 15+, (% of total population)' and the 'Employment in agriculture by gender (% of gender employment)'. Employment to population ratio is the proportion of a country's population that is employed. Employment is defined as persons of working age who, during a short reference period, were engaged in any activity to produce goods or provide services for pay or profit, whether at work during the reference period (i.e. who worked in a job for at least one hour) or not at work due to temporary absence from a job, or to working-time arrangements. Ages 15 and older are generally considered the working-age population. The International Labour Organization (ILO) classifies economic activity using the International Standard Industrial Classification (ISIC) of All Economic Activities, revision 2 (1968), revision 3 (1990), and revision 4 (2008).

Source: International Labour Organization, ILOSTAT database (ILOSTAT, 2021[14]). ILO Estimates as presented in the World Development Indicators (WDI, 2021[15]).

As observed in Figure 6.1, overall OECD countries have a much smaller workforce in the agriculture sector. However in Turkey, Colombia, Mexico and Greece the agricultural sector continues to represent more than 9% of the total employment, while Luxembourg and Belgium employment in agriculture represents less than 1% of total employment. Figure 6.2 shows the gender distribution of the agricultural workforce for all OECD countries. Turkey is the only OECD Member country where women's employment has a higher representation in the agricultural workforce than men's', by almost 25%. Of those countries where agriculture employs more than 9% of the total population, Mexico and Colombia stand out for their low female representation, barely 25% of the total agricultural workforce. This situation explain calls by civil society for greater inclusiveness of women in these countries' agricultural sectors, such as in the coffee and bean production sectors in Colombia, where women report to be constrained to specific gender roles (Global Coffee Platform (GCP), 2018[16]); (Avila-Santamaria and Del Pilar Useche, 2016[17]).

6.3.2. Women as small-scale holders

Food security is a growing problem in much of the developing world while food waste continues unabated in advanced countries (FAO, 2015[18]). Hunger often affects those directly involved in producing food. Sex-disaggregated data on undernourished people at global or regional levels are not readily available, but research shows that women are at higher risk of being undernourished than men (UNDP, 2012[19]); (Sethuraman and Duvvury, 2007[20]).

Gender discrimination is the root cause of this challenge. Despite women's role in agriculture and farming, women farmers have limited rights to inherit, access and use land and other productive resources, leading to smaller production by 20-30% when compared to that of men1 (more on women and land in Chapter 14). Differences in yields between men and women in agriculture reduce significantly when both sexes have equal access to resources (Croppenstedt, Goldstein and Rosas, 2013[21]).

Across low and middle income countries, women engaged in farming hold mainly small pieces of land and cultivate mostly traditional food for subsistence and sale, while men generally hold larger pieces of land and focus mainly on trade activities (World Bank, 2020[22]). Women do not only struggle to participate in the production chain but also have a harder time to store, transform, transport and sell, further hindering gender equality in the agriculture sector. Women are also particularly affected by the destruction of 'marginal' land, which is often perceived as less important and less useful than agricultural land. Yet, marginal lands perform key subsistence functions and are of particular importance to women and indigenous peoples (CBD, 2008[23]).

Land tenure is another challenge for female farmers. The FAO Gender and Land Rights database shows that women who hold land generally have less secure rights even if land ownership is for many women a source of economic security, especially in societies lacking safety nets and an inclusive labour market (FAO, 2021[24]). For instance, a 2019 national agricultural census in Mexico shows that out of 4.9 million people in the country who own agrarian units, more than 3.6 million are men, while only 1.3 million are women (RAN, 2019[25]). Where land ownership rights are exercised mainly by men, women are not represented in decision-making spaces with no voice or vote in decisions related to agricultural and livestock practices.

Female farmers are more exposed to gender-based violence, as the majority of agricultural work often takes place out of the purview of others (Castañeda Carney et al., 2020[26]). Evidence shows that this is the case both in low and middle income countries and higher income countries, and it often involves sexual harassment from male superiors and being forced to give sexual favours to employers to secure contracts (Henry and Adams, 2018[27]); (FIAN International, 2014[28]).

In the context of the COVID-19 pandemic, restrictions on the movement of people and goods and other measures to contain the spread of the virus are disrupting agricultural value chains and food systems (FAO, 2020[29]). The negative and gender-differentiated impact on women has become visible through dimensions of food security, decreased purchasing power and diminished distribution capacities. While this affects rural farmers in general, women face greater disadvantages because they have limited access to different products and markets, services such as finance, and information. Research shows that women's assets are more likely to be impacted under an illness shock or a family death (Quisumbing, Kumar and Behrman, 2017[30]).

6.3.3. Health effects on women of unsustainable agriculture

Agriculture also affects health through the use of pesticides, which are most common in large-scale farming but also used by many smallholder farms. According to World Health Organization (WHO) data, an estimated 3 million cases of pesticide poisoning occur every year, resulting in over 250 000 deaths worldwide (Thundiyil et al., 2008[31]). Sex-disaggregated data on the use, exposure and impact of pesticides is not readily available, but women may be at greater risk of adverse effects due to a number of factors including insufficient knowledge of the negative effects, limited access to training and lack of personal protective equipment (Mrema et al., 2017[32]); (Garrigou et al., 2020[33]).

An example from the People's Republic of China shows that there are gender differences regarding knowledge of pesticide impacts, pesticide use practices and protective behaviours which result in men having better awareness regarding associated health risks but adopting less protective measures or behaviours when using pesticides than women. The research suggested that gender-sensitive educational programmes should be implemented to increase the safety awareness amongst farmers, together with increased data availability and research on this topic (Wang et al., 2017[34]).

Additionally, biological factors (size, physiological, hormonal and enzyme differences between women and men, and between adults and children) can create higher susceptibility to health damage from exposure to toxic chemicals for women (UNDP, 2011[35]). Exposure to chemicals generally occurs through food consumption, with evidence linking a higher intake of organic fruit and vegetables with a lower pesticide residue in the body (Berman et al., 2016[36]). Working in the field or living in the vicinity of crops can also lead to direct chemical exposure, putting female workers in direct contact with endocrine-disrupting properties of some pesticides. The harmful impacts on health have become evident through the connection between pesticides and breast cancer rates (Watts, 2007[37]); (Watts, 2013[38]).

In a context of climate change, as more women enter agricultural production, the intensification of agriculture and the resulting environmental damage worsens women's conditions as yields decline due to droughts and water gathering – a mainly female activity - become increasingly arduous. There is therefore an urgent need to transform agriculture towards more sustainable practices.

6.4. The role of women in sustainable agriculture

Evidence from Africa shows that women adapt as well or more effectively than men to changes that affect their farming, even though women farmers have less access to land, credit, modern technology, improved seeds, and education (Perez et al., 2015[39]). The FAO estimates that enabling women to access productive resources to the same extent as men in the agricultural sector could increase yields on women's farms by 20-30%. This would translate to an increase in total agricultural output in developing countries by 2.4-4%, followed by a reduction of hungry people in the world by 12-17% (FAO, 2011[40]).

In addition, applying gender-smart solutions for small-scale farming could allow more women to join the agricultural value chains (OECD/WTO, 2019[41]). This would have knock-on effects of reducing poverty, improving health, and food security. Additionally, increased productivity by sustainable farming practices in agriculture will also support the reduction of emissions. This will also require increased support to close the digital gender divide and broaden the application of digital tools in agricultural production – for instance, tools ensuring more sustainable water management and enabling the reduction of pesticide use - and access to an online market.

Women in rural areas and indigenous peoples play an important role in the conservation and management of biodiversity. In developing countries, women often are key users and custodians of natural resources (TEEB, 2015[42]). Their dependence on natural resources and surrounding environments to provide food, medicine and fuel for their families serves as a strong incentive to preserve and protect those resources. Further data collection on women's farming practices that considers their traditional knowledge is key for ensuring the successful adoption of more sustainable agricultural practices.

Mainstream research is lacking on women's role in environmental preservation, and gender disaggregated data is more scarce than in other sectors. However, there is growing evidence that women – as well as indigenous communities - may play a key role in environmental preservation, often through their traditional knowledge and agricultural methods (Kennedy et al., 2017[43]); (Winniefridah and Manuku, 2013[44]). There are also case studies demonstrating women's interest in sustainable farming practices for instance in Kenya's slum Kibera, where women use vertical farms due to the lack of space for farming, or women in Niger where they participate in the Africa Market Garden where they use technologies such as solar-power drip irrigation to grow vegetables for both self-consumption and distribution (UNEP, 2016[45]). The global community is mobilising to advance this agenda, particularly via the Convention on Biological Diversity (CBD), as part of the discussion on the conservation of biodiversity for food and agriculture (FAO, 2019[46]). This underlines the importance of collecting data beyond head of household, time-use surveys, and asking women specific questions about their needs and the impacts so as to help tailor policy measures accordingly.

Eliminating gender discrimination and otherwise facilitating and promoting women's engagement in sustainable agriculture could help drive forward action to meet all relevant targets under SDG 2, in particular Target 2.3 on small scale farming, Target 2.4 on resilient and sustainable agriculture, and Target 2.5 on conservation of plant and animal genetic resources, especially those in danger of extinction. Introducing gender-sensitive and gender-inclusive aspects in agricultural investment, trade and value chains, and rural infrastructure policies, could support achieving Targets 2.a and 2.b. Guidance on responsible business conduct (RBC) can help enterprises operating in agricultural supply chains identify and prevent adverse impacts to ensure that agricultural investments contribute to sustainable development. Governments could actively promote guidance such as the OECD-FAO Guidance for Responsible Agricultural Supply Chains, which includes specific recommendations to companies to promote gender equality by eliminating discrimination against women, enhancing their meaningful participation in decision-making, and facilitating women's equal access and control over natural resources, financial services and markets (OECD/FAO, 2016[47]).

In terms of investment, projects such as the FAO Multi-Partner Programme Support Mechanism (FMM) on gender-sensitive value chain development, which was specifically designed to enable women to benefit more equally from agri-food value chains, provides technical assistance and policy support to address barriers that hinder rural women's access to, and benefits from local, national and global markets (FAO, 2019[12]). The programme aims to develop women's capacities and increase women's economic opportunities and benefits from more efficient and inclusive agri-food chains, triggering multiplier effects on food and nutrition security, education and health. The tri-fold approach followed, supports field-level activities targeting women's associations and individual enterprises to access labour- and time-saving technologies; enhances skills in on- and off-farm activities, business management and enterprise development; and assists policy makers in designing tools that increase women's participation in the higher-value segments of the value chains; while acknowledging the key role women play in promoting sustainable farming practices (FAO, 2019[12]). In developing countries, women are responsible for producing staple crops (such as rice, wheat and maize), which produce between 60% and 80% of food, and may cover up to 90% of food intake in poor rural areas (FAO, 2011[40]); (FAO, 2014[48]); (Menon, Van der Meulen Rodgers and Kennedy, 2017[49]).

Women are often in charge of the selection, improvement and adaptation of plant varieties when seed selection is done in situ, using criteria based on their genetic characteristics. Women safeguard and maintain seeds and germplasm to be used as planting material in smallholder agricultures (Howard and Cuijpers, 2013[50]); (Vernooy et al., 2017[51]). They choose to grow different crops than men, contributing to farm biodiversity and food security (Kennedy et al., 2017[43]). Women – and children - are also often in charge of small livestock production and milk processing (FAO, 2013[52]); (Subrahmanyeswari and Chander, 2013[53]). In addition, in developing countries, women cover about 80% of the healthcare needs of their families, through traditional medicine, using a variety of plants (Shewamene, Dune and Smith, 2020[54]).

Better agricultural practices could help reduce pesticide use and their associated risks, including for human health. In countries where farmers have adopted Integrated Pest Management techniques, results show that reduced use of pesticides can also have a positive effect on yields, farm profits and incomes (OECD, 2016[55]). Skilling women in these fields offers an opportunity to make them key players in the transition to more sustainable practices, while higher productivity offers safeguards to ensure food security objectives. However, women are not a homogeneous group, and their roles, rights and needs, as well as their relationship with seeds, plants and land, may differ between regions and countries. These differences or special characteristics, need to be taken into consideration when introducing agricultural practices.

Gender-sensitive policies that target the promotion of healthy diets can benefit the transition to more sustainable agricultural practices. Healthier diets do not only prevent many non-communicable diseases, but also create synergies for reducing environmental pressure on agricultural systems, through reduced demand and consumption of organic products (FAO, 2019[56]). As women are often the household member in charge of diets, targeted food policy could contribute to maximising such opportunity.

A gender perspective is also critical to promoting sustainable farming in OECD countries. On average, only 21.35% of agricultural landholders are women in OECD countries, based on FAO data. Yet, in the European Union, women in rural areas are almost half of the rural population, representing 45% of the economically active population (about 40% of them are formally occupied in their family farms, while informal employment is not documented) (Franić and Kovačićek, 2019[57]). In Central and Eastern Europe (non-EU), women outnumber men in rural areas, with the exception of 15-49 year olds, where the figures are reversed. They also appear to be more dependent on gains from agricultural labour as in many cases there is no clear distinction between their domestic and labour-related tasks (FAO, 2018[58]).

In OECD countries, discrimination may also be the result of gender-blind policies or measures. Iceland offers an interesting experience as it is considered a gender equality frontrunner and has been using gender mainstreaming and gender budgeting tools since 2009. Through gender budgeting, the government recently changed the conditions by which farmers received state funding affecting their pensions. Based on 2012 data, Iceland officials realised that, even though both men and women worked equally on the farm, only the men applied for the funding; only one farmer per farm has the right to register for a grant (EC, 2019[59]). By allowing two farmers to register per farm, both family members have now access to the state funding and, subsequently, to a pension. Nevertheless, even countries like Iceland need to reconsider their general farm support policies, given their environmental impact (OECD, 2019[60])). An analysis on the impact of agriculture support policies on the environment from a gender equality perspective may further highlight the need to consider the differentiated impact of these policies on women and men.

As pandemic lockdowns are lifted and stimulus packages implemented, recovery strategies should integrate gender-responsive elements that ensure women's food security and support to their economic activities in the agri-food value chains. The OECD has issued different policy briefs on safeguarding progress on gender- related SDGs during the COVID-19 pandemic as well as to ensure a green recovery (OECD, 2020[61]); (OECD, 2020[9]). Guaranteeing access to basic services to rural women and providing them with immediate cash –transfers can mitigate the economic impact of COVID-19. Understanding that not all groups of society will benefit from job creation to the same extent is also important. Establishing a Gender Observatory and using Policy Coherence for Sustainable Development data and methodologies to map and monitor the gender impact of the crisis can help identify good policy practices.

6.5. Key actions for advancing the agenda and ongoing work

Despite women's strong engagement in agriculture, there is still a need for better gender mainstreaming in agricultural policy. Possible actions in this regard include:

- Collecting evidence on women's sustainable agricultural methods at local level. Supporting such initiatives by breaking legal and cultural barriers limiting their activity. Building gender-sensitive place-based approaches which allow for women's role in managing local communities to be acknowledged.
- Eliminating legal barriers to land ownership by women and their access to natural resources.

- Engaging women and indigenous communities in decision-making regarding farming policies and practices, based on their role as custodians of natural resources, and their representation in the agricultural sector. Their traditional knowledge may help identify issues and difficulties that the local population is confronted with, and may also provide alternatives in providing solutions.
- Strengthening women's leadership in the agricultural sector, including both government and the private sector.
- Ensuring gender mainstreaming when providing finance, financial literacy, digital skills and other incentives for scaling up sustainable agricultural production methods and market access. Governments should follow a gender-responsive approach when providing financial and other incentives for scaling up sustainable agricultural production methods and market access. This requires taking into consideration women's needs and care responsibilities, including the changes that a continuous increase in the proportion of agricultural production that is marketed, may bring to women.

References

Avila-Santamaria, J. and M. Del Pilar Useche (2016), *Women's Participation in Agriculture and Gender Productivity Gap: The Case of Coffee Farmers in Southern Colombia and Northern Ecuador.* [17]

Bélanger, J. and D. Pilling (eds.) (2019), *The State of the World's Biodiversity for Food and Agriculture*, FAO Commission on Genetic Resources for Food and Agriculture Assessments, Rome, http://www.fao.org/3/CA3129EN/CA3129EN.pdf. [46]

Berman, T. et al. (2016), "Urinary concentrations of organophosphate and carbamate pesticides in residents of a vegetarian community", *Environment International*, Vol. 96, pp. 34-40, http://dx.doi.org/10.1016/j.envint.2016.08.027. [36]

CBD (2008), *Gender Equality and the Convention on Biological Diversity: A COMPILATION OF DECISION TEXT.* [23]

Croppenstedt, A., M. Goldstein and N. Rosas (2013), "Gender and agriculture: Inefficiencies, segregation, and low productivity traps", *World Bank Research Observer*, Vol. 28/1, pp. 79-109, http://dx.doi.org/10.1093/wbro/lks024. [21]

EC (2019), *Females in the field: more women managing farms across Europe*, European Commission, https://ec.europa.eu/info/news/queens-frontage-women-farming-2019-mar-08_en (accessed on 13 November 2020). [59]

FAO (2021), *Realizing Women's Rights to Land in the Law - A Guide for Reporting on SDG Indicator 5.a.2*, FAO, Rome, http://www.fao.org/3/i8785en/I8785EN.pdf. [24]

FAO (2020), *Gendered impacts of COVID-19 and equitable policy responses in agriculture, food security and nutrition*, FAO, http://dx.doi.org/10.4060/ca9198en. [29]

FAO (2020), *The State of Food and Agriculture 2020*, FAO, http://dx.doi.org/10.4060/cb1447en. [3]

FAO (2019), *Good practices for integrating gender equality and women's empowerment in climate-smart agriculture programmes.*. [12]

FAO (2019), *Sustainable healthy diets*, FAO and WHO, http://dx.doi.org/10.4060/ca6640en. [56]

FAO (2018), *Realizing women's rights to land in the law. A guide for reporting on SDG indicator 5.a.2*, Food and Agriculture Organization of the United Nations, Rome. [58]

FAO (2016), "PART I Agriculture in Sub-Saharan Africa: Prospects and challenges for the next decade", http://dx.doi.org/10.1787/888933381341. [1]

FAO (2015), *The State of Food Insecurity in the World*, http://www.fao.org/publications. [18]

FAO (2014), *Rural Women in Eastern Europe and Central Asia*, http://www.fao.org/publications. [48]

FAO (2013), *Understanding and integrating gender issues into livestock projects and programmes : a checklist for practitioners.*, Food and Agriculture Organization of the United Nations. [52]

FAO (2011), *FAO in the 21st century : ensuring food security in a changing world.*, Food and Agriculture Organization of the United Nations. [40]

FAO (2011), "Prospects for the Environment", http://www.fao.org/3/y3557e/y3557e11.htm (accessed on 28 October 2020). [8]

FAO et al. (2020), *The State of Food Security and Nutrition in the World 2020: Transforming food systems for affordable healthy diets*, FAO, Rome, https://doi.org/10.4060/ca9692en. [5]

FIAN International (ed.) (2014), *Women Agricultural Workers and the Right to Adequate Food and Nutrition*, https://www.tni.org/files/download/women_agricultural_workers.pdf. [28]

Franić, R. and T. Kovačićek (2019), *The professional status of rural women in the EU*, European Parliament, Policy Department for Citizens' Rights and Constitutional Affairs. [57]

Garrigou, A. et al. (2020), "Critical review of the role of PPE in the prevention of risks related to agricultural pesticide use", *Safety Science*, Vol. 123, http://dx.doi.org/10.1016/j.ssci.2019.104527. [33]

Global Coffee Platform (GCP) (2018), *Gender Equality analysis in Colombia's coffee sector - Voices of men and women engaged in coffee growing and their organizations*, http://www.globalcoffeeplatform.org. [16]

Group, W. (ed.) (2021), *World Bank Development Indicators*, https://databank.worldbank.org/source/world-development-indicators. [15]

Henry, C. and J. Adams (2018), *Spotlight on Sexual Violence and Harassment in Commercial Agriculture: Lower and Middle Income Countries*, ILO, Rome, https://www.ilo.org/wcmsp5/groups/public/---dgreports/---inst/documents/publication/wcms_630672.pdf. [27]

Howard, P. and W. Cuijpers (2013), *Gender and the management and conservation of plant biodiversity*, https://www.researchgate.net/publication/40792278. [50]

Human Rights Watch (2020), "My Fear is Losing Everything", *The Climate Crisis and First Nations' Right to Food in Canada*. [11]

ILOSTAT (2021), *ILOSTAT*, ILO, https://ilostat.ilo.org/. [14]

IPCC (2019), "Summary for Policymakers", in Shukla, P. et al. (eds.), *Climate Change and Land: an IPCC special report on climate change, desertification, land degradation, sustainable land management, food security, and greenhouse gas fluxes in terrestrial ecosystems*. [7]

Kennedy, G. et al. (2017), "Food biodiversity for healthy, diverse diets", in Biodiversity International (ed.), *Food Mainstreaming Agrobiodiversity in Sustainable Food Systems: Scientific Foundations for an Agrobiodiversity Index*. [43]

Menon, N., Y. Van der Meulen Rodgers and A. Kennedy (2017), "Land Reform and Welfare in Vietnam: Why Gender of the Land-Rights Holder Matters", *Journal of International Development*, Vol. 29/4, pp. 454-472, http://dx.doi.org/10.1002/jid.3203. [49]

Mrema, E. et al. (2017), "Pesticide Exposure and Health Problems Among Female Horticulture Workers in Tanzania", *Environmental Health Insights*, Vol. 11, http://dx.doi.org/10.1177/1178630217715237. [32]

OECD (2021), "The triple challenge", in *Making Better Policies for Food Systems*, OECD Publishing, Paris, https://dx.doi.org/10.1787/edf73cce-en. [13]

OECD (2020), *Biodiversity and the economic response to COVID-19: Ensuring a green and resilient recovery*. [10]

OECD (2020), "Making the Green Recovery work for jobs, income and growth", *OECD Policy Responses to Coronavirus (COVID-19)*, https://doi.org/10.1787/a505f3e7-en. [9]

OECD (2020), *Women at the Core of the Fight Against COVID-19 Crisis*, OECD publishing, Paris, https://www.oecd.org/coronavirus/policy-responses/women-at-the-core-of-the-fight-against-covid-19-crisis-553a8269/. [61]

OECD (2019), *Agricultural Policy Monitoring and Evaluation 2019*, OECD Publishing, Paris, https://dx.doi.org/10.1787/39bfe6f3-en. [60]

OECD (2016), "Unleashing the green growth potential of integrated pest management", in *Farm Management Practices to Foster Green Growth*, OECD Publishing, Paris, https://dx.doi.org/10.1787/9789264238657-6-en. [55]

OECD/FAO (2020), *OECD-FAO Agricultural Outlook 2020-2029*, OECD Publishing, Paris/Food and Agriculture Organization of the United Nations, Rome, https://dx.doi.org/10.1787/1112c23b-en. [6]

OECD/FAO (2016), *OECD-FAO Guidance for Responsible Agricultural Supply Chains*, OECD Publishing, Paris, https://dx.doi.org/10.1787/9789264251052-en. [47]

OECD/WTO (2019), *Aid for Trade at a Glance 2019: Economic Diversification and Empowerment*, OECD Publishing, Paris, https://dx.doi.org/10.1787/18ea27d8-en. [41]

Perez, C. et al. (2015), "How resilient are farming households and communities to a changing climate in Africa? A gender-based perspective", *Global Environmental Change*, Vol. 34, pp. 95-107, http://dx.doi.org/10.1016/j.gloenvcha.2015.06.003. [39]

Quisumbing, A., N. Kumar and J. Behrman (2017), "Do shocks affect men's and women's assets differently? Evidence from Bangladesh and Uganda", *Development Policy Review*, Vol. 36/1, pp. 3-34, http://dx.doi.org/10.1111/dpr.12235. [30]

RAN (2019), *Sujetos de Núcleos Agrarios Certificados y No Certificados - Estadística con Perspectiva de Género*, http://www.ran.gob.mx/ran/indic_gen/nucag-certynocert-resultados-2020.pdf. [25]

Rapsomanikis, G. (2015), *Food and Agriculture Organization of the United Nations Rome*, http://www.fao.org/publications. [2]

Sethuraman, K. and N. Duvvury (2007), "The nexus of gender discrimination with malnutrition: an introduction", *Economic and Political Weekly, Sameeksha Tust, Mumbai; India*, Vol. 42, pp. 49-53. [20]

Shewamene, Z., T. Dune and C. Smith (2020), "Use of traditional and complementary medicine for maternal health and wellbeing by African migrant women in Australia: a mixed method study", *BMC complementary medicine and therapies*, Vol. 20/1, p. 60, http://dx.doi.org/10.1186/s12906-020-2852-6. [54]

Subrahmanyeswari, B. and M. Chander (2013), *Integrating indigenous knowledge of farmers for sustainable organic farming: An assessment in Uttarakhand state of India*. [53]

TEEB (2015), *TEEB for Agriculture & Food Interim Report*, United Nations Environment Programme, Geneva. [42]

Thundiyil, J. et al. (2008), "Acute pesticide poisoning: a proposed classification tool", *Bulletin of the World Health Organization*, Vol. 86/3, pp. 161-240. [31]

UN Women (2019), "Facts and Figures: Economic Empowerment". [4]

UNDP (2012), *Gender and Climate Change Africa*. [19]

UNDP (2011), *Chemicals and gender Energy & Environment Practice Gender Mainstreaming Guidance Series Chemicals Management*. [35]

UNEP (2016), *Global gender and environment outlook*. [45]

Vernooy, R. et al. (2017), "The roles of community seed banks in climate change adaption", *Development in Practice*, Vol. 27/3, pp. 316-327, http://dx.doi.org/10.1080/09614524.2017.1294653. [51]

Wang, W. et al. (2017), "Gender differences in pesticide use", *Science of The Total Environment*, Vol. 590-591, pp. 22-28, http://dx.doi.org/10.1016/j.scitotenv.2017.03.053. [34]

Watts, M. (2013), *Breast Cancer, Pesticides and YOU!*, Pesticide Action Network Asia and the Pacific (PAN AP), http://www.panap.net. [38]

Watts, M. (2007), *Pesticides & Breast Cancer: A Wake up Call*, Pesticide Action Network Asia & the Pacific (PAN AP). [37]

Wen, J. (ed.) (2020), *Gender-based violence and environment linkages: The violence of inequality*, IUCN, International Union for Conservation of Nature, http://dx.doi.org/10.2305/iucn.ch.2020.03.en. [26]

Winniefridah, M. and M. Manuku (2013), *Traditional Science of Seed and Crop Yield Preservation: Exploring the Contributions of Women to Indigenous Knowledge Systems in Zimbabwe*. [44]

World Bank (2020), "Agriculture and Food", https://www.worldbank.org/en/topic/agriculture/overview (accessed on 28 October 2020). [22]

Notes

[1] http://www.fao.org/fileadmin/templates/nr/sustainability_pathways/docs/Factsheet_SMALLHOLDERS.pdf

7 Women and SDG 6 – Clean Water and Sanitation: Ensure availability and sustainable management of water and sanitation for all

Lack of access to clean water, sanitation and hygiene affects mainly developing countries, particularly in Sub-Saharan Africa and South Asia. Women are disproportionately affected by growing water scarcity and inadequate sanitation, both because of their specific hygiene needs and their role in collecting water. Tackling discrimination and social norms in relation to water management would allow societies to leverage the role of women in better-functioning water systems, wider access and inclusive economic benefits for communities.

7.1. Key findings

This chapter provides a description of the links between gender equality and water management and proposes some key actions to improve access to water and adequate sanitation facilities. Its main findings include the following:

- Currently more than 2 billion people live with restricted access to water resources. By 2050, at least one in four people (2.8 billion) are likely to live in a country affected by severe water shortages.
- In much of the developing world, women are mainly responsible for collecting water, a task with a high opportunity cost and risk of potential health problems. Inadequate sanitation decreases the likelihood that girls attend school, particularly during menstruation.
- In many developing countries, the burden placed on women and girls by exposure to unsafe water, sanitation and hygiene (WASH) services is multifaceted. Travel to water resources and culturally defined expectations in relation to water management can leave women vulnerable to gender-based violence.
- Better gender-disaggregated data is needed on women's access to clean water and sanitation, as well as on the extent of women's involvement and impact in water, sanitation and hygiene decision making.
- More gender-sensitive assessment of water management projects, in particular shared river flows, lakes and other sources of fresh drinking water and irrigation, is needed. Women can be vulnerable to the effects of dam projects, including across borders.
- Development co-operation actions, including aid disbursement, should integrate a gender dimension into water management projects, in particular through gender impact assessments.
- Women's knowledge of local natural resources and household water management skills can be leveraged to shape conservation efforts. Governance arrangements for water management projects should be reviewed to promote gender equality in decision making and ensure consultation of groups representing women's voices.

7.2. Key interlinkages between gender equality, sustainable water management and other SDGs

Water scarcity is a growing problem that will be exacerbated by population growth, increased urbanisation, pollution and climate change. It is estimated that currently more than two billion people live with restricted access to water resources, and that by 2050, at least one in four people (2.8 billion) are likely to live in a country affected by severe water shortages (UN-Water and FAO, 2007[1]) (UNDP, 2006[2]). Rising populations' demand for water goes hand in hand with increased demand for food. With 70% of the world's freshwater used for agriculture, feeding a planet of 9 billion people by 2050 is estimated to require a 15% increase in water withdrawals. By 2050, it is estimated that world demand for water will exceed supply by 40% (World Bank, 2016[3]).

At the same time, and despite progress made over the past 20 years, 30% of the global population lacks access to safe water, and over 50% to safe sanitation and hygiene facilities (UNICEF and WHO, 2019[4]). These issues are more prominent in developing countries, particularly in Sub-Saharan Africa and South Asia (WHO and UNICEF, 2017[5]).

Limited access to clean water, sanitation and hygiene (SDG 6) is usually linked to poverty (SDG 1) and hunger (SDG 2). Such access is essential for well-being, affecting health and education outcomes (SDG 3 and SDG 4), and is a key determinant for sustainable food production, industrial development and urbanisation (SDGs 2, 9 and 11). SDG 6 is also linked to SDG 15, in particular Target 15.1 on conservation and sustainable use of freshwater, as well as to climate-related hazards and natural disasters (SDG 13).

Humanity faces a dismal future if it is unable to tackle climate change and properly manage water resources. An estimated 1.6 billion people will be at risk from floods by 2050, especially in coastal cities. Meanwhile, increasing droughts will generate tensions across users in particular urban dwellers, as in the recent cases of Rio de Janeiro, São Paulo and Cape Town (C40 Cities, 2020[6]).

Water resources and water scarcity are also strongly linked to energy production and consumption, and hence SDG 7. The expected increase in energy demand over the coming years – with electricity consumption expected to rise by 80% by 2040 – could further disrupt water-stressed areas around the globe. This could be especially problematic in the case of low-carbon technologies, which, if not properly managed, could increase water stress or be limited by it. For instance, while wind and solar photovoltaic (PV) require very little water, other technologies, such as biofuels, concentrating solar power (CSP), carbon capture and nuclear power are relatively water-intensive. At the same time, provision of freshwater from surface water, groundwater or desalination, its transportation and distribution, and the collection and treatment of water and wastewater all depend on energy. Nevertheless, achieving access to clean water and sanitation worldwide would only add about 1% to global energy demand in 2030 (IEA, 2018[7]).

There are well-established linkages between women, sanitation, hygiene and health, especially in low-income countries (Bouzid, Cumming and Hunter, 2018[8]). Women more often face the negative health effects of poor water quality and untreated wastewater because of household roles such as cooking, cleaning, and childcare. Additionally, women are particularly affected by lack of access to clean water and sanitation due to hygienic needs and increased vulnerability to infection around menstruation and reproduction (Graham, Hirai and Kim, 2016[9]) (Unilever Domestos, 2013[10]).

Women are also highly dependent on efficient water management, though they are rarely included in decision making in the relevant sectors. Women could be important actors in driving more sustainable use of water resources, both in developed and developing countries, due to their roles in agriculture and domestic labour. Yet, currently only SDG Target 6.1, on universal and equitable access to safe and affordable drinking water for all, and Target 6.2, on equitable sanitation and hygiene, are linked to women and girls. It should be noted, however, that SDG Target 3.9 calls for reducing the number of deaths and illnesses from water pollution and contamination, specifically referencing exposure to unsafe water, sanitation and hygiene (WASH) services.

7.3. Key water-related challenges for women

7.3.1. Inadequate access to clean water

Social norms in many countries are more likely to impose a water management role for women. The UN estimates that women and girls are responsible for water collection in 80% of households without access to water on premises (UNEP, 2016[11]). In a study of 48 countries, adult women and girls were found to be responsible for water collection more than twice as often as their male counterparts in Sub-Saharan Africa and Asia (UN, 2010[12]). Inequality in terms of water management was particularly high in rural sub-Saharan Africa, where adult women fetch water in 63% of households compared to 11% of adult men (Figure 7.1) (UN, 2010[12]). Women with responsibilities as household and family caretakers are often severely affected by inadequate access to water and sanitation.

According to the UN, in a single day in 25 sub-Saharan African countries, women spend 16 million hours collecting water – often to the detriment of education or paid work – compared to only 6 million hours spent by men and 4 million hours spent by children. There are also differences in water usage, with women prioritising domestic and health and hygiene needs, while men prioritise water use for farming and raising livestock (UNEP, 2016[11]).

Figure 7.1. Women are overly responsible for water collection (latest data available 2005-13)

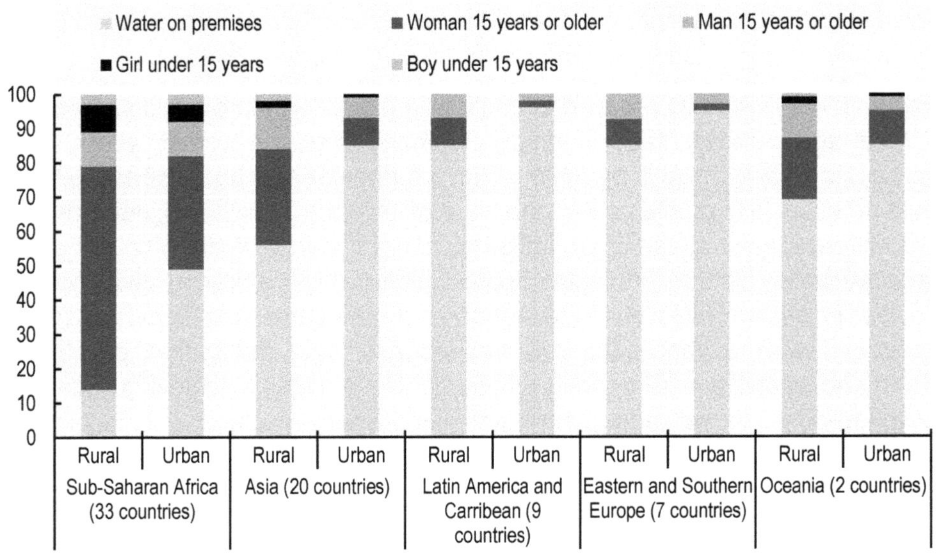

Note: Unweighted averages of the amount of time spent collecting water. The number in parenthesis indicates the number of countries averaged. Data presented by Millennium Development Goal (MGD) regions.
Source: United Nations, 2015. The World's Women 2015: Trends and Statistics. New York: United Nations, Department of Economic and Social Affairs, Statistics Division. Sales No. E.15.XVII.8, Statistical Annex. (United Nations, 2015[13]).

The lack of safe water makes women and girls vulnerable to gender-based-violence (GBV) in much of the developing world. Poor water connections force women to walk long distances in sometimes unsafe circumstances. Women have reported systematic violent attacks and sexual abuse while completing these domestic tasks. Women and girls also face the threat of GBV when walking to shared sanitation facilities. Fear of sexual violence can restrict freedom of movement and affect equal opportunities (Kayser et al., 2019[14]). Moreover, failure of women to fulfil their socially defined expectations in relation to fetching water greatly increases the risk of experiencing violence at home if men feel they have not delivered in their duties (Pommells et al., 2018[15]).

Women's health is also at risk where water work is concerned. In societies where women are responsible for collecting water, carrying heavy buckets of 30 to 40 kg on average has detrimental effects on the spine and can lead to deformation and disease. Water collection expends 30% of daily calorie intake, thus putting women and girls with poor nutritional intake at risk (Abid et al., 2018[16]).

Women suffer disproportionately from desiccation and its consequences, as they are often left to take care of the household while men migrate for work or look for job opportunities elsewhere (International Organization for Migration, 2020[17]). For instance, water scarcity resulting from the Aral Sea Crisis led to an increase in maternal morbidity and mortality, infertility, and pregnancy and foetal development complications (Ataniyazova, 2003[18]). Chronic exposure to high concentrations of minerals and toxic pollutants through unsafe drinking water was found to cause dangerous concentrations of heavy metals and pesticides in the blood of pregnant women, umbilical cords and breast milk in affected areas (Wæhler and Sveberg Dietrichs, 2017[19]).

Agriculture is increasingly feminised, with women accounting for 43 % of all farmworkers in Asia (more than 50% in Southeast and East Asia) and 47% in Africa (Agarwal, 2018[20]); (FAO, IFAD and ILO, 2010[21]). Women are also primarily responsible for subsistence farming (Sections 6.3.2, 11.3.2, and 14.5.1). Since agriculture accounts for most freshwater use, growing water restrictions will put increasing pressure on many women who depend on subsistence farming for their food and income. In many countries, women are also affected by insecure water rights (UN WomenWatch, 2009[22]). As a result, mismanagement of water resources, including depletion due to climate change, disproportionately affects women who already devote high amounts of time providing for their families.

7.3.2. Inadequate sanitation facilities

Access to sanitation facilities is of greater importance for women due to both health concerns and cultural norms. Environmental sanitation plays a major role in the transmission of endemic diseases, such as malaria, that disproportionally affect women, and particularly pregnant women (Shapiro-Mendoza et al., 2017[23]). Improved sanitation facilities can reduce mortality caused by diarrhoeal diseases, severely affecting both girls and boys (UNICEF, 2021[24]). Cultural biases favouring caring for boys over girls may lead to differentiated impacts for them (Jarman et al., 2018[25]). Gender-specific sanitation issues are not limited to health concerns, however; in countries such as India, where sanitation facilities are not easily accessible and open defecation is more common, privacy concerns force women to wait until after dark, negatively affecting their well-being and comfort (Saleem, Burdett and Heaslip, 2019[26]).

The availability of sanitation facilities also influences school attendance. According to UNICEF, in 2013, only 47% of schools in least-developed countries had adequate sanitation facilities. Inadequate sanitation, particularly during menstruation, decreases the likelihood that girls attend school (UNICEF, 2015[27]). In a study on the relation between access to adequate sanitation facilities, menstruation and school absenteeism in India, 40% of girls were found to remain absent from school during their menstruation due to lack of clean toilets, clean water, privacy, soap and sanitary supplies (Vashisht et al., 2018[28]).

Inadequate sanitation and water access in the context of natural disasters and emergencies also has a gendered aspect, as women often carry a disproportionate burden for restoring basic WASH services. For instance, following the 2017 hurricane in Puerto Rico, when technological appliances and sanitation facilities such as water pipes, washing machines and toilets became unavailable, women and men fell back into traditional methods of performing household tasks. This meant that while men contributed to water transportation, women took on increased domestic work including collecting and cleaning with rainwater, bathing children with water from buckets and emptying improvised toilets. In the absence of toilet facilities, women also reported facing privacy challenges as opposed to men who relieved themselves in the open (Oxfam, 2018[29]). While humanitarian interventions often focus on restoring WASH infrastructure and services, they sometimes ignore the differentiated effects on women and on their domestic work, which is more difficult to measure, yet can be alleviated by providing financial and physical tools that ease domestic tasks.

7.3.3. Transboundary waters and gender mainstreaming

Transboundary basins cover over half of our planet's land surface, account for about 60% of global freshwater flow and provide a home for over 40% of the world's population (UNECE, n.d.[30]). Co-operation between and among riparian countries could therefore be key for achieving SDG 6. More specifically, SDG Target 6.5 calls for the implementation "by 2030 [of] integrated water resources management at all levels including through transboundary cooperation as appropriate". Taking into consideration a gender sensitive approach during the design and implementation of countries' relevant strategies, policies and programmes, while considering each transboundary basin's own topographic characteristics and particular features, may have a positive effect on co-operation.

As an example, the UNESCO-IHP Governance of Groundwater Resources in Transboundary Aquifers (GGRETA) project applies a gender-sensitive assessment approach on three transboundary aquifers located in Central America, Southern Africa and Central Asia. In the case of the Stampriet Transboundary Aquifer System (Botswana, Namibia and South Africa) the project focuses on providing science-based gender data. For the Ocotepeque-Citala Transboundary Aquifer (El Salvador and Honduras) the focus was on examining gender issues as part of stakeholder involvement in water governance (UN and UNESCO,

2018[31]). The project is linked to the UNESCO World Water Assessment Programme (WWAP), mentioned below (Section 7.4).

7.4. The role of women in sustainable water management

The role of women in effective water management has been recognised in global water fora for decades.[1] Particularly in developing countries, women are the primary water decision makers at the household level. United Nations Development Programme (UNDP) research shows that communities where women are included in water management achieve measurably better outcomes, including better-functioning water systems, expanded access and economic and environmental benefits (UNDP, 2006[32]). Enhancing women's access to safe water has positive effects on social inclusion, poverty alleviation, health, environmental sustainability and food security. Involving women in water and sanitation management, taking their needs into account, and including them in budgeting decisions can help orientate scarce funding towards sustainable solutions that benefit communities as a whole (Sandys, 2005[33])

Women's knowledge of local natural resources and skills in household water management could be leveraged to shape conservation efforts through awareness-building campaigns (OECD, 2018[34]); (Benedict and Hussein, 2019[35]). Moreover, their experience in primary caregiving puts women in a unique position to instil water-saving values for future generations. A 2006 study on water and sanitation projects conducted by the International Water and Sanitation Centre (IRC) across 15 countries found that projects that ensured the full participation of women at all stages were more sustainable and effective than those that did not (UNESCO, 2006[36]). Evidence from 121 rural water supply projects studied by the World Bank shows that the projects are 6 to 7 times more effective than others when women are involved (World Bank, 1995[37]). Hence, women should be acknowledged as key agents in water management, especially in the context of climate change mitigation.

UNDP research on 44 water projects across Asia and Africa shows that communities use water services more sustainably when both men and women are engaged in policy-design. When faced with scarcity in these communities, women are key in ensuring equity and justice in resource management as well as peace and stability (Trivedi, 2018[38]).

There is also evidence of similar positive outcomes when women assume leadership roles in the water sector. For instance, in Uganda, gender strategies developed by Maria Mutagamba during her term as Minister of State for Water ensured women's role in decision-making committees and led to an increase in access to safe water from 51% to 61% in two years (Government of Uganda Ministry of Water and Environment, 2010[39]). Similarly, in Tanzania, women altruistically share water resources regardless of availability, further reinforcing differentiated management of the commons (Lecoutere, D'Exelle and Van Campenhout, 2015[40]).

Despite these positive examples, on a broader scale women are marginalised in water governance and have poor access to agricultural inputs and productive resources (e.g. irrigation, technology, credit), which can have implications for sustainable water management (Njie and Ndiaye, n.d.[41]) (Sadoff, Borgomeo and De Waal, 2017[42]). Globally, women comprise less than 17% of the hygiene, sanitation and water force (Spencer et al., 2017[43]).

The link between gender equality, climate change and water resources management is addressed by UNESCO and its World Water Assessment Programme (WWAP). The 2020 World Water Development Report co-ordinated by WWAP highlights the differentiated effects of droughts, waterborne diseases and water contamination between women and girls, and men. It also argues for the need to collect better gender-disaggregated data on climate change to support gender-sensitive policy solutions. Increasing women's participation in decision making around water management is also highlighted, as it can lead to gender mainstreaming in disaster risk reduction strategies (UNESCO and UN-Water, 2020[44]).

Looking at the proportion of climate-related aid that also supports the achievement of gender equality, the water supply and sanitation sector falls second to agriculture, forestry and fishing, with 46% targeting gender equality as a significant or principal objective, on average per year in 2018-19 (GENDERNET, 2021[45]). Gender equality is increasingly becoming integrated in climate-related aid to water. A five-year project in Mexico, supported by the Inter-American Development Bank's Multilateral Investment Fund, led to the avoidance of 212 000 tons of CO_2 emissions by improving the sanitary facilities in about 17 000 households. The project also led to the elimination of water losses and to a 60% reduction of energy costs (electricity and gas) used to heat water. Fifty-two women, trained in plumbing, were the ones who carried all technical works (BID, 2016[46]).

With rising tensions surrounding water-resources, ensuring women's equality and role in water management is essential for national security and social justice. Both intra and interstate conflict could be avoided if such conflict is targeted at the source, empowering women as necessary (Carpioli et al., 2007[47]). Women's engagement in cross-country water negotiations can bring about agreements, supporting long-term political stability and sustainable growth. Peace and democracy are challenged in countries with high gender inequality (Hudson and den Boer, 2004[48]); (Caprioli, 2004[49]). Improved access to water for agriculture and domestic consumption will allow women more time for income-generating activities and to become more involved in governance and policy-making structures (FAO, 2016[50]).

Acknowledging women's role in water management also means working with local communities to protect women from gender-based violence. Better infrastructure that ensures water points are local, well regulated and have community-managed pathways that provide safe routes for women when fetching water could help alleviate GBV risk (Pommells et al., 2018[15]).

While the gendered effects of water scarcity are mainly a concern in developing countries, some middle and high income countries also suffer from water stress. Engaging more women in the water sector can bring about more effective and sustainable water management. The Netherlands has been integrating gender equality in water management in both the public and private sectors. Of the ten companies handling the nations' drinking water supply, five CEOs are women, who themselves encourage other women to enter and pursue careers in water management (Women for Water Partnership, 2014[51]). Surveys in industrialised countries also show that women are more responsible water users than men in household settings (OECD, 2014[52]).

7.5. Key actions for advancing the agenda and ongoing work

A number of actions can be taken to better mainstream gender into the water agenda:

- As with other SDGs, the application of a gender equality perspective to SDG 6 is hampered by a lack of readily available quantitative evidence. There is a clear need to breach the data gap, building on other international organisations' efforts such as UNESCO's World Water Assessment Programme.
- Development co-operation actions, including aid disbursement, should integrate gender considerations into water management projects and ensure consultation and joint participation of communities where projects are developed.
- Considering the high stakes, governance arrangements for water management projects should be reviewed to promote gender equality in decision making and ensure consultation of groups representing women's voices. While this may already be the case in some OECD countries, it could be further promoted as guidance when implementing the OECD Recommendation on Water (OECD, n.d.[53]).
- Environmental and social assessments of large water management projects, including dam construction, should include a gender dimension.

References

Abid, Z. et al. (2018), "Detrimental Effects of Climate Change on Women", *Earth Systems and Environment*, Vol. 2/3, pp. 537-551, http://dx.doi.org/10.1007/s41748-018-0063-9. [16]

Agarwal, B. (2018), *The challenge of gender inequality*, Springer International Publishing, http://dx.doi.org/10.1007/s40888-018-0092-8. [20]

Ataniyazova, O. (2003), *Health and Ecological Consequences of the Aral Sea Crisis Panel III: Environmental Issues in the Aral Sea Basin Health and Ecological Consequences of the Aral Sea Crisis.* [18]

Benedict, S. and H. Hussein (2019), "An Analysis of Water Awareness Campaign Messaging in the Case of Jordan: Water Conservation for State Security", *Water*, Vol. 11/6, http://dx.doi.org/10.3390/w11061156. [35]

BID (2016), *Informe sobre Efectividad en el Desarrollo*, Banco Interamericano de Desarrollo, https://publications.iadb.org/publications/spanish/document/Informe-sobre-efectividad-en-el-desarrollo-2016.pdf (accessed on 13 April 2021). [46]

Bouzid, M., O. Cumming and P. Hunter (2018), *What is the impact of water sanitation and hygiene in healthcare facilities on care seeking behaviour and patient satisfaction? A systematic review of the evidence from low-income and middleincome countries*, BMJ Publishing Group, http://dx.doi.org/10.1136/bmjgh-2017-000648. [8]

C40 Cities (2020), *The Future we don't want for cities - The heat is on*, https://www.c40.org/other/the-future-we-don-t-want-for-cities-the-heat-is-on. [6]

Caprioli, M. (2004), "Democracy and Human Rights versus Women's Security: A Contradiction?", *Security Dialogue*, Vol. 35/4, pp. 411-428, https://www.jstor.org/stable/26298581. [49]

Carpioli, M. et al. (2007), "Putting Women in Their Place", *Baker Center Journal of Applied Public Policy*, Vol. 1/1, http://trace.tennessee.edu/utk_bakecentpubs/2. [47]

FAO (2016), *How can women control water?*, Social Policies and Rural Institutions Division (ESP) - Land and Water Division (AGL), http://water.org/water-crisis/women-children-facts/. [50]

FAO, IFAD and ILO (2010), *Gender dimensions of agricultural and rural employment : differentiated pathways out of poverty : status, trends and gaps.*, Food and Agriculture Organization of the United Nations. [21]

GENDERNET (2021), *Development Finance for Gender Equality and Women's Empowerment: A 2021 Snapshot*, OECD DAC Network on Gender Equality, https://www.oecd.org/development/gender-development/Development-finance-for-gender-equality-2021.pdf (accessed on 6 April 2021). [45]

Government of Uganda Ministry of Water and Environment (2010), *WATER AND SANITATION SUB-SECTOR- Gender Strategy.* [39]

Graham, J., M. Hirai and S. Kim (2016), "An analysis of water collection labor among women and children in 24 sub-Saharan African countries", *PLoS ONE*, Vol. 11/6, http://dx.doi.org/10.1371/journal.pone.0155981. [9]

Hudson, V. and A. den Boer (2004), "Bare Branches: The Security Implications of Asia's Surplus Male Populations", *Japanese Journal of Political Science 5(02)* Cambridge, MA: The MIT Press, http://dx.doi.org/DOI: 10.1017/S146810990522162X. [48]

IEA (2018), *World Energy Outlook 2018*, International Energy Agency, Paris, https://dx.doi.org/10.1787/weo-2018-en. [7]

International Organization for Migration (2020), *World Migration Report 2020*, United Nations, Geneva, http://dx.doi.org/ISSN 1561-5502. [17]

Jarman, A. et al. (2018), "Sex and Gender Differences in Acute Pediatric Diarrhea: A Secondary Analysis of the DHAKA Study", *Journal of Epidemiology and Global Health*, Vol. 8/1-2, http://dx.doi.org/10.2991/j.jegh.2018.08.102. [25]

Kayser, G. et al. (2019), "Water, sanitation and hygiene: Measuring gender equality and empowerment", *Bulletin of the World Health Organization*, Vol. 97/6, pp. 438-440, http://dx.doi.org/10.2471/BLT.18.223305. [14]

Lecoutere, E., B. D'Exelle and B. Van Campenhout (2015), "Sharing Common Resources in Patriarchal and Status-Based Societies: Evidence from Tanzania", *Feminist Economics*, Vol. 21/3, pp. 142-167, http://dx.doi.org/10.1080/13545701.2015.1024274. [40]

Njie, N. and T. Ndiaye (n.d.), *Women and Agricultural Water Resource Management*, UN Chronicle, https://www.un.org/en/chronicle/article/women-and-agricultural-water-resource-management. [41]

OECD (2018), *Policy Coherence for Sustainable Development and Gender Equality: Fostering an Integrated Policy Agenda*, http://www.oecd.org/gov/gender-mainstreaming/policy-coherence-for-sustainable-development-and-gender-equality.pdf. [34]

OECD (2014), *Greening Household Behaviour: Overview from the 2011 Survey - Revised edition*, OECD Studies on Environmental Policy and Household Behaviour, OECD Publishing, Paris, https://dx.doi.org/10.1787/9789264214651-en. [52]

OECD (n.d.), *Recommendation of the Council on Water*. [53]

Oxfam (2018), "The Weight of Water on Women: The Long Wake of Hurricane Maria in Puerto Rico", https://www.oxfamamerica.org/explore/research-publications/research-backgrounder-wash-gender-report-puerto-rico/. [29]

Pommells, M. et al. (2018), *Gender Violence as a Water, Sanitation, and Hygene Risk: Uncovering Violence Against Women and Girls as it Pertains to Poor WaSH Access*, https://doi.org/10.1177/1077801218754410. [15]

Programme, U. (ed.) (2006), *Human development report 2006 : beyond scarcity : power, poverty and the global water crisis*, Palgrave Macmillan. [2]

Sadoff, C., E. Borgomeo and D. De Waal (2017), *Turbulent Waters. Pursuing Water Security in Fragile Contexts*, World Bank, Washington, http://www.worldbank.org/water. [42]

Saleem, M., T. Burdett and V. Heaslip (2019), "Health and social impacts of open defecation on women: A systematic review", *BMC Public Health*, Vol. 19/1, http://dx.doi.org/10.1186/s12889-019-6423-z. [26]

Sandys, E. (2005), *Women 2000 and beyond.* [33]

Shapiro-Mendoza, C. et al. (2017), *Morbidity and Mortality Weekly Report Pregnancy Outcomes After Maternal Zika Virus Infection During Pregnancy-U*, https://www.cdc.gov/zika/. [23]

Spencer, B. et al. (2017), "Case studies in co-benefits approaches to climate change mitigation and adaptation", *Journal of Environmental Planning and Management*, Vol. 60/4, pp. 647-667, http://dx.doi.org/10.1080/09640568.2016.1168287. [43]

Trivedi, A. (2018), "Women Are the Secret Weapon for Better Water Management", *World Resources Institute*, https://www.wri.org/blog/2018/10/women-are-secret-weapon-better-water-management. [38]

UN (2010), *The Right to Water*, United Nations Human Rights, UN Habitat and World Health Organisation. [12]

UN WomenWatch (2009), "Women and Climate Factsheet", pp. 1-11, https://www.un.org/womenwatch/feature/climate_change/downloads/Women_and_Climate_Change_Factsheet.pdf. [22]

UNDP (2006), *Mainstreaming Gender in Water Management.* [32]

UNECE (n.d.), *Many more operational arrangements for transboundary water cooperation needed across the world, shows 2021 UN-Water SDG6 progress report*, https://unece.org/circular-economy/press/many-more-operational-arrangements-transboundary-water-cooperation-needed (accessed on 8 April 2021). [30]

UNEP (2016), *Global gender and environment outlook*, United Nations Environment Programme, http://dx.doi.org/10.18356/0b979453-en. [11]

UNESCO (2006), *Gender, Water and Sanitation: A Policy Brief*, http://www.wsscc.org. [36]

UNESCO and UN-Water (2020), *The United Nations World Water Development Report 2020: Water and Climate Change*, UNESCO, Paris. [44]

UNICEF (2021), *Diarrhoea*, https://data.unicef.org/topic/child-health/diarrhoeal-disease/ (accessed on 13 April 2021). [24]

UNICEF (2015), "Advancing WASH in Schools Monitoring", pp. 1-68, https://www.unicef.org/wash/schools/files/Advancing_WASH_in_Schools_Monitoring(1).pdf. [27]

UNICEF and WHO (2019), *Progress on household drinking water, sanitation and hygiene 2000-2017. Special focus on inequalities*, United Nations Children's Fund (UNICEF) and World Health Organization (WHO), New York, https://washdata.org. [4]

Unilever Domestos, W. (2013), *We Can't Wait A report on sAnitAtion And hygiene for women And girls Photo: WSSCC/Saskia Castelein.* [10]

United Nations (2015), *The World's Women 2015: Trends and Statistics*, United Nations, Department of Economic and Social Affairs, Statistics Division, http://dx.doi.org/10.18356/9789210573719. [13]

UN and UNESCO (2018), *Progress on Transboundary Water Cooperation 2018 Global baseline for SDG indicator 6.5.2*, United Nations and United Nations Educational, Scientific and Cultural Organization. [31]

UN-Water and FAO (2007), *Coping with water scarcity - Challenge of the twenty-first century.* [1]

Vashisht, A. et al. (2018), "School absenteeism during menstruation amongst adolescent girls in Delhi, India.", *Journal of family & community medicine*, Vol. 25/3, pp. 163-168, http://dx.doi.org/10.4103/jfcm.JFCM_161_17. [28]

Wæhler, T. and E. Sveberg Dietrichs (2017), *The vanishing Aral Sea: health consequences of an environmental disaster | Tidsskrift for Den norske legeforening*. [19]

WHO and UNICEF (2017), *Progress on drinking water, sanitation and hygiene: 2017 update and SDG Baselines*, World Health Organization (WHO) and the United Nations Children's Fund (UNICEF), Geneva, http://apps.who.int/bookorders. [5]

Women for Water Partnership (2014), *Five women leading a male dominated water management world in the Netherlands*, 7 Women, Water, and Leadership, ADB Briefs No.24, https://www.womenforwater.org/five-women-leading-a-male-dominated-water-management-world-in-the-netherlands.html. [51]

World Bank (2016), *Annual freshwater withdrawals, agriculture (% of total freshwater withdrawal)*, https://data.worldbank.org/indicator/er.h2o.fwag.zs. [3]

World Bank (1995), "The Contribution of People's Participation Evidencefrom 121 Rural Water Supply Projects", *Environmentally Suistainable Development Occasional Paper Series No. 1 ESD The World Bank, Washington, D.C.*. [37]

Notes

[1] The importance of involving both women and men in the management of water and sanitation has been recognised at the global level, in the 1977 United Nations Water Conference at Mar del Plata, the International Drinking Water and Sanitation Decade (1981-90) and the 1992 International Conference on Water and the Environment, which explicitly recognised the central role of women in the provision, management and safeguarding of water. Reference to the involvement of women in water management is also made in Agenda 21 (Chapter 18) and the Johannesburg Plan of Implementation.

8 Women and SDG 7 – Affordable and Clean Energy: Ensure access to affordable, reliable, sustainable and modern energy for all

Energy poverty is a worldwide phenomenon with a strong gender dimension. In developing countries, lack of access to energy is an obstacle to women's and girls' well-being and economic opportunities, as it strongly affects their living conditions and time-use, and undermines their educational and economic opportunities. Gender energy inequality may be further accentuated by national energy policies and labour market patterns. Seeing as energy is the primary source of GHG emissions, extending access to green energy and promoting affordability can therefore be central to the achievement of more inclusive and sustainable development. Women can also play a key role in the green energy transition as responsible consumers, particularly in the household, but also in business and policy making. Women's empowerment and leadership in the energy sector could help accelerate the transition to a low-carbon economy by promoting clean energy and more efficient energy use, as well as help to tackle energy poverty. The "just transition" should also include a gender perspective, to guarantee equal opportunities for both men and women in the workforce.

8.1. Key findings

Access to affordable, sustainable and clean energy is a precondition for gender equality and well-being. Currently, gender gaps in energy are substantial across the world. The key findings and recommendations of this chapter include the following:

- Seven hundred seventy million people, about three-quarters of them in Sub-Saharan Africa, lack access to electricity. Despite an improvement in recent years, data from the International Energy Agency shows that COVID-19 is reversing this positive trend in Africa after six years of steady decline and the rise in poverty levels worldwide may have already made basic electricity services unaffordable for more than 100 million previous electricity users in Asia and Africa (IEA, 2020[1]); (OECD, 2020[2]).
- Energy poverty is a worldwide phenomenon, although it is most intense in developing countries and especially affects women, who are the main users and producers of household energy. In some OECD countries, it is estimated that up to 30% of households live in energy poverty, limiting women's and girls' access to education and economic opportunities, and disproportionally exposing them to health risks.
- Women can play a central role in the transition to clean energy as consumers, helping to shift energy consumption - and by leading transformative change in the energy industry. Energy is a largely male-dominated sector, although women are in general better represented in the renewable energy sector.
- Achieving greater gender diversity in company boards and senior management positions could help to accelerate the green transition, as it would allow for a more effective integration of environmental and gender goals.
- More systematic evidence is needed on the linkages between gender equality and clean energy goals and for aligning energy policies with the needs of women, especially in countries with a high incidence of energy poverty.

8.2. Interlinkages between gender equality, affordable and clean energy (SDG 7), and other SDGs

According to the IEA, 770 million people, about three-quarters of them in Sub-Saharan Africa, lack access to electricity (IEA, 2020[3]). About 3 billion people around the world lack access to clean-cooking solutions and are exposed to dangerous levels of air pollution from using wood, coal, charcoal or animal waste for cooking and heating (WHO, 2018[4]).

Sustainable Development Goal 7, affordable and clean energy, sets targets to ensure universal access to affordable, reliable and modern energy services (Target 7.1). It highlights the need to expand the share of clean renewable energy (Target 7.2) and emphasizes the importance of improving energy efficiency (Target 7.3). The SDG framework acknowledges the need to increase substantially the share of renewable energy in the global energy mix by 2030. The rationale behind acknowledges the differentiated impacts that energy poverty and pollution can have on women and children (UN, 2016[5]).

Sustainable Development Goal 7 interacts with many other SDGs. Energy is needed for many elements of basic well-being, from heating and cooking, to education (SDG 4), health (SDG 3), and transport, and hence for labour market participation. As lack of access to energy creates a development and poverty trap, ensuring affordable energy for all also supports the achievement of SDG 1 (eliminate poverty). The COVID-19 pandemic has also shown that energy access is key for healthcare provision and well-being (SDG 3), as affordable electricity is needed to keep people connected at home and to run life-saving equipment in hospitals (Ogunbiyi D, 2020[6]). A growing supply of renewable, clean energy is also essential for achieving sustainable economic growth (SDG 8), building sustainable cities (SDG 11), ensuring sustainable consumption and production patterns (SDG 12) as well as the transition towards a low-carbon economy and hence, the achievement of SDG 13 on climate action.

8.3. Gendered effects of energy poverty

Energy poverty is a worldwide phenomenon. Though its definition varies according to context, location and population, it affects both the Global North and the Global South. In most advanced economies, energy poverty is a matter of affordability rather than access. In least-advanced economies, considerations of availability, access and reliability precede those of affordability and sustainability. In both cases, energy poverty has a strong gender equality dimension.

Energy poverty is an issue for OECD countries. In the United States, it is estimated that around 30% of households live in energy poverty (USEA, 2019[7]). In the European Union, in 2012, more than 54 million people, almost 11% of the population, had difficulty heating their homes and paying their utility bills on time. Women, especially single mothers and elderly single women, were the most affected due to lower income, physiological characteristics and behavioural patterns (Clancy, Feenstra and Daskalova, 2017[8]), (EIGE, 2020[9]).

In developing countries, lack of access to energy is an obstacle to women's and girls' well-being and economic opportunities. Women and girls in rural areas spend a large part of their day collecting fuelwood, which translates not only into perpetuating poverty and inequality (Dutta, Kooijman and Cecelski, 2017[10]), but also into lost opportunities for education and remunerated labour (OECD, 2018[11]). This is the case throughout much of Africa, with particularly high figures in Sierra Leone, Niger and Cameroon (see Figure 8.1) (IEA, 2017[12]). In India, Bangladesh and Nepal, women spend up to 20 or more hours per week collecting biomass fuel for cooking and heating (Bloomfield, 2014[13]).

Figure 8.1. Average number of hours spent collecting fuel per day per household in selected countries in Africa (2015)

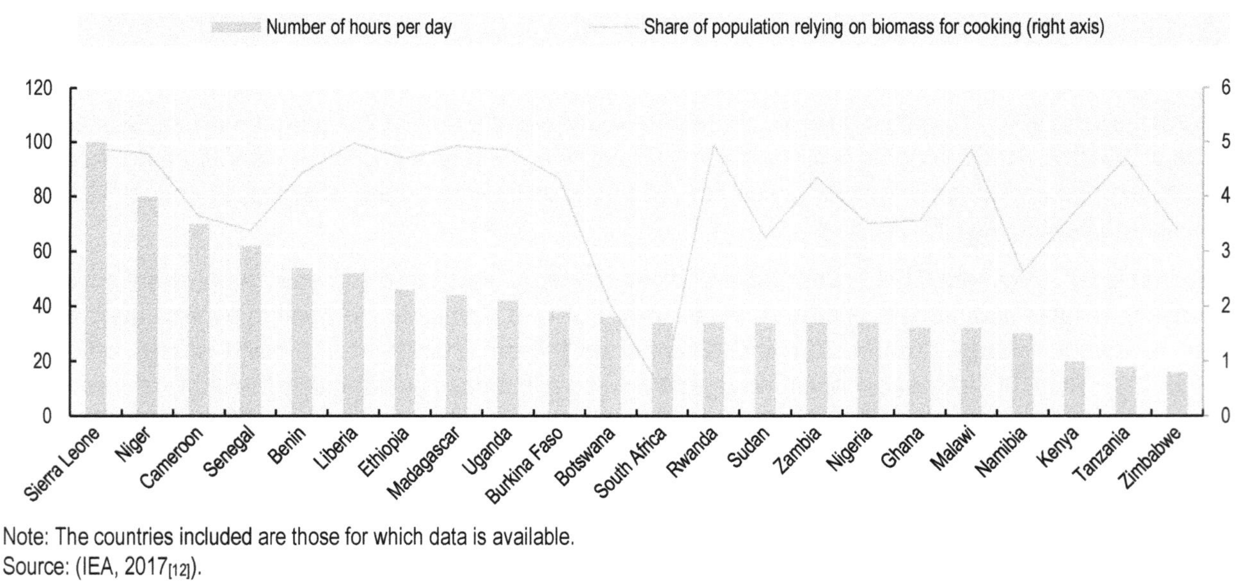

Note: The countries included are those for which data is available.
Source: (IEA, 2017[12]).

The time spent by girls on gathering biomass fuel limits their access to education. Household electrification improves school attendance for girls and, in the long-run, women's employment opportunities (Lewis et al., 2013[14]). Research in Brazil shows that girls in rural areas with access to electricity are 59% more likely to complete primary education by the time they are 18 years old than those without (O'Dell et al, 2015[15]). It also shows that increased access to electricity ameliorated employment opportunities for both men and women, but that women benefitted the most, as use of electric appliances freed up time spent on household chores.

The impact of energy poverty on educational outcomes also has negative intergenerational effects. Links between mothers' education and children's health are well established. Lower education rate of mothers is correlated with high infant stunting levels (Abuya, Ciera and Kimani-Murage, 2012[16]) and lower levels of immunisation (Özer, Fidrmuc and Eryurt, 2018[17]). A study of child mortality in 175 countries between 1970 and 2009 concluded that half of the reductions of child mortality could be attributed to improved women's education (Gakidou et al., 2010[18]). Limited access to education discourages schooling in future generations, thus perpetuating the vicious cycle (Azomahou and Yitbarek, 2016[19]) (Mare and Maralani, 2006[20]).

Energy poverty has a significant direct impact on women's and girls' health and well-being. People in low- and middle-income countries, and in lower-income communities in higher-income countries, who rely on polluting sources of energy for basic needs disproportionally bear the effects of air pollution (WHO, 2018[21]). This impact is particularly felt among women and girls, who are the main users and producers of household energy around the world. As stated in Chapter 3, pregnant women are at greater risk from air pollution. Exposure to ambient air pollution is linked to adverse impacts on fertility, pregnancy and newborns, with recent evidence of fine particles crossing the placenta and leading to foetal exposure. (Bové et al., 2019[22]).

Dangerous work deriving from accessing energy resources is linked to gender-based violence (GBV). Collection of fuelwood and other resources can create tensions within communities, especially when competing over scarce resources or entering private land. Especially in humanitarian settings, fuel collection tasks come with the risk of sexual harassment or assault (UNHCR, 2016[23]). A study found that in Chad, 42% of the 673 refugee households surveyed reported incidents of GBV during firewood collection over a six-month span (Global Alliance for Clean Cookstoves, 2016[24]).

8.3.1. Energy and indoor pollution

As noted in Chapter 2, women and children are the main casualties from indoor pollution generated by inefficient cooking stoves widely used in the Global South. As women generally spend more time at home than men, they are more exposed to pollutant fuels and inadequate heating, especially if they cannot rely on modern cooking facilities. According to the World Health Organization (WHO), over 4 million people – mainly women and children – die every year as a result of indoor air pollution, as it increases the risk of stroke, pneumonia, lung disease, cancer, asthma, and other diseases (WHO, 2018[4]).

More than a quarter of the world's population rely on traditional use of biomass for cooking and heating (see Figure 8.2), and have limited access to clean and efficient energy for lighting (IEA, 2017[12]). The negative effects of the use of traditional biomass such as the burning of wood, dung, and crop residues have been widely reported on both human health, and agriculture and ecosystems (Venkataraman et al., 2010[25]). Kerosene is often advocated as a cleaner alternative to solid fuels, biomass and coal, for cooking, and kerosene lamps are widely used for lighting in much of the developing world. Kerosene hazards include poisonings, fires, and explosions and some less investigated health impacts from kerosene's combustion products include lung dysfunction and infectious illness (Lam et al., 2012[26]).

Figure 8.2. Share of population relying on different cooking fuels (2017)

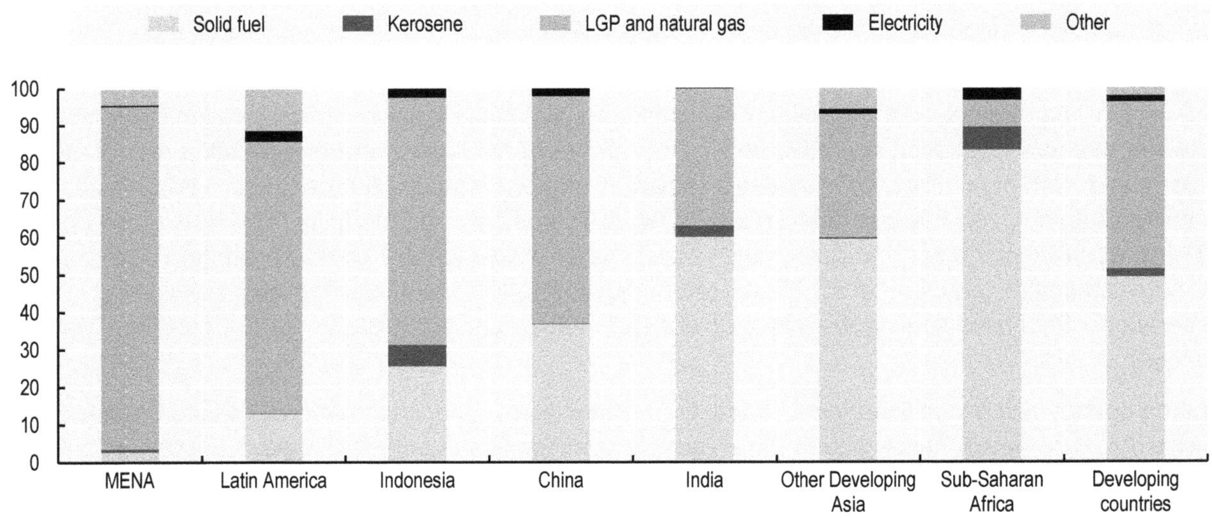

Note: Solid Fuels include: (i) traditional biomass (wood, charcoal, agricultural residues, and dung), (ii) processed biomass (pellets, briquettes); and (iii) other solid fuels (such as coal and lignite)
Source: (IEA, 2018[27])

More sustainable energy sources that guarantee fuel efficiency, reduce pollution, health risks and climate impacts are being widely developed. By 2017, 32 countries had included an improved cookstove initiative in their Nationally Determined Contributions (NDCs), as well as other initiatives to promote the use of renewable energy in specific sectors (Graichen et al., 2017[28]). These efforts need to be multiplied, especially in Sub-Saharan Africa, where more than 80% of the population still relies on solid cooking fuels (Box 8.1). The transition to more sustainable fuel sources requires special attention, given that some technologies might entail trade-offs with air quality, as is the case for biofuels. Hence, greener technologies should be assessed not only according to their ability to reduce emissions but also to reduce health risks and air pollution.

Box 8.1. Promoting women's access to renewable energy

Research by the International Energy Agency (IEA World Energy Outlooks 2017 and 2018, and Africa Energy Outlook 2019) finds that the most cost-effective strategy for providing universal access to electricity and clean cooking facilities in developing countries is compatible with meeting global climate goals, and would prevent millions of premature deaths each year (IEA, 2019[29]). To provide universal electricity for all, decentralised systems led by solar photovoltaic (PV) in off-grid and mini-grid systems will be the least-cost solution for many regions. This shift would especially benefit women, as it would free up billions of hours currently lost to gathering fuelwood.

Recently updated data on energy access shows that the number of people with electricity access fell below 1 billion for the first time in 2017, down from 1.6 billion in 2000. However, due to the COVID-19 pandemic, latest updates show a reverse in this progress, with the number of people lacking electricity in Africa rising to more than 590 million in 2020, an increase of 13 million, or 2%, from the previous year (IEA, 2018[27]); (IEA, 2020[30]). While fossil fuels, mainly coal, have remained the main new source for electricity access since 2000, renewables are growing rapidly, providing more than a third of new connections in the last five years. This shift is expected to accelerate in coming years, and by 2030 renewables are set to provide new electricity access for three-quarters of the additional connections needed and contribute to a cleaner environment due to their low carbon emissions, according to the IEA report (IEA, 2018[27]). While the crisis has put a dampener on the growth of decentralised renewable energy solutions like solar home systems and mini-grids, their expansion is expected to continue once economic conditions recover.

The most recent IEA report estimates that providing universal access to energy by 2030 would require an additional investment of USD 24 billion per year (on top of the USD 31 billion invested under current and planned policies), equivalent to less than 2% of global energy investment (IEA, 2020[30]). The overwhelming majority of this extra investment would need to be directed to sub-Saharan Africa, and most of it to renewables in order to speed up the transition. Of this, the investment required for clean cooking facilities, including liquefied petroleum gas, is modest and amounts to less than one-tenth of the total.

There are many benefits to achieving energy for all and doing so primarily via renewables. Women will save one hour per day when they do not need to collect fuelwood, freeing up the equivalent of a workforce of 80 million people. Increasing the share of renewables would reduce household air pollution, avoiding premature deaths and limiting carbon emissions.

8.3.2. Gender inequalities caused by energy policies

Gender energy inequality may be further exacerbated by national energy policies and labour market patterns. Such inequalities can be appreciated through the allocation of fossil fuel subsidies and its impacts are visible through women's access to transport and land use. For example, fossil fuel production subsidies often benefit more large energy producers, industries that are traditionally male-dominated. In developing countries, priority for energy access is often given to large industrial, export-oriented activities, which are typically owned by men. Women are more likely to work in the informal sector and therefore face greater difficulties in accessing energy for their economic activities. Studies from Africa confirm that woman-headed businesses often have less access to finance and energy-related services than those headed by men (UNDP, 2012[31]). Fossil fuel consumer subsidies have a demonstrated regressive effect, mostly felt by low-income women with limited access to – or who are unaware of – such subsidies (for more see Chapter 11).

Energy consumption subsidies also tend to benefit men more in both developing and developed countries, as they are bigger users of private transport. Due to their often higher economic status, but also to their behavioural preferences, men are more likely to use private cars rather than public transport. In Sweden, for instance, 70% of cars are owned and used by men (ITF, 2011[32]). A study of consumption patterns in four European countries (Germany, Norway, Greece and Sweden) found that men use considerably more energy than women for transport, ranging from 70% more in Germany to over 350% more in Greece, a gender difference largely due to the average single man spending more money on vehicles and fuel than the average single woman (Räty and Carlsson-Kanyama, 2009[33]).

The growing demand for biofuels in an attempt to reduce greenhouse gas emissions has affected land use in developing countries, in particular the marginal lands and small plots harvested by women (EIGE, 2016[34]). These land transfers have deprived vulnerable households of their means of energy subsistence and often with no compensation mechanisms (Clancy, 2012[35]).

8.4. Women's role in greening energy

Achieving universal energy access by 2030 via clean, renewable energy can deliver triple wins: economic (investment and employment in the renewables sector), social (including women's empowerment and improved health impacts) and environmental (lower emissions and pollution). In particular, greening energy infrastructure is a *sine qua non* for tackling the climate crisis and reducing pollution, two phenomena that affect women disproportionally.

Many countries are taking measures to transition away from fossil fuel use. In 2017, 13.5% of the total primary energy supply came from renewable energy sources (Statistical Office of the European Communities, 2019[36]). Currently, about 71.5% of global renewable energy is supplied by non-OECD countries (see Figure 8.3). Yet, much of the renewable energy in developing countries is not clean. Solid biofuels and charcoal cover almost 61% of the global renewables supply, and no major fluctuation has been measured since 1990 (IEA, 2019[37]). Countries need to seize the opportunity to leapfrog brown technologies altogether and move towards greener technologies, developing low-cost, renewable energy facilities based on solar and wind.

Within this transition, women have a central role to play as energy professionals, energy decision-makers and energy consumers. For instance, women and men reveal different preferences for energy policy options, especially when it comes to the energy transition and the adaptation of renewable energy (Fraune, 2016[38]). However, energy policy is often gender-blind and women tend to be underrepresented in the energy sector at all levels, including in bottom-up approaches such as community-based solutions (Fraune, 2015[39]). Acknowledging the benefits of a green transition for gender equality and the role women could play in the clean energy sector due to their behavioural preferences, calls for an urgent action to eliminate structural barriers for women's participation in labour force and decision-making in the energy sector (Clancy and Feenstra, 2019[40]).

Figure 8.3. Share of renewable energy in regional total primary energy supply

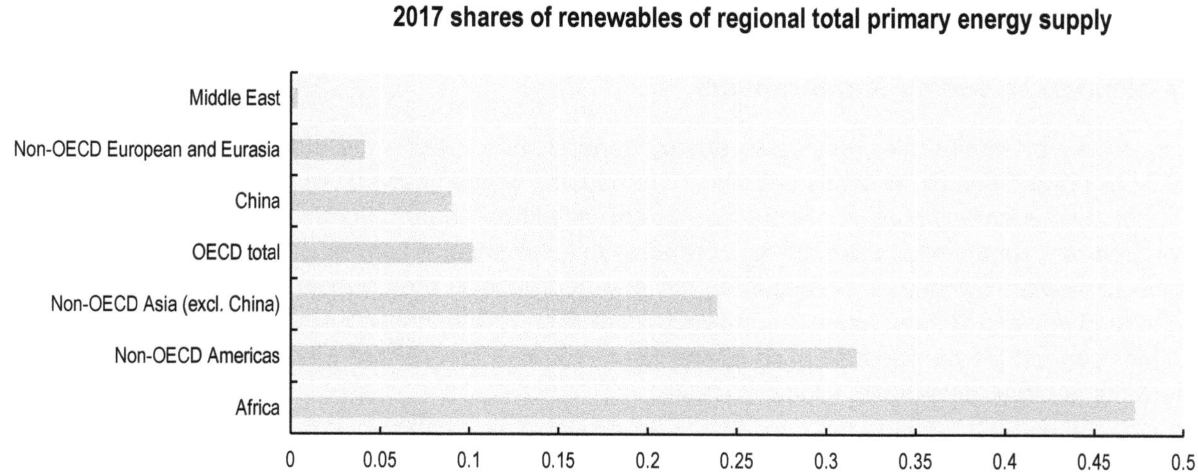

Note: Renewable energy includes: Solar PV, Wind, Hydropower, bioenergy, CSP and geothermal, Transport biofuels, Renewable heat.
Source: (IEA, 2019[29]).

8.4.1. Women as sustainable energy consumers

As primary energy managers in households, women in both developed and developing countries can play a key role in promoting sustainable energy consumption and accelerating the shift to renewable energy.

Evidence suggests that women are more responsible users of energy than men. A 2015 Canadian study on the relationship between consumers' environmental concerns, carbon footprint and socio-economic status showed that women tend to be more environmentally concerned and engaged in pro-environmental household behaviour. Results also showed that women-led households are more likely to have a smaller carbon footprint, likely due to smaller house size, and limited vehicle ownership and use (Huddart Kennedy, Krahn and Krogman, 2015[41]). In a recent study in the United Kingdom, women reported engaging in activities with a higher energy footprint than men, but performing them using less electricity (Grünewald and Diakonova, 2020[42]). Other studies in Europe have shown that single men directly or indirectly use up to 22% more energy than single women. Women could be more receptive than men to energy conservation efforts and demonstrate a greater willingness to change their everyday behaviour to save energy (Räty and Carlsson-Kanyama, 2010[43]).

Consumer behaviour and consumption patterns vary not only according to gender, but also based on income and location. Extensive qualitative research exists on household energy consumption and time use in relation to household income and location, but more quantitative analysis at a disaggregate level (per person within household) would help build more the evidence regarding differentiated gender patterns of sustainable energy use. Research shows a link between an increase in household income and less time spent on energy-intensive household activities such as meal preparation, food expenditure, and cleaning (De Lauretis, Ghersi and Cayla, 2017[44]). Considering that these activities are traditionally carried out by women, further analysis is required on how gender equality and women's economic empowerment may change energy household consumption.

Targeted action is needed to engage women consumers in energy efficiency practices. Connecting potential customers of clean technologies with financing opportunities available through financial institutions and NGOs is a key step in both tackling issues of energy poverty and gender inequality (IRENA, 2019[45]). Specific policy action and support mechanisms require better evidence on the gender dimension of energy use. Sex-disaggregated data is needed in order to draft specific policy recommendations based on: per capita energy consumption for men and women; the share of non-commercial energy used by men and women; the purposes for which energy is used; the amount of time spent and the effort made by men and women in providing energy for their activities; and the amount that each pays for energy (Lambrou and Piana, 2006[46]).

8.4.2. Women as energy entrepreneurs

The possibility of small-scale, renewable energy generation is making the industry more accessible to women. As off-grid energy solutions become more popular, women have an opportunity to become more active not only as energy consumers but also as energy entrepreneurs. For instance, Windfang E.G, the first women-run, community-based energy co-operative established in Germany, began in 1991 as a small initiative of women committed to supporting the energy transition through wind energy. Today, it owns 11 wind turbines and 3 solar panels, supplying more than 3 000 households. In Germany, legislative provisions support the participation of co-operatives in auctions for onshore wind and solar PVs by setting lower tariffs for small developers (Botta, 2019[47]).

Women in developing countries are also entering the retail market for more efficient renewable energy solutions (Botta, 2019[47]). Renewable energy co-operatives provide an opportunity for women to engage all along the value chain, including in production. An example is Solar Mamas, an initiative by India-based Barefoot College that uses colour coding and sign language to teach rural women to assemble their own equipment and install lighting systems in their villages. The programme is now present in 93 countries, including in Africa and Latin America (Barefoot College, 2020[48]). Further analysis on gender-responsive policies and measures supporting women's co-operatives could provide policy makers with the necessary tools to actively enhance women's economic empowerment through sustainable solutions.

To support governments in creating an enabling environment for finance and investment in renewable energy and energy efficiency in emerging economies, in 2019 the OECD launched the Clean Energy Finance and Investment Mobilisation (CEFIM) programme, a five-year project funded by the Danish government (Tam, 2019[49]). One area being explored by CEFIM is whether clean energy finance and investment policies promote gender diversity and women's empowerment. Women entrepreneurs are often disadvantaged in debt finance, as they generally have fewer assets to guarantee loans. To support a just transition and encourage innovative business models for clean energy, it is important to ensure that women and men have equal access to finance and consideration in public engagement programmes.

The same considerations apply for the financing provisions of multilateral development banks (MDBs), where allocation of funds for climate change mitigation, adaptation and resilience should have a gender component encompassing labour, social, and industry and economic changes in existing production systems (GGCA, 2016[50]). MDBs are the most advanced donors in terms of integrating gender and climate change in their energy finance operations – the European Investment Bank (EIB) and European Bank for Reconstruction and Development (EBRD) do so routinely (EIB, 2020[51]) (EBRD, 2019[52]).

8.4.3. A just transition for women and men

Energy is a largely male-dominated sector. For instance, in the EU, women account for less than a quarter (22.1%) of the energy sector workforce (EIGE, 2016[53]). Women are in general better represented in the renewable energy sector. A global survey conducted in 2018 by the International Renewable Energy Agency (IRENA) shows that women account for 32% of the workforce in the renewable energy sector, compared to 22% in the oil and gas industry sector, indicating that women may have a higher interest in environmental sustainability fields (IRENA, 2019[45]).

However, the study also shows that women occupy almost half of the administrative positions in the renewables sector and 35% of the non Science, Technology, Engineering, Mathematics (STEM) technical roles, but only 28% of the STEM-related roles.[1] This is linked to perceptions of gender roles – common also in other sectors - that hamper women's participation in STEM and Research and Development (R&D)

related fields, exclusion and harassment by male colleagues, and obstacles in reaching decision-making positions due to lack of supportive measures to address such gender-based barriers.[2]

The IEA is supporting the Clean Energy Education and Empowerment (C3E) initiative, launched at the Clean Energy Ministerial in 2010. C3E focuses on enabling greater gender diversity in the clean energy professions. It brings together experts in public administration, industry and research organisations, which work together to identify best practices and share data, experiences and career development programmes. The Equal by 30 Campaign is operated under the C3E initiative, and its signatories (9 countries and more than 80 energy companies) have committed to equal pay, equal leadership and equal opportunities by 2030. Based on their analysis, on average 23% of total employees in 135 energy companies are female (C3E International, 2019[54]). Additionally, in 2018, the International Finance Cooperation (IFC) partnered with the European Commission and 17 leading technology companies to promote opportunities for women via the digital2equal initiative that encourages gender equality while supporting technological advancements (Eunice Ahairwe and Bilal, 2020[55]).

Greater representation of women in top management and leadership positions in the energy sector would support more "green" decisions in both the public and private sectors. As discussed in Chapter 2, private firms with gender diversity in their boards and senior management usually take more sustainable initiatives than those that do not. Yet fewer women reach senior management roles in the energy sector when compared to senior officials and managers in government and business (corporate and small enterprises) (IEA, 2020[56]).

Moving away from carbon-intensive industries in the transition to a low-carbon economy is expected to create changes in employment in different sectors, even if projections show that, at the aggregate level, employment should remain at the same levels (Albrizio et al., 2014[57]). Independently of the different scenarios analysed, disruption is expected in energy-intensive industries, but also, potentially, in construction or business services. The most affected seem to be low-skilled workers (Chateau, Bibas and Lanzi, 2018[58]).

Furthermore, Botta's (2019) analysis on low-carbon transition shows a possible shift of workers from fossil-fuel intensive industries to low-carbon ones. Botta (2019) also argues that the transition has differential effects based on a company's location, and on the workforce's gender and age. International Labour Organisation (ILO) calculations project an 11-15% decrease of the workforce in "brown" industries (Botta, 2019[47]). In the case of the United Kingdom coal-mining sector, the transition affected primarily the male workers in the sector, 90% of which were displaced. Evidence shows, however, that female workers in manufacturing were crowded out, as men engaged in activities previously occupied by them (Aragón, Rud and Toews, 2018[59]).

A just transition should, therefore, guarantee equal opportunities for both men and women in the workforce. More research in coal regions, where structural changes are expected, would help identify the trends and the needs for more inclusive and sustainable job creation. This could expand beyond skills development and training, to financing and investment priorities.

Hence, considering women's already higher engagement in the renewables sector, but low participation in STEM-related roles, new skills development should consider how to build upon existing good trends and empower women to strengthen their presence in areas that were traditionally male dominated. Governments could further promote research and innovation to create jobs and entrepreneurship opportunities for women in renewable energy value chains.

Another potential challenge of the energy transition is avoiding the 'climate change gap' between those who can invest in sustainability and those who cannot. For instance, energy efficiency is not only about changing attitudes but also about affordability. However, those who have access to energy efficiency technologies can increase their incomes, bridging a gap between rich and poor. While in Europe many municipalities are providing subsidies and tax benefits for house insulation, only home-owners who have the means to make an investment can benefit from such policies. Considering that women are often economically disadvantaged and that men are over-represented as tenants, such insulation and retrofitting programs might not be inclusive of women. A gender analysis is, therefore, important for spotting similar gender effects of energy policy (Clancy and Feenstra, 2019[60]).

Lastly, a just transition should also take into account the role of indigenous peoples. The 18th session of the UN Permanent Forum on Indigenous Issues (PFII) highlighted how indigenous knowledge and traditional legal systems can enable sustainable climate solutions and good governance (UN, 2019[61]). The Free Prior and Informed Consent principle, an instrument that requires bottom-up consultation and co-operation with indigenous peoples prior to developing a project, can enable synergies between indigenous knowledge and the development of cleaner technologies. In this line of work, more projects such as the Canadian government-funded project 'A SHARED Future' can foster engagement with indigenous women who are renewable energy leaders in their communities (A SHARED Future, 2019[62]).

8.5. Key actions for advancing the agenda and ongoing work

A number of actions can be taken to foster synergies between gender equality and energy goals:

- More systematic evidence gathering on the linkages between gender quality and clean energy goals.
- Energy policies should be aligned with the needs of women, especially in countries with a high incidence of energy poverty.
- Policy makers should take into account the implications of their energy policies on other countries, including how they affect sustainability goals and gender inequality.
- A gender perspective should be integrated in all elements of energy planning and policy-making. There is also a need to promote the presence of women, including those from indigenous communities, within local, national and international decision-making bodies and in the energy industry itself at all policy-making stages.
- It is essential to address structural and behavioural gender inequities to allow women participate in the energy sector at all levels: first, by encouraging more girls' to study STEM subjects in order to develop specialised knowledge, and, second, by promoting more equal sharing of unpaid household work by men and women to allow women to apply their skills in the decision-making, both the professional and in the community setting.
- Donors should promote the integration of gender equality in aid to climate change, as more needs to be done to improve women's opportunities to participate in the green economy, notably through ensuring that women benefit equally from development projects focusing on clean technology and renewable energy (GENDERNET, 2015[63]).

References

A SHARED Future (2019), *A SHARED Future*, http://asharedfuture.ca/ (accessed on 14 March 2021). [62]

Abuya, B., J. Ciera and E. Kimani-Murage (2012), "Effect of mother's education on child's nutritional status in the slums of Nairobi", *BMC Pediatrics*, Vol. 12, http://dx.doi.org/10.1186/1471-2431-12-80. [16]

Albrizio, S. et al. (2014), "Do Environmental Policies Matter for Productivity Growth?: Insights from New Cross-Country Measures of Environmental Policies", *OECD Economics Department Working Papers*, No. 1176, OECD Publishing, Paris, https://dx.doi.org/10.1787/5jxrjncjrcxp-en. [57]

Aragón, F., J. Rud and G. Toews (2018), "Resource shocks, employment, and gender: Evidence from the collapse of the UK coal industry", *Labour Economics*, Vol. 52, pp. 54-67, http://dx.doi.org/10.1016/j.labeco.2018.03.007. [59]

Azomahou, T. and E. Yitbarek (2016), "Intergenerational Education Mobility in Africa: Has Progress Been Inclusive?", *World Bank Group, Development Research Group* Policy Research Working Paper 7843, http://documents1.worldbank.org/curated/en/379961475169190879/pdf/WPS7843.pdf. [19]

Barefoot College (2020), "Solar Mamas", https://www.barefootcollege.org/approach/ (accessed on 10 December 2020). [48]

Bloomfield, E. (2014), *Gender and Livelihoods Impacts of Clean Cookstoves in South Asia*, https://www.cleancookingalliance.org/binary-data/RESOURCE/file/000/000/363-1.pdf. [13]

Botta, E. (2019), "An experimental approach to climate finance: the impact of auction design and policy uncertainty on renewable energy equity costs in Europe", *Energy Policy*, Vol. 133, http://dx.doi.org/10.1016/j.enpol.2019.06.047. [47]

Bové, H. et al. (2019), "Ambient black carbon particles reach the fetal side of human placenta", *Nature Communications*, Vol. 10/1, http://dx.doi.org/10.1038/s41467-019-11654-3. [22]

C3E International (2019), *STATUS REPORT ON GENDER EQUALITY IN THE ENERGY SECTOR MAPPING GENDER DIVERSITY IN THE ENERGY SECTOR.* [54]

Chateau, J., R. Bibas and E. Lanzi (2018), "Impacts of Green Growth Policies on Labour Markets and Wage Income Distribution: A General Equilibrium Application to Climate and Energy Policies", *OECD Environment Working Papers*, No. 137, OECD Publishing, Paris, https://dx.doi.org/10.1787/ea3696f4-en. [58]

Clancy, J. (2012), "Biofuels and Rural Poverty", http://dx.doi.org/10.4324/9780203128473. [35]

Clancy, J. and M. Feenstra (2019), *Women, Gender Equality and the Energy Transition in the EU*, http://www.europarl.europa.eu/supporting-analyses. [40]

Clancy, J. and M. Feenstra (2019), *Women, Gender Equality and the Energy Transition in the EU*, http://www.europarl.europa.eu/supporting-analyses. [60]

Clancy, J., M. Feenstra and V. Daskalova (2017), "Gender perspective on access to energy in the EU.", https://doi.org/10.13140/RG.2.2.14577.02406. [8]

De Lauretis, S., F. Ghersi and J. Cayla (2017), "Energy consumption and activity patterns: An analysis extended to total time and energy use for French households", *Applied Energy*, Vol. 206, http://dx.doi.org/10.1016/j.apenergy.2017.08.180. [44]

Dutta, S., A. Kooijman and E. Cecelski (2017), *SEAR ENERGY ACCESS AND GENDER GETTING THE RIGHT BALANCE*, http://www.worldbank.org. [10]

EBRD (2019), *GENDER-RESPONSIVE INVESTMENT CLIMATE REFORM IN TAJIKISTAN Making policies work for women in business A toolkit for policymakers and advocates*. [52]

EIB (2020), "Delopment Solutions: How to fight climate change with gender equality", *Development Solutions*, https://www.eib.org/en/essays/climate-change-gender-investment (accessed on 11 December 2020). [51]

EIGE (2020), *Gender Equality Index 2019 - Work-life balance*, http://dx.doi.org/10.2839/852588. [9]

EIGE (2016), "Gender and Energy" : Publications Office of the European Union. [53]

EIGE (2016), "Gender in environment and climate change", http://dx.doi.org/10.2839/51996. [34]

Eunice Ahairwe, P. and S. Bilal (2020), *A gender-sensitive sustainable COVID-19 recovery: The role of development finance institutions (ECDPM Discussion Paper 284)*. [55]

Fraune, C. (2016), "The politics of speeches, votes, and deliberations: Gendered legislating and energy policy-making in Germany and the United States", *Energy Research & Social Science*, Vol. Volume 19, https://doi.org/10.1016/j.erss.2016.06.007. [38]

Fraune, C. (2015), "Gender matters: Women, renewable energy, and citizen participation in Germany", *Energy Research & Social Science*, Vol. 7, http://dx.doi.org/10.1016/j.erss.2015.02.005. [39]

Gakidou, E. et al. (2010), "Increased educational attainment and its effect on child mortality in 175 countries between 1970 and 2009: a systematic analysis.", *Lancet (London, England)*, Vol. 376/9745, pp. 959-74, http://dx.doi.org/10.1016/S0140-6736(10)61257-3. [18]

GENDERNET (2015), *Making climate finance work for women: Overview of the integration of gender equality in aid to climate change*, https://www.oecd.org/dac/gender-development/Making-Climate-Finance-Work-for-Women.pdf. [63]

GGCA (2016), *Gender and Climate Change: A Closer Look at Existing Evidence*, https://wedo.org/gender-and-climate-change-a-closer-look-at-existing-evidence-ggca/. [50]

Global Alliance for Clean Cookstoves (2016), *Gender-Based Violence in Humanitarian Settings: Cookstoves and Fuels. A Systematic Review of the Evidence Base*, Global Alliance for Clean Cookstoves, https://www.cleancookingalliance.org/resources/478.html (accessed on 22 March 2021). [24]

Graichen, J. et al. (2017), *International Climate Initiatives - A way forward to close the emissions gap? Initiatives' potential and role under the Paris Agreement Final Report*, Umweltbundesamt, https://www.umweltbundesamt.de/publikationen. [28]

Grünewald, P. and M. Diakonova (2020), "Societal differences, activities, and performance: Examining the role of gender in electricity demand in the United Kingdom", *Energy Research & Social Science*, Vol. 69, http://dx.doi.org/10.1016/j.erss.2020.101719. [42]

Huddart Kennedy, E., H. Krahn and N. Krogman (2015), "Are we counting what counts? A closer look at environmental concern, pro-environmental behaviour, and carbon footprint", *Local Environment*, Vol. 20/2, http://dx.doi.org/10.1080/13549839.2013.837039. [41]

IEA (2020), *Gender diversity in energy: what we know and what we don't know*, https://www.iea.org/commentaries/gender-diversity-in-energy-what-we-know-and-what-we-dont-know (accessed on 23 March 2021). [56]

IEA (2020), *SDG7: Data and Projections*, International Energy Agency, http://IEA (2020), SDG7: Data and Projections, IEA, Paris https://www.iea.org/reports/sdg7-data-and-projections (accessed on 11 March 2021). [3]

IEA (2020), "The Covid-19 crisis is reversing progress on energy access in Africa", *IEA*, http://IEA, Paris https://www.iea.org/articles/the-covid-19-crisis-is-reversing-progress-on-energy-access-in-africa (accessed on 2 December 2020). [1]

IEA (2020), "World Energy Outlook 2020", *IEA*, https://www.iea.org/reports/world-energy-outlook-2020 (accessed on 4 December 2020). [30]

IEA (2019), "Africa Energy Outlook 2019", https://www.iea.org/reports/africa-energy-outlook-2019 (accessed on 4 December 2020). [29]

IEA (2019), "Renewables Information 2019, IEA, Paris https://www.iea.org/reports/renewables-information-2019". [37]

IEA (2018), *World Energy Outlook 2018*, International Energy Agency, Paris, https://dx.doi.org/10.1787/weo-2018-en. [27]

IEA (2017), "Energy Access Outlook 2017, IEA, Paris https://www.iea.org/reports/energy-access-outlook-2017". [12]

IRENA (2020), *Wind energy: A gender perspective*, IRENA, Abu Dhabi, http://www.irena.org. [64]

IRENA (2019), *Renewable Energy: A Gender Perspective*, http://www.irena.org. [45]

ITF (2011), *Gender and Transport*, OECD, Paris, http://dx.doi.org/Discussion Paper 2011.11. [32]

Lambrou, Y. and G. Piana (2006), *Energy and Gender Issues in Rural Sustainable Development*. [46]

Lam, N. et al. (2012), "Kerosene: A Review of Household Uses and their Hazards in Low- and Middle-Income Countries", *Journal of Toxicology and Environmental Health Part B*, Vol. 15/6, pp. 396-432, http://dx.doi.org/10.1080/10937404.2012.710134. [26]

Lewis, J. et al. (2013), *The short-run and long-run effects of household technological change **. [14]

Mare, R. and V. Maralani (2006), "The Intergenerational Effects of Changes in Women's Educational Attainments", *Am Sociol Rev.* 71(4): 5542–564., https://www.ncbi.nlm.nih.gov/pmc/articles/PMC4381439/. [20]

O'Dell et al (2015), *Women, energy, and economic empowerment Applying a gender lens to amplify the impact of energy access.* [15]

OECD (2020), *OECD Economic Outlook, Volume 2020 Issue 2: Preliminary version*, OECD Publishing, Paris, https://dx.doi.org/10.1787/39a88ab1-en. [2]

OECD (2018), *Policy Coherence for Sustainable Development and Gender Equality: Fostering an Integrated Policy Agenda*, http://www.oecd.org/gov/gender-mainstreaming/policy-coherence-for-sustainable-development-and-gender-equality.pdf. [11]

Ogunbiyi D (2020), *Damilola Ogunbiyi: Power in a Pandemic - Why Energy Access Matters During Coronavirus*, Sustainable Energy for All, https://www.seforall.org/news/power-in-a-pandemic-why-energy-access-matters-during-coronavirus. [6]

Özer, M., J. Fidrmuc and M. Eryurt (2018), "Maternal education and childhood immunization in Turkey", *Health Economics (United Kingdom)*, Vol. 27/8, pp. 1218-1229, http://dx.doi.org/10.1002/hec.3770. [17]

Räty, R. and A. Carlsson-Kanyama (2010), "Energy consumption by gender in some European countries", *Energy Policy*, Vol. 38(1):646-649, http://dx.doi.org/DOI: 10.1016/j.enpol.2009.08.010 ·. [43]

Räty, R. and A. Carlsson-Kanyama (2009), *Comparing energy use by gender, age and income in some European countries.* [33]

Statistical Office of the European Communities (2019), *Energy, transport and environment statistics: 2019 edition.* [36]

Tam, C. (2019), *Clean energy finance and investment mobilisation programme*, OECD, http://www.oecd.org/cgfi. [49]

UN (2019), *Permanent Forum on Indigenous Issues - Report on the eighteenth session (22 April–3 May 2019)*, https://undocs.org/en/E/2019/43 (accessed on 14 March 2021). [61]

UN (2016), *Affordable and Clean Energy: Why It Matters*, https://www.un.org/sustainabledevelopment/wp-content/uploads/2016/08/7_Why-It-Matters-2020.pdf. [5]

UNDP (2012), *Gender and Climate Change Africa.* [31]

UNHCR (2016), *SGBV Prevention and Response: A Training Package*, https://www.unhcr.org/583577ed4.pdf (accessed on 14 April 2021). [23]

USEA (2019), "USEA BRIEFING: ADDRESSING ENERGY POVERTY IN THE US: A FEDERAL/STATE/UTILITY COLLABORATION. https://www.usea.org/event/usea-briefing-addressing-energy-poverty-usfederalstateutility-collaboration". [7]

Venkataraman, C. et al. (2010), "The Indian National Initiative for Advanced Biomass Cookstoves: The benefits of clean combustion", *Energy for Sustainable Development*, Vol. 14/2, pp. 63-72, http://dx.doi.org/10.1016/j.esd.2010.04.005. [25]

WHO (2018), *Air pollution and child health – prescribing clean air*, World Health Organization Regional Office for Europe, Copenhagen, https://www.who.int/ceh/publications/air-pollution-child-health/en/ (accessed on 12 March 2021). [21]

WHO (2018), "Household air pollution and health", *WHO Factsheet*, https://www.who.int/news-room/fact-sheets/detail/household-air-pollution-and-health. [4]

Notes

[1] A more recent IRENA report on women's engagement in the wind energy sector reaches equivalent results, also showing women less engaged in the sector in Africa (9%) and Asia-Pacific (15%) in comparison to Latin America and the Caribbean (19%), and Europe and North America (26%) (IRENA, 2020[64]).

[2] In the IRENA 2019 survey, these measures include mainstreaming gender through audits and awareness raising in the private sector; setting supportive networks, mentorships and awards; providing better access to education and vocational training by adapting curricula; introducing gender quota and targets; breaking gender barriers by adapting workplace policies and regulations; and, ensuring better work-life balance.

9 Women and SDG 9 – Industry, Innovation and Infrastructure: Build resilient infrastructure, promote inclusive and sustainable industrialisation and foster innovation

Industrialisation and infrastructure development have underpinned economic growth for decades and allowed for major improvements in many aspects of well-being across all segments of the population. Infrastructure is essential for gender equality, as it provides women with better access to essential services and fosters economic opportunities. However, industrialisation and infrastructure have also been the source of major health and environmental costs and can create adverse social spillovers, which often affect women most. Applying a gender lens to infrastructure development is essential to close persistent gender gaps in use and employment. Women can also play a critical role in green and digital innovation, but there are a number of challenges to be addressed, especially in relation to skills gaps, social biases and outright discrimination. There is also a persistent gender gap in decision-making positions in the private sector in the infrastructure, green and digital sectors.

9.1. Key findings

This chapter provides a description of the links between gender equality and the empowerment of women on the one hand and industrialisation, infrastructure and innovation on the other. A number of issues are addressed:

- Infrastructure development is fundamental to economic growth and to creating economic opportunities for vulnerable groups. Access to safe, multimodal transport, modern digital services, and social infrastructure like public parks, and health and care centres, are essential to close gender gaps and promote the economic empowerment of women.
- At the same time, major infrastructure projects, in particular in the transport sector, could harm local communities and the environment, especially in countries with low standards of protection and enforcement. The vast share of construction projects in the transport sector are concentrated in developing countries, including in areas where there is high biodiversity. Women are often most affected by land displacements, human rights abuses (including sexual crime and violence), weak labour rights, and safety and health risks caused by unsustainable infrastructure projects.
- The growth of industrial sectors, and the move to service and knowledge-based economies are rarely gender neutral. While industrialisation has created employment opportunities for women in the developing world, many women are still in low-skilled, low-paid assembly-line type jobs.
- Important gender gaps persist in the more dynamic and innovative sectors of the economy. Surveys show that women have less access to the Internet and are less likely to own a mobile phone than men. The gap is largest in developing countries.
- Another concern is the low take-up of STEM (science, technology, engineering and mathematics) subjects among women, which leads to a low percentage of women participating in technology development (inventive activity), reaching only 15% on average across all countries and all technology domains. This translates into more limited opportunities for women to contribute to green innovation.
- Skill gaps, social norms, biases and labour market discrimination translate into a large gender gap in decision-makers in the infrastructure, green innovation and digital sectors.
- Gender inequalities can combine with discrimination over race, disabilities or other personal attributes to deepen gender gaps. Assessing the intersectionality of the gender-infrastructure nexus is fundamental to the development of effective policies.
- Policy action is required in these different areas to tackle gender-specific risks, address gender labour gaps and promote the economic empowerment of women. Regarding infrastructure, a key requirement is to ensure that major projects undergo an independent, comprehensive environmental and social impact assessment, including a gender impact assessment. Infrastructure strategies and plans, in particular in the transport and digital sectors, must include a gender dimension.
- Policy makers must consider options, including reporting, targets and quotas, for increasing the participation of women in senior management positions in industry and infrastructure. More resources and action are needed to promote programmes to increase the uptake of scientific research and innovation by women, and to tackle the barriers to their participation in STEM subjects.

9.2. Key interlinkages between gender equality; industrialisation, sustainable infrastructure and innovation and other SDGs

Manufacturing, technological progress, innovation and infrastructure development are at the core of human progress and well-being. They underpin higher productivity, income generation and wage growth, jobs, and better living standards through access to basic services such as health and education services. They are therefore at the heart of many other SDGs, including SDG 8 on decent work and economic growth, SDG 10 on inequalities, SDG 1 on poverty eradication and SDG 2 on zero hunger.

However, most economic production processes are also natural resource and energy intensive, and have contributed to the destruction of ecosystems, including deforestation and the extinction of millions of animal and plant species. They also generate waste, pollution and greenhouse gas (GHG) emissions.

Achieving SDG 9, therefore, requires a transformation in production processes, especially in energy intensive industries such as mining, chemicals and materials manufacturing, as well as fossil-fuel based transport. Air transport is particularly polluting and is experiencing rapid growth. Maritime transport is also of great concern to environmental sustainability especially for the oceans. It also requires technological innovation to transform the current industrialisation trends to more sustainable and resilient infrastructure and production methods.

The industrial development and growth of economic sectors, and the move to service and knowledge-based economies are rarely gender neutral. Women in rural areas, indigenous groups and traditional societies have been affected most by these trends. Manufacturing tends to be a male dominated industry, even though the "feminisation" of the workforce is becoming more and more apparent. Women are integrating more in manufacturing, especially in developing countries, while in some cases labour conditions and protection are not up to standards. In addition, there is also a large gender gap in new technologies and innovation, leading to female exclusion from the technological innovation necessary to move towards more sustainable industrialisation. Women entrepreneurs also face greater obstacles to operate from regulatory barriers to access to finance.

Under SDG 9 there are three gender-related indicators, all of which cover environmental issues (9.1.1 on the proportion of the rural population who live within 2 km of an all-season road, 9.5.2 on the number of researchers per million inhabitants, and 9.c.1 on the proportion of population covered by a mobile network, by technology). These cover different gender issues, namely rural women's access to road infrastructure; the role of women researchers and inventors; and women's access to digital technology and mobile networks. Yet, achieving all other indicators under SDG 9 could potentially have positive effects towards women's and girls' empowerment, should inclusive and sustainable industrialisation and infrastructure encompass gender equality. Collecting gender-disaggregated data on these indicators, which also have a strong environmental component – such as on modes of transport, manufacturing and small-scale industries – is imperative, considering women as users, workers or entrepreneurs.

9.3. Gendered effects of industrialisation, infrastructure and new technologies

9.3.1. Industrialisation and its impact on women and the environment

The growth of industrial sectors, and the move to service and knowledge-based economies are rarely gender neutral. Export-oriented industrialisation and assembly-line type jobs have created new employment opportunities in manufacturing for women across much of the developing world. As also discussed in Chapter 6, women in manufacturing tend to concentrate in low-skilled and low-paid assembly-line type jobs (ILO, 2016[1]). Women tend to move from agriculture to manufacturing, without having guaranteed better paid or more secure positions (Tran, 2019[2]).

The expanding services sector around the world has opened up career opportunities in formal, skill-intensive employment for a minority of highly educated women. Yet, mostly in developing countries, the majority of women continue to be trapped in poorly paid or part-time jobs due to household chores and care burden (ILO, 2016[1]). Jobs in research and innovation that are driving the transformation towards the knowledge economy continue to be dominated by men.

Major gender gaps also persist in OECD countries. For instance, in the case of the United States, women's share of employment in the manufacturing industry decreased from 33.2% in 1990 to 29.0% in 2016 (U.S. Census Bureau, 2016[3]). Furthermore, major wage gaps remain, with unequal access to opportunities. Women are also subject to discrimination and in some instances unsafe working environments.

As described in more detail in Chapter 4, industrialisation has also contributed to environmental damage, including pollution and other environmental hazards, with specific negative effects on women's health.

9.3.2. Infrastructure development and its social and environmental spillovers

Infrastructure plays a key role in trade and access to markets and is closely linked to economic growth and well-being. Infrastructure is also essential for gender equality, as it may provide women with better access to transport, energy, clean water, and sanitation and hygiene facilities. It can therefore reduce the time women spend in household and care responsibilities, providing them with an opportunity – and the means – to move into paid labour. Other social infrastructure developments, such as education and health, can support women's economic empowerment and well-being. When developed with gender equality considerations, well-planned projects can additionally benefit women by ensuring better personal safety in public spaces (see for example urban transportation in Section 10.3.4). Across the world, the sector is also a major employer. Ensuring a gender lens in infrastructure development is therefore essential. At every stage, there can be further integration of women's role in infrastructure, starting with project scoping. Project assessment, approval, construction and maintenance must all include a gender dimension (Open Development, 2020[4]) to guarantee that women's needs and perceptions are taken into consideration. Initiatives like Gender-based Analysis Plus applied to the National Trade Corridors Fund in Canada show women, men and gender diverse people[1] can all benefit from more sustainable infrastructure (ITF, 2019[5]).

Infrastructure projects need to integrate ecosystem, environmental and social considerations, including gender impacts. While major infrastructure projects can bring great benefits in economic development and opportunities for different groups, including women, they also create risks to the environment and to women affected by construction projects (OECD, 2019[6]). In developing countries, women's low levels of education and gender discrimination make rural women disproportionately vulnerable (Mortensen and Boyland, 2019[7]).

Policy makers are increasingly focused on promoting sustainable infrastructure, taking into account environmental and social considerations. Infrastructure development can have profound implications for the environment, as it may contribute to changes in the air quality, in water quality and quantity, and in biodiversity and local ecosystems. Infrastructure projects, if not sufficiently consulted and designed, could lead to disproportionate costs for local communities and indigenous populations; leading to their displacement, loss of ancestral lands or even violation of human and labour rights (UNDESA, 2009[8]). Women in rural areas and among indigenous peoples are more often than not additionally affected due to the marginalisation and lack of ownership and voice they experience. At the same time, infrastructure development may create new or different jobs, changing the labour patterns and the economic development of the given region. This may have gender implications that would need to be considered.

The G20 Principles for Quality Infrastructure Investment, and the OECD-developed G20 Reference Note on Environmental and Social Considerations in Quality Infrastructure, integrate both environmental, social and particularly gender considerations in infrastructure development. The Reference Note proposes possible measures to help minimise the negative environmental and social impacts, and to make future infrastructure development and investment more sustainable. Among the points raised is also a gender perspective in infrastructure planning, design and development (OECD, 2019[9]).

In 2015, the OECD developed a Framework for the Governance of Infrastructure, which identified 10 "success factors" for getting infrastructure right and provided policy options for an enabling environment, building on several OECD instruments such as public procurement, budgeting, integrity framework etc. (OECD, 2017[10]). In 2020, OECD members endorsed a Recommendation on the Governance of Infrastructure, which allows for more gender inclusive infrastructure projects, and ensures gender mainstreaming and direct involvement of women throughout the infrastructure governance cycle (OECD, n.d.[11]).

The risks of transport infrastructure construction on local communities and the environment are highest in countries with low standards of protection and enforcement. The vast share of construction projects in the transport sector are concentrated in developing countries. By 2050 global freight and passenger travel are expected to double, for which 25 million km of new paved roads and more than 300 000 km of rail tracks will be needed worldwide. This will lead to additional 85% infrastructure development, of which 90% will be roads (Duloc, 2013[12]).

Such major growth in infrastructure, besides the economic benefits it is expected to bring, will certainly have environmental and social effects, potentially damaging tropical environments with high biodiversity and environmental value (Alamgir et al., 2017[13]). For example, in Brazilian Amazonia, 95% of all deforestation occurs within 5.5 km of a paved or unpaved road (Dulac, n.d.[14]). The same trend has been found in other tropical and sub-tropical countries. In these regions, roads can also bring poachers and other undesirable activities including illicit mining, smuggling and drug production, and migrant movements that affect the often delicate balance of local communities, especially among isolated indigenous groups.

Such effects may touch upon the female population in these areas more than others, as women are often the main caretakers of small subsistence farms from which they may be displaced by road works. Women also often have specific roles in traditional societies such as gathering food and ingredients for medicines from forests which may be affected by infrastructure projects. They are affected most by human rights abuses (including sexual crimes and violence) and weak labour rights, safety and health risks caused by infrastructure projects (OHCHR and Heinrich-Böll-Stiftung, 2019[15]). Projects with a large influx of workers may increase the demand for sex work and the risks of gender-based violence (World Bank, 2018[16]).This is not only the case in least developed countries. Recent reports on the impact of hydro-electric projects in Manitoba, Canada, and in wind energy projects in Mexico, have been associated with increased numbers of sexual abuse and harassment (CBC, 2018[17]); (Castañeda Carney et al., 2020[18]).A key goal for policy makers should be to use the large and broad benefits of infrastructure projects to improve the economic opportunities and well-being of women, while tackling these potential risks at the project level. These impacts should be assessed and discussed upfront during the infrastructure investment decision-making process. Integrating gender into sustainable infrastructure policies could be advanced by considering the social and environmental spillovers of infrastructure projects to women.

Comprehensive, pre-construction social and environmental risk assessments with an integrated gender-sensitive analysis are essential to ensure effective management of these risks. Such assessments should examine the impact of infrastructure projects on the well-being of women living in communities. Unfortunately, both environmental impact assessments that take into account indirect risks (so-called strategic environmental assessments) and social risk analyses are expensive and therefore applied to only a minority of projects. As a minimum, government intervention is needed to ensure that such comprehensive assessments are carried out for the highest-risk projects, such as major roads cutting through forested regions and wetlands or communities. Furthermore, assessments need to be as independent as possible. In practice, their quality varies widely, as responsibility for choosing an evaluator often falls on the operator who may influence the consultant to ensure a lenient assessment.

Throughout the implementation of infrastructure projects in urban and rural areas, mitigation, reporting and monitoring require the development of specific gender indicators. These should reflect information on the role of women both as users, workers or entrepreneurs, and must also measure women's organisational capacity, access to information and decision-making. Moreover, as highlighted in the World Bank's Good Practice Note for addressing gender-based violence in major civil works, projects should include a response mechanism for gender-based violence cases that provides essential services for survivors and has effective and confidential reporting channels (World Bank, 2018[16]).

The private sector also has a key responsibility in mitigating and responding to social and environmental risks from their infrastructure investments and projects. The OECD Due Diligence Guidance for Responsible Business Conduct[2] should be promoted in infrastructure projects and related public procurement procedures to reinforce the social and environmental sustainability of such projects and to mitigate adverse impacts on gender equality and the environment.

9.3.3. Gender gaps in access to digital services

Enhancing women's access to communications infrastructure, from mobile to broadband networks, is crucial to ensuring that they can harness the benefits of the digital transformation. Access to digital networks increases economic opportunities and it may also help address environmental issues by, for example, facilitating teleworking and reducing the need for commuting.

Connectivity is not yet ubiquitous or evenly distributed by gender nor by geographic location. Surveys show that globally, women access the Internet less than men do, with 45% of women using the Internet compared to about 51% for men – which corresponds to having 250 million fewer women than men online (ITU, 2017[19]). In OECD countries, Internet usage among women in 2018 was at 86%, equal to that among men. However, even among some OECD countries, disparities persist. For instance, in Turkey, the gender gap was around 14 percentage points, with women having less access when compared to men (OECD, 2019[20]). Worldwide, women are on average 26% less likely than men to have a smartphone. In South Asia and Africa, these proportions stand at 70% and 34%, respectively. Worldwide, some 327 million fewer women than men have a smartphone and can access the mobile Internet (OECD, 2018[21]).

To ensure an inclusive digital transformation, it is essential to enhance access and reduce digital divides, including by age, education, gender, income, and geography, that persist across and within countries (OECD, 2020[22]). The 2016 OECD-IDB Latin America and the Caribbean Broadband Toolkit sets out a comprehensive agenda for policies that can help broaden access to digital technologies in the region, addressing both major supply and demand issues in a holistic and coherent manner (OECD/IDB, 2016[23]).

Several good practices exist in terms of promoting connectivity to rural populations, based on the experience and outcomes in OECD countries. Some effective options to improve access are to subsidise national and rural broadband networks, promote municipal networks and design competitive tenders for private sector network deployment and management, and to implement open access arrangements (OECD, 2018[24]). Beyond fostering sound regulatory frameworks, certain policies such as universal service frameworks and state aid mechanisms can help address the specific needs of women. Well-designed, appropriately located and affordably priced broadband infrastructure can be a powerful tool in the pursuit of gender equality.

Improving women's access to communication networks and services can contribute substantially to greater gender equality. The use of the Internet, digital platforms, mobile phones and digital financial services, for example, can help women earn additional income, increase employment opportunities, and access knowledge and digital government services. In Australia, fast broadband connection at home has encouraged more people to work from home, access education, have smart devices in their homes, and to start their own business. The effects were found to be particularly strong in rural areas and for women. Upon the broadband roll-out, the number of self-employed women grew on average 2.3% every year, compared to only 0.1% on average in non-National Broadband Network areas (NBN, 2018[25]). The use of digital platforms has also helped reduce barriers to participation in the labour market for women, increasing flexibility and work-life balance, even though these are often linked to part-time employment (OECD, 2017[26]). Some of the benefits of increased flexibility, as well as of 'teleworking', are currently being tested during the COVID-19 pandemic, as extended lockdown periods are changing daily work- and family- life habits. Even though it has been argued that teleworking could both improve productivity, gender equality and work-life balance for both women and men in the long-run, it is yet to be determined whether these benefits are also applicable in the short-run (OECD, 2020[27]). Evidence from Germany before the COVID-19 pandemic show that teleworking was preferred by either men without children or by women with children. Irrespective of the case, teleworking is seen as a possible barrier for career advancement, an issue which could rather affect women more than men, due to existing biases (Zhang et al., 2020[28]). Mandatory teleworking as experienced currently, could also improve men's work-life balance in a way that they can contribute more easily in the home and reduce care burdens on women. Digital services can also facilitate the delivery of medical services, especially for elderly people in remote places, if accessibility is guaranteed (Taylor, 2015[29]).

A fundamental barrier for women to access the Internet is the lack of availability of broadband services. Policies to promote competition and private investment, as well as independent and evidence-based regulation, have been tremendously effective in extending coverage. Scarcely populated areas, such as rural areas, may be more challenging in terms of profitability for market players. In these cases, the cost of deploying some types of infrastructure may be high compared to the expected return on investment (OECD, 2018[24]). This can disproportionally affect more women in developing countries as they seem to surpass men located in rural areas in numbers, whereas working age men mainly tend to be in urban areas (UNDESA, 2018[30]). Affordability of communication services in both rural and urban areas is a challenge for all but also disproportionally affects more women and girls, and is one of the key hurdles in accessing Information and Communication Technologies (ICTs) (OECD, 2018[21]). With it come difficulties to obtain health information and tele-health services, which remain crucial healthcare tools as illustrated by the COVID-19 pandemic.

In addition to hurdles related to access, such as availability and affordability, women may also lack sufficient education and there may be inherent biases and socio-cultural norms that curtail their ability to benefit from the opportunities offered by the digital transformation (OECD, 2019[31]).

Safety-related issues are also one of the reasons leading families to oppose the use of the Internet or the ownership of a mobile phone for women and girls. For example, for women in China, Colombia and Mexico, harassment is a key concern and among the top barriers to owning and using a mobile phone. Women and girls using the Internet can be exposed to additional risks, including cyberstalking, online harassment or even sexual trafficking, and it thus becomes crucial to develop measures to protect and prevent gender-based violence online (GSMA, 2015[32]); (OECD, 2018[21]). The European Institute for Gender Equality estimates that 1 in 10 women have already experienced some form of cyber violence at the age of 15 (EIGE, 2017[33]). The paucity of data that exist calls for the need to collect harmonised data, on a recurrent basis, related to cyber violence against women and girls, for effective actions to be designed and implemented and progress monitored (c.f. (OECD, 2018[21])).

Enhanced and gender-sensitive applications on top of the infrastructure layer are critical, as are policy interventions addressing long-term structural biases. For example, applications (apps) such as the "SafetiPin" in India could contribute to addressing issues related to sexual harassment, and to improving security for women in India by helping them navigate the city with less risk (see section 5.4.3). In addition, similar apps could provide the aggregated data from its users to local governments and planners to improve services and make cities safer for women (SafetiPin, n.d.[34]).

Developing digital infrastructure could also support the empowerment of women in greener economic activities and enable them to tackle climate change. For instance, ICT can help farmers receive more accurate information on weather forecasts, climate trends and new production practices. The Shamba Shape-up broadcasts, viewed in Kenya, Tanzania and Uganda, provide practical information on how to improve farming practices and approaches, ranging from livestock health and agronomy to climate change adaptation. The broadcasts target mainly women farmers, as they are aired at times when women and children are at home. Through the broadcast's website women and men are equally encouraged to share their experiences and ask for information. An impact evaluation has estimated that the net economic impact of the websites reached USD 25 million, mainly from dairy farming in which women are heavily engaged (World Bank Group, FAO and IFAD, 2015[35]).

Technology and innovation can also support women in rural areas by reducing the time spent in household chores, and thus providing women with free time to engage in other, income generating activities. A project promoting solar-powered drip irrigation systems in Benin found that introducing such an innovative and energy efficient solution provided food security and increased household income with the increase of production. The project benefited women and girls in rural off-grid areas, who are usually the ones both collecting water and, as smallholders or in charge of community gardens, facing higher risks in their production. Despite initial high investment costs, this type of technology has proved more cost-effective when compared to alternative technologies in the long-term (Burney et al., 2010[36]).

9.4. Benefits of gender equality for industry, innovation and infrastructure: Women's role in innovation and the development of digital infrastructure

9.4.1. Women's leadership in the green and digital sectors

The OECD Analytical Database on Individual Multinationals and their Affiliates (ADIMA) shows that women are under-represented in boardrooms across all industries, although there has been some improvement in recent years. Women make up only 16% of board members in the top 500 multinational enterprises (MNEs) (by market capital) according to ADIMA, with shares as low as 12% in the technology sector (Figure 9.1) (OECD, n.d.[37]).

Figure 9.1. Boards of Directors in all industries remain largely male dominated

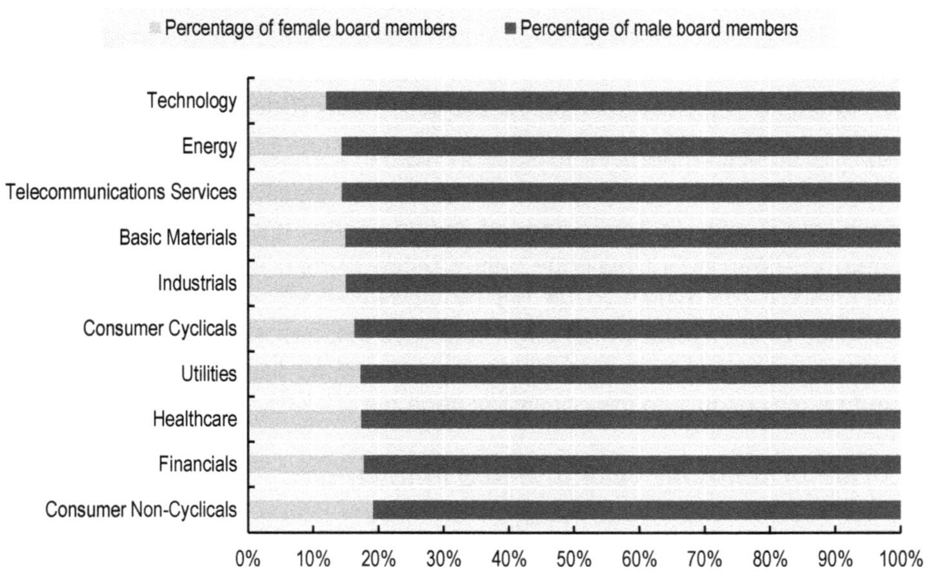

Source: OECD Analytical Database on Individual Multinationals and their Affiliates (ADIMA), (OECD, n.d.[37])

Whilst a number of national and indeed international efforts to improve female participation exist (e.g. The G20/OECD Principles of Corporate Governance (OECD, 2015[38])), gaps remain across all countries, although they are smaller – but still significantly large – in countries that have introduced specific policies, such as quotas (see also the OECD Corporate Governance Factbook, 2019 (OECD, 2019[39])).

There is a similar gender gap in self-employment and entrepreneurship. For instance, in the European Union (EU), less than one in ten (9.6%) working women were self-employed in 2018, significantly below the share for men (16.9%). Although this gender gap has closed slightly over the past decade, it is due to a decline in the number of self-employed men. Over the period 2014-18, 5.3% of women across OECD economies were actively working to start a business, compared to 7.9% of men (OECD/European Union, 2019[40]).

Women face several barriers to entrepreneurship, notably in the area of perceived skills and risk aversion. Over the 2014-2018 period, only 37.7% of women in OECD countries reported they had the knowledge and skills to start a business, compared to about half of men. Furthermore, women in OECD countries were more likely to indicate a fear of failure than men (42.2% vs. 36%). The gap was greater in EU countries, and non-existent in Korea, Japan and Israel (OECD/European Union, 2019[40]).

There are many examples of how greater gender equality in senior management in industry and infrastructure can help bring about a faster move towards sustainability. Using a dataset of all Fortune 500 CEOs and boards of directors for a ten-year period, (Glass, Cook and Ingersoll, 2016[41]) find that firms characterised by gender diverse leadership teams are more effective than other firms at pursuing environmentally friendly strategies (Chapter 2).

Women can play an active role in decision making related to digital infrastructure and help shape the future digital landscape. However, women are currently under-represented in ICT jobs and top management, and men are four times more likely than women to be ICT specialists. In OECD countries on average, only 0.5% of girls at 15 years of age wish to become ICT professionals, compared to 5% of boys (OECD, 2018[21]). Perhaps, unsurprisingly, there are also fewer female entrepreneurs in the ICT sector – and those women that do start ICT businesses face socio-cultural gender biases when raising capital (OECD/European Union, 2019[40]).

Yet, women can be crucial contributors to expanding access and use of broadband networks in underserved areas. In India, Wireless for Communities (W4C) fostered the creation of barefoot women network engineers and wireless women entrepreneurs in communities to help transfer knowledge and develop local content. This project helped to raise women's empowerment and to create safe spaces, while also making these networks more socially viable by demystifying technology and transferring the control, management and ownership of the technologies to the community (Srivastava, 2018[42]).

In OECD countries it is equally imperative to support women's engagement in leading green business initiatives. For instance, the Canadian government has made significant investments to increase the consideration of gender diversity in environmental issues. Under Impact Canada, a government-wide initiative, the Women in CleanTech Challenge was created to help support the creation of six, highly impactful clean technology companies to be led by women. Each entrepreneur receives more than USD 600K over a period of 2.5 years, which cover business incubation support, science and technology support from federal laboratories, as well as an annual stipend for living and travel expenses, allowing women to dedicate themselves fully to their business ventures (OECD, 2020[43]).

9.4.2. Women's role in scientific research and innovation

Science is fundamental in informing environmental management. Ensuring the sustainable management of ecosystems will require massive progress in science and innovative technologies. The digital transformation under way and the related advances in biology and materials science have a tremendous potential to help tackle the negative side-effects of economic activity, including climate change and pollution, as well as improve the management of natural resources and ecosystems and support biodiversity. The application of artificial intelligence is also bringing about a transformation in research and innovation, and could become an important tool in environmental management. According to the 2018 OECD Science, Technology and Innovation Outlook, the national government budget for research and development (R&D) on issues relating to environmental concerns has been steadily increasing over the past 35 years (OECD, 2018[44]).

Women's participation in sciences and innovation can both enrich the outcomes and help overturn long-held beliefs and social norms regarding their role. For instance, there is a well-established research field on male-female differences in cognitive thinking and socio-emotional skills. An often quoted generalisation that men are better at analytical thinking while women score better at empathy was demonstrated in one study on newborn babies conducted in 2000 (Connellan et al., 2000[45]). However, when scrutinised by female researchers, they found that the research methodology of the study did not meet psychological research standards and the results may simply have reflected the social and cultural gender biases of researchers rather than a biological reality (Nash and Grossi, 2007[46]).

Women's participation in science can also change the quality and outcomes of research beyond human sciences. To illustrate, female evolutionary biologists have changed the way a species behaviour is interpreted. A study undertaken in Sweden shows that academic literature on the traits and behaviours of animals and plants in sexual conflicts is often framed from a human viewpoint, the male often described as proactively searching for a partner, and the female as the passive one reflecting certain societal norms, but such frames may affect research conclusions (Karlsson Green and Madjidian, 2011[47]). Beyond evolutionary biology, it is difficult to assess how women's presence could change the outcomes of research due to their limited participation.

The digital transformation of science is also bringing to the forefront differences in the way male and female scientists conduct scientific research. Under the OECD International Survey of Scientific Authors, female authors are less likely to use advanced tools and data or code sharing practices compared to their male colleagues. On the contrary, they appear more willing to engage in activities relating to their digital identity or to share information about their work online.[3]

Box 9.1. Women's participation in science

While there was some progress in the representation of women in science in some countries and sectors (e.g. biology), overall they are less present, in particular in technical sectors such as physics, computational molecular biology and the digital technology, such as computer science. These technologies are increasingly relevant for innovation in environmental issues.

The gender gap starts to widen among PhD graduates and peaks at the researcher level. According to UNESCO data, less than 30% of the world's researchers (those employed in research and development) in 2017 were women (UNESCO, 2019[48]). The lowest ratio is found in East and South Asia (less than 20%) and the highest in Latin America and the Caribbean, and Central Asia (over 45%). Within OECD countries, one of the lowest ratios is Japan's, at 16.2%, while Lithuania and Latvia had the highest, at above 50%.

There are a number of reasons for this, from gender stereotyping in childhood and youth – which affect choices of study and cause self-selection among female students – to social norms, and inherent gender biases in the academic community. For example, in the United States, women often make up nearly half of the biology faculty, and within the department of behavioural and social sciences, 70% of faculty members are women. Yet, more often than not women are dissuaded from following more technical subjects related to environmental management, which may hamper the quality of overall biodiversity research and management (Sheltzer and Smith, 2014[49]).

Women are under-represented in most STEM-related professions, despite the fact that girls do as good as or even better than boys in these fields at school (Stoet and Geary, 2018[50]). Based on 2016 data, in OECD countries, only one third of graduates in natural sciences, engineering and ICTs were women (Figure 9.2). Such a large gap among graduates drives the gender gap for professionals in these fields (Box 9.1). The gender disparities in science-related careers may also be affected by other factors, such as women's additional household and caring responsibilities that may create barriers to career advancement, or biased performance evaluation which is often influenced by gender stereotypes on women's abilities in STEM, as well as the lack of women in high ranking positions (OECD, 2018[51]).

Figure 9.2. Tertiary graduates in natural sciences, engineering and ICTs (NSE & ICT), by gender, 2016

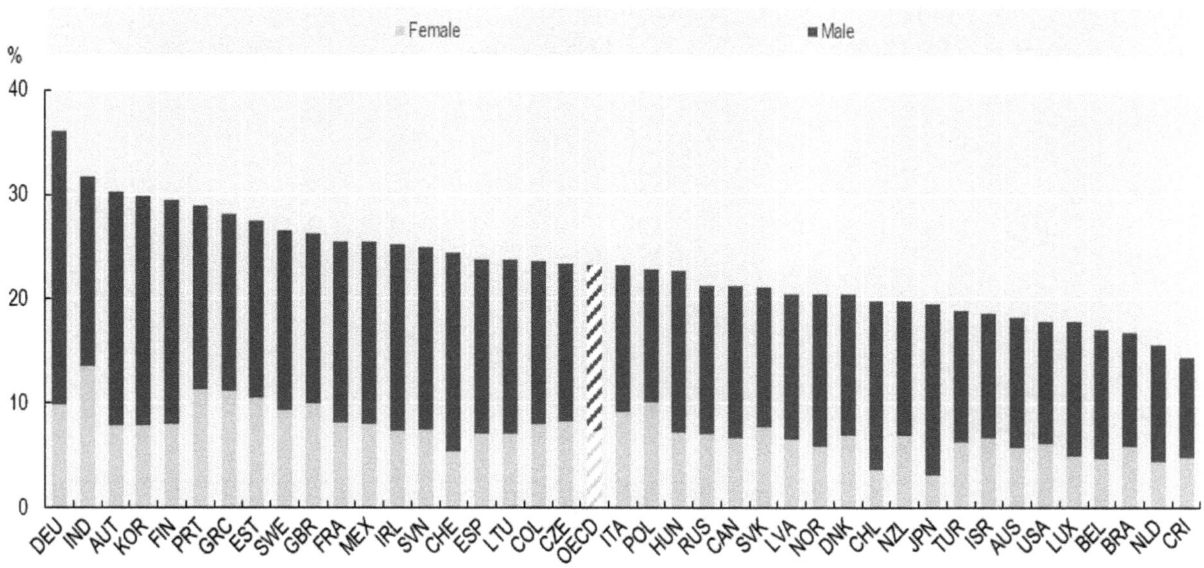

Source: OECD (2019), Measuring the Digital Transformation, (OECD, 2019[20])

An OECD report proposed a first-time analysis of the participation of women in science and technology developments, especially those related to the digital transformation. An analysis of the extent to which women contribute to developing patentable inventions and open-source software shows that women's participation in inventive activities has been increasing over the last 15 years, although at a very slow pace. Female participation in patenting activities has increased at a faster pace than the average rate at which all patent applications grew over the period 2004-15, – and in ICTs it increased relatively more than in all other technological domains (OECD, 2018[21]).

Women's participation has grown remarkably in many technology domains, as reflected in patent applications globally. For instance, in Canada, compared with the 1980s, there are now four times more patents including at least one woman inventor and five times more in the case of ICTs (Canadian Intellectual Property Office., 2017[52]).

Still, the gender gap remains significant. The percentage of women participating (as professionals and technicians) in technology development (inventive activity) remains low, reaching only 15% on average across all countries and all technology domains worldwide (Figure 9.3). There is a relatively higher participation observed for chemistry and health-related technologies (20% and 24% respectively), while environment-related technologies are just below the average participation and the rate is even lower for power generation and general engineering technologies (10% and 8% respectively).

Figure 9.3. Female participation in inventive activities worldwide

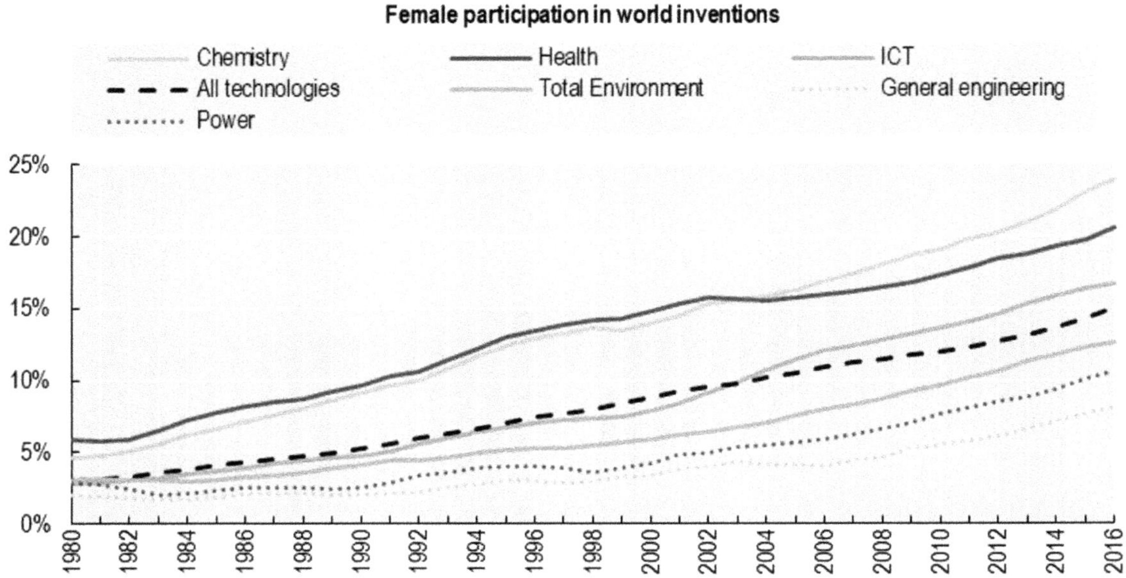

Note: Showing a 3-year moving average of counts of priority patent applications (simple patent families), by inventor's country of residence, with patent family size of two or more (excluding singletons). Data for 2016 are provisional. ICT = Information and Communication Technologies, CCM = Climate Change Mitigation, CCA = Climate Change Adaptation.
Source: OECD (2020) OECD Environment Statistics (database); OECD calculations based on extractions from EPO (2019) and using Dictionaries from (Laz Martinez, Raffo and Saito, 2016[53]) and search strategies developed by OECD.

Within the range of environment-related inventions, there are important variations both in the levels and in their growth rates (Figure 9.4). Women's participation is higher in some of the relatively new domains such as climate change adaptation technologies and solar photovoltaics, which is in contrast to domains such as climate change mitigation technologies in transport and wind power where there is a persistently low rate of women inventors. The latter could be partly explained by the need for engineering skills for developing many transport and wind power technologies. Moreover, road transport in particular is a domain where more inclusiveness efforts might be needed.

Figure 9.4. Female participation is higher in some of the less mature 'green' technologies

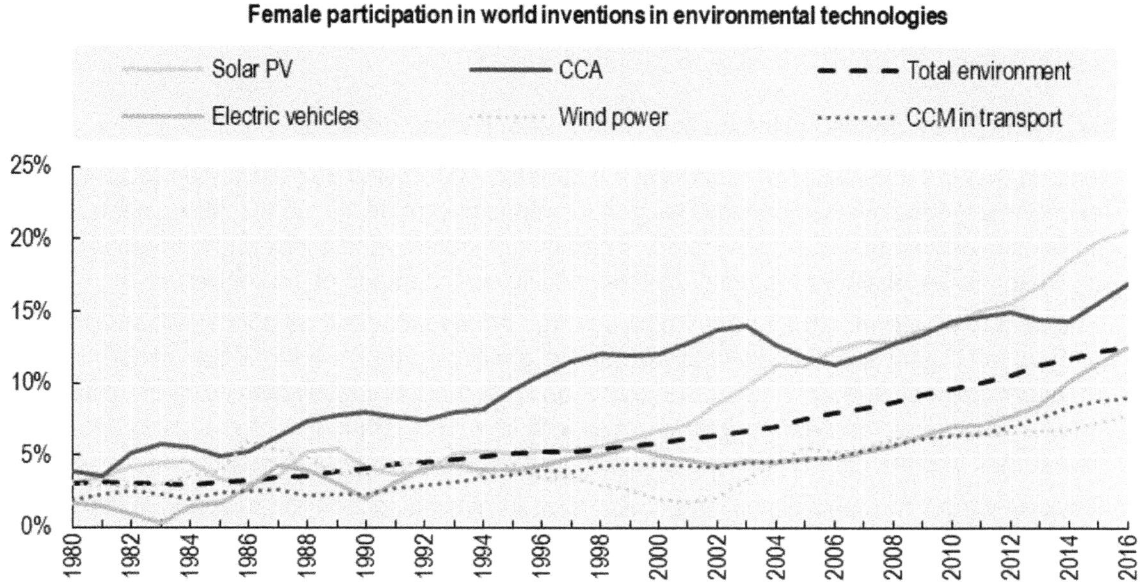

Note: Showing a 3-year moving average of counts of priority patent applications (simple patent families), by inventor's country of residence, with patent family size of two or more (excluding singletons). Data for 2016 are provisional. ICT = Information and Communication Technologies, CCM = Climate Change Mitigation, CCA = Climate Change Adaptation.
Source: OECD (2020) OECD Environment Statistics (database); OECD calculations based on extractions from EPO (2019) and using Dictionaries from (Laz Martinez, Raffo and Saito, 2016[53]) and search strategies developed by OECD.

Differences in women's involvement across these domains could be explained by their traditionally rather low participation in STEM courses, and this trend is likely to continue: the OECD 2020 PISA report shows that among students who score highly in the PISA tests, it is overwhelmingly boys who more often expect to work in science and engineering (Mann et al., 2020[54]).

Greater inclusion of women in inventive activities is good not only for women themselves, but also good for stronger economic growth and enhanced societal well-being. Evidence shows that inventions arising out of mixed teams, or women-only groups, appear to have wider technological breadth (and may therefore be more economically valuable) and higher impact from a technological viewpoint than those in which only men are involved (OECD, 2018[21]).

Despite being able to bring value for all, the presence of women also remains scarce in a fundamental component of the digital economy: software and algorithms. Analysis focusing on one well-known open-source software (R) shows that software remains very much a male-dominated world, especially in companies. Women are few and far between in the software world: of the top 1 000 software package contributors, only 92 were women. Women also play a relatively less important role, with many of them less connected to the network of software developers than their male colleagues. Especially in companies, very few (15%) female software (R) authors can be found (OECD, 2018[21]).

Greater efforts to tackle gender skills gaps in green innovation are also needed in developing countries. USAID, for instance, is providing financial support to researchers in developing countries. Through the Partnerships for Enhanced Engagement in Research (PEER), these researchers are linked with major academic institutions and research in the United States in the fields of Sciences, Engineering and

Medicine. Researchers receive help to build capacity and produce new research to fill existing knowledge gaps. Half of the researchers supported through PEER are women (USAID, 2020[55]).

9.5. Key actions for advancing the agenda and ongoing work

A number of actions are needed to integrate a gender lens in these domains:

- Ensure that the application of responsible business conduct and due diligence in supply chains in environment-sensitive sectors address gender impacts, in particular on the labour rights and health conditions of women. OECD standards, in particular the MNE Guidelines and the Recommendation on Responsible Business Conduct, call for specific consideration of gender issues.
- Ensure that major infrastructure projects undergo an independent, comprehensive environmental and social impact assessment that includes a gender angle, that there are gender-responsive monitoring and evaluation indicators in place, and that there is consultation with potentially affected groups, including women groups, in line with the G20 Principles for Quality Infrastructure Investment and the OECD Recommendation for the Governance of Infrastructure.
- Develop a more inclusive digital infrastructure by enhancing access and reducing digital divides for women, especially in rural areas.
- Consider mechanisms, including quotas and affirmative measures, for increased participation by women in senior management positions in industry and infrastructure. Specific measures that are applicable in favour of groups in situations of discrimination should also be considered.
- Develop programmes to increase the uptake of scientific research and innovation by women, and to tackle the barriers to their participation in STEM subjects.

References

Alamgir, M. et al. (2017), *Economic, Socio-Political and Environmental Risks of Road Development in the Tropics*, Cell Press, http://dx.doi.org/10.1016/j.cub.2017.08.067. [13]

Burney, J. et al. (2010), "Solar-powered drip irrigation enhances food security in the Sudano–Sahel", *Proceedings of the National Academy of Sciences*, Vol. 107/5, http://dx.doi.org/10.1073/pnas.0909678107. [36]

Canadian Intellectual Property Office. (2017), *Women's participation in patenting : an analysis of Patent Cooperation Treaty applications originating in Canada.*, Innovation, Science and Economic Development Canada, Canadian Intellectual Property Office. [52]

CBC (2018), "Allegations of Sexual Abuse, Racism revealed in Report of Hydro Projects impact in Northern Manitoba" (21 August 2018), https://www.cbc.ca/news/canada/manitoba/abuse-racism-report-hydro-1.4793749. [17]

Connellan, J. et al. (2000), "Sex differences in human neonatal social perception", *Infant Behavior and Development*, Vol. 23/1, http://dx.doi.org/10.1016/S0163-6383(00)00032-1. [45]

Dulac, J. (n.d.), *2013 GLOBAL LAND TRANSPORT INFRASTRUCTURE REQUIREMENTS Estimating road and railway infrastructure capacity and costs to 2050 INFORMATION PAPER*, http://www.iea.org. [14]

Duloc, J. (2013), "Global Land Transport Infrastructure Requirements: Estimating road and railway infrastructure capacity and costs to 2050". [12]

EIGE (2017), *Cyber Violence Against Women and Girls*, European Institute for Gender Equality. [33]

Glass, C., A. Cook and A. Ingersoll (2016), "Do Women Leaders Promote Sustainability? Analyzing the Effect of Corporate Governance Composition on Environmental Performance", *Business Strategy and the Environment*, Vol. 25/7, http://dx.doi.org/10.1002/bse.1879. [41]

Government of Canada (n.d.), *Gender-Based Analysis Plus*, https://cfc-swc.gc.ca/gba-acs/index-en.html#what (accessed on 11 February 2020). [56]

GSMA (2015), *Bridging the gender gap: Mobile access and usage in low-and middle-income countries*, http://www.altaiconsulting.com. [32]

ILO (2016), *Non-standard employment around the world : understanding challenges, shaping prospects.*, International Labour Organization, Geneva. [1]

ITF (2019), *Transport Connectivity: A Gender Perspective*, OECD Publishing, Paris, http://www.itf-oecd.org. [5]

ITU (2017), *ICT Facts and Figures 2017*, https://www.itu.int/en/ITU-D/Statistics/Documents/facts/ICTFactsFigures2017.pdf (accessed on 12 November 2020). [19]

Karlsson Green, K. and J. Madjidian (2011), "Active males, reactive females: stereotypic sex roles in sexual conflict research?", *Animal Behaviour*, Vol. 81/5, http://dx.doi.org/10.1016/j.anbehav.2011.01.033. [47]

Laz Martinez, G., J. Raffo and K. Saito (2016), "Identifying the gender of PCT inventors. Economic Research Working Paper No. 33", *Economics and Statistics Series*. [53]

Mann, A. et al. (2020), *Dream Jobs? Teenagers' Career Aspirations and the Future of Work*, OECD. [54]

Mortensen, S. and M. Boyland (2019), *Integrating gender in transitions to renewable energy in the Lower Mekong Region*, Stockholm Environment Institute, https://www.jstor.org/stable/pdf/resrep22986.pdf. [7]

Nash, A. and G. Grossi (2007), "Picking Barbie™'s Brain: Inherent Sex Differences in Scientific Ability?", *Journal of Interdisciplinary Feminist Thought*, Vol. 2/1, http://escholar.salve.edu/jift/vol2/iss1/5. [46]

NBN (2018), *Connecting Australia Report*, National Boradband Network, http://www.connectingaustralia.com.au/pdf/Connecting_Australia_Report.pdf (accessed on 12 November 2020). [25]

OECD (2020), *EPOC Survey on integrating gender in environmental policies*, https://one.oecd.org/document/ENV/EPOC(2020)9/en/pdf. [43]

OECD (2020), *OECD Digital Economy Outlook 2020*, OECD Publishing, Paris, https://dx.doi.org/10.1787/bb167041-en. [22]

OECD (2020), *Productivity gains from teleworking in the post COVID-19 era: How can public policies make it happen?*, OECD Publishing, Paris. [27]

OECD (2019), *Measuring the Digital Transformation: A Roadmap for the Future*, OECD Publishing, Paris, https://dx.doi.org/10.1787/9789264311992-en. [20]

OECD (2019), *OECD Corporate Governance Factbook 2019*, http://www.oecd.org/corporate/corporate-governance-factbook.htm. [39]

OECD (2019), *OECD Reference Note on Environmental and Social Considerations in Quality Infrastructure*, https://www.oecd.org/g20/summits/osaka/OECD-Reference-Note-on-Environmental-and-Social-Considerations.pdf (accessed on 12 November 2020). [9]

OECD (2019), "Sustainable connectivity: Closing the gender gap in infrastructure", *OECD Environment Policy Papers*, No. 15, OECD Publishing, Paris, https://dx.doi.org/10.1787/6350ba66-en. [6]

OECD (2019), *The role of education and skills in bridging the digital gender divide. Evidence from APEC economies*, https://www.oecd.org/sti/education-and-skills-in-bridging-the-digital-gender-divide-evidence-from-apec.pdf (accessed on 12 November 2020). [31]

OECD (2018), *Bridging the Digital Gender Divide*, http://www.oecd.org/internet/bridging-the-digital-gender-divide.pdf. [21]

OECD (2018), "Bridging the rural digital divide", *OECD Digital Economy Papers*, No. 265, OECD Publishing, Paris, https://dx.doi.org/10.1787/852bd3b9-en. [24]

OECD (2018), "Gender in a changing context for STI", in *OECD Science, Technology and Innovation Outlook 2018: Adapting to Technological and Societal Disruption*, OECD Publishing, Paris, https://dx.doi.org/10.1787/sti_in_outlook-2018-12-en. [51]

OECD (2018), “STI policies for delivering on the Sustainable Development Goals”, in *OECD Science, Technology and Innovation Outlook 2018: Adapting to Technological and Societal Disruption*, OECD Publishing, Paris, https://dx.doi.org/10.1787/sti_in_outlook-2018-9-en. [44]

OECD (2017), *Getting Infrastructure Right: A framework for better governance*, OECD Publishing, Paris, https://dx.doi.org/10.1787/9789264272453-en. [10]

OECD (2017), *Going Digital: The Future of Work for Women. Policy Brief*, http://www.oecd.org/els/. [26]

OECD (2015), *G20/OECD Principles of Corporate Governance*, OECD Publishing, Paris, https://dx.doi.org/10.1787/9789264236882-en. [38]

OECD (n.d.), *Recommendation of the Council on the Governance of Infrastructure*, http://legalinstruments.oecd.org. [11]

OECD (n.d.), *What data can tell us about women on boards*, https://www.oecd.org/gender/data/what-big-data-can-tell-us-about-women-on-boards.htm (accessed on 12 November 2020). [37]

OECD/European Union (2019), *The Missing Entrepreneurs 2019: Policies for Inclusive Entrepreneurship*, OECD Publishing, Paris, https://dx.doi.org/10.1787/3ed84801-en. [40]

OECD/IDB (2016), *Broadband Policies for Latin America and the Caribbean: A Digital Economy Toolkit*, OECD Publishing, Paris, https://dx.doi.org/10.1787/9789264251823-en. [23]

OHCHR and Heinrich-Böll-Stiftung (2019), *The Other Infrastructure Gap: Sustainability. Human Rights and Environmental Perspectives*, Office of the United Nations High Commissioner for Human Rights and Heinrich Böll Foundation. [15]

Open Development (2020), *Gender and Infrastructure*, https://opendevelopmentmekong.net/topics/gender-and-infrastructure-development/#ref-15179015-3. [4]

SafetiPin (n.d.), *SafetiPin: Supporting Sager Cities (website)*, https://safetipin.com/ (accessed on 12 November 2020). [34]

Sheltzer, J. and J. Smith (2014), “Elite male faculty in the life sciences employ fewer women”, *Proceedings of the National Academy of Sciences*, Vol. 111/28, http://dx.doi.org/10.1073/pnas.1403334111. [49]

Srivastava, R. (2018), “Women Creating Socially Sustainable Wireless Community Networks in India”, in *Global Information Society Watch 2018 - Community Networks*, https://giswatch.org/sites/default/files/giswatch18_web_0.pdf (accessed on 12 November 2020). [42]

Stoet, G. and D. Geary (2018), “The Gender-Equality Paradox in Science, Technology, Engineering, and Mathematics Education”, *Psychological Science*, Vol. 29/4, http://dx.doi.org/10.1177/0956797617741719. [50]

Taylor, K. (2015), *Connected health: How digital technology is transforming health and social care*, Deloitte Centre for Health Solutions. [29]

Tran, T. (2019), "The Feminization of Employment through Export-Led Strategies: Evidence from Viet Nam.Féminisation de l'emploi dans les stratégies axées sur l'exportation : l'exemple du Viet NamFeminización del empleo en las estrategias basadas sobre la exportación: el ejemplo de Viet nam", *Revue de la régulation* 25, http://dx.doi.org/10.4000/regulation.14589. [2]

U.S. Census Bureau (2016), *1970, 1980, 1990 and 2000 Decennial Censuses and 2010 2016 American Community Surveys*, https://www.census.gov/programs-surveys/decennial-census/data/datasets.html. [3]

UNDESA (2018), *United Nations demographic yearbook 2017*, United Nations. Department of Economic and Social Affairs, https://unstats.un.org/unsd/demographic-social/products/dyb/dybsets/2017.pdf (accessed on 12 November 2020). [30]

UNDESA (2009), *State of the World's Indigenous Peoples*, United Nations, Department of Economic and Social Affairs, Division for Social Policy and Development, Secretariat of the Permanent Forum on Indigenous Issues. [8]

UNESCO (2019), *Women in Science, Fact Sheet No. 55*, UNESCO Institute for Statistics, http://uis.unesco.org. [48]

USAID (2020), *PARTNERSHIPS FOR ENHANCED ENGAGEMENT IN RESEARCH (PEER)*, https://www.usaid.gov/GlobalDevLab/fact-sheets/partnerships-enhanced-engagement-research-peer (accessed on 12 November 2020). [55]

Wen, J. (ed.) (2020), *Gender-based violence and environment linkages: The violence of inequality*, IUCN, International Union for Conservation of Nature, http://dx.doi.org/10.2305/iucn.ch.2020.03.en. [18]

World Bank (2018), *Good Note Practice on Addressing Gender Based Violence in Investment Project Financing Involving Major Civil Works*, http://documents1.worldbank.org/curated/en/399881538336159607/Environment-and-Social-Framework-ESF-Good-Practice-Note-on-Gender-based-Violence-English.pdf. [16]

World Bank Group, FAO and IFAD (2015), *Gender in Climate-Smart Agriculture. Module 18 for the Gender in Agriculture Sourcebook*. [35]

Zhang, S. et al. (2020), "A work-life conflict perspective on telework", *Transportation Research Part A: Policy and Practice*, Vol. 141, http://dx.doi.org/10.1016/j.tra.2020.09.007. [28]

Notes

[1] Canada states that the Gender-based Analysis Plus (GBA+) is a process "that provides a rigorous method for the assessment of systemic inequalities, as well as a means to assess how diverse groups of women, men, and gender diverse people may experience policies, programs and initiatives" (Government of Canada, n.d.[56])

[2] http://mneguidelines.oecd.org/OECD-Due-Diligence-Guidance-for-Responsible-Business-Conduct.pdf.

[3] http://oe.cd/issa.

10 Women and SDG 11 – sustainable cities and communities: Make cities and human settlements inclusive, safe, resilient and sustainable

Women and men relate to urban and settlement design and transport infrastructure differently due to different social roles, occupational patterns and preferences. The risks of uncontrolled urbanisation, urban sprawl and slums, as well as inadequate and unsafe transport are greater for women for a variety of factors, ranging from the effects of indoor and outdoor pollution to gender-based violence. This chapter reviews the evidence on how urban life and design affects men and women differently, looks into women's role in promoting sustainable and inclusive cities and transport, and provides a series of policy recommendations to better integrate gender and sustainability considerations in urban design and infrastructure strategies and policies.

10.1. Key findings

This chapter focuses on the interaction between gender equality (SDG 5) and the promotion of inclusive and sustainable communities, with a focus on urban areas (SDG 11). The main findings and recommendations include the following:

- Growing urbanisation, combined with the continuous expansion of world population, are exacerbating a number of social and environmental challenges, including housing shortages, urban sprawl, carbon emissions, air pollution and land degradation.
- Air pollution is most damaging for the health of children, the elderly and women, in particular during pregnancy. Furthermore, women account for an over-proportionate share of low-income citizens, which tend to be closest to the most polluted parts of cities.
- Natural disasters tend to kill more women than men. Women appear to be among the most affected by natural disasters occurring in urban areas, especially when they live in the poorer neighbourhoods. They are more likely to be the last ones to leave home (or stay at home) in cases of natural disasters, due to existing gender inequality in terms of access to resources and the gendered division of labour.
- Inadequate and unsafe transport infrastructure has a greater negative impact on women's economic opportunities, when compared to those of men. Women are generally more sensitive to time constraints and put a higher opportunity cost on travel time because of their different household, family and work responsibilities. Safety is also a top priority for women which increases the attractiveness of public transport.
- Women's transport and mobility preferences are often more sustainable than those of men, as women follow more sustainable travel patterns. Adapting public transport to women's needs (in particular regarding safety and multimodality), could therefore lead to more sustainable transport patterns, enhance women's well-being and improve their economic opportunities.
- The interaction between gender equality and urban and transport development requires an intersectional analysis that takes into account other factors such as race and socio-economic status.
- Better representation of women in urban design and planning related decision-making and professions could help make cities and settlements more women-sensitive, and in turn, help optimise infrastructure investments to meet the needs of all the population.
- There is a need to collect evidence at the local level on women's transport and mobility patterns, as well as preferences and time use statistics. Understanding better women's travel needs is a prerequisite for making the right decisions regarding sustainable urban and transport development.
- Cities should develop comprehensive strategies on safety, with a specific focus on violence against women. More broadly, transport, land-use strategies, policies and projects need to take into account the needs of women, and their role should be promoted in developing national urban policies. Strategies and measures concerning resilience against natural disasters would also benefit from gender mainstreaming.

10.2. Key interlinkages between gender equality, urban and settlement development, and other SDGs

Fifty-five percent of the world's population lives in cities and the share is growing rapidly, could reach 60% by 2030 and 70% by 2050 (86% in OECD countries) (UN, 2018[1]). Cities are the source of well-paid, high quality jobs, education, health and social services. However, they are also linked to a high concentration of inequalities and are the source of much of the world's growing environmental problems. Cities account for more than 70% of the total global energy use and greenhouse gas (GHG) emissions (OECD, 2017[2]); (United Nations, 2017[3]). Growing urbanisation, combined with the continuous expansion of world population, will exacerbate a number of social and environmental challenges, including congestion, housing shortages, carbon emissions, air pollution and land degradation.

The problems are more intense in cities undergoing very rapid expansion where housing construction and public infrastructure developments are not keeping up with the rapidly growing population. In low income countries (LICs), 66% of the urban population in 2018 lived in slum conditions without access to clean water, sanitation, education and social services. Sub-Saharan Africa is the geographical region with most slum households in cities, reaching 54% (Figure 10.1). Even though there seems to be a decrease in the percentage of people living in slums, the absolute number of the world's slum population has been rising over the past 25 years, from 650 million in 1990 to nearly 1 billion in 2016 (Clos, 2016[4]).

Figure 10.1. Population living in slums (Percentage of urban population)

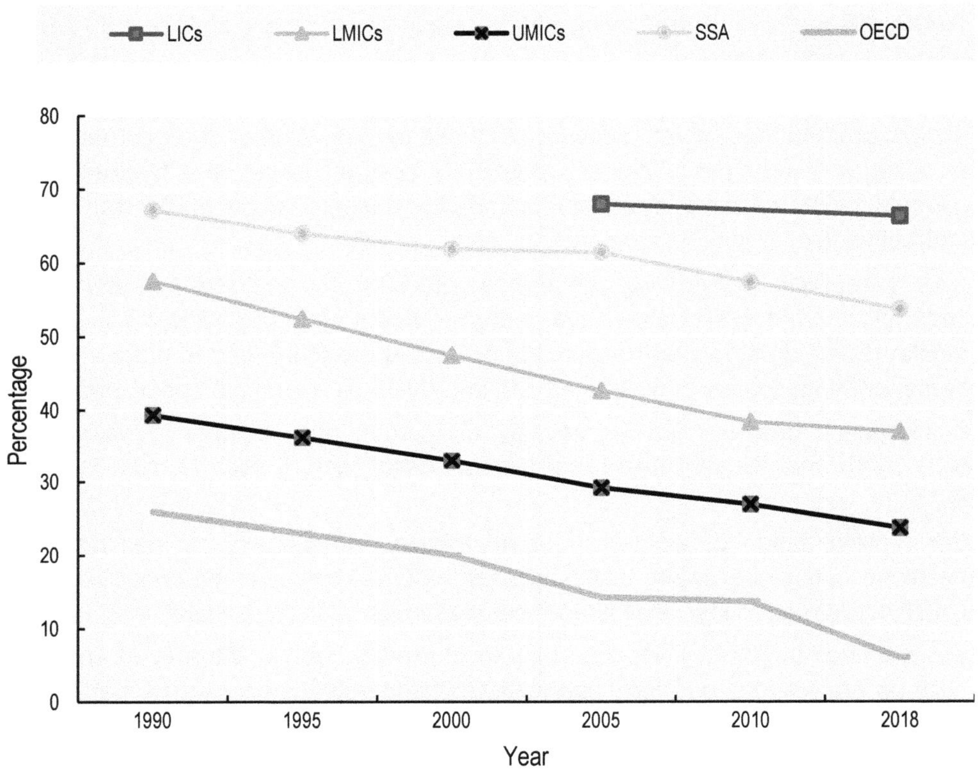

Note: Population living in slums is the proportion of the urban population living in slum households. A slum household is defined as a group of individuals living under the same roof lacking one or more of the following conditions: access to improved water, access to improved sanitation, sufficient living area, and durability of housing. Information presented for Low Income Countries (LICs), Lower Middle Income Countries (LMICs), Upper Middle Income Countries (UMICs), OECD members (OECD) and Sub-Sahara Africa region (SSA).
Source: World Bank Group World Development Indicators, last updated 15/10/2020.

The way cities are designed and governed, including the services offered, have implications for most SDGs. For instance, access to health care (SDG 4) and education (SDG 3) depend on the location of the respective health and education centres and their accessibility (i.e. transport network). At the same time, increased urbanisation has led to high levels of air and water pollution (SDG 3 and SDG 6), pressures on waste management (SDG 12) and a growing reliance on fossil fuels as a source of energy (SDG 7).

Urban planning and infrastructure development have traditionally been considered gender-neutral. However, women and men relate to urban and settlement design, and transport infrastructure differently due to different social roles, occupational patterns and preferences (SDG 5). Urban and settlement planning and transport infrastructure do not take into account the needs and the lives of its different users including women and girls, as documented in the World Bank's *Handbook for Gender-Inclusive Urban Planning and Design* (WBG, 2020[5]). This can in turn significantly reduce economic opportunities and well-being of these users by increasing the time and means they spend on commuting, and at the same time, contribute to air pollution and inefficient resource use. They could also lead to increasing safety and security risks, intensifying phenomena such as violence against women.

Urban and settlement development sectors - housing, transport, and land use – have marked implications on gender equality goals through three key dimensions: user patterns (accessibly, safety and affordability), labour market participation (employment and participation in decision-making), and spill over effects (social and environmental). Women's greater involvement in decision-making in these sectors could help reduce the overall environmental footprint of infrastructure in urban areas, and make it more gender-inclusive.

Sustainable urban planning and transport systems encompass in their definition both environmental sustainability and inclusiveness. Inclusiveness is, in turn, created by prioritising accessibility, instead of mobility (OECD, 2019[6]). Women's mobility patterns benefit much more from a turn to accessibility, hence a turn to more sustainable urban planning, design, and transport. This also applies to access to social infrastructure.

10.3. How unsustainable urban life and design affects men and women differently – key challenges

10.3.1. Gender-specific impact of urban pollution, natural disasters and other health hazards

The risks of uncontrolled urbanisation, urban sprawl and slums are greater for women for a variety of factors, ranging from higher exposure to or effects of pollutants in housing and outdoors, to gender-based violence. Women and children are most exposed to indoor air pollution in developing countries, where biomass is still used for heating and cooking, causing about 4 million deaths a year (WHO, 2018[7]). As women spend more time at home than men and are more frequent users of household cleaning products, they are also more exposed to certain hazardous chemicals (Hertz-Picciotto et al., 2010[8]).

The growth of cities and expansion of urban areas has also led to a growing exposure of the population to outdoor air pollution. Studies have consistently shown that air pollution is most damaging for the health of children, the elderly and women, in particular during pregnancy (Section 3.2.1). Furthermore, women account for an over-proportionate share of low income citizens, which tend to be closest to the most polluted parts of cities (e.g. heavy traffic, factories, etc.).

Pollution has more intense effects on women through other channels. As they are mainly responsible for caring obligations in the household, they are more likely to be the ones staying at home with children during high pollution days, reducing their employment opportunities (Aragón, Miranda and Oliva, 2017[9]) (Montt, 2018[10]). Research also provides a link between air pollution and psychological factors affecting mental and physical health (Zhang, Zhang and Chen, 2015[11]) (Kioumourtzoglou et al., 2017[12]), cognitive performance (Chen, Zhang and Zhang, 2017[13]) and even violent behaviour, of which women are the main victims (Truman, Morgan and Statisticians, 2014[14]) (Burkhardt et al., 2019[15]).

Gender inequality in urban pollution exposure and other environmental stressors can benefit from an intersectional analysis that takes into account other factors such as race and socio-economic status. For example, persistent environmental injustice means that disproportionately high numbers of ethnic-minority households in North America and Europe live near incinerators and landfills, and schools with high proportions of ethnic or national minority students are located near highways and industrial sites (Martuzzi, Mitis and Forastiere, 2010[16]) (Kweon et al., 2016[17]). In the United States, research shows that racial and ethnic minorities, especially in metropolitan areas with high residential segregation, are more exposed to higher levels of air pollution (NO_2, $PM_{2.5}$ and PM_{10}) than Whites[1], because these groups are closely located to roads, industrial and construction sites (Woo et al., 2019[18]). Understanding how these urban inequalities might interplay with gender inequality is crucial for conceptualising the burden on women.

Women's health is also particularly sensitive to the lack of sanitation and clean water (mainly in developing countries) (WHO and UNICEF, 2017[19]), smog and other forms of pollution (including chemicals contamination) during times of pregnancy (Inyinbor Adejumoke et al., 2018[20]) (Bergman, Rüegg and Drakvik, 2019[21]) (Leiser et al., 2019[22]) (Freia Project, 2020[23]). Obesity and related diseases such as diabetes and cardiovascular problems are also more likely to arise in an urban setting. People's sedentary lifestyles and changing eating habits in cities are key drivers of such health effects (Smith S. et al, 2012[24]) (Gassasse et al., 2017[25]) (Congdon, 2019[26]). This is becoming the trend also in developing countries, where the phenomena of malnutrition (over-nutrition or under-nutrition) are more and more frequent (Kuddus, Tynan and McBryde, 2020[27]) (Yarahmadi et al., 2013[28]). Women in urban areas seem to be the ones more affected by obesity in low income countries; whereas in high income countries obesity is widespread among both women and men in disadvantaged groups (Swinburn et al., 2011[29]). Among other policies such as changing nutritional habits, better access to sports and recreation facilities for both children and adults is necessary, as it would allow for more exercise and a turn to healthier life-styles for urban dwellers. Other infrastructure such as bicycle lanes and public green spaces could also offer an incentive for people to exercise more, in addition to further supporting women's mobility which is more sustainable than that of men (Section 10.3.3).

Studies of the impact of natural disasters have also shown that on average they kill more women than men (Neumayer and Plümper, 2007[30]); (Islam, 2012[31]). Such phenomena are becoming more frequent, driven by the effect of climate change on extreme weather events. Women appear to be among the most affected by natural disasters occurring in urban areas, especially when they live in poorer neighbourhoods. For instance, the 2011 floods at the coastal city of Lagos, Nigeria, killed 100 people, and displaced thousands, causing about USD 320 million worth of damages. Women living in the city's slums were highly affected by the floods, which caused damages to their homes and properties, illness and injuries; leading to increasing caring responsibilities and lack of sanitation and health; when compared with women in other affected areas (Ajibade, McBean and Bezner-Kerr, 2013[32]). In an Oxfam study on deaths resulting from the 2004 Tsunami in coastal Indonesia, women and girls accounted for more than three-quarters of deaths in most of the surveyed villages (Oxfam International, 2005[33]). In 1991, during the cyclone disasters in Bangladesh, of the 140 000 people who died, 90% were women (Ikeda, 1995[34]). In industrialised countries, more women than men died during the heat wave that affected Europe in 2003, and in France most deaths were among elderly women (Pirard et al., 2005[35]). Natural disasters also affect the city structure, as they destroy houses and livelihoods. In the case of the heatwave in Europe, the existing housing structures and facilities were inefficient to deal with the high temperatures (Ogg, 2005[36]).

The disproportionately high female death rate in natural disasters results from women staying in risk-prone zones to pursue domestic duties, while men are more likely to be away from home or have access to transport and thus flee quickly. Women are more likely to be the last ones to leave home (or stay at home) in cases of natural disasters, due to existing gender inequality in terms of access to resources and the gendered division of labour. In coastal Indonesia and Sri Lanka women spent precious seconds looking for relatives and children when the wave hit, and that more men than women knew how to swim (Oxfam International, 2005[37]).

Women and girls also face a heightened risk of gender-based violence during and following natural disasters. In the absence of social protection schemes and in situations in which there is food insecurity combined with impunity for gender-based violence, women and girls are often exposed to sexual violence and exploitation as they attempt to gain access to food and other basic needs for family members and themselves. Women and girls with disabilities are at a particular risk of gender-based violence and sexual exploitation during and following disasters, due to discrimination on the basis of physical limitations and barriers to communication and the inaccessibility of basic services and facilities (Castañeda Carney et al., 2020[38]).

The Sendai Framework for Disaster Risk Reduction (2015-30) acknowledges women's role in risk management and reduction and resilience building. It includes references to promoting gender equality (participation in decision making and resource management, and access to social protection measures, education, health and early warning etc.). The 2015 Paris Agreement emphasised the contribution of gender equality and empowerment of women to fighting climate change as well as the specific impact of climate change on women. Improved coherence between climate and disaster risk reduction frameworks is considered imperative for more effective policy deployment (OECD, 2020[39]). Looking at the differentiated effects of extreme weather events and natural hazards to women, gender-sensitive risk prevention and adaptation measures should be also prioritised. Such measures should build on including women in the administrative, decision-making and development of preventive measures; as well as addressing inequalities that exacerbate the vulnerability of certain population groups to such events. Mainstreaming gender equality in financing disaster relief is also key.

For instance, after the 2005 earthquake in the Pakistan-administered Azad Kashmir region which left over 85,000 people dead, the Earthquake-Displaced People Livelihood Assistance Restoration Program included a Gender Vulnerability Action Plan. Funds were directed specifically to improving women's access to rights and entitlements of land and home ownership. All new houses were registered under the names of both wife and husband. The plan also set targets to provide equitable access to housing reconstruction by ensuring a 50% female representation in the Village Reconstruction Committees. In addition, women had to make up 50% of participants trained in housing reconstruction and other non-traditional skills. While the programme had positive effects and allowed a large number of women rebuild their homes, results fell short of expectations. It showed, however, that while gender-specific plans are an important start, they cannot alone ensure gender equality and hence, additional time and resources need to be allocated to ensure that gender mainstreaming in disaster reconstruction plans are truly successful (WBG, 2020[5]).

10.3.2. Improving social infrastructure contributes to gender equality

Typical city design, with segregated areas for residences, workplaces and shopping, reflects the one-earner household paradigm and smaller cities of the 20th century; commute time between these areas makes it particularly difficult for a single individual to take on a double or triple burden of childcare, breadwinning and elderly care. While in some countries, policies and societal norms are adapting to improve burden-sharing, women's participation in economic activities is still more restricted than men's because of the way urban areas are designed and how they have expanded over the years.

In developed countries, women more often than men find themselves with the double (or triple) burden of looking after their children and elderly family members, while providing income to the household at the same time. Worldwide, women spend on average three times more time on unpaid care work than men do. In South Asia, the gap is much greater, with women spending 7.5 times more time than men (Figure 10.2). In the United Kingdom, for instance, one in four women are responsible for taking care of an elder with a chronic illness or disability as well as a child, as opposed to one in six men. There are currently 2.4 million people who are "sandwiched" into providing for both generations.

Figure 10.2. Average time spent on unpaid care work varies by gender and region

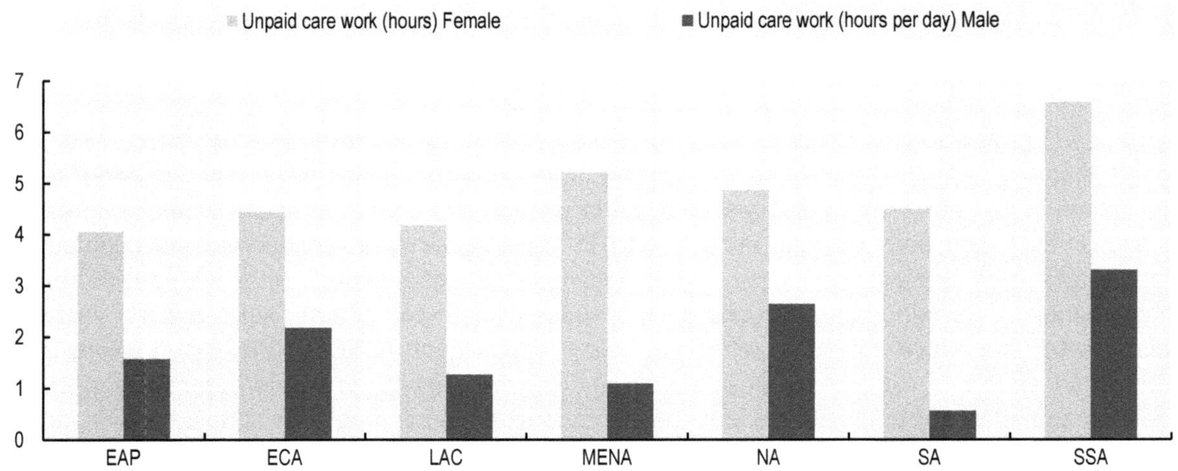

Note: This chart presents the average hours per day spent on unpaid care work by women and men by regions of the world: East Asia and Pacific (EAP), Europe and Central Asia (ECA), Latin America and the Caribbean (LAC), Middle East and North Africa (MENA), North America (NA), South Asia (SA) and Sub-Saharan Africa (SSA).
Source: OECD (2019), Gender, Institutions and Development Database.

Due to this added pressure, women are twice as likely as men to give up their work and four times more likely to take on part-time jobs (Holzhausen, 2014[40]). Women are also more often than men obliged to combine multiple jobs. For instance, in the United States 6.7% of women aged 20 to 24 work multiple jobs compared to 4.6% of men in the same age group (Wilson, 2015[41]) (Figure 10.3). The burden is greatest for single mothers, who account for almost 6% of all households in OECD countries – four times more prevalent than single father households (OECD, 2011[42]). In the United States, 82.2% of custodial parents are mothers compared to 17.8% custodial fathers (Grall, 2013[43]).

Figure 10.3. Women in the United States are more likely to work multiple jobs than men

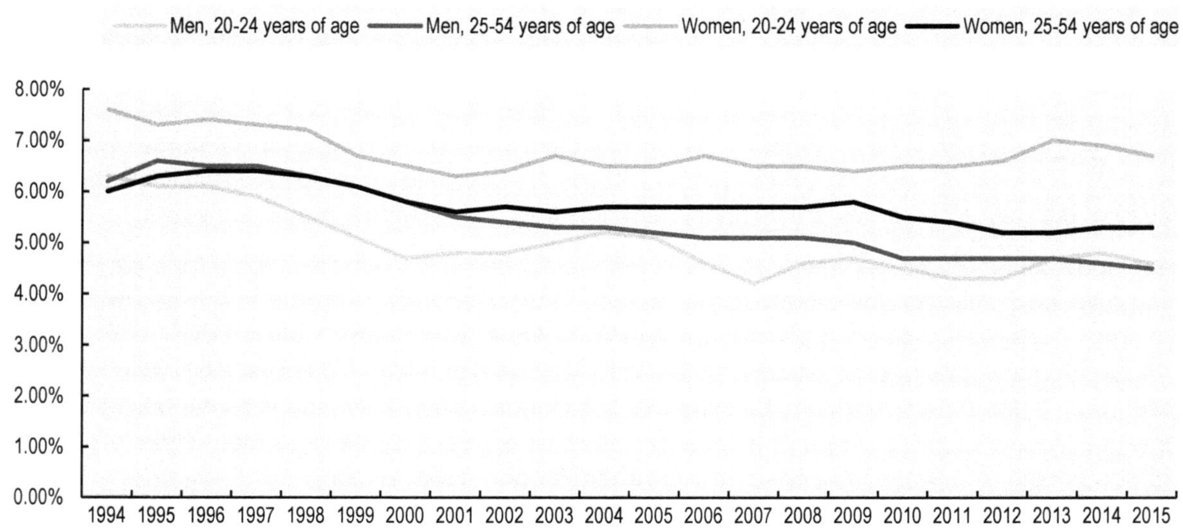

Note: Multiple job holders as a percent of employed by sex and age, for the period 1994-2015. Rates for 2015 are the average for the period January-June 2015.
Source: Wilson (2015). Women are more likely to work multiple jobs than men.

Easy access to affordable children and elderly care facilities are essential to facilitate women's participation in the economy, while allowing them to fulfil their family responsibilities. Yet, in many countries, access to such facilities is limited, too expensive, or inconveniently located. Developing such services can bring about immediate benefits. In Hamburg, Germany, the abolishment of a range of fees associated with schooling and day-care, and a guaranteed place in kindergarten crèche, or other day care institution for children over one year of age, has led to more children staying in school until late afternoon. This has also had the effect of supporting women to participate in the labour force, and providing choice and flexibility to families (OECD, 2016[44]). In addition to the cost, the location of such care services is critical, as women and men display different mobility preferences and patterns.

10.3.3. Women show more sustainable mobility patterns and preferences than men

Men and women typically use transport differently, but in the past transport policies have not considered gender-specific patterns of transport use (Sarmiento, 1996[45]). In some countries, women still face some legal and social barriers to travel freely, as it is the example of Qatar, where guardianship rules still limit women's ability to travel. Even when women have legal access to transport, they still face the disproportionate effects of inadequate transport which limit can limit their economic opportunities, when compared to those of men, as women are generally more sensitive to time constraints and put a higher opportunity cost on travel time (OECD, 2012[46]). For example, changes in commuting distances may have greater impacts on women, who have different mobility patterns, as they are usually responsible for double or triple burden of childcare, breadwinning and elderly care (Kwan, 1999[47]); (Kwan and Kotsev, 2015[48]).

Travel patterns may also be influenced by the density of urban sprawl. Urban sprawl generally leads to longer commuting distances, causing loss of time and productivity (OECD, 2018[49]). It usually creates greater public infrastructure requirements, including sufficient road network and public transportation, leading to higher public service provision costs and higher living costs for the local population. Taking into consideration that women are the ones in charge of the majority of non-work related travelling within a household, especially when it relates to children, and irrespective of the income disparities between the two sexes, more multifunctional land use and better local transport services can enhance gender equality and women's economic empowerment, while at the same time boosting more sustainable forms of transport (Boarnet and Hsu, 2015[50]).

Neglecting women's preferences of transport and mobility may limit women's economic participation. In particular, high commuting costs may have a negative effect on women's access to full-time employment in large metropolitan areas. In Tokyo, for instance, women with lower incomes usually live further from the business districts than men while higher commuting costs, or high housing prices in the city centre, create obstacles for women to enter the full-time labour market (Abe, 2011[51]). When making employment decisions, women put greater importance on the convenience of commuting than men, who generally prioritise salary over commute time (Nafilyan, 2019[52]).

Studies have found a negative correlation between commuting time and women's participation in the labour force. An increase of one minute in commuting time in metropolitan areas is associated with approximately 0.3 percentage point decline in the women's labour force participation – reflecting women's mobility patterns: they do not simply commute but do a lot of additional travel (Black, Kolesnikova and Taylor, 2014[53]). Another study from the Office for National Statistics in the United Kingdom found that men tend to have longer commutes than women and the commuting gap follows the same age-pattern as the gender pay gap. Commuting time is more important in women's decision to leave one's job while hourly rate has a greater impact on men, which suggests women prefer jobs with shorter commutes and higher flexibility, at the expense of pay. This is often an indicator of their need to perform other non-paid labour roles such as dealing with family and caring responsibilities (ONS, 2019[54]).

Women and men also display different mobility patterns. Women on average travel less often and for shorter distances than men (Moriarty and Honnery, 2005[55]) and are more willing to reduce vehicle use than men (Polk, 2003[56]) (Polk, 2004[57]). A recent study of eight European and Asian cities confirms that women travel shorter trips on average than men, use public transport more and travel more during off-peak hours (Ng and Acker, 2018[58]). A 2019 study on Santiago, Chile using big data collected by passengers' mobile phone use, shows that women and girls often engage in multi-purpose trips, covering different chores linked to household groceries, childcare and work. Women also tend to spread their trips between a smaller number of destinations when compared to men, and they also tend to visit locations closer to home. Female mobility patterns also vary based on income and employment (Gauvin et al., 2019[59])

Since women have more complex travel patterns, they tend to prefer more flexible modes. At the same time, since they have a higher preference for public transport, emerging trends such as shared mobility or mobility as a service, could attract more female than male users. Such solutions would also help mitigate the environmental costs of transport (Ng and Acker, 2018[58]).

Some travel surveys and limited gender-based data available for OECD and European countries seem to indicate that women follow a more sustainable travel behaviour (Samek Lodovici et al., 2012[60]). When given better alternatives, women may choose to give up driving altogether. If cities want to further encourage the development of flexible and sustainable modes of transport, policies to address women users' preferences should be implemented as women will be the dominating users.

Furthermore, research shows that women are more interested in making decisions for environmental or ecological reasons. This can be seen by their choice of private vehicles (i.e. in developed countries, women influence heavily the final decision of the purchase of a family vehicle). They tend to choose fuel- efficient smaller cars, with safety aspects being crucial, but are less interested with the status the vehicle may bring. That said, as women often play an important role in the purchase of the main family vehicle, they may be influenced to buy heavier cars, which are promoted as being safer. Often women prioritise safety above fuel economy in relation to transport. From their perspective, fuel economy may appear to be less important than safety (SUM4All, 2019[61]).

However, women's more sustainable travel patterns have not been examined thoroughly enough to see how they could further support the decline of private car usage, nor to see how they could set the scene for a shift in the travel patterns of men. Also, more analysis would be welcomed to show how these travel patterns are aligned with fluctuations in income, fuel prices and environment-related tax-policies, which lead to changes in demand. Hence, implementing a gender equality lens to the development of public transport networks and emerging mobility services could boost women's economic empowerment. At the same time, a dialogue with women users could help policy-makers with integrating gender-based analysis in developing the public transport networks, as well as prioritising more sustainable travel, thus potentially limiting cities' adverse environmental impacts, including carbon emissions.

10.3.4. Transport safety as a top priority for women

Safety is a major concern for women, more so than men, which determines their choices across all transport modes. Safety is also the top priority insisted upon by women as a condition for their use of public transport (Bray, Holyoak and Bray, 2015[62]); (Ng and Acker, 2018[58]); (Civitas, n.d.[63]). This is notably the case in urban areas where more women than men use public transport and heavily depend on these systems for their mobility needs. Guaranteeing women's safety in cities and public transport will further increase usage of more sustainable modes of transport, such as walking, cycling and public transport. Modes often preferred by women.

Women in both developed and developing countries have reported feeling unsafe using public transport services (Yavuz and Welch, 2010[64]) (OECD, 2019[65]). Violence against women and girls affects multiple aspects of their lives. In 2011 a Gallup survey with data from 143 countries found that on average only 62% of women responded positively when asked whether they feel safe walking alone at night. Men giving the same response rose to 72%. The gap was much higher in high income countries, with only 59% of women responding positively, compared to 82% of men (Crabtree and Nsubuga, 2011[66]). A NGO 2018 study on sexual harassment and assault in the United States found that 81% of females had experienced harassment in public spaces and public transport (SSH, 2018[67]). In Mexico, 71% of women report feeling insecure in public transport (OECD, 2017[68]).

This is not only morally unacceptable in itself; it also causes economic and social harm, reinforcing inequality (ITF, 2019[69]). A 2017 International Labour Organisation (ILO) study on safety involving a large-scale survey of women's use of transport in developing countries shows that limited access to safe transportation is the greatest challenge to greater participation by women in the labour market, reducing their participation by 15.5 percentage points (ILO, 2017[70]). Unsafe public transport also creates additional environmental costs, to the extent that men and women who would have otherwise used it turn instead to private vehicles.

Examples provided in the International Transport Forum's (ITF) "Compendium on Women's Safety and Security: A Public Transport Priority" (2018) show that a large majority of women worldwide feel unsafe in public transport and have been victims of some type of physical or verbal harassment and other forms of violence in public spaces (ITF, 2018[71]). As a result, women often prefer driving when faced with a modal choice, using taxis or other forms of for-hire ride services rather than walking, cycling or using public transport.

For instance, ITF (2018) reports a London survey that found that 28% of women who have used public transport in the past 12 months say they experienced unwarranted staring, sexual comments, bodily contact, wolf-whistling and exposure (ITF, 2018[71]). In Latin America alone, six-in-ten women say they have been physically harassed while using public transport. The statistics are alarming in many Asian countries as well. Women in Bangladesh face high levels of inequality in livelihood opportunities and access to economic assets. Women's participation in the workforce remains low, at an estimated 34%, while in rural areas women own only 8% of productive assets. According to estimates, around 94% of women commuting in public transport have experienced sexual harassment in verbal, physical and other forms. In Jakarta, nearly 90% of women found the safety of trains to be poor or very poor, whereas only 35% of men held a similar concern for security (Turner, 2011[72]).

If cities want to increase their public sustainable transport use and occupancy rates, and therefore reduce GHG emissions from road transport, the safety of their services must be ensured. This will both attract more women passengers and improve the experience of the substantial share of existing women users.

10.3.5. Making transport gender-responsive and sustainable

Most cities do not have transport programmes or policies that are focused on improving the user experience of women transit riders considering their off-peak time of travel and non-commute trip purpose. Yet, by better tailoring public transport to women's preferences and needs, its appeal can increase, leading to cleaner cities and greater economic opportunities for women. One city that does consider gender aspects in its urban planning is Vienna. Prompted by a survey in the late 1990s on the use of public transport by men and women, data is now collected to determine how different groups of people use public transport and spaces before an infrastructure project gets underway (Foran, 2013[73]).

The Los Angeles METRO bus system noted a 39% decrease in total crime and a 60% decrease in operator assaults between 2017 and 2018 thanks to implementing the safety measures that included greater presence of transit and local police, video cameras to document and deter assaults, and training for transit operators on the best ways to de-escalate confrontations (ITF, 2018[71]).

Women's mobility and use of public transport is also affected by comfort and physical accessibility (Civitas, n.d.[63]). Beyond guaranteeing safe access to bus and metro stations, many times women – as well as elderly or other vulnerable groups - have different needs concerning the vehicle's design and technology.

Added to the specific route patterns of women (with bus stops placed close to schools and nurseries for example), and to security in public transportation, public transportation also have shortcomings concerning the "comfort measures". For example, given that women are more likely to travel with children or elderly dependents, they would benefit from buses with a lowering platform, appropriate railings for safe holding, ramps and designated space for access with baby-strollers or shopping bags. In Santiago, Chile, women's needs and preferences have been taken into consideration when upgrading the bus fleet (ITF, 2019[74]).

10.4. Women's role in promoting sustainable and inclusive cities and transport

While women are more exposed to the risks of urban living they are also in a unique position to make urban life more inclusive and safe. As more vulnerable users, they can help identify and support better policies for all.

While women account for a large proportion of employment in the public sector in regional and local governments, they are underrepresented in decision-making responsibilities. There is a growing number of female mayors, such as Barcelona, Madrid, Paris and Singapore, but there is no internationally available data. Preliminary data for nine OECD countries show an average 5% of mayors are female – ranging from 0% to 32% (OECD, 2020[75]). A 2016 survey in 100 cities in the United States indicated that only 25% of mayors were female (Levine Einstein, Glick and LeBlanc, 2017[76]).

10.4.1. Increasing women's workforce participation and leadership in the transport sector would improve sustainability

In order to plan and design transport systems and infrastructure with women in mind, the sector needs more women in the transport workforce. Women passengers also feel safer when they ride with women drivers, who are considered to be safer drivers (Marsh, 2004[77]); (IFC, 2020[78]). This is especially critical in developing cities, where efficient, equitable and safe public transport modes play an important role in regulating the growing share of private vehicle use, including motorcycles.

Yet, in research recently conducted by the ITF on 47 countries across the world, it was found that female participation in the transport sector was 17% on average in 2018, and some of the countries with the smallest gender gaps are experiencing declines in female participation in the sector (Ng and Acker, 2020[79]). In OECD countries women account on average for only 22% of employment in the transport sector, with a larger percentage of them occupying positions in air transport and postal and courier activities (Figure 10.4). In Mexico, Colombia and Turkey men account for over 90% of transport jobs. On the other hand, women in the transport sector surpass 30% in Iceland, and 28% in the United States. In the 21 APEC economies, fewer than 20% of transport jobs are held by women (OECD, 2019[65]). Despite women's presence in the sector, they usually occupy administrative, catering and low-paid positions, while they are almost absent from international road haulage or maritime services (SUM4All, 2019[61]). In the United States, in 2015 women comprised only 15% of transport and related occupations and only 4.6% of commercial truck drivers were women (Olczak-Rancitelli, 2015[80]). Increasing female participation in the transport workforce will require measures addressing problems in recruitment, retention and long-term career advancement.

Figure 10.4. Only 22% of the OECD transport workforce is female

2017 data

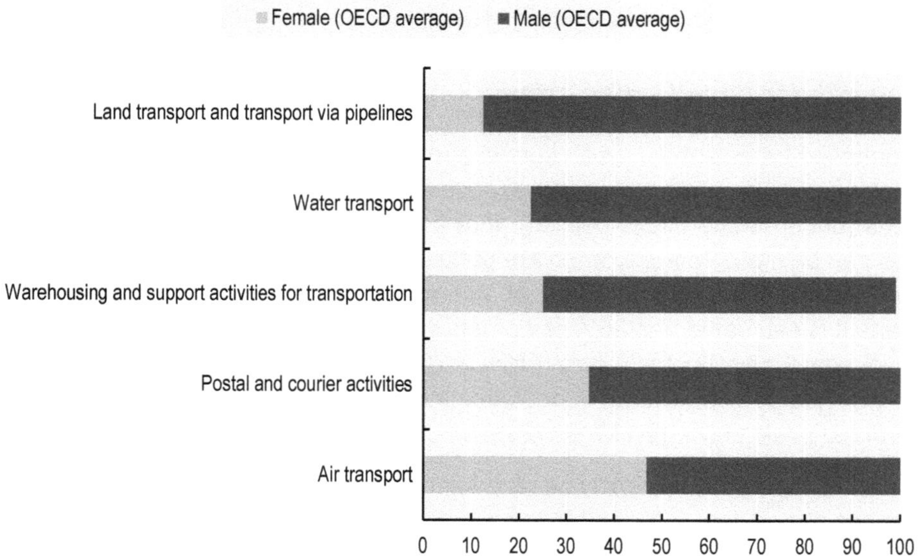

Note: All data for 2017, under "Economic activity (ISIC-Rev.4), 2 digit level: 49 - Land transport and transport via pipelines", except for Israel (2016). Data for Chile and Colombia under Economic activity (ISIC-Rev.3.1), 2 digit level: 60 - Land transport; transport via pipelines.
Source: ILOSTAT (2017).

In most countries, women are also hardly represented in decision-making positions in infrastructure development. Globally, females only make up 18% of leadership in infrastructure ministries (energy, transport and communications) compared to 38% in socio-cultural ministries (health, education, family and youth) (Wilson Center, 2018[81]). Moreover, they only make up 16% of leadership in economy and finance ministries, thus having a limited influence in investment decisions in infrastructure development at the national level (for more on women in leadership positions see Section 2.3). Out of the 62 member countries of the ITF, only 11 countries have female Ministers of Transport in 2020. Having more women on boards of transport companies can also help increase the use of public transport (and hence deliver environmental gains) by focusing more on women's needs such as the availability of public transport at off-peak hours, specific transport routes, flexible transport modes and personal safety.

10.4.2. Making settlements safer and more peaceful by engaging women

Until recently, the role of women in safeguarding settlements and cities had not been acknowledged or much researched. However, new research and case studies reveal how, for instance, women in particular can make settlements safer and more inclusive when they participate in the police force and peacekeeping operations.

Many communities have adopted the community policing approach that stresses the importance of involving the community in a practical way so that the police and the public can co-operate to prevent and solve crimes. Through this framework, more women have entered the police force. Women officers have been shown to use less physical force and to better promote co-operation and trust. With a shift in the perception of good policing as being less about physical force and more about preventing violence, women are particularly suited for the position. In Sierra Leone, for instance, increasing the participation of women in the police force has made lawmakers more conscientious of gender violence, and has enabled more women to be informed about their human and legal rights (Ibrahim, 2012[82]).

There is also evidence that women's engagement in peace processes contributes to their success and durability, thereby contributing to the security and resilience of cities. The Geneva Graduate Institute's Broadening Participation Project studied over 180 peace agreements across countries and found that women's involvement in the peace process increased the probability of reaching a peace deal and its duration (O'Reilly, Súilleabháin and Paffenholz, 2015[83]).

10.4.3. Tackling gender-based urban crime

The risks of uncontrolled urbanisation, urban sprawl and slums are greater for women, in particular due to gender-based violence. Women are especially exposed to urban living risks in parts of cities which lack safe public spaces (under-lit and under-policed), that are poorly connected to safe public transport, and where crime rates can be high. Poorer women are particularly exposed. In both developed and developing countries women represent the largest share of victims of criminal deaths, assaults, kidnappings and sexual harassment. It is estimated that 35% of women worldwide have experienced either physical and/or sexual violence at some point in their lives (WHO, 2017[84]). Furthermore, in some countries, sexual harassment and violence against women is not criminalised (OECD, 2019[85]). Victims of sexual assaults are also often afraid to seek justice (WHO, 2012[86]).

While sprawling metropolises cannot simply be razed and rebuilt with a gender lens, a number of measures can be taken to make streets feel safer and to keep women more secure when moving around the city. By making cities safer, women can prioritise more sustainable mobility including public transport, cycling and walking. For example, in India, SafetiPin, founded in 2013, is an application ("app") that aims to help women stay safe by letting users' rate streets and areas for safety criteria such as lighting, visibility, people density, gender diversity, security and transportation. It also aggregates safety data, partly provided by its users, for use by local government and planners. SafetiPin now has 51 000 points of data for Delhi alone, and offers users "safest routes", helping them navigate the city with less risk (SafetiPin, n.d.[87]).

10.4.4. Greening cities from a gender perspective

Cities can help champion a place-based and territorial approach to global agendas, and rethink policies for sustainable development from the ground up. They are well-placed to experiment, pilot and replicate ambitious policies that can be tailored to the places where people work and live, and generate complementarities, co-benefits and synergies.

The transition to a low-carbon economy is an opportunity to leverage the potential of cities to advance environmental quality, while fostering inclusive growth. For instance, improvements in air quality (by reducing CO_2 emissions from private cars) which is called for under SDG 11 (cities and communities) also helps minimise health cost as targeted by SDG 3 (good health and well-being).

Feminist urban designers claim that men and women experience space differently, and are requesting a gender-responsive approach to urban planning, and to the design and construction of public spaces and amenities (Casanovas et al., 2015[88]). These differences are not only influenced by the socially and culturally constructed productive, reproductive, personal or community gendered roles, but also by other characteristics such as age, income, race etc.

Introducing a more gender-sensitive approach to urban design, may also lead to more sustainable infrastructure. In Wallhagen, Eriksson and Sörqvist (2018), for example, female urban designers participating in a competition in Sweden placed greater importance on environmental aspects than men, even though they felt that their possibility to influence them was rather low. Male urban designers, on the other hand, felt they could influence, even though they rated environmental aspects as of the lowest importance (Wallhagen, Eriksson and Sörqvist, 2018[89]).

A more participatory approach, by including women in all stages of infrastructure planning design and development, could help include perspectives that might not have been otherwise considered. (Ortiz

Escalante and Gutiérrez Valdivia, 2015[90]) and (Fleming, 2018[91]) present the case of Col-lectiu Punt 6, an organisation of female architects and urban planners in the city of Barcelona, which over the last decade have included local women in all stages of urban transformation in the city. As a main constraint to a gender-sensitive approach in urban planning they identify the inability of the relevant public authorities to integrate such an approach in their work, and thereby mainstream gender in urban development.

Elsewhere, women's groups have also been pursuing the goal, sometimes successfully, of empowering local women and turning them into agents of change in their neighbourhoods and cities. This is the case both in Europe, as seen in the case of Berlin (Droste, 2011[92]), and in developing countries. The Gender Inclusive Cities Programme (GIPC), implemented in Petrozavodsk, Russia; Dar es Salaam, Tanzania; Delhi, India; and Rosario, Argentina, worked with local women to fill in knowledge gaps on why women and girls felt unsafe is some parts of their cities, and were therefore excluded from city life (Women in Cities International, 2012[93]).

Better representation of women in urban design and planning related decision-making and professions could help make cities and settlements more women-sensitive, and, in turn, help optimise infrastructure investments to meet the needs of all the population.

Examples of cities led by female mayors who have embarked in major greening campaigns include Paris and Singapore, involving for instance a large expansion of cycle lanes and a closure of parts of the city to motor vehicles. In the City of Kitakyushu, Japan, a historical example shows how the active role of women's associations led the city on a new path of sustainable development, due to their heightened apprehension about the health risks caused by the city's industrial structure (Box 10.1).

Box 10.1. Women's activism to reduce pollution in the City of Kitakyushu, Japan

The City of Kitakyushu developed as a manufacturing city in the beginning of the 1900s and soon became one of the four main industrial zones in Japan, focusing on industries like steel, chemicals, ceramics and cement. Although these heavy industries had a positive impact on the economic development of the city, as well as on Japan as a whole, they also resulted in negative externalities on the environment, generating high levels of air and water pollution, which reached their peak in the 1960s.

Civil society, and in particular associations of women concerned about the health of their families, started a protest against the high level of pollution in the city and launched the slogan "We want our blue skies back". The movement later involved universities, the business community and local government to seek common solutions to overcome pollution. The campaign achieved remarkable results, with joint efforts contributing to clearing up both the skies and sea water around Kitakyushu in only a couple of decades (end of 1970s).

The movement towards a more environment-friendly economy, combined with the need to rethink the industrial structure of the city due to the crisis of the steel industry, brought the City of Kitakyushu towards new industries, including assembly and automobile industry, renewable energy and recycling industry.

More recently, some cities have taken initiatives to develop specific gender-responsive urban plans. For example, the city of Umeå, Sweden has been developing a gender-based landscape ("gendered landscape" approach) since 2009, mapping all changes in the city with a gender and a sustainability lens. The city has been collecting gender-disaggregated data for the past 30 years, and uses the data to develop mobility and infrastructure policies and projects, taking into consideration women's more sustainable travel patterns, different income levels, and different interests and needs (Kneeshaw and Norman, 2019[94]). This has led to changes in the cities public areas, more lighting in streets that would facilitate access for men, women and children, and changes in the public transport network.

Vienna, as seen above, has been pioneering 'gender mainstreaming' for nearly 30 years, and has developed a Manual for Gender Mainstreaming in Urban Planning and Urban Development (Urban Development Vienna, 2013[95]). When developing social or subsidised housing, which constitutes a large part of the city's total housing market, it uses a four-pronged approach comprising of planning, economic, ecological and socially sustainable pillars. The city's Housing Fund follows gender-sensitive planning criteria. Wohnprojekt Wien, in the north part of Vienna, is a self-run complex of 40 flats, with low energy consumption, shared mobility options, bike garages, shared rooms and gardens (Kail, 2018[96]). This model is taking into consideration gender aspects, as many common activities are shared between the inhabitants (such as cooking, shopping and occasionally childcare). Each inhabitant contributes 11 hours of unpaid work per month to the community, a model copied from previous gender-responsive development examples in the city, which has proven to facilitate both men and women living in these areas (Littig and Leitner, 2017[97]).

Key to urban planning and design is the methodology, which often tends to take male-centred participant recruitment, language, and hypotheses. There are now several examples of gender-responsive methodologies that reflect women's mobility patterns and preferences. For instance, Lille, France, has been conducting research on women's cycling patterns in Lille, the barriers they face and their perceived risks. From the results they understood that to encourage women to cycle more, and hence move in a more sustainable way, there needs to be more protected bicycle infrastructure, traffic-calming, additional street lighting and dedicated bike workshops for women (POLIS, 2021[98]).

In Madrid, the public transport operator EMT has made gender inclusiveness a long standing priority for many years. Through the Women STEM Chair (launched in October 2020), EMT has been working with Comillas Pontifical University and Iberdrola to improve women's education, training and professional careers. The partnership seeks to support women in accessing public transport professions, including technical and managerial roles. In addition, the public operator also recently launched the EMT's Observatory for Women and Safe Transport, which studies the way women use transport and takes active steps to improve women's safety while using public transport services (POLIS, 2021[99]).

Some cities in developing countries are also starting to make the urban environment more women-friendly. For instance, the city of Maputo, Mozambique, has launched a Safe City and Safe Public Spaces Programme as part of the UN Women's Safe Cities Global Initiative. This initiative, organised together with youth activists, includes improving street lighting as well as rebuilding abandoned public buildings with a gender perspective in mind (UN Women, 2019[100]).

A more systematic collection of disaggregated data at the regional, local and city level, as well as integrating gender-responsive budgeting and gender and environmental impact assessments in infrastructure programmes and projects, could help systematise gender-mainstreaming in infrastructure development.

Green and blue spaces can help to address the impacts of climate change, such as the urban heat island effect and floods. They can also stabilise urban temperatures and reduce energy requirements for the heating and cooling of buildings, thus reducing greenhouse gas emissions. Green spaces can increase noise attenuation and they have proven key in attenuating mental health issues and stress during the COVID-19 pandemic (Pouso et al., 2021[101]). Some cities are also expanding green spaces within residential areas and increasing the availability of sports facilities. Such initiatives can especially benefit adult women who, globally, are almost 32% insufficiently physically active, in comparison to 23% of men (WHO, 2016[102]) (Box 10.2).

Box 10.2. Well-designed urban environments can promote active lifestyles

Insufficient physical activity are risk factors for a range of chronic diseases, including heart disease, stroke, diabetes, osteoporosis and cancer. Chronic diseases caused by these risk factors also lead to significant economic costs, including medical treatment, reductions in productivity and increases in work-related absenteeism.

In OECD countries, there is a significant gender gap in physical activity levels, as 30% of men and 37% of women do not meet the WHO physical activity recommendations. This is mostly because women are less likely to do sports than men. For example, women are 10% less likely to report sports participation in Germany and the United States, 16% less likely in Canada, and up to 36% less likely in France. There is also a sizeable socioeconomic gradient in sports participation. In France, women with post-secondary education are almost six times more likely to participate in sports compared to women without such education. Many causes underpin increasing levels of sedentary behaviours including, particularly in the case of women, perception of safety.

Effective public health actions can help increase total physical activity. Taking France as a case study, the OECD SPHeP-NCD (Strategic Public Health Planning for NCDs) model was adapted to assess six policy actions targeting different groups in the adult population. The interventions comprised public spending on sports and recreation, prescribing physical activity in primary care, mass media campaigns, mobile apps, public transportation and workplace sedentary interventions.

All the interventions were found to reduce the number of new cases of diabetes, cancer and cardiovascular diseases. Public spending on sports and recreation was found to lead to the largest reductions in health spending compared with other modelled interventions, with EUR 1.2 billion saved in France compared to the baseline scenario within 32 years after the start of the intervention in 2019. Overall, three interventions - spending on sports and recreation, mass media campaigns and mobile apps - were found to be cost-effective within ten years from the start of their implementation

10.5. Key actions for advancing the agenda and ongoing work

There are a number of actions that can be taken to mainstream gender into urban development and transport infrastructure and thereby contribute to make cities safer and cleaner, and more inclusive and sustainable:

- Collect evidence at the local level on women's transport and mobility patterns and preferences. Time use surveys linked to users' trip purpose would allow for a better understanding of women's travel needs, and would set the ground for more gender-responsive urban development.
- Develop a whole-of-city initiative on safety and fighting crime and violence, with a specific focus on violence against women.
- Ensure that transport and land use strategies, policies and projects take into account the needs of women, promote the role of women in developing national urban policies, and incorporate gender mainstreaming into strategies and actions concerning resilience against natural disasters.
- A city design based on multi-functional neighbourhoods with short travel distances and proximity to work, childcare and schools, health care, shopping and services, along with safe pedestrian and recreation environments (including public parks) and frequent and easily accessible public transport, would help parents combine work and family duties, increasing opportunities for working parents to access the labour market and reduce time lost to commuting. This will also ensure lower air pollution, greater environmental protection and a more sustainable use of resources

- Promoting corporate practices such as flexible working hours and "teleworking", that can facilitate women's access to (and possibly to stay in) full-time work, while reducing carbon footprint and pollution.
- Promote the development of community networks that promote sharing of responsibilities and gender equality. Local support networks are particularly important in this context and can also bring about change in men's attitudes to childcare and household chores. A communal setting not only fosters mutual support but also validates changes in behaviour as men see their friends and peers taking up greater family caregiving responsibilities.

References

Abe, Y. (2011), "Family labor supply, commuting time, and residential decisions: The case of the Tokyo Metropolitan Area", *Journal of Housing Economics*, Vol. 20/1, pp. 49-63, http://dx.doi.org/10.1016/j.jhe.2010.12.001. [51]

Ajibade, I., G. McBean and R. Bezner-Kerr (2013), "Urban flooding in Lagos, Nigeria: Patterns of vulnerability and resilience among women", *Global Environmental Change*, Vol. 23/6, http://dx.doi.org/10.1016/j.gloenvcha.2013.08.009. [32]

Aragón, F., J. Miranda and P. Oliva (2017), "Particulate matter and labor supply: The role of caregiving and non-linearities", *Journal of Environmental Economics and Management*, Vol. 86, pp. 295-309, http://dx.doi.org/10.1016/j.jeem.2017.02.008. [9]

Bergman, Å., J. Rüegg and E. Drakvik (2019), *Final technical report Report: Final Technical Report of EDC-MixRisk*, http://ec.europa.eu/environment/endocrine/documents/4_SOTA%20EDC%20Final%20Report%20V3%206%20Feb%2012.pdf. [21]

Black, D., N. Kolesnikova and L. Taylor (2014), "Why do so few women work in New York (and so many in Minneapolis)α Labor supply of married women across US cities", *Journal of Urban Economics*, Vol. 79, pp. 59-71, http://dx.doi.org/10.1016/j.jue.2013.03.003. [53]

Boarnet, M. and H. Hsu (2015), "The gender gap in non-work travel: The relative roles of income earning potential and land use", *Journal of Urban Economics*, Vol. 86, pp. 111-127, http://dx.doi.org/10.1016/j.jue.2015.01.005. [50]

Bray, D., N. Holyoak and D. Bray (2015), *Motorcycles in Developing Asian Cities: A Case Study of Hanoi*, https://www.researchgate.net/publication/282332097. [62]

Burkhardt, J. et al. (2019), "The effect of pollution on crime: Evidence from data on particulate matter and ozone", *Journal of Environmental Economics and Management*, Vol. 98, http://dx.doi.org/10.1016/j.jeem.2019.102267. [15]

Casanovas, R. et al. (2015), *Women Working. Urban assessment guide from a gender perspective*, Col-lectiu Punt 6, https://issuu.com/punt6/docs/ww_issuu_simple (accessed on 4 November 2020). [88]

Chen, X., X. Zhang and X. Zhang (2017), *Discussion PaPer series Smog in Our Brains: Gender Differences in the Impact of Exposure to Air Pollution on Cognitive Performance*, http://www.iza.org. [13]

Civitas (n.d.), *Smart choices for cities.* [63]

Clos, J. (2016), "A New Urban Agenda for the 21st century: The role of urbanisation in sustainable development", in *OECD Regional Outlook 2016: Productive Regions for Inclusive Societies*, OECD Publishing, Paris, https://dx.doi.org/10.1787/9789264260245-9-en. [4]

Congdon, P. (2019), "Obesity and Urban Environments", *International Journal of Environmental Research and Public Health*, Vol. 16/3, http://dx.doi.org/10.3390/ijerph16030464. [26]

Crabtree, S. and F. Nsubuga (2011), *Women Feel Less Safe Than Men in Many Developed Countries*, https://news.gallup.com/poll/155402/women-feel-less-safe-men-developed-countries.aspx (accessed on 17 December 2020). [66]

Droste, C. (2011), *Gender in Mainstreaming Urban Development. Berlin on the path towards becoming a metropolis worth living in for women and men*, Senate Department for Urban Development, Berlin, https://www.stadtentwicklung.berlin.de/soziale_stadt/gender_mainstreaming/download/gender_broschuere_englisch.pdf (accessed on 4 November 2020). [92]

Fleming, A. (2018), "What would a city that is safe for women look like?", *The Guardian*, https://www.theguardian.com/cities/2018/dec/13/what-would-a-city-that-is-safe-for-women-look-like (accessed on 4 November 2020). [91]

Foran, C. (2013), *How to Design a City for Women. A fascinating experiment in "gender mainstreaming."*, https://www.bloomberg.com/news/articles/2013-09-16/how-to-design-a-city-for-women (accessed on 4 November 2020). [73]

Freia Project (2020), *Polystic Ovary Syndrome (PCOS) Irregular Menstrual Cycles : Advancing EDC Testing For More Protective Chemical Regulations*. [23]

Gassasse, Z. et al. (2017), "Association between urbanisation and type 2 diabetes: an ecological study", *BMJ Global Health*, Vol. 2/4, http://dx.doi.org/10.1136/bmjgh-2017-000473. [25]

Gauvin, L. et al. (2019), "Gender gaps in urban mobility", http://arxiv.org/abs/1906.09092. [59]

Grall, T. (2013), *Custodial Mothers and Fathers and Their Child Support: 2011 Current Population Reports*, http://www.census.gov/people/childsupport/data. [43]

Hertz-Picciotto, I. et al. (2010), "Study of Use of Products and Exposure-Related Behaviors (SUPERB):Study design, methods, and demographic characteristics of cohorts", *Environmental Health: A Global Access Science Source*, Vol. 9/1, http://dx.doi.org/10.1186/1476-069X-9-54. [8]

Holzhausen, E. (2014), *Sandwich generation concern is growing*, https://www.carersuk.org/for-professionals/policy/expert-comment/4604-sandwich-generation-concern-is-growing (accessed on 3 November 2020). [40]

Ibrahim, A. (2012), *The Integration of a Gender Perspective in the Sierra Leone Police*, DCAF, Geneva, http://www.alicehammond.com. [82]

IFC (2020), *Gender-Segregated Transportation in Ride-Hailing: Navigating the Debate*, International Finance Corporation, Washington DC. [78]

Ikeda, K. (1995), "Gender Differences in Human Loss and Vulnerability in Natural Disasters: A Case Study from Bangladesh", *Indian Journal of Gender Studies*, Vol. 2/2, pp. 171-193, https://doi.org/10.1177/097152159500200202. [34]

ILO (2017), *World employment and social outlook : trends for women 2017*, International Labour Office. [70]

Inyinbor Adejumoke et al. (2018), "Water Pollution: Effects, Prevention, and Climatic Impact", in *Water Challenges of an Urbanizing World*, InTech, http://dx.doi.org/10.5772/intechopen.72018. [20]

Islam, M. (2012), *Vulnerability and Coping Strategies of Women in Disaster: A Study on Coastal Areas of Bangladesh*. [31]

ITF (2019), *Transport Connectivity: A Gender Perspective*, OECD Publishing, http://www.itf-oecd.org. [69]

ITF (2019), *Transport Connectivity: A Gender Perspective*, OECD Publishing, Paris, http://www.itf-oecd.org. [74]

ITF (2018), *Women's Safety and Security: A Public Transport Priority*, International Transport Forum, Paris, http://www.itf-oecd.org. [71]

Kail, E. (2018), *Vienna acts against the climate change*, http://www.energetskiportal.rs. [96]

Kioumourtzoglou, M. et al. (2017), "The association between air pollution and onset of depression among middle-aged and older women", *American Journal of Epidemiology*, Vol. 185/9, pp. 801-809, http://dx.doi.org/10.1093/aje/kww163. [12]

Kneeshaw, S. and J. Norman (2019), *Gender equal cities*, URBACT, http://urbact.eu/secretariat. [94]

Kuddus, M., E. Tynan and E. McBryde (2020), "Urbanization: a problem for the rich and the poor?", *Public Health Reviews*, Vol. 41/1, http://dx.doi.org/10.1186/s40985-019-0116-0. [27]

Kwan, M. (1999), *Gender, the Home-Work Link, and Space-Time Patterns of Nonemployment Activities Gender, the Home-Work Link, and Space-Time Patterns of Nonemployment Activities* Gender, the Home-Work Link, and Space-Time Patterns of Nonemployment Activities**. [47]

Kwan, M. and A. Kotsev (2015), "Gender differences in commute time and accessibility in Sofia, Bulgaria: A study using 3D geovisualisation", *Geographical Journal*, Vol. 181/1, pp. 83-96, http://dx.doi.org/10.1111/geoj.12080. [48]

Kweon, B. et al. (2016), "Proximity of public schools to major highways and industrial facilities, and students' school performance and health hazards", *Environment and Planning B: Urban Analytics and City Science*, Vol. 45/2, pp. 312-329, http://dx.doi.org/10.1177/0265813516673060. [17]

Leiser, C. et al. (2019), "Acute effects of air pollutants on spontaneous pregnancy loss: a case-crossover study", *Fertility and Sterility*, Vol. 111/2, pp. 341-347, http://dx.doi.org/10.1016/j.fertnstert.2018.10.028. [22]

Levine Einstein, K., D. Glick and C. LeBlanc (2017), *2016 Menino Survey of Mayors*, Boston University, Boston, http://www.bu.edu/ioc. [76]

Littig, B. and M. Leitner (2017), "Combining Methods in Practice Oriented Research", in *Methodological Reflections on Practice Oriented Theories*, Springer International Publishing, Cham, http://dx.doi.org/10.1007/978-3-319-52897-7_11. [97]

Marsh, P. (2004), *Sex differences in driving and insurance risk: An analysis of the social and psychological differences between men and women that are relevant to their driving behaviour.*, Social Issues Research Centre. [77]

Martuzzi, M., F. Mitis and F. Forastiere (2010), "Inequalities, inequities, environmental justice in waste management and health", *The European Journal of Public Health*, Vol. 20/1, pp. 21-26, http://dx.doi.org/10.1093/eurpub/ckp216. [16]

Montt, G. (2018), "Too polluted to work? The gendered correlates of air pollution on hours worked", *IZA Journal of Labor Economics*, Vol. 7/1, http://dx.doi.org/10.1186/s40172-018-0067-6. [10]

Moriarty, P. and D. Honnery (2005), *Determinants of urban travel in Australia*, https://www.researchgate.net/publication/233779196. [55]

Nafilyan, V. (2019), *Gender differences in commute time and pay.* [52]

Neumayer, E. and T. Plümper (2007), "The gendered nature of natural disasters: The impact of catastrophic events on the gender gap in life Expectancy, 1981-2002", *Annals of the Association of American Geographers*, Vol. 97/3, pp. 551-566, http://dx.doi.org/10.1111/j.1467-8306.2007.00563.x. [30]

Ng, W. and A. Acker (2020), "The Gender Dimension of the Transport Workforce", *International Transport Forum Discussion Papers*, No. 2020/11, OECD Publishing, Paris, https://dx.doi.org/10.1787/0610184a-en. [79]

Ng, W. and A. Acker (2018), "Understanding Urban Travel Behaviour by Gender for Efficient and Equitable Transport Policies", *International Transport Forum Discussion Papers*, No. 2018/01, OECD Publishing, Paris, https://dx.doi.org/10.1787/eaf64f94-en. [58]

OECD (2020), *Common Ground Between the Paris Agreement and the Sendai Framework : Climate Change Adaptation and Disaster Risk Reduction*, OECD Publishing, Paris, https://dx.doi.org/10.1787/3edc8d09-en. [39]

OECD (2020), *OECD Champion Mayors: Gender inequality in numbers*, http://www.oecd-inclusive.com/wp-content/uploads/2020/03/OECD-Champion-Mayors-March-on-Gender-flyer.pdf. [75]

OECD (2019), *Accelerating Climate Action: Refocusing Policies through a Well-being Lens*, OECD Publishing, Paris, https://dx.doi.org/10.1787/2f4c8c9a-en. [6]

OECD (2019), *Society at a Glance 2019: OECD Social Indicators*, OECD Publishing, Paris, https://dx.doi.org/10.1787/soc_glance-2019-en. [85]

OECD (2019), "Sustainable connectivity: Closing the gender gap in infrastructure", *OECD Environment Policy Papers*, No. 15, OECD Publishing, Paris, https://dx.doi.org/10.1787/6350ba66-en. [65]

OECD (2018), *Rethinking Urban Sprawl: Moving Towards Sustainable Cities*, OECD Publishing, Paris, https://dx.doi.org/10.1787/9789264189881-en. [49]

OECD (2017), *Building an Inclusive Mexico: Policies and Good Governance for Gender Equality*, OECD Publishing, Paris, https://dx.doi.org/10.1787/9789264265493-en. [68]

OECD (2017), *Investing in Climate, Investing in Growth*, OECD Publishing, Paris, https://dx.doi.org/10.1787/9789264273528-en. [2]

OECD (2016), *2015 OECD Recommendation of the Council on Gender Equality in Public Life*, OECD Publishing, Paris, https://dx.doi.org/10.1787/9789264252820-en. [44]

OECD (2012), *Gender Equality in Education, Employment and Entrepreneurship: Final Report to the MCM 2012*, https://www.oecd.org/employment/50423364.pdf (accessed on 17 December 2020). [46]

OECD (2011), *OECD Family Database, Family size and composition*, http://www.oecd.org/social/family/database.htm (accessed on 4 November 2020). [42]

Ogg, J. (2005), *Heatwave: Implications of the 2003 French Heatwave for the Social Care of Older People*, https://youngfoundation.org/wp-content/uploads/2013/04/Heatwave-October-2005.pdf (accessed on 12 April 2021). [36]

Olczak-Rancitelli, M. (2015), *Women in transport*, http://oecdinsights.org/2015/06/12/women-in-transport/ (accessed on 4 November 2020). [80]

ONS (2019), *Gender Differences in Commute Time and Pay: A Study Into the Gender Gap for Pay and Commuting Time*, UK Office for National Statistics, https://www.ons.gov.uk/employmentandlabourmarket/peopleinwork/earningsandworkinghours/articles/genderdifferencesincommutetimeandpay/2019-09-04. [54]

O'Reilly, M., A. Súilleabháin and T. Paffenholz (2015), *Reimagining Peacemaking: Women's Roles in Peace Processes*, International Peace Institute, New York, http://www.ipinst.org. [83]

Ortiz Escalante, S. and B. Gutiérrez Valdivia (2015), "Planning from below: using feminist participatory methods to increase women's participation in urban planning", *Gender & Development*, Vol. 23/1, http://dx.doi.org/10.1080/13552074.2015.1014206. [90]

Oxfam International (2005), *The tsunami's impact on women*, https://oxfamilibrary.openrepository.com/bitstream/handle/10546/115038/bn-tsunami-impact-on-women-250305-en.pdf?sequence=1&isAllowed=y (accessed on 3 November 2020). [33]

Oxfam International (2005), *The tsunami's impact on women*, https://oxfamilibrary.openrepository.com/bitstream/handle/10546/115038/bn-tsunami-impact-on-women-250305-en.pdf?sequence=1&isAllowed=y (accessed on 3 November 2020). [37]

Pirard, P. et al. (2005), *Summary of the mortality impact assessment of the 2003 heat wave in France*, http://www.eurosurveillance.org. [35]

POLIS (2021), *Lille: Expanding Research Into Women's Cycling*, https://www.polisnetwork.eu/news/lille-expanding-research-into-womens-cycling/. [98]

POLIS (2021), *Under Her Own Steam: Closing the Mobility Gender Gap*, https://www.polisnetwork.eu/news/under-her-own-steam-closing-the-mobility-gender-gap/. [99]

Polk, M. (2004), "The influence of gender on daily car use and on willingness to reduce car use in Sweden", *Journal of Transport Geography*, Vol. 12/3, http://dx.doi.org/10.1016/j.jtrangeo.2004.04.002. [57]

Polk, M. (2003), "Are women potentially more accommodating than men to a sustainable transportation system in Sweden?", *Transportation Research Part D: Transport and Environment*, Vol. 8/2, http://dx.doi.org/10.1016/S1361-9209(02)00034-2. [56]

Pouso, S. et al. (2021), "Contact with blue-green spaces during the COVID-19 pandemic lockdown beneficial for mental health", *Science of The Total Environment*, Vol. 756, p. 143984, http://dx.doi.org/10.1016/j.scitotenv.2020.143984. [101]

SafetiPin (n.d.), *SafetiPin: Supporting Sager Cities (website)*, https://safetipin.com/ (accessed on 12 November 2020). [87]

Samek Lodovici, M. et al. (2012), *The role of women in the green economy-The issue of mobility-NOTE.* [60]

Sarmiento, S. (1996), *Household, Gender, and Travel*, United States Department of Transportation Federal Highway Administration. [45]

Smith S. et al (2012), *Urbanization and cardiovascular disease Raising heart-healthy children in today's cities*, The World Heart Federation, Geneva, http://www.worldheart.org. [24]

SSH (2018), *The Facts Behind the #MeToo Movement: A National Study on Sexual Harassment and Assault*, Stop Street Harassment, Reston, Virginia. [67]

SUM4All (2019), *Global Roadmap of Action Toward Sustainable Mobility - Gender, Paper 3*, Sustainable Mobility for All, http://www.sum4all.org. [61]

Swinburn, B. et al. (2011), *The global obesity pandemic: Shaped by global drivers and local environments*, Lancet Publishing Group, http://dx.doi.org/10.1016/S0140-6736(11)60813-1. [29]

Truman, J., R. Morgan and B. Statisticians (2014), *Nonfatal Domestic Violence, 2003-2012.* [14]

Turner, J. (2011), "Urban Mass Transit and Social Sustainability in Jakarta , Indonesi". [72]

UN (2018), *The World's Cities in 2018 - Data Booklet (ST/ESA/SER.A/417)*, United Nations, Department of Economic and Social Affairs, Population Division, https://www.flickr.com/photos/thisisin. [1]

UN Women (2019), *Youth activists call for safer streets in Maputo*, https://www.unwomen.org/en/news/stories/2019/3/feature-story-youth-activists-call-for-safer-streets-in-maputo (accessed on 4 November 2020). [100]

United Nations (2017), *New Urban Agenda.* [3]

Urban Development Vienna (2013), *Gender Mainstreaming in Urban Planning and Urban Development*, https://www.wien.gv.at/stadtentwicklung/studien/pdf/b008358.pdf (accessed on 4 November 2020). [95]

Wallhagen, M., O. Eriksson and P. Sörqvist (2018), "Gender differences in environmental perspectives among urban design professionals", *Buildings*, Vol. 8/4, http://dx.doi.org/10.3390/buildings8040059. [89]

WBG (2020), *Handbook for Gender-Inclusive Urban Planning Design*, International Bank for Reconstruction and Development / The World Bank, https://openknowledge.worldbank.org/handle/10986/33197 (accessed on 17 December 2020). [5]

Wen, J. (ed.) (2020), *Gender-based violence and environment linkages: The violence of inequality*, IUCN, International Union for Conservation of Nature, http://dx.doi.org/10.2305/iucn.ch.2020.03.en. [38]

WHO (2018), *Household air pollution and health*, https://www.who.int/news-room/fact-sheets/detail/household-air-pollution-and-health (accessed on 3 November 2020). [7]

WHO (2017), *Violence against women*, https://www.who.int/news-room/fact-sheets/detail/violence-against-women (accessed on 4 November 2020). [84]

WHO (2016), *Prevalence of insufficient physical activity among adults aged 18+ years (age-standardized estimate) (%)*, https://www.who.int/data/gho/data/indicators/indicator-details/GHO/prevalence-of-insufficient-physical-activity-among-adults-aged-18-years-(age-standardized-estimate)-(-) (accessed on 8 April 2021). [102]

WHO (2012), *Understanding and addressing violence against women (WHO/RHR/12.37)*, World Health Organization, https://apps.who.int/iris/bitstream/handle/10665/77434/WHO_RHR_12.37_eng.pdf;jsessionid=EC78DA827E071D258101BDA48204CFF4?sequence=1 (accessed on 21 December 2020). [86]

WHO and UNICEF (2017), *Progress on drinking water, sanitation and hygiene: 2017 update and SDG Baselines*, World Health Organization (WHO) and the United Nations Children's Fund (UNICEF), Geneva, http://apps.who.int/bookorders. [19]

Wilson Center (2018), *Roadmap to 50x50*, http://www.wilsoncenter.org/program/global-womens-leadership-initiative (accessed on 11 September 2020). [81]

Wilson, V. (2015), *Women Are More Likely to Work Multiple Jobs than Men*, https://www.epi.org/publication/women-are-more-likely-to-work-multiple-jobs-than-men/ (accessed on 3 November 2020). [41]

Women in Cities International (2012), *Tackling Gender Exclusion: Experiences from the Gender Inclusive Cities Programme*, http://www.kittenrocket.com. [93]

Woo, B. et al. (2019), "Residential Segregation and Racial/Ethnic Disparities in Ambient Air Pollution", *Race and Social Problems*, Vol. 11/1, http://dx.doi.org/10.1007/s12552-018-9254-0. [18]

Yarahmadi, S. et al. (2013), *Urbanization and Non-Communicable Risk Factors in the Capital City of 6 Big Provinces of Iran*, http://ijph.tums.ac.ir. [28]

Yavuz, N. and E. Welch (2010), "Addressing Fear of Crime in Public Space: Gender Differences in Reaction to Safety Measures in Train Transit", *Urban Studies*, Vol. 47/12, http://dx.doi.org/10.1177/0042098009359033. [64]

Zhang, X., X. Zhang and X. Chen (2015), *Happiness in the Air: How Does a Dirty Sky Affect Subjective Well-being?*. [11]

Notes

[1] The United States census defines as White “a person having origins in any of the original peoples of Europe, the Middle East, or North Africa” (https://www.census.gov/topics/population/race/about.html).

11 Women and SDG 12 – Responsible Consumption and Production: Ensure sustainable consumption and production patterns

A move towards more sustainable consumption and production patterns is the essential condition for reducing environmental damage, protecting ecosystems and biodiversity and tackling climate change. Because of their social and economic position in societies, women are differentially affected by such patterns. At the same time, women can be key drivers of change, as consumers and as decision-makers, in both the public and private sectors. Integrating gender equality is essential for the successful implementation of a circular economy strategy. Empowered women, with access to information and availing of incentives, can be key agents of change to help decouple economic growth from environmental degradation, increasing resource efficiency and promoting sustainable lifestyles.

11.1. Key findings

This chapter addresses the interaction between gender equality (SDG 5) and sustainable consumption and production patterns. The main findings include the following:

- At a global level, there is no evidence of materials use decoupling from economic growth, while the negative impact of environmental damage, waste generation, and climate change is rapidly accumulating.
- Because of their overrepresentation among vulnerable groups of the population, women are often severely affected by unsustainable production patterns through various channels. Women are dependent for subsistence on strained natural resources; women are affected by poor labour conditions in a "feminised" workforce; women provide a large amount of informal and sometimes unpaid work related to waste management; and women are involuntarily and without their knowledge exposed to harmful products and chemicals.
- In developing countries, women are overrepresented in assembly-line type jobs, which tend to be low-paid, characterised by poor working conditions (long and irregular working hours and exposure to harmful products), and weak social protection. Much of this employment is located in export processing zones, in which between 70-90% of workers – around 50 million - are women.
- Surveys from around the world show that women tend to be more sustainable consumers and are more sensitive to ecological, environmental and health concerns. Women are more likely to recycle, minimise wastage, buy organic food and eco-labelled products, and engage in water and energy savings initiatives at the household level. They also place a higher value on energy-efficient transport and in general have a higher preference for public transport than men.
- Engaging women in the circular economy – raising awareness on sustainable consumption and encouraging participation in leadership and managerial roles – is indispensable to create good circular systems.
- There is a need to systematically collect gender-disaggregated evidence on the environmental damage caused by unsustainable production and consumption patterns and on the role of women in driving change towards more sustainable production and consumption patterns. A focus on vulnerable groups and intersectionality issues should be an essential aspect of evidence-based analysis and policy action.
- Rationalising inefficient fossil-fuel subsidies that encourage wasteful consumption is integral to sustainable consumption and production patterns, but further work is needed to better understand and address any gender-disaggregated distributional impacts of reform, and how these might be successfully addressed.

11.2. Key interlinkages between gender equality and sustainable consumption and production

The growth in raw materials use, together with the environmental impact of their extraction, processing and disposal, has put tremendous pressure on our limited natural resources and damaged the Earth's ecosystems. According to the OECD, the use of materials resources rose from 27 billion tonnes in 1970 to 90 billion tonnes in 2017, which is practically equal to the growth of GDP over the same period (2.6% and 2.7% annual average, respectively) (OECD, 2019[1]). If this lack of decoupling of materials use from economic growth continues, the consumption of materials is expected to double by 2060, substantially worsening environmental consequences (OECD, 2019[1]). Global energy demand is projected to be 80% higher by 2050 – 85% of it covered by fossil fuels - while global water demand is expected to increase by 55% (OECD, 2012[2]).

In 2015, the annual per capita material consumption in OECD countries was 60% above the world average (OECD, 2015[3]). An average person consumed about 46 kg of materials – mainly construction and industrial minerals, fossil energy carriers and biomass – and produced 1.45 kg of waste on a daily basis in 2011 (OECD, 2015[3]) (OECD, n.d.[4]). Rapidly increasing population and industrialisation in developing countries is expected to intensify environmental and social challenges in these countries, as they put further pressure on natural resources.

Unsustainable production and consumption is ultimately behind the human factors causing environmental degradation and natural resource depletion, as it is linked to overconsumption of natural resources such as water, soil, forest, energy and minerals, and an increase in pollution and industrial development. Therefore, production and consumption levels, and the ways humans produce and consume, determine all other environment-related SDGs. Sustainable production and consumption could support the transition towards sustainable agriculture and food systems (SDG 2) and sustainable fishing practices (SDG 14), enhance sustainable use of water (SDG 6) and energy (SDG 7) resources in the production cycle, and drive the transition towards inclusive and sustainable industrialisation and more resilient infrastructure (SDG 9). It could also support more sustainable urbanisation, improving air quality and municipal waste management (SDG 11). It could improve the capacity of rural communities to pursue sustainable livelihood opportunities in parallel to reversing land degradation and halting biodiversity loss (SDG 15), and strengthen resilience capacity against climate-related hazards through efficient use of natural resources (SDG 13). Beyond the environment-related SDGs, sustainable production and consumption could have positive health effects (SDG 3), lead to a reduction of poverty levels (SDG 1), and support achievement of decent work and advancing economic progress through diversification, technological upgrading and innovation (SDG 8).

While there are no SDG 12 targets or indicators explicitly linked to gender equality or gender disaggregation, mainstreaming gender equality in SDG 12 would help achieve its underlying targets. SDG 12 is closely linked to gender equality and women's empowerment, as women's access to education (SDG 4), and to land and other assets (SDG 2, SDG 15, and SDG 5), are necessary prerequisites for a better integration of the female population in global and local production and consumption. The role of women in sustainably managing natural resources (see Chapter 6 and Chapter 14), reducing waste generation, and moving towards more sustainable production and consumption patterns at national, local and household levels is not sufficiently acknowledged. Nor is the effect of unsustainable business practices or fossil-fuel subsidies to women's and men's economic, health and social conditions. In particular, there is room for further research on the effect of fossil fuel subsidy reform through a gender equality lens. While a substantial amount of research has been conducted on the differentiated consumption of fossil fuels by gender, research on the impact of energy policy reform on gender equality is limited. As with other SDGs, there is a lack of systematic data collection on this key pillar of the gender-environment nexus.

11.3. Women are worst affected by unsustainable production patterns

Unsustainable production, waste generation and pollution have distinct harmful impacts on women, in particular those from socially disadvantaged societal and economic layers. Women are affected by the strain on natural resources on which they depend for subsistence. Women also often experience poor labour conditions in areas of the workforce becoming more and more "feminised". Women in developing countries provide increasing amounts of unpaid and informal work related to economic activities such as the textile industry and waste management, leading to a greater involuntary and uninformed exposure to harmful products and chemicals.

Women are more likely to experience the negative side-effects of unsustainable production, such as pollution, hazardous waste, and the destruction of common public space such as forests (more on women and forests under Chapter 14).

The costs of the linear economy which brought about degradation of the environment are particularly heavy for disadvantaged groups of the population. Poor people tend to live closer to polluted waters, factories and transport hubs, suffering more directly the negative consequences of pollution and climate change. This is the case both in developed and developing countries, and it becomes more obvious at the local and city level (Finkelstein et al., 2003[5]); (Hajat, Hsia and O'Neill, 2015[6]); (Kioumourtzoglou et al., 2015[7]); (Li, Konisky and Zirogiannis, 2019[8]); (Jiang, Kim and Woo, 2020[9]). Women tend to be at higher risk of poverty than men in many countries, leading to women usually suffering most from poverty and social exclusion, especially in single-headed households with dependent children (Millar, 2003[10]) (World Bank, 2011[11]).

11.3.1. Risks from waste management

Due to social norms in many cultures, women are more often in charge of waste management. More waste means more work for them. In developing countries, the waste management sector has a high percentage of female participation, in some cities surpassing that of men, though this is often limited to informal work and unregulated employment (Dias and Fernandez, 2013[12]); (Krishnan et al., 2019[13]). Women engaged in these activities usually come from the poorer population groups (Krishnan et al., 2019[13]), and waste picking may not even be a sufficient income-generating activity for them and their dependents (Marello and Helwege, 2018[14]).

Health risks in the waste sector are widely acknowledged, with increasing attention to the consequences of heavy metals exposure from E-Waste on women's and maternal health (Heacock et al., 2016[15]) (Kim et al., 2020[16]). These are often exacerbated by gender inequality, as equipment used to collect or transport waste is owned by men, which implies that women may lack access to the equipment and hence face additional challenges, which are usually exacerbated due to physical differences between the two sexes (Ziraba, Haregu and Mberu, 2016[17]); (Krishnan et al., 2019[13]). In the formal sector there is a preference for women to cover tasks like material processing and sorting, while men cover activities that require lifting, loading and other heavy work tasks (Krishnan et al., 2019[13]).

In cities where women cover the majority of informal economic activities, they also constitute the majority of informal waste pickers, a high-risk activity that can lead to injury and infection because of physical contact with chemicals directly disposed in landfills. There is also a risk of long-term exposure to solid waste, although there is a lack of available data to measure such health impacts (Ziraba, Haregu and Mberu, 2016[17]). The major landfill collapses that took place in Addis Ababa, Ethiopia in 2017 and Maputo, Mozambique in 2018, illustrate these inequalities; of the hundreds of casualties, women made up more than 65% and 75%, respectively (Moshenberg, 2018[18]).

In several developing countries there have been attempts to formalise the activity of casual waste pickers through waste and recycling co-operatives, associations, and micro-enterprises. In some cases women-led co-operatives have provided a safe space for women to get more involved in waste picking, guaranteeing better income and childcare facilities for working mothers (Dias and Fernandez, 2013[12]). Yet inequalities seem to persist, as women continue to face different forms of discrimination in the workplace compared to their male colleagues (Dias and Ogando, 2015[19]).

11.3.2. Inadequate labour and occupational safety conditions

The operation of multinational enterprises (MNEs) in developing countries is of particular concern, as often labour, health and environmental standards are less stringent or less effectively applied. MNEs may move their operations in search of more flexible or less strict regulations, and lighter controls and reporting standards than in their home countries (Morimoto, 2005[20]). Some MNEs have been responsible for egregious damage to the environment, in particular deforestation in countries within the tropical region to develop mining operations or to open up land for grazing and farming, much of which is export-oriented

(Harvey, 1995[21]); (Sonter et al., 2017[22]); (Digdowiseiso and Sugiyanto, 2020[23]). Deforestation and forest degradation has a negative effect on communities and peoples dependent on forest natural resources. In many cases these are women, who see their work burden increase (fuelwood collection, increase of agricultural land distance from home, need to shift cultivation) (Mishra and Mishra, 2012[24]).

Rapid industrialisation and investment inflows in some parts of the developing world have led to the "feminisation" of labour in export-oriented production, meaning an increase in the number of female workers in specific sectors, as well as a move towards less protective practices in some cases (duplicating characteristics of informal female labour to formal labour) (Ghosh, 2004[25]); (Otobe, 2015[26]). In developing countries women are overrepresented in assembly-line type jobs, which tend to be low-paid, have bad working conditions (long and irregular working hours and exposure to harmful products) and weak employment and social protection. Much of this employment is located in export processing zones (EPZs) (Murayama and Yokota, 2009[27]); (Cirera and Lakshman, 2017[28]), in which between 70-90% of workers – around 50 million - are women (Wick, 2010[29]). Sectors with a particularly high representation of women include textiles, clothing, food processing, horticulture, pharmaceuticals, household goods and toy production.

Reports on the conditions in textile factories and the garment sector in particular highlight the vulnerability of women. In Viet Nam, 80% of the 700 000 garment factory workers are women. They work for longer hours than men, are less likely to receive training and benefits, and earn only 85% of men's wages (Rees, 2014[30]). Even in factories that supply some of the best-known companies in the world, working conditions have sparked human rights violation allegations. In the span of three days in November 2016, 360 workers collapsed in Cambodia. They reported working in 37°C heat, being overworked and underfed (McVeigh, 2017[31]). Human Rights Watch similarly revealed that women were refused bathroom breaks, denied sick leave and suffered from sexual and physical abuse (Kashyap and Human Rights Watch (Organization), n.d.[32]). In some cases, women suffer a double or triple burden given their race and religion. Recent reports by a coalition of human rights groups has brought attention to international textile industry links with forced Uighur labour in China (Xiuzhong Xu, 2020[33]). In India, exploitation of Dalit girls in the garment industry has been widely reported (INC and SOMO, 2014[34]).

Women in many countries represent the majority of garment factory workers. As such, they are more exposed to the use of hazardous products in the textile and footwear industries (ILO, 2019[35]), chemical substances (pigments, dyes, adhesives and primers), some of which may affect the health of both textile workers and wearers of clothes, and can also end up in the environment (Ahmed et al., n.d.[36]); (Mahmud, Rajath D. and Jahan, 2018[37]). Evidence has shown that maternal health can also be impacted by exposure to occupational health stressors in the textile industry (Wong et al., 2009[38]).

Due to public pressure, companies increasingly report on social and environmental aspects of their activities. Through initiatives such as the UN Global Compact Principles, the Global Reporting Initiative Sustainability Reporting Standards, the OECD Guidelines for Multinational Enterprises, and the OECD Due Diligence for Responsible Business Conduct, multinationals and their related companies across global supply chains are increasingly being held accountable for their operations in developing countries, including their carbon footprint, broader environmental impact and the labour and human rights conditions of their employees (OECD, 2018[39]). All these initiatives include a specific reference to gender equality or women's rights, with the exception of the UN Global Compact where it focuses on human rights more generally.

A stronger effort is needed to enhance awareness about the unmeasured costs of business operations, in particular multinationals, with a specific focus on any potential negative impacts on women, vulnerable groups and the environment. More also needs to be done to improve transparency and corporate accountability for environmental impact and human rights and workplace conditions along global supply chains.

11.4. Consumption patterns and attitudes to the environment differ by gender

Consumption patterns at the level of the end-user are important to explore, as consumers – through their actions and purchasing habits – can influence how products are being developed, produced, used and potentially reused. Social norms highly influence consumer behaviour and attitudes (Melnyk et al., 2019[40]), including towards more sustainable behaviours (Yamin et al., 2019[41]). Women and men also have different environmental attitudes and behaviours (Zelezny, Chua and Aldrich, 2000[42]), as well as different interests regarding environmental improvement based on the different purposes for which they use natural resources. There is, however, an increased willingness by women to pay for improved services (Bulle, 1999[43]).

There are several key areas of consumption that have a strong gender dimension, and where influencing behaviour needs a gender equality perspective to be effective in improving sustainability. For example, traditional division of household responsibilities influences consumption patterns, as women are often responsible for buying short-term use products (household products, food, etc.), while men tend to decide on the purchase of more durable items (e.g. cars) (Yaccato and Jaeger, 2003[44]); (Kelan, 2008[45]). This traditional work-home division of responsibilities persists to some extent in dual-earner households. Estimates from Canadian companies show that women make over 80% of consumer purchasing decisions, but men spend over 80% of household income, although this balance is changing as women's economic and social situation advances (Yaccato and Jaeger, 2003[44]). This pattern has been confirmed in other studies (Kelan, 2008[45]).

Women tend to be more sustainable consumers and are more sensitive to ecological, environmental and health concerns (OECD, 2008[46]); (Johnsson-Latham, 2007[47]); (Kaenzig, Heinzle and Wüstenhagen, 2013[48]); (Khan and Trivedi, 2015[49]); (Bulut, Kökalan Çımrin and Doğan, 2017[50]). Women are more likely to recycle, minimise waste, buy organic food and eco-labelled products and engage in water and energy savings initiatives at the household level (Yaccato and Jaeger, 2003[44]). They also place a higher value on energy-efficient transport and in general are more likely to use public transport than men. Men are more often the ones taking the credit decisions within a household, and are usually the ones to take up credit (Kirchler, Hoelzl and Kamleitner, 2008[51]). The reasons behind this phenomenon are women's lower income levels, men's greater impatience towards making a purchase, and women's higher risk aversion. Women also have higher credit scores than men – 675 compared to 670, despite conscious or unconscious bias (Rivera, 2016[52]).

When asked about preferences for goods and services, for instance when selecting electronic products, women in Denmark seem to prefer those that have an end-of-life feature (that is, the ability of the product to be reused, remanufactured or recycled). Additionally, they would also be willing to pay a supplementary amount if the product purchased was more environmentally friendly. Men would also be willing to pay a premium price, but only if that was very low (Atlason, Giacalone and Parajuly, 2017[53]).

Women in Denmark also seem to be more responsive to more sustainable waste management solutions. Depending on location and income, women are more likely to accept sorting recyclables and bio-waste as part of their household waste disposal ritual when compared to men; men, on the other hand, seem to not be very engaged in recycling and pay less consideration to the environmental impact of their lifestyle choices (Nainggolan et al., 2019[54]).

The main OECD work on this matter involves a periodic household survey dating from 2008 and 2011 that showed that in some countries - Australia, Canada, Chile, Japan, Korea, Sweden and Switzerland - women were likely to see environmental issues as more pressing than men, whereas in other countries – France, Israel, Netherlands and Spain – men were more likely to be concerned about the environment (OECD, 2014[55]). Furthermore, the survey showed differences in energy consumption behaviour: men are more likely to take special measures to buy renewable energy from their electricity provider, while women – depending on the country and the distribution of household tasks – are more likely to engage in energy saving activities such as turning off lights, energy metering and shifting to renewable energy. In the study, it was concluded that respondents responsible for the economic charges of energy in households are more likely to engage in energy saving practices. Based on the self-assessment based study, men appear to be more familiar with energy-efficient labels, while women have an overall better knowledge of eco labels.

Another study presented by the United Nations shows that women consumers in OECD countries have a marginally more environment-focused or "greener" attitude than men concerning recycling and driving less (Table 11.1). In particular, women seem to recycle more than men in Austria, the Czech Republic, Latvia, Mexico, Korea, Sweden and the United Kingdom, even though this behaviour may also be linked to the gender division of domestic labour. In all countries in the survey, with the exception of Japan, women tend to drive less than men for the purpose of protecting the environment. The information available on the willingness of men and women to pay higher prices or taxes to protect the environment vary between countries. For example, in Germany, Israel, Korea, and the United Kingdom, data showed men were more willing to pay higher prices. Conversely, in Denmark, Finland, New Zealand and Norway, women were more willing to pay higher prices. As for higher taxes, in addition to the countries mentioned above, men in France, Spain, and Turkey also showed more willingness to pay, probably linked to their higher income when compared to women. Only in Denmark and Norway were women more willing to pay higher taxes than men to protect the environment. Finland is the only country where a significant difference exists between men and women that contributed to environmental groups, with 31% of women and 21% of men contributing in 2010 (United Nations, 2015[56]).

Table 11.1. Women in OECD countries have a marginally "greener" attitude than men when it comes to recycling and driving less

OECD	2000		2010	
	Male	Female	Male	Female
Percentage of persons who are recycling	59	62	72	76
Percentage of persons who drive less to protect the environment	15	15	22	26
Percentage of persons who gave money to an environmental group in the last five years	19	19	14	14
Percentage of persons that are willing to pay higher taxes to protect the environment	28	25	24	23
Percentage of persons that are willing to pay higher prices to protect the environment	40	39	33	33

Note: Analysis on data used for United Nations, 2015. The World's Women 2015: Trends and Statistics. New York: United Nations, Department of Economic and Social Affairs, Statistics Division. Sales No. E.15.XVII.8, Statistical Annex. OECD countries for which data were available from the survey Austria, Canada, Chile, Czech Republic, Denmark, Finland, France, Germany, Ireland, Israel, Japan, Korea, Latvia, Lithuania, Mexico, Netherlands, Norway, Portugal, Slovak Republic, Slovenia, Spain, Switzerland, Turkey, United Kingdom, and United States.
Source: ISSP (International Social Survey Programme) Research Group, 2014. Environment I and II - ISSP 2010. GESIS Data Archive, Cologne. ZA5500. www.issp.org/index.php

Studies in developing countries have also found major differences between men's and women's consumption preferences. Women are more likely to use income and debt for food products, health and education for their families. Conversely, men spend a higher share of income on things that personally benefit them – such as snacks, alcohol or luxuries. Such trends explain the success of microfinance initiatives, such as the Grameen Bank which lends practically only to women and has a 97% repayment rate (Esty, 2013[57]).

Studies from Africa also show that across cultures, women are usually assigned domestic waste management roles, as part of their unpaid activities, even when these activities extend beyond the home to community cleaning. Men, on the other hand, generally only tend to handle waste as part of their paid activities (Scheinber, Muller and Tasheva, 1999[58]); (Poswa, 2004[59]). Women and men also treat solid waste differently; women having developed knowledge and skills in managing natural resources, and sorting and recycling solid waste (Woroniuk and Schalkwyk, 1998[60]); (Almasi et al., 2019[61]); (Krishnan et al., 2019[13]).

Women can therefore be key actors to move consumption towards more sustainable patterns. In this regard, public policies and new approaches to influence consumption decisions, such as behavioural insights, should take into consideration a gender perspective. For instance, a 2016 study of 2 000 American and Chinese individuals found that socially accepted notions of masculinity were at odds with much of the eco-friendly marketing and recommended making such marketing more masculine to counter this tendency (Brough et al., 2016[62]).

As consumers, women can play a central role in the move to a circular economy. About 50% of household consumption worldwide covers food and beverages, clothing and footwear, and other household products (World Bank, n.d.[63]). Around 50% of global plastic waste generated is plastic packaging, with single-use plastic for food and beverages being most common (UNEP, 2018[64]). Women are considered to be the decision-makers when it comes to 70-80% of household purchases: as such, they could determine the shift to more sustainable consumption patterns and can therefore become key drivers of eco-friendly behaviour (Brennan, 2015[65]). Such a move towards mainstreaming women's consumer behaviour towards plastic may be more important than ever, with the effect the COVID-19 crisis is having on plastic waste. Recent information show a slow-down in implementing policies against single-use plastics (Prata et al., 2020[66]); (Brock, 2020[67]).

At the same time, however, women disproportionately use potentially toxic cosmetics and household cleaning products that can harm their health and the environment. In some countries where the use of such chemicals is permitted, women expose themselves to "skin-lightening creams that contain mercury, vaginal douches containing phthalates, and talcum powder," in sync with feminine norms and societal pressure to be beautiful (Heise et al., 2019[68]). The skin lightening industry is a multi-billion dollar global enterprise, and the mercury sometimes found in cosmetics (eye makeup, mascara, cleansing products) is eventually discharged into the environment via wastewater, where it "becomes methylated and enters the food-chain as the highly toxic methylmercury in fish" (WHO, 2019[69]).

The women's wear industry, worth about EUR 500 billion, is the largest segment of the whole textiles industry (Stotz and Kane, 2015[70]). The clothing industry, of which women are the largest consumer group, uses numerous chemical substances (such as formaldehyde, dyes, residues of cleaning products and fabric and hygiene conditioner), some of which may affect the health of both textile workers (see Section 11.3.2) and wearers of clothes, and can also end up in the environment during manufacturing, use and disposal phases. When washed, some garments release plastic microfibers, of which around half a million tonnes every year contribute to ocean pollution – 16 times more than plastic microbeads from cosmetics (Ellen MacArthur Foundation, 2017[71]). Plastic microfibers also have direct effects on human health from chronic exposure, particularly visible in manufacturing workers (Buzzi and Börkey, n.d.[72]). Environmental and health concerns, such as carcinogenicity, mutagenicity and skin sensitisation arise in the cosmetics and cleaning products sectors, which also employ millions of women and target them as their main consumers (Nijkamp et al., 2014[73]).

Women also bear the brunt of childcare and along with this comes the responsibilities of it, such as changing nappies. Carrying the double-burden of paid and unpaid work – women are driven toward time-saving options, one of which is disposable nappies which generate a lot of waste. According to the United Kingdom's Environment Agency, nappies accounted for 2-3% of all household waste in the country in 2005 (Aumonier and Collins, 2005[74]). Later calculations estimated that a single child's disposable nappies results in a global warming impact equivalent to about 550 kg of carbon dioxide within a period of two and a half years, amounting to approximately 700 Mt of carbon dioxide equivalents per year for the United Kingdom (Aumônier, Collins and Garrett, 2008[75]). In Australia an estimated 3.75 million nappies enter landfills per year, and an estimated 4.2 million tonnes of nappies are discarded per year in the United States (Sustainability Victoria, 2020[76]). Wet wipes are also problematic and the build-up of discarded wipes in the United Kingdom is even changing the shape of British riverbeds as they accumulate in mounds (Van der Zee, 2018[77]).

Women also utilise an array of disposable products, such as tampons and sanitary pads, which often consist of plastic. Over the course of her lifetime, a woman may use between five and 15 000 pads or tampons. Knowing exactly how much waste these products create is not so easy to track, but the amount of tampons sold per year are in the tens of billions, with a third sold in the United States alone in 2018 (Borunda, 2019[78]).

Hence, while women may in general have a predisposition to engage in environmental matters, they have a long way to go to achieve more sustainable consumption. The concern arises partially from the lack of awareness and education on sustainability, and partially from the lack of alternatives for basic necessities that are more sustainable but still affordable, as well as from cultural and societal norms that impose unsustainable consumption patterns on women and men.

11.5. Women and the circular economy

Agenda 2030 has set out some ambitious targets under SDG 12, including substantially reducing waste generation by 2030 through prevention, reduction, recycling and reuse, and halving per capita global food waste at the retail and consumer levels. The concept of the circular economy is indispensable to achieving sustainable resource management and reducing carbon emissions through fundamental shifts in the way we produce and consume. As identified in the OECD RE-CIRCLE project, transitioning towards a circular economy, through business models that are more resource efficient and promote the reduce-recycle-reuse triptych, is expected to strengthen growth prospects, increase the competitiveness of domestic firms and create jobs in innovative sectors. When the circular economy is supported by advancements in the Information and Communications Technology (ICT) sector and digitalisation, it can contribute to both resource productivity growth and non-resource and externality benefits. For Europe, this has been calculated to a 7% GDP increase up to 2030, equivalent to an 11% increase in household disposable income, not to mention the positive effects on employment (Ellen MacArthur Foundation, 2015[79]).

A report by the Carbon Trust, UK Knowledge Transfer Network and Coventry University (Knowledge Transfer Network (KTN) et al., 2014[80]) estimated that remanufacturing typically uses 85% less energy than manufacturing, and that on a global scale it could offset more than 800 000 tonnes of CO_2 emissions per annum. The circular economy can also boost growth and employment opportunities. The World Economic Forum and the Ellen MacArthur Foundation estimate that a shift in reusing, remanufacturing and recycling products could create more than half a million jobs in the recycling industry across Europe (Ellen MacArthur Foundation, 2013[81]).

Yet, so far, work on the circular economy has largely focused on the environmental and business aspects of circularity, while there has been little analysis of the social implications, in particular the role of women in leading the necessary transformations in the circular economy, the skill set needed, and the impact on women's job opportunities. As Murray et al (2015) point out, "key social equality aspects such as gender, racial and financial equality, inter- and intra-generational equity and equality of social opportunities are [still] often absent in the existing conceptualizations of the circular economy" (Murray, Skene and Haynes, 2017[82]).

On the production side, the circular economy needs to look at all the steps of the chain to minimise the use of resources and their ecological footprint; to keep resources in circulation for as long as possible; and to recover as much as possible of those resources at the product's end of service life via recycling. Products are therefore designed in a way to facilitate reuse and recycling. A well-designed circular economy also needs to promote sustainable consumption practices that minimise waste by extending the service life of products and promoting the sharing economy and second hand markets. Without understanding consumer behaviour, it is not possible to design sustainable circular economy models.

A move towards a more circular economy can enable gender equality and women's empowerment. Considering women's role in the local community, their engagement with household tasks, including waste management, and their consumption patterns, they are likely to benefit greatly from a shift towards circular economy and better waste management. Such a shift would not only reduce the environmental damage, waste generation and pollution caused by the production and consumption of materials, but could also support women's efforts in the waste management business to increase their income (through recycling and reusing) in a safer environment (minimising danger from toxic substances and contaminated products). Hence, circular economy could generate economic opportunities for women, boosting female employment and green entrepreneurship. In addition, developing financial support mechanisms that could promote such female entrepreneurship and employment, together with the necessary upskilling that the shift to green jobs might entail, could further support women to be equally represented in the sector. Integrating a gender perspective is therefore essential for the successful implementation of a circular economy strategy.

Engaging women in the circular economy – awareness-raising on sustainable consumption and encouraging participation in leadership and managerial roles - is indispensable to create good circular systems. A move towards a more circular economy can be designed to encourage gender equality. As women are more often segregated into jobs with low pay, low security and limited social mobility, the rise of green jobs as part of the circular economy movement offers an opportunity to empower women (ILO, 2015[83]).

11.5.1. The role of women in promoting sustainable production

The development of more economically and environmentally sustainable value chains is interlinked with achieving gender equality. Women's social responsibilities make them ideally positioned to manage natural resources, such as land, water and air, and contribute to local and global value chains. In developing countries, given their role in collecting water and biofuel and growing subsistence crops, women have a unique repertoire of knowledge and skills. However, the gender gap in access to resources, assets and decision-making undermines women's ability to efficiently contribute to the economy and promote sustainable development.

With the development of global value chains, production and sourcing take place on an increasingly global scale. Women generally have less of a say in production, as they have fewer assets and less access to leadership positions, especially in manufacturing activities and natural resource sectors, such as mining and energy. In 2013, only 10% of employees in large-scale extractive industry were women. Furthermore, studies show that in countries with high dependence on mining, oil and gas extraction, women were much less likely to be in leadership positions than men (World Bank, 2015[84]).

Improving gender equality and sustainable economies is mutually reinforcing. For instance, closing the gender gap in agriculture (by increasing access to assets, land and opportunities) would enable women to increase their yield by 20% to 30%, leading to a rise in total agricultural production in developing countries by 2.5% to 4%, and thus reducing the number of food insecure people worldwide by 12% to 17% (FAO, 2016[85]). Improving efficiency in agriculture also helps women free up time for other responsibilities and alleviates the triple burden of caring for children, the elderly and working. In addition, the integration of women in local value chains enables regional suburban development, thereby reducing urban resettlement and the pressures of urban living.

11.5.2. Transforming the fashion industry

Women could play a central role in the circular economy as consumers, by steering companies towards production methods based on the circular economy. There have been important efforts recently in women-focused industries such as the fashion industry. So-called sustainable fashion is becoming more apparent, and covers clothing, shoes and accessories that are produced, marketed and consumed in a sustainable way, both from an environmental and a socio-economic aspect. Apart from the choice of materials, companies are taking initiatives with the potential to reduce materials use, embrace the fashion reuse market, set up their own recycling system, or manufacture clothes from certified textiles. Many new and some repositioned old clothing brands are now focusing more on a greater sustainable production of clothes, on recycling, on using sustainable and responsible materials. Standards against "greenwashing" are being developed. The EU only recently approved the so-called "Taxonomy Regulation" for financial activities [Regulation (EU) 2020/852], and the OECD has developed sustainable finance definitions and taxonomies (OECD, 2020[86]). It would be worth examining how to expand such approach to other economic activities currently not covered by it, such as apparel manufacturing.

The current COVID-19 crisis is expected to change consumer behaviour towards the apparel industry. First of all, the changes in everyday habits and needs, due to restrictions in moving, is estimated to bring a 27-30% fall in revenues in 2020 compared to 2019 (McKinsey, 2020[87]). The 2020 McKinsey report also foresees a change in the type of apparel items people consume, estimating a shift towards more sustainable products. In the United States and Europe alone 15% of consumers are expected to buy more sustainable clothing. Fashion companies are also expected to change their business models, moving towards more sustainable design (clothes with multiple uses, which may be adapted to seasons and needs) (McKinsey, 2020[87]).

Additionally, the circular economy is increasingly getting attention as 71% of customers are expressing a greater interest in circular business models, such as rental, resale, and refurbishment, and many are showing interest in investing in higher quality apparel after the pandemic (GFA and McKinsey, 2020[88]). Moreover, there are a lot of gains which could be saved from circular business models considering that more than USD 500 billion of value is lost annually due to clothing under-utilisation and lack of recycling (Ellen MacArthur Foundation, 2017[71]).

When it comes to fashion companies that self-define as sustainable and ethical, women seem to occupy more senior management positions in this part of the clothing sector. In 60 sustainable brands that are active internationally, 52% of CEOs are women (Figure 11.1). According to a 2019 report, only 12.5% of Fortune 1000 companies in the apparel industry have female CEOs, even though women do occupy a larger percentage in middle management positions (PwC, 2019[89]).

Figure 11.1. Fifty-two percent of CEOs in today's sustainable brands are women

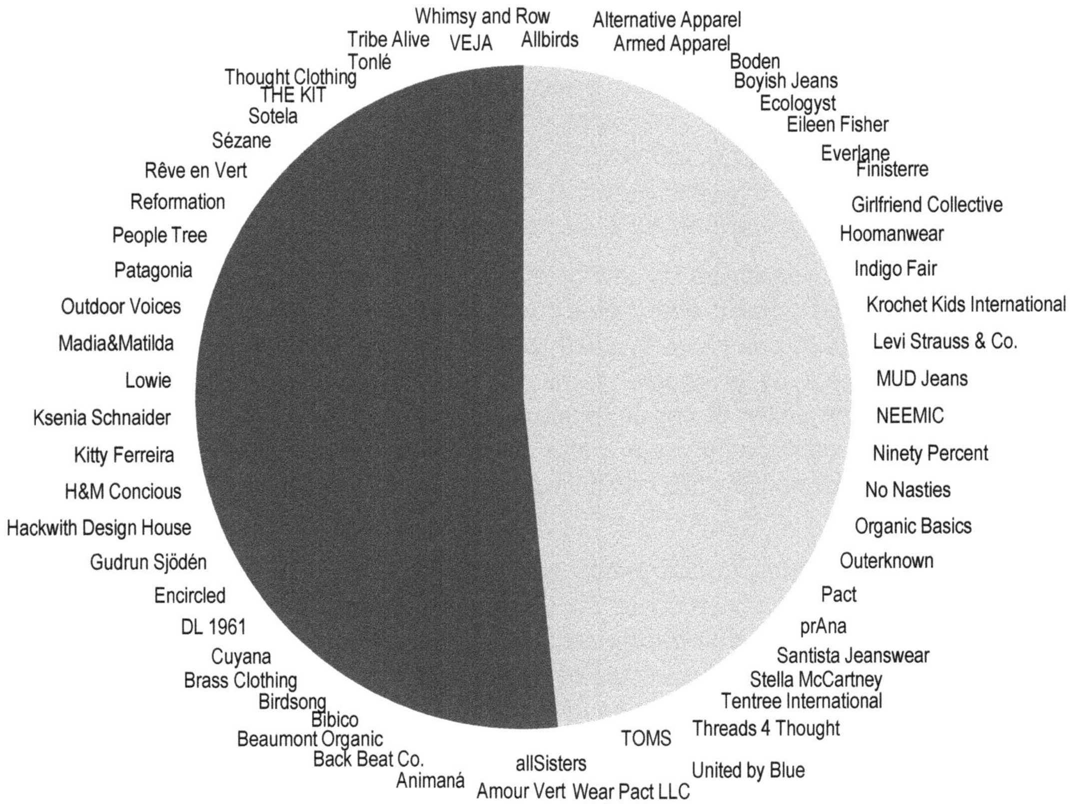

Note: In green the companies with male CEOs. In red the companies with female CEOs. For Patagonia, the female CEO who occupied the position for the past decade has recently resigned and not yet replaced. The size of the chart slices are not indicative of companies' size or shares.
Source: Authors' own research (data assessed 10/11/2020).

11.5.3. Transforming materials use, recycling and waste management

Women have parlayed their unique experiences into the development and advocacy of eco-friendly and sustainable products that reduce waste. Notable are reusable alternatives to one-use, disposable sanitary pads, tampons, and nappies pioneered by women. Innovative solutions such as Thinx underwear, or Mooncups (reusable silicone menstrual cup) were created by women. The Mooncup is used by women in over 50 countries and is estimated to have reduced the use of 2.4 billion tampons that would have ended up in waste streams (Stewart, n.d.[90]).

In modern times, women have eschewed reusable cloth nappies due to the dirty and time consuming task of cleaning and sanitising them. Nevertheless, women around the world are now entering the cloth nappy business through their own start-ups, and promote their products that result in cost savings over-time, are more easily maintained, and reduce overall waste that enters waste streams (such as Bumpadum, Cotton Babies, Superbottoms, Esembly, Magabi etc.).

In developing countries, waste handling represents a considerable source of income, especially for the more disadvantaged female groups. The transition to more sustainable waste management can generate economic opportunities for women in recycling and waste management, and in parallel the move to better organising informal waste pickers could help to tackle the risks of waste picking and manual recycling of products. Leveraging these opportunities requires a consideration of a gender perspective in the development of national and local circular economy strategies and measures, as well as relevant initiatives at the business level (OECD, 2019[91]).

An example where initiatives engaging women resulted in improved sanitation and sustainable consumption took place in Harare, Zimbabwe (Davies and Kudzai, 2016[92]). By including women in solid waste management, proper sanitation behaviour across the community improved, together with household income as waste management generates returns. A similar initiative took place in Bangalore, India (Huysman, 1994[93]). In Indonesia, the government launched a Waste Bank initiative in 2008, which has created employment opportunities for women as well as increased their income (OECD, 2019[91]) (Box 11.1).

Box 11.1. Women-led waste management businesses in Indonesia

The Indonesian Waste Bank Associations

The Waste Bank Associations is a social entrepreneurship initiative on circular economy and waste management in Indonesia. By processing waste, the waste banks are producing secondary raw material, as well as end consumer products. Through reducing, sorting, utilising, recycling and upcycling waste, these women-managed associations are integrating traditional knowledge with new technology. Eighty percent of the more than 8 000 waste banks currently in operation in Indonesia are female led. Such initiatives are providing economic empowerment and education for local women, especially those that were previously engaged in informal waste picking activities. This initiative has been transforming women from users to business owners, and has provided economic improvement for local communities. Transforming waste to energy (fuel, biodiesel, bioethanol), livestock feed and fertiliser. This systematic and whole-of-country approach has been endorsed by local communities and the government, scaling up small action for big impact.

The Mountain Mamas

The "Bye Bye Plastic Bag" initiative in Indonesia was founded by two sisters, Melati and Isabel Wijsen, with the initial goal to inspire youth to put a stop on plastic waste in the ocean and freshwater. The initiative has now initiated other projects, such as Mountain Mamas. The Mountain Mamas project started in 2017 with the aim of empowering local women on the slopes of Mount Batu Karu. Women were provided with sewing machines and training, and are now voluntarily producing bags out of donated or recycled material, on their own time and based on their skills level. This activity provides a return to the community, as half of the profits from the bags sold return to the village and are: (i) used to set up a local waste management system; (ii) invested in the local schools (English classes, computers etc.); and (iii) distributed as health care packages to every family.

Note: Information presented during the OECD Global Forum on Environment "Mainstreaming Gender and Empowering Women for Environmental Sustainability", Paris, 5-6 March 2020.

Another example is a company in Uttar Pradesh, India, which employs over 150 women from the lower social and economic strata to collect flowers daily from more than 30 temples and mosques. The company detoxifies the flowers of all the major insecticides and pesticides and uses them to make incense and soaps. The flowers would have normally ended up in the Ganges River, polluting the water (Lewandowska, 2019[94]).

Despite these positive examples, women generally remain absent in the ownership and senior management of large recycling companies and landfill operators, where marginal profits appear to be the highest (Krishnan et al., 2019[13]). Also, the modernisation of waste management generally makes it capital and technology intensive, with reduced employment opportunities for less qualified labour (Durgekar, 2016[95]), such as women when compared to men.

A focus on women and vulnerable groups, should be at the core of initiatives to modernise waste management (Groh, 2017[96]). Guaranteeing women that they will also benefit from initiatives that support skills development or innovation in the sector would make sure that they would not be marginalised or excluded in the next steps. Civil society organisations also have a key role to play in championing labour rights and the empowerment of women, including via stakeholder consultations and campaigns to raise awareness raising (Samson, 2010[97]).

11.5.4. Mainstreaming gender into national circular economy strategies

SDG Target 12.1 calls for the implementation of the 10-year Framework of Programmes on Sustainable Consumption and Production (SCP) Patterns. According to the UN Statistics Division, 71 countries around the world – and the European Union - have developed such action plans or mainstreamed sustainable consumption and production as a priority in national policies (Figure 11.2). Yet, few countries effectively integrate a gender perspective into their SCP strategies and policies. For instance, the EU Circular Economy Action Plan does not report any differentiated gender actions, and there are few references in other national plans to the differentiated impacts of unsustainable production and consumption by gender or the specific conditions for empowering women as more responsible consumers (EC, 2020[98]).

Figure 11.2. Countries with sustainable consumption and production national action plans in 2017

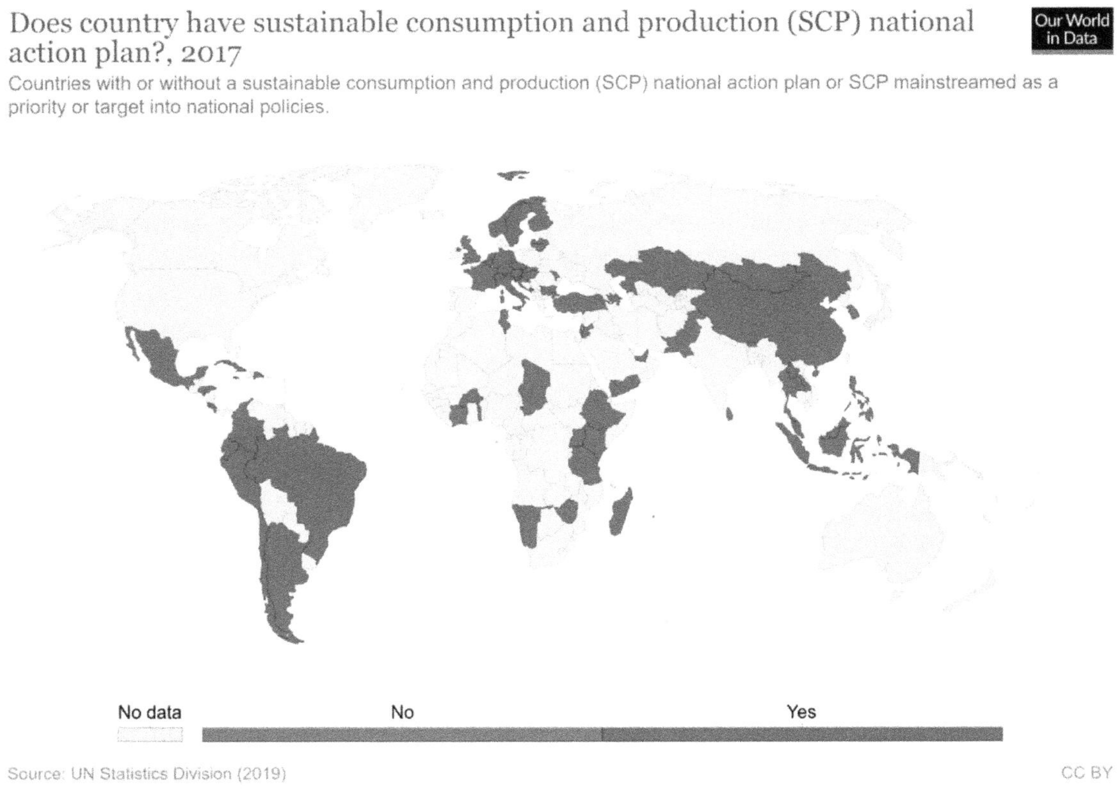

Note: Data for 2017 published by United Nations Statistics Division. Last update 14 February 2018. Data refer to SDG indicator 12.1.1 "Number of countries with sustainable consumption and production (SDC) national action plans or SDC mainstreamed as a priority or a target in national policies".
Source: UN Statistics Division (2019) as presented by (Richie et al., 2018[99])

11.5.5. Promoting women's role in the circular economy in cities

Regions and cities, where most of the people live and will be living in the future (70% of the global population by 2050), are taking actions towards the transition to the circular economy. Cities like London, Paris, Amsterdam, but also smaller cities in size like Valladolid, Granada, Umeå and Groningen, to name a few, are developing and implementing circular economy strategies (UNDESA, 2018[100]). Projections show that greenhouse gas emissions are likely to decrease by half a million tonnes of CO_2 per year in the City of Amsterdam (Circle Economy, 2018[101]); that circular approaches applied to the built environment, food, textiles, electronics and plastics in London are estimated at USD 9.3 billion every year by 2036 (LWARB, 2015[102]); finally, in the Île-de-France about 50 000 jobs linked to the circular economy are estimated to be created (Mairie de Paris, 2019[103]) (OECD, 2020[104]).

The OECD Programme on the Circular Economy in Cities and Regions supports them in defining their role as promoters, facilitators and enablers of the circular economy (OECD, n.d.[105]). As such, it is widely recognised that transitioning from a linear to a circular economy is a shared responsibility across governments and a wide range of stakeholders, including women.

11.5.6. Behavioural insights to 'nudge' women and men into sustainable consumption

Communications policies, financial incentives, and behavioural policies are part of the toolkit to 'nudge' consumers towards the SDGs. As highlighted in the 2018 Western Cape Government-OECD Behavioural Insights Conference in Cape Town, South Africa, behavioural insights could be used to promote better outcomes in key policy areas such as improving education and youth policies; creating safer communities; making better choices in water, energy and transport; and delivering better health services and results. Given women's role in consumption decisions, their sensitivity to sustainability concerns and the different roles women and men play in the household, behaviourally-informed policy solutions may help promote sustainable choices that provide better outcomes for all (OECD, 2017[106]); (Western Cape Government and OECD, 2018[107]).

Consumption patterns can be heavily influenced via effective public communications campaigns and labelling. Building on behavioural insights can support consumers in reaching more sustainable consumption choices by adapting messages across different social groups. Businesses, media and citizen engagement can play a significant role in changing unsustainable consumption patterns and in transitioning towards a sustainable economy.

11.6. Gender equality and fossil fuel subsidy reform

Although fossil fuel subsidies are not gender-specific, discriminatory effects can arise where policies fail to address the social barriers that women face in accessing services (Elson and United Nations Development Fund for Women., 2006[108]).

Despite the redistributive intent behind many fossil fuel subsidies, the literature shows them to be, on the whole, regressive. This is due to wealthier segments of the population capturing the majority of consumer subsides, given their higher consumption and access to energy. This is notably the case for liquefied petroleum gas (LPG) in India and kerosene in Bangladesh and Nigeria (Merrill et al., 2019[109]). The IEA has pointed out the regressive impact of fossil fuel subsidies, estimating that in 2010, the poorest 20% received only 5% of subsidies for LPG, 9% of subsidies for electricity, 10% of subsidies for natural gas and 15% of subsidies for kerosene (IEA, 2011[110]). This observed regressive effect is especially felt by low-income women, who have limited access to currently subsidised fuels (such as LPG in India) and many are not aware of the existence of such subsidies (such as in Bangladesh and Nigeria - (Merrill et al., 2019[109])).

As responsibility for cooking decisions tends to be gendered in countries surveyed by research [Nigeria, India, Bangladesh, Indonesia (Kusumawardhani et al., 2017[111]); (Merrill et al., 2019[109]); (Zinecker et al., 2020[112])], subsidy reform for fossil fuels used for cooking such as kerosene in Nigeria, or LPG in India should target women when planning mitigation measures. In low-income households, fuel price was found to be the most significant factor when determining household consumption. Thus, subsidised fossil fuels have the effect of locking poorer households into use (kerosene subsidies in Nigeria and Bangladesh – (Merrill et al., 2019[109])), where women are often found to bear the detrimental health effects and loss of time linked to using a cheaper fuel. This effect is amplified in rural areas where households have access to 'free energy'. For example, 51% of households in Imo State, Nigeria, stated that they would use more biomass to cope with price increases (Merrill et al., 2019[109]). Fossil fuel subsidies should be removed to align fuel prices with the social cost they incur, a cost which is heavily borne by women. Nevertheless, reforms solely based around cooking fuels and women may further reinforce existing gender roles within households.

At the same time, OECD analysis on Indonesia's fossil fuel subsidy reform and its distributional impacts has indicated that redistribution schemes such as cash transfers are the most progressive from a social perspective while also meeting environmental and economic goals (Durand-Lasserve et al., 2015[113]). Schemes such as food subsidies and labour support are less progressive. Applying a gender lens when designing redistribution schemes, by focusing on single-parent households, or by moving to more disaggregated analysis in the household, could help provide clearer guidance to guarantee that such schemes do not discriminate against women and girls in the household.

Limitations to be overcome in this area of research include establishing a causal link between reform and witnessed impacts, and estimating the magnitude of said impacts. Kitson et al., (2016) addresses this shortfall by surveying the literature and beginning to tackle the issue by hypothesising on the gender effects of fossil fuel subsidy reform, given it results in a fuel price rise (Kitson et al., 2016[114]). Further research can build on this by relaxing this assumption and exploring scenarios other than a fuel price rise.

11.7. Key actions for advancing the gender-environment nexus in sustainable consumption and production, and ongoing work

A number of policy actions are needed to better integrate a gender perspective into global, national and local efforts to shift production and consumption towards more sustainable patterns:

- Collect gender-disaggregated evidence on the environmental damage caused by unsustainable production and consumption patterns, with a focus on vulnerable groups and taking intersectionalities into account. Greater awareness is needed on women's exposure to environmental damage in certain sectors such as garments and waste management, where they are overrepresented in the workforce.
- Develop a better understanding of consumer behaviour across genders, integrating lessons learned from behavioural insights and traditional sustainable practices, of which women are often knowledge holders, and leveraging local value chains for sustainability. In particular, there is a need for an up-to-date survey on gender differences in consumer attitudes to sustainability and their drivers. This would allow developing policies that ensure a "just transition" for all, but would also inform how to make the new economic paradigm operational and sustainable.
- Ensure a systematic gender equality perspective on the circular economy strategies and action plans. Targeting gender roles and behavioural preferences in consumption as well as waste generation and prevention could be a key pillar in the transition to a circular economy not only by reducing waste but also by addressing some gender inequalities through recognising the value of jobs supporting circular economies. Women's exposure to environmental and health stressors need to be considered in this effort in order to guarantee their health and safety.

- Develop gender-responsive skills strategies to strengthen women's career opportunities in green economy sectors. Equipped with the right information, knowledge, and competences, women can play a growing role in transforming industrial practices towards more sustainable methods.
- There is a need to mobilise business, media and civil society to ensure more responsible business conduct that integrates gender and environmental considerations. Along with public communication campaigns and behavioural policies by governments, businesses and the media should play an active role in promoting sustainable and ethical business practices and encouraging responsible consumer behaviour. This also requires taking an integrated gender-sustainability angle in the monitoring and management of social and environmental risks, including in international initiatives such as the OECD Guidelines for Multinational Enterprises, the OECD's work on Responsible Business Conduct and the UN's Global Compact. Policymakers should also consider a gender lens when designing environmental regulations, carbon pricing and other climate policies that lead to more sustainable production and consumption patterns.
- There is room for further research on the effect of fossil fuel subsidy reform, through a gender lens. While a substantial amount of research has been conducted on the differentiated consumption of fossil fuels by gender, research on the impact of energy policy reform on gender equality is limited, further still concerning fossil fuel subsidy reform.
- Subsidy reform needs to be undertaken with care, and mitigation measures are needed to protect poor women: Increasing the price of subsidised fuels without any support measures could hurt poor women, especially where they are using subsidised cooking fuels. Secondary impacts, such as on studying or leisure time, should also be taken into consideration.
- Education and information campaigns must accompany fossil fuel subsidy reform in order to ensure access to clean fuels for women. This is because the level of education of women has been found to be a significant factor when switching between fuels (Nigeria - (Zinecker et al., 2020[112])); (Guatemala, India, Indonesia, Kenya, Pakistan and Sri Lanka - (Kojima, 2011[115])).
- A focus on connection over consumption subsidies can encourage gender empowerment around decisions to purchase new cooking equipment for LPG and overcome upfront connection costs (Merrill et al., 2019[109]).

References

Ahmed, S. et al. (n.d.), *Health and Safety in the Textile Dyeing Industry*, http://www.sei.se/water/beel.Tel:+4684121400Fax:+4687230348Web:www.sei.se. [36]

Almasi, A. et al. (2019), "Assessing the knowledge, attitude and practice of the kermanshahi women towards reducing, recycling and reusing of municipal solid waste", *Resources, Conservation and Recycling*, Vol. 141, http://dx.doi.org/10.1016/j.resconrec.2018.10.017. [61]

Atlason, R., D. Giacalone and K. Parajuly (2017), "Product design in the circular economy: Users' perception of end-of-life scenarios for electrical and electronic appliances", *Journal of Cleaner Production*, Vol. 168, pp. 1059-1069, http://dx.doi.org/10.1016/j.jclepro.2017.09.082. [53]

Aumonier, S. and M. Collins (2005), *Life cycle assessment of disposable and reusable nappies in the UK*, Environment Agency UK. [74]

Aumônier, S., M. Collins and P. Garrett (2008), *An updated lifecycle assessment study for disposable and reusable nappies*, Environment Agency. [75]

Borunda, A. (2019), *How tampons and pads became so unsustainable*, https://www.nationalgeographic.com/environment/2019/09/how-tampons-pads-became-unsustainable-story-of-plastic/ (accessed on 10 November 2020). [78]

Brennan, B. (2015), *Top 10 Things Everyone Should Know About Women Consumers*, https://www.forbes.com/sites/bridgetbrennan/2015/01/21/top-10-things-everyone-should-know-about-women-consumers/?sh=68c02f806a8b (accessed on 9 November 2020). [65]

Brock, J. (2020), "The Plastic Pandemic: COVID-19 trashed the recycling dream", *Reuters Special Report*, https://www.reuters.com/investigates/special-report/health-coronavirus-plastic-recycling/ (accessed on 10 December 2020). [67]

Brough, A. et al. (2016), "Is Eco-Friendly Unmanly? The Green-Feminine Stereotype and Its Effect on Sustainable Consumption", *Journal of Consumer Research*, Vol. 43/4, pp. 567-582, https://doi.org/10.1093/jcr/ucw044. [62]

Bulle, S. (1999), *Issues and Results of Community Participation in Urban Environment. Comparative analysis of nine projects on waste management A*, Urban Waste Expertise Programme. [43]

Bulut, Z., F. Kökalan Çımrin and O. Doğan (2017), "Gender, generation and sustainable consumption: Exploring the behaviour of consumers from Izmir, Turkey", *International Journal of Consumer Studies*, Vol. 41/6, pp. 597-604, http://dx.doi.org/10.1111/ijcs.12371. [50]

Buzzi, E. and P. Börkey (n.d.), "Mitigating microplastics in marine and freshwaters. A sectoral focus on textiles and tyres (forthcoming)", OECD Working Paper. [72]

Circle Economy (2018), *Circular Amsterdam - A vision and action agenda for the city and metropolitan area.* [101]

Cirera, X. and R. Lakshman (2017), "The impact of export processing zones on employment, wages and labour conditions in developing countries: systematic review", *Journal of Development Effectiveness*, Vol. 9/3, http://dx.doi.org/10.1080/19439342.2017.1309448. [28]

Davies, N. and N. Kudzai (2016), *The Usefulness of Including Women in Household Solid Waste Management. A Case Study of Dzivaresekwa High Density Suburb; Harare.* [92]

Dias, S. and L. Fernandez (2013), "Waste Pickers - A Gendered Perspective", in Cela, B., I. Dankelman and J. Stern (eds.), *Powerful Synergies. Gender Equality, Economic Development and Environmental Sustainability*, United Nations Development Programme. [12]

Dias, S. and A. Ogando (2015), *Engendering Waste Pickers Cooperatives in Brazil*, https://www.researchgate.net/publication/291334401_Cooperatives_and_the_World_of_Work_Engendering_Waste_Pickers_Cooperatives_in_Brazil_1 (accessed on 8 December 2020). [19]

Digdowiseiso, K. and E. Sugiyanto (2020), "The Effects of Multinational Companies on Deforestation: The Building Block or Stumbling Block", *Journal of Environmental Management and Tourism*, Vol. XI, pp. 5-11. [23]

Durand-Lasserve, O. et al. (2015), "Modelling of distributional impacts of energy subsidy reforms: an illustration with Indonesia", *OECD Environment Working Papers*, No. 86, OECD Publishing, Paris, https://dx.doi.org/10.1787/5js4k0scrqq5-en. [113]

Durgekar, V. (2016), "Towards Sustainable Waste Management Through Technological Innovations, Effective Policy, Supply Chain Integration & Participation", *Procedia Environmental Sciences*, Vol. 35, http://dx.doi.org/10.1016/j.proenv.2016.07.061. [95]

EC (2020), *A new Circular Economy Action Plan - For a cleaner and more competitive Europe*, European Commission, Brussels, https://www.un.org/sustainabledevelopment/sustainable-consumption-production/. [98]

Ellen MacArthur Foundation (2017), *A new textiles economy: Redesigning fashion's future*, http://www.ellenmacarthurfoundation.org/publications (accessed on 9 November 2020). [71]

Ellen MacArthur Foundation (2015), *Growth Within: A Circular Economy Vision for a Competitive Europe*, Ellen MacArthur Foundation. [79]

Ellen MacArthur Foundation (2013), *Towards the circular economy. The Economic and business rationale for an accelerated transition*, Ellen MacArthur Foundation. [81]

Elson, D. and United Nations Development Fund for Women. (2006), *Budgeting for women's rights : monitoring government budgets for compliance with CEDAW*, United Nations Development Fund for Women. [108]

Esty, K. (2013), *Twenty-Seven Dollars and a Dream: How Muhammad Yunus Changed the World and What It Cost Him*, Katharine Esty Company. [57]

FAO (2016), *Developing gender-sensitive value chains: A guiding framework.*, Food and Agriculture Organization of the United Nations. [85]

Finkelstein, M. et al. (2003), "Relation between income, air pollution and mortality: a cohort study", *Canadian Medical Association Journal*, Vol. 169/5, pp. 397-402. [5]

GFA and McKinsey (2020), *Fashion on Climate - How the Fashion Industry can Urgently Act to Reduce its Greenhouse Gas Emissions*, Global Fashion Agenda and McKinsey & Company. [88]

Ghosh, J. (2004), "Globalization, Export-oriented Employment for Women and Social Policy: A Case Study of India", in *Globalization, Export-oriented Employment and Social Policy*, Palgrave Macmillan UK, London, http://dx.doi.org/10.1057/9780230524217_4. [25]

Groh, K. (2017), "Chemicals and waste in the circular economy", *Food Packaging Forum*, https://www.foodpackagingforum.org/news/chemicals-and-waste-in-circular-economy (accessed on 14 December 2020). [96]

Hajat, A., C. Hsia and M. O'Neill (2015), "Socioeconomic Disparities and Air Pollution Exposure: a Global Review", *Current Environmental Health Reports*, Vol. 2/4, http://dx.doi.org/10.1007/s40572-015-0069-5. [6]

Harvey, M. (1995), "The MNCs' Role and Responsibility in Deforestation of Tropical Forests", *Journal of Macromarketing*, Vol. 15/2, http://dx.doi.org/10.1177/027614679501500208. [21]

Heacock, M. et al. (2016), "E-Waste and Harm to Vulnerable Populations: A Growing Global Problem", *Environmental Health Perspectives*, Vol. 124/5, pp. 550-555, http://dx.doi.org/10.1289/ehp.1509699. [15]

Heise, L. et al. (2019), *Gender inequality and restrictive gender norms: framing the challenges to health*, Lancet Publishing Group, http://dx.doi.org/10.1016/S0140-6736(19)30652-X. [68]

Huysman, M. (1994), "Waste picking as a survival strategy for women in Indian cities", *Environment and Urbanization*, Vol. 6/2, http://dx.doi.org/10.1177/095624789400600209. [93]

IEA (2011), *World Energy Outlook 2011*, https://www.iea.org/reports/world-energy-outlook-2011 (accessed on 1 December 2020). [110]

ILO (2019), "The future of work in textiles, clothing, leather and footwear", No. 326, International Labour Office, Sectoral Policies Department. [35]

ILO (2015), *Gender equality and green jobs*, International Labour Organization. [83]

INC and SOMO (2014), "Flawed Fabrics: The Abuse of Girls and Women Workers in the South Indian Textile Industry", http://www.indianet.nl/FlawedFabrics.html. [34]

Jiang, M., E. Kim and Y. Woo (2020), "The relationship between economic growth and air pollution—a regional comparison between China and South Korea", *International Journal of Environmental Research and Public Health*, Vol. 17/8, http://dx.doi.org/10.3390/ijerph17082761. [9]

Johnsson-Latham, G. (2007), *A study on gender equality as a prerequisite for sustainable development*, Report to the Environment Advisory Council, Stockholm, http://www.sou.gov.se/mvb/. [47]

Kaenzig, J., S. Heinzle and R. Wüstenhagen (2013), "Whatever the customer wants, the customer gets? Exploring the gap between consumer preferences and default electricity products in Germany", *Energy Policy*, Vol. 53, http://dx.doi.org/10.1016/j.enpol.2012.10.061. [48]

Kashyap, A. and Human Rights Watch (Organization) (n.d.), *"Work faster or get out" : labor rights abuses in Cambodia's garment industry..* [32]

Kelan, E. (2008), "Bound by stereotypes?", *Business Strategy Review*, Vol. 19/1, http://dx.doi.org/10.1111/j.1467-8616.2008.00509.x. [45]

Khan, N. and P. Trivedi (2015), *Gender Differences and Sustainable Consumption Behavior*, http://www.eajoutrnals.org. [49]

Kim, S. et al. (2020), "Birth outcomes associated with maternal exposure to metals from informal electronic waste recycling in Guiyu, China", *Environment International*, Vol. 137, p. 105580, http://dx.doi.org/10.1016/j.envint.2020.105580. [16]

Kioumourtzoglou, M. et al. (2015), "PM2.5 and mortality in 207 US cities", *Epidemiology*, http://dx.doi.org/10.1097/EDE.0000000000000422. [7]

Kirchler, E., E. Hoelzl and B. Kamleitner (2008), "Spending and credit use in the private household", *The Journal of Socio-Economics*, Vol. 37/2, http://dx.doi.org/10.1016/j.socec.2006.12.038. [51]

Kitson, L. et al. (2016), *Gender and Fossil Fuel Subsidy Reform: Current status of research*, Global Subsidies Initiative-IISD, IRADe, S4C, BIDS, http://www.iisd.org. [114]

Knowledge Transfer Network (KTN) et al. (2014), *Supporting Excellence in UK Remanufacturing Stakeholder dialogue on opportunities and challenges*. [80]

Kojima, M. (2011), *The Role of Liquefied Petroleum Gas in Reducing Energy Poverty*, The World Bank, http://www.worldbank.org/ogmc. [115]

Krishnan, S. et al. (2019), *The role of gender in waste management. Gender perspectives on waste in India, Indonesia, the Philippines and Vietnam*, Ocean Conservancy, http://www.gacircular.com. [13]

Kusumawardhani, N. et al. (2017), *Gender and Fossil Fuel Subsidy Reform - An audit of data on energy subsidies, energy use and gender in Indonesia*, Global Subsidies Initiative-IISD, http://www.iisd.org. [111]

Lewandowska, E. (2019), *The next big opportunity for gender equality?*, pp. 36-39, https://www.unido.org/sites/default/files/files/2019-10/makingit_26_web.pdf (accessed on 10 November 2020). [94]

Li, Z., D. Konisky and N. Zirogiannis (2019), "Racial, ethnic, and income disparities in air pollution: A study of excess emissions in Texas", *PLOS ONE*, Vol. 14/8, http://dx.doi.org/10.1371/journal.pone.0220696. [8]

LWARB (2015), *London, the circular economy capital. Towards a circular economy - context and opportunities*, London Waste and Recycling Board, London, https://www.lwarb.gov.uk/wp-content/uploads/2015/12/LWARB-circular-economy-report_web_09.12.15.pdf (accessed on 10 November 2020). [102]

Mahmud, M., V. Rajath D. and M. Jahan (2018), "Health Issues of Female Garment Workers: Evidence from Bangladesh", *Journal of Population and Social Studies*, Vol. 26/3, http://dx.doi.org/10.25133/JPSSv26n3.013. [37]

Mairie de Paris (2019), *Deuxième feuille de route de l'économie circulaire*, https://www.paris.fr/pages/economie-circulaire-2756 (accessed on 10 November 2020). [103]

Marello, M. and A. Helwege (2018), "Solid Waste Management and Social Inclusion of Wastepickers: Opportunities and Challenges", *Latin American Perspectives*, Vol. 45/1, http://dx.doi.org/10.1177/0094582X17726083. [14]

McKinsey (2020), *The State of Fashion 2020 - Coronavirus Update.* [87]

McVeigh, K. (2017), “Cambodian female workers in Nike, Asics and Puma factories suffer mass faintings”, *The Guardian*, https://www.theguardian.com/business/2017/jun/25/female-cambodian-garment-workers-mass-fainting (accessed on 9 November 2020). [31]

Melnyk, V. et al. (2019), “The Mechanisms of Social Norms’ Influence on Consumer Decision Making”, *Zeitschrift für Psychologie*, Vol. 227/1, http://dx.doi.org/10.1027/2151-2604/a000352. [40]

Merrill, L. et al. (2019), *Gender and fossil fuel subsidy reform: Findings from and recommendations for Bangladesh, India and Nigeria*, ENERGIA. [109]

Millar, J. (2003), “Gender, Poverty and Social Exclusion”, *Social Policy and Society*, Vol. 2/3, http://dx.doi.org/10.1017/S1474746403001246. [10]

Mishra, A. and D. Mishra (2012), “Deforestation and Women’s Work Burden in the Eastern Himalayas, India: Insights from a Field Survey”, *Gender, Technology and Development*, Vol. 16/3, http://dx.doi.org/10.1177/0971852412459428. [24]

Morimoto, T. (2005), “Growing industrialization and our damaged planet. The extraterritorial application of developed countries’ domestic environmental laws to transnational corporations abroad”, *Utrecht Law Review*, Vol. 1/2, http://dx.doi.org/10.18352/ulr.12. [20]

Moshenberg, D. (2018), *Women bear the brunt of Africa’s urban disasters, such as the collapse of landfills*, https://theconversation.com/women-bear-the-brunt-of-africas-urban-disasters-such-as-the-collapse-of-landfills-92854 (accessed on 10 November 2020). [18]

Murayama, M. and N. Yokota (2009), *Revisiting Labour and Gender Issues in Export Processing Zones: Cases of South Korea, Bangladesh and India*, pp. 73-83, https://www.jstor.org/stable/40279060 (accessed on 9 November 2020). [27]

Murray, A., K. Skene and K. Haynes (2017), “The Circular Economy: An Interdisciplinary Exploration of the Concept and Application in a Global Context”, *Journal of Business Ethics*, Vol. 140/3, http://dx.doi.org/10.1007/s10551-015-2693-2. [82]

Nainggolan, D. et al. (2019), “Consumers in a Circular Economy: Economic Analysis of Household Waste Sorting Behaviour”, *Ecological Economics*, Vol. 166, http://dx.doi.org/10.1016/j.ecolecon.2019.106402. [54]

Nijkamp, M. et al. (2014), *Hazardous substances in textile products*, National Institute for Public Health and the Enviornment, The Netherlands. [73]

OECD (2020), *Developing Sustainable Finance Definitions and Taxonomies*, Green Finance and Investment, OECD Publishing, Paris, https://dx.doi.org/10.1787/134a2dbe-en. [86]

OECD (2020), *The Circular Economy in Cities and Regions: Synthesis Report*, OECD Urban Studies, OECD Publishing, Paris, https://dx.doi.org/10.1787/10ac6ae4-en. [104]

OECD (2019), *Global Material Resources Outlook to 2060: Economic Drivers and Environmental Consequences*, OECD Publishing, Paris, https://dx.doi.org/10.1787/9789264307452-en. [1]

OECD (2019), *OECD Green Growth Policy Review of Indonesia 2019*, OECD Environmental Performance Reviews, OECD Publishing, Paris, https://dx.doi.org/10.1787/1eee39bc-en. [91]

OECD (2018), *OECD Due Diligence Giudance for Reponsible Business Conduct*. [39]

OECD (2017), *Behavioural Insights and Public Policy: Lessons from Around the World*, OECD Publishing, Paris, https://dx.doi.org/10.1787/9789264270480-en. [106]

OECD (2015), *Material Resources, Productivity and the Environment*, OECD Green Growth Studies, OECD Publishing, Paris, https://dx.doi.org/10.1787/9789264190504-en. [3]

OECD (2014), *Greening Household Behaviour: Overview from the 2011 Survey - Revised edition*, OECD Studies on Environmental Policy and Household Behaviour, OECD Publishing, Paris, https://dx.doi.org/10.1787/9789264214651-en. [55]

OECD (2012), *OECD Environmental Outlook to 2050: The Consequences of Inaction*, OECD Publishing, Paris, https://dx.doi.org/10.1787/9789264122246-en. [2]

OECD (2008), *Household Behaviour and the Environment. Reviewing the evidence*, http://www.oecd.org. [46]

OECD (n.d.), “Municipal waste (indicator)”. [4]

OECD (n.d.), *The Circular Economy in Cities and Regions*, https://www.oecd.org/regional/cities/circular-economy-cities.htm (accessed on 10 November 2020). [105]

Otobe, N. (2015), “Export-led development, employment and gender in the era of globalization”, No. 197, International Labour Office, Geneva, http://www.ilo.org/global/about-the-ilo/mission-and-objectives/WCMS_099766/lang--en/index.htm. [26]

Poswa, T. (2004), *The importance of gender in waste management planning: A challenge for solid waste managers*. [59]

Prata, J. et al. (2020), “COVID-19 Pandemic Repercussions on the Use and Management of Plastics”, *Environmental Science & Technology*, Vol. 54/13, http://dx.doi.org/10.1021/acs.est.0c02178. [66]

PwC (2019), *Tracking female leadership in the apparel industry*, https://www.pwc.com/us/en/industries/consumer-markets/assets/pwc-unraveling-the-fabric-ceiling.pdf (accessed on 11 December 2020). [89]

Rees, D. (2014), “Improving conditions for women workers has a domino effect”, *The Guardian*, https://www.theguardian.com/sustainable-business/women-garmet-workers-conditions (accessed on 9 November 2020). [30]

Richie et al. (2018), *Measuring progress towards the Sustainable Development Goals*, SDG-Tracker.org, website. [99]

Rivera, K. (2016), *Men vs. Women: Who Wins the Credit Game?*, https://www.experian.com/blogs/insights/2016/03/men-vs-women-credit-trends/ (accessed on 9 November 2020). [52]

Samson, M. (2010), *Women in Informal Employment: Globalizing and Organizing. Reclaiming Reusable and Recyclable Materials in Africa*, WIEGO Urban Policies Research Report Series. [97]

Scheinber, A., M. Muller and E. Tasheva (1999), *Gender and Waste. Integrating gender into community waste management: project management insights and tips from an e-mail conference, 9-13 May 1998*, Urban Waste Expertise Programme. [58]

Sonter, L. et al. (2017), "Mining drives extensive deforestation in the Brazilian Amazon", *Nature Communications*, Vol. 8/1, http://dx.doi.org/10.1038/s41467-017-00557-w. [22]

Stewart, L. (n.d.), *How is the Mooncup environmentally friendly?*, https://www.mooncup.co.uk/blog/how-is-the-mooncup-environmentally-friendly/ (accessed on 11 December 2020). [90]

Stotz, L. and G. Kane (2015), *Global Garment Industry Factsheet Facts on The Global Garment Industry*, http://www.somo.nl/publications-en/Publication_4110. [70]

Sustainability Victoria (2020), "Eco-friendlier alternatives to disposable nappies", *Victoria State Government*, https://www.sustainability.vic.gov.au/nappies (accessed on 14 December 2020). [76]

UNDESA (2018), *World Urbanization Prospects. The 2018 Revision.* [100]

UNEP (2018), *Single-use plastics, a roadmap for sustainability..* [64]

United Nations (2015), *The World's Women 2015: Trends and Statistics*, United Nations, Department of Economic and Social Affairs, Statistics Division, http://dx.doi.org/10.18356/9789210573719. [56]

Van der Zee, B. (2018), "Wet wipe pollution 'changing the shape of British riverbeds'", *The Guardian*, https://www.theguardian.com/environment/2018/may/02/wet-wipes-boom-is-changing-the-shape-of-british-riverbeds (accessed on 10 November 2020). [77]

Western Cape Government and OECD (2018), *Making a real difference: Nudging for policy change. Key messages & summary.* [107]

WHO (2019), *Mercury in skin lightening products*, World Health Organization. [69]

Wick, I. (2010), *The informal economy and export processing zones Women Working in the Shadows.* [29]

Wong, E. et al. (2009), "Dust and chemical exposures, and miscarriage risk among women textile workers in Shanghai, China", *Occupational and Environmental Medicine*, Vol. 66/3, pp. 161-168, http://dx.doi.org/10.1136/oem.2008.039065. [38]

World Bank (2015), *Women's Employment in the Extractive Industry*, https://usilive.org/another-woman-minework-. [84]

World Bank (2011), *Poverty and Social Exclusion in India*, The World Bank, http://dx.doi.org/10.1596/978-0-8213-8690-3. [11]

World Bank (n.d.), *Global Consumption Database*, http://datatopics.worldbank.org/consumption/ (accessed on 9 November 2020). [63]

Woroniuk, B. and J. Schalkwyk (1998), *Waste disposal & equality between women and men*, prepared for Sida, http://www.sida.se. [60]

Xiuzhong Xu, V. (2020), "Uyghurs For Sale: Re-education, Forced Labour and Surveillance Beyond Xinjiang", *International Cyber Policy Center* Policy Brief, Report No. 26/2020. [33]

Yaccato, J. and J. Jaeger (2003), *The 80% Minority: Reaching the Real World of Women Consumers*, Viking Canada. [44]

Yamin et al. (2019), "Using Social Norms to Change Behavior and Increase Sustainability in the Real World: A Systematic Review of the Literature", *Sustainability*, Vol. 11/20, http://dx.doi.org/10.3390/su11205847. [41]

Zelezny, L., P. Chua and C. Aldrich (2000), *Elaborating on Gender Differences in Environmentalism.* [42]

Zinecker, A. et al. (2020), *Gender and Fossil Fuel Subsidy Reform in Nigeria: Findings and recommendations GSI REPORT*, Global Subsidies Initiative-IISD, BIDS, IRADe and Spaces for Change, http://www.iisd.org/gsi. [112]

Ziraba, A., T. Haregu and B. Mberu (2016), "A review and framework for understanding the potential impact of poor solid waste management on health in developing countries", *Archives of Public Health*, Vol. 74/1, http://dx.doi.org/10.1186/s13690-016-0166-4. [17]

12 Women and SDG13 – Climate Action: Take urgent action to combat climate change and its impacts

The impact of climate change and large-scale environmental hazards is intensifying and taking a growing toll on economies and livelihoods. The impacts are not gender neutral, and women often bear a greater burden because of their more vulnerable social and economic status and their role in society. At the same time, women can be powerful agents for climate action, both at the grassroots level and as decision-makers in the public and private sectors. Climate strategies and policies, therefore, need to incorporate a gender perspective, and better gender disaggregated data on climate impact and action is needed.

12.1. Key findings

This chapter analyses the relationship between gender equality (SDG 5) and climate change (SDG 13). It considers both gender-specific impacts of climate change as well as the role of women tackling it. The main findings are the following:

- In general, women are more vulnerable to climate change due to their dependence on natural resources and structural inequity in their access to and control of such resources. Women are more likely to be victims of increasingly severe environmental hazards (droughts, fires and floods), accounting for more than 75% of displaced persons. Social and economic norms tend to exacerbate the cumulative effects of climate related events.
- While the Paris Agreement stresses the contribution of gender equality and women's empowerment to fighting climate change as well as the specific impact of climate change on women, few countries are effectively integrating a gender perspective in their impact assessments and response strategies and collecting the necessary data to implement this goal.
- National climate strategies, including National Adaptation Plans (NAPs) need to include a gender dimension, including the use of Gender Impact Assessment training as a key tool to support adaptation and mitigation actions, with a focus on areas such as transport planning, urban safety, consumption patterns, health and energy use.
- The role of women in climate-related grassroots movements is increasing, and there is close to gender parity in a number of environment-related UN processes such as the United Nations Framework Convention on Climate Change (UNFCCC). Yet, women remain underrepresented in formal decision-making in both the public and private sectors on issues that have a key impact on climate change, such as finance, health, energy and transport.
- Increasing the presence of women in leadership positions in both the public and private sectors can accelerate climate action, as women in such positions often put a strong focus on tackling climate change and ensuring environmental sustainability.

12.2. Key interlinkages between gender equality, climate action and other SDGs

The impact of climate change and large-scale environmental hazards is intensifying and taking a growing toll on economies and livelihoods. A number of tipping points in climate change will soon be or are already being reached, triggering feedback loops with catastrophic consequences for life on Earth. The United Nations Office for Disaster Risk Reduction (UNDRR) together with UC Louvain note that natural disaster occurrence has almost doubled in the past 20 years compared to the previous 20, leading to approximately 1.23 million deaths, that is an estimated 60,000 deaths per year, and almost doubled cost in damages (UN, 2020[1]). More specifically, developing nations experienced deaths rates more than four times higher than developed ones. Take for instance, the growing intensity and frequency of storms, floods, droughts, earthquakes, heatwaves and wildfires in the world – which have collectively quadrupled since the 1970s (Easterling et al., 2012[2]).

Over 450 disasters occurred in the United States alone in 1995-2015 (UNISDR, 2015[3]). An April 2019 report pegged the economic cost of climate-related impacts to be USD 224 billion per annum by 2090 in the United States, considering impacts across "health, infrastructure, electricity, water resources, agriculture, and ecosystems," (Nuccitelli, 2019[4]). One-third of the cost estimate is attributable to heat-related deaths, with the report estimating an additional 1 300 to 9 300 mortalities per year across 49 cities in the United States, depending on the level of climate action taken (Nuccitelli, 2019[4]).The global cost of delayed action to the increasing challenges of climate change, considering a 2°C stabilisation target, would reach 17% of global GDP in 2070, if accounting for a 1990 start to climate mitigation, and 35% in 2035 for a 2020 start (Sanderson and O'Neill, 2020[5]). Climate change will also impact health considerably, with estimates forecasting approximately 250 000 climate-change related additional deaths per year between 2030 and 2050; 38,000 due to heat exposure in elderly people, 48,000 due to diarrhoea, 60,000 due to malaria, and 95,000 due to childhood undernutrition (WHO, 2018[6]).

Climate change has far-reaching impacts and cuts across all SDGs, endangering health, essential resources, food security and biodiversity, and in turn economies and global security. SDG 13 on climate action is essential for achieving all other sustainability development goals, in particular, SDG 2 (zero hunger), SDG 3 (good health and well-being), SDG 6 (clean water and sanitation), SDG 7 (clean energy), SDG 9 (sustainable and inclusive infrastructure), and SDG10 (reduced inequalities), SDG 11 (safe, sustainable and inclusive cities), SDG 12 (responsible consumption and production), and Goals 14 and 15 on protection, restoration and sustainable use of land and water resources.

Tackling climate change is also intrinsically linked to SDG 5. However, there is only one SDG 13 target specifically with a gender equality angle: raise capacity climate-change related planning and management including focusing on women (13.b).

Climate justice, in the context of the Paris Agreement, is understood as the process of integrating inclusive adaptation into socio-economic and environmental action. Most importantly, both the Paris Agreement and UN bodies such as the UNFCCC take into consideration gender equality and empowerment of women to fight climate change and acknowledge the differentiated impacts from climate change on women and girls. Efforts to integrate the gender and climate action agendas are increasingly being recognised through initiatives such as the 'Action Coalition on Feminist action for Climate Justice' recently inaugurated in March at the Generation Equality Forum organised by Mexico, France and UN Women.

Nevertheless – studies and data remain sparse on the differential impacts climate change and environmental hazards have on men and women – as well as the crucial role women can and do play in climate action. While various UN bodies have well-documented work of the disproportionate impact climate change has on women in developing countries, the same cannot be said for OECD countries and more gender-disaggregated data is needed across the board. It was recently announced that the COP 26 team of politicians and negotiators who will host the negotiations in Glasgow 2021 will be composed of all men (The Grantham Institute, 2020[7]). The latter is reflective of - and also perpetuates - a lack of awareness by local, national, and even global decision-makers on the gender dimension of climate change.

12.3. Gendered effects of climate change

There is a significant body of literature on gender equality and climate change, which shows that women and men experience and respond to climate change differently. In general, women are more vulnerable due to their greater dependence on natural resources and structural inequity in their access and control of such resources (Ravera et al., 2016[8]) and their more limited mobility and income buffers. Multiple social, economic, and cultural characteristics interact with gender in influencing power inequities and explaining how and why people face and manage climate change and environmental stresses in different ways (Ravera et al., 2016[8]); (Ogra and Badola, 2015[9]).

Physiological differences between genders may also explain why climate-related hazards may affect women more. A 2019 study focusing on Spain, showed women – across all age ranges - are more susceptible to death from cardiovascular disease linked to climate change related temperature increases (Achebak, Devolder and Ballester, 2019[10]). Emissions of pollutants into the air from vehicles, buildings and industrial processes is also both a source of climate damage and harms human health. As shown in Chapter 3, air pollution resulting from emissions is a major health threat for pregnant women and is also associated with respiratory and developmental problems in their children. Other factors may also intersect with gender, such as age and ethnicity. For instance, the heatwave that hit France in 2003 claimed over

15 000 lives – with the excess mortality rate for women 75% higher than that for men (Fouillet et al., 2006[11]), due to differences in life expectancy between the two sexes.

There are gender differences stemming from the cumulative economic, social and health impacts of climate change. Some potent cases point to the need to further investigate these differences. For instance, in 2013, Austrian StartClim - a research programme dealing with climate change and its effects – looked at gender issues in the context of natural hazards, in particular flooding, and found disproportionate effects on women (StartClim, 2013[12]). In the aftermath of Hurricane Katrina in 2005, 83% of low-income single mothers displaced were unable to return to their homes when the storm displaced more than a million people in the Gulf Coast region. (Sastry, 2009[13]); (Bryner, Garcia-Lozano and Bruch, 2017[14]). After the 2017 Hurricane Maria in Puerto Rico, the disruption of modern water and electrical infrastructure left many households without the most basic services, a burden that fell significantly on women. While men contributed to finding and transporting water, women were found to do the arduous labour of caretaking, looking after the sick and maintaining households without water and power, including the improvisation of WASH services (OXFAM, 2018[15]). Research conducted in Brazil further shows that women are both vulnerable in the face of environmental disasters and essential to overcoming the impact of such situations and in recovery efforts (De Araujo Pinheiro, 2011[16]).

On the other hand, farmer suicide, partly due to drought or severe and unpredictable weather threatening agricultural income, is a predominately-male phenomenon (Sorensen et al., 2018[17]). Harmful stereotypes, such as maintaining a macho persona, prevent men from seeking help. Men account for 87% of farmer suicides in Australia (Bryant, 2018[18]), 96% in the United Kingdom (ONS UK, 2019[19]), and around 86% in France (Grosclaude et al., 2018[20]). In India, in 2019, a total of 10,281 farmers and agricultural labourers died by suicide in India. Government's data shows that these suicides were mainly linked to despair over their livelihoods, with recent calls made by farmers complaining about loan sharking, the privatisation of the rural credit system, and agriculture monopolies among other issues (NCRB, 2020[21]).This is a deep-rooted crisis that has led many farmers to take their own lives by consuming a pesticide, particularly during COVID-19 (Shivji, 2021[22]).

In the developing country context, climate change disproportionately affects women and children. They are more likely to be victims of increasingly severe environmental hazards (droughts, fires and floods), accounting for more than 75% of displaced persons (IPCC, 2012[23]). Socio-economic and cultural norms tend to exacerbate the cumulative effects of climate-related events. Traditional gender roles dictate that women become the primary caretakers for those affected by disasters – including children, the injured and sick, and the elderly – substantially increasing their emotional and material workload (WHO, 2020[24]).

Nevertheless, worldwide natural disasters impact men and women disproportionately. Stemming both from physiological differences and cultural norms across societies, disasters can and have disproportionally impacted women and girls. During a major disaster, this could result in women being reluctant to seek shelter because shared communal facilities may not provide separate private spaces (UFCOP, 2016[25]).

In general, the gender equality aspects of climate change remain a largely under-researched agenda and national climate strategies often lack a gender equality perspective. Some countries have started to take action to correct this deficit. For instance, in September 2017, the Government of Finland approved its Midterm (2030) Climate Policy Plan and included Gender Impact Assessment training as a key tool for its actions, with a focus on areas such as transport planning, urban safety, consumption patterns and energy use (OECD, 2020[26]).

The Government of Chile, with the support of UN Women and the Food Agriculture Organisation (FAO), has recently launched a study to gather evidence on gender equality and climate change in the country. The initiative will include an Atlas of Information on Gender and Climate Change and sectoral gender indicators (still under development) to identify gender gaps and climate change in certain sectors which call for the design and updating of adaptation and mitigation plans. Additionally, there are other projects underway, such as Austria's study on "Climate and Energy Strategy 2030" ("mission2030"), which includes a gender angle (OECD, 2020[26]).

The UNDP Nationally Determined Contributions (NDC) Support Programme is supporting countries to improve their focus on gender equality as they plan for implementing, enhancing or revising their National Determined Contributions. In Costa Rica, the new National Policy for Equality (2018-2030) includes goals related to strengthening the climate resilience of women and their participation in risk management. The national women's institute (INAMU) is playing an active role in climate change related policy. They have participated in the Inter-ministerial Committee on Climate Change, which is an advisory body and they have provided support to MINAE for monitoring the National Strategy on Climate Change, Moreover, INAMU has also been involved in strengthening a gender focus in the National Adaptation Policy (UNDP, 2019[27]).

In Côte d'Ivoire, the National Climate Change Programme (NCCP) has included a climate and gender unit working to develop the Gender and Climate Change Strategy. In partnership with the UNDP and the NAP Global Network, they have produced a gender analysis and recommendations for mainstreaming gender in climate action policy (MINEDD, 2019[28]).

12.4. Gender equality and the role of women in climate action

Tackling the impact of climate change requires a bevy of innovative solutions, strategies and changes in behaviour. Targeted policy action accounting for gender, alongside socio-economic, cultural and physiological factors, can decrease negative outcomes of climate-related health impacts (Sorensen et al., 2018[17]). Understanding gender roles, discrimination and inequalities in the context of climate change and climate action supports a more informed approach to mitigation and adaptation that can galvanise women's social agency, and the efficacy of initiatives.

12.4.1. Gender equality measures reinforce climate action

Direct connections can be made between gender equality and climate action, but a gender-responsive approach also requires thinking outside the box. Project Drawdown – a consortium of companies committed to finding solutions to reduce greenhouse gases and sequestering carbon already in the atmosphere – has compiled a list of 80 solutions modelled and measured through to 2050 (Table 12.1). Educating Girls and Family Planning ranks 6 and 7 on the list, with the potential to reduce Carbon Dioxide Equivalent (CO2-EQ) by 103 gigatonnes. These solutions fall just behind restoring and preserving tropical forests (61.23 gigatonnes) and above solar farms (36.90 gigatonnes).

Table 12.1. Solutions by Rank

Rank	Solution	Sector	Total Atmospheric CO2-EQ Reduction (GT)	Net Cost (Billions US $)	Savings (Billions US $)
1	Refrigerator Management	Materials	89.74	N/A	$-902.77
2	Wind Turbines (Onshore)	Electricity Generation	84.6	$1,225.37	$7,425.00
3	Reduced Food Waste	Food	70.53	N/A	N/A
4	Plant-Rich Diet	Food	66.11	N/A	N/A
5	Tropical Forests	Land Use	61.23	N/A	N/A
6	Educating Girls	Women and Girls	51.48	N/A	N/A
7	Family Planning	Women and Girls	51.48	N/A	N/A
8	Solar Farms	Electricity Generation	36.9	$-80.6	$5,023.84
9	Silvopasture	Food	31.19	$41.59	$699.37
10	Rooftop Solar	Electricity Generation	24.6	$453.14	$3,457.63

Source: Project Drawdown (https://www.drawdown.org/solutions).

Population growth in the context of unsustainable consumption patterns is one of the main causes of climate change. A comprehensive framework of sexual reproductive health and rights, including voluntary family planning solutions, access to contraception and reproductive health services, together with improved access to education, can therefore have a substantial effect on population growth, slowing the increase of the carbon footprint of humans (i.e. reduced demand for food and resources, waste and transportation) (Murtaugh and Schlax, 2009[29]). It also has the knock-on effect for improving health, poverty, and hunger outcomes by reducing pregnancy in high risk groups (the young and old), maternal mortality rates, and freeing up time for women and girls to pursue other goals (Smith et al., 2014[30]).

The funding gap for implementing voluntary family planning is estimated at USD 5.3 billion, making it a relatively low-cost solution and one that pales in comparison to the cost of inaction and other, more costly solutions (Bixby Center, 2017[31]). In 2017, OECD Development Assistance Committee (DAC) figures show that 8% - or USD 3.31 billion - of Official Development Assistance (ODA) was directed towards population and reproductive health (OECD, 2017[32]). ODA has nevertheless been incorporating gender equality and women's empowerment in developing countries with bilateral aid steadily increasing and reaching an average of USD 48.7 billion per year in 2017-18, corresponding to 42% of aid (GENDERNET, 2020[33]). Additionally, the DAC gender equality policy marker monitors and accounts for all bilateral aid in support of the implementation of the Sustainable Development Goals (SDGs) commitments on gender equality, further supporting gender oriented ODA (UNDP, 2016[34]). Climate aid that targets gender equality has increased rapidly in recent years from USD 4.4 billion in 2010 to USD 8 billion in 2014. Different programmes include the Solar Sister programme, through which donors have supported women across rural Africa to sell solar lamps that provide safe, clean energy and employment for women, or the TransMilenio, a project that establishes a low-emission rapid bus transit system in Bogotá, Colombia (OECD, 2016[35]).

Arriving at these seemingly unrelated, but sensible solutions requires adopting wide visibility of the synergies and trade-offs between well-being outcomes and climate action. The OECD Climate Change Mitigation through a Well-Being Lens initiative advocates for this approach where policies and decisions are taken with multiple well-being objectives in mind, rather than focusing on singular or a narrow range of objectives (OECD, 2019[36]). The Well-being Lens provides for a two-way alignment: "action in non-climate policy is supportive of and does not undermine the pursuit of climate change mitigation goals," while "climate action meets other important societal goals" without negatively impacting key aspects of well-being.

12.4.2. Men and women express different preferences, perceptions and beliefs towards climate change

Men and women express different preferences, perceptions and beliefs when it comes to acting in environmentally friendly ways. While consumer behaviour towards environmental sustainability has been discussed in Chapter 11, here the focus is mostly on gender differences in people's preferences and perceptions towards climate change.

For instance, substantially reducing meat consumption, particularly red meat, can bring about massive reductions in GHG emissions. While more people are turning to a vegan or vegetarian lifestyle, men making this change trail behind women. An Ipsos MORI survey in the United Kingdom found that women are significantly more likely to be vegetarian than men (IPSOS, 2018[37]). Strong associations exist between meat and masculinity across regions and culture, as does an affinity for fast, fuel-guzzling cars (Love and Sulikowski, 2018[38]).A study of men and women's energy consumption in Germany, Greece, Norway and Sweden found that men eat more meat, use cars more frequently and drive longer distances than women (Räty and Kanyama, 2010[39]). Results concluded that "men consumed 70-80% more energy on transport than women in Germany and Norway, 100% more in Sweden and 350% more in Greece" and single male households consumed 6-38% more total energy that single female households (Räty and Kanyama, 2010[39]). A study conducted by France's National Institute of Statistics and Economics (INSEE) found that, based on daily activity, men produce 7 kilograms more of CO_2 emissions per day (INSEE, 2020[40]). An OECD study also found that women are more likely to recycle, minimise wastage and buy organic food and eco-labelled products (OECD, 2008[41]).

Focusing on environmental objectives to change behaviour and steer men and women toward more environmentally-friendly choices will not be enough. These efforts must be broadly underpinned by gender equality measures to breakdown harmful gender stereotypes/roles and discriminatory social institutions, so that men and women feel more comfortable embracing more green lifestyles.

12.4.3. Women's engagement in climate action

Women and girls can be proactive and experienced agents with expertise in adaptation and mitigation in the face of climate change (Sinharoy and Caruso, 2019[42]); (Yadav, Han and Rho, 2016[43]). As discussed in Chapter 5, women and girls are increasingly engaged in climate change action. Women are raising their own voice in the debate on climate change adaptation, not only because they experience the vulnerabilities depicted by climate change at a greater scale (due to the gender divide), but also because they have a different sense of what constitutes a bigger climate risk than men, based on their role at the household and the local community (UN, 2020[44]); (Terry, 2009[45]).

Women have been advocating for climate justice since the COP 13 in Bali, (GenderCC Network, 2007[46]) and they are continuing to do so, raising awareness and campaigning for a gender-just transition. Throughout the world, there are examples of women's groups taking climate action in their hands (Chapter 4). In South Asia for instance, during the 1970s, the Chipko movement mobilised popular opposition to large-scale commercial forestry in the Indian Himalaya (Uttarakhand). This movement opposed commercial loggers and certain agricultural practices and local ecology (Price, 2018[47]). In 1997 in the Headwaters Forest of Northern California, the young Julia Butterfly Hill made history when she climbed up and lived for 738 days on the branches of a tree to protest tree-felling in the Pacific Northwest's old-growth forests. Today's climate justice activism amongst the youth is also represented by a female face, Greta Thunberg.

Indigenous women, in particular, have become key agents in defending nature and taking climate action. They have, however, also become the main targets of environmental-related violence. In 2017, roughly half of all female activists were murdered for defending community land and environmental rights (Ervin, 2018[48]). Despite the numerous challenges facing women environmental defenders, they continue to demonstrate leadership, resiliency, and flexibility in their efforts to support their communities and be at the forefront of driving change, innovation, and progress. Providing access to indigenous women to decision-making spaces remains key for climate action. Examples include Hindou Oumarou Ibrahim, who was not only selected as the speaker representing civil society in COP 21 but has also pioneered many climate action projects, including a 3D mapping project in Chad that has contributed in the protection of natural resources (McCarthy, 2020[49]).

There is a lack on women's representation in public and private sector decision-making, especially in sectors that have key impacts on climate change (finance, energy and transport) (UNDP, 2016[34]) However in climate-related grassroots movements and environment-related UN processes such as the UNFCCC women's role is increasing, and gender parity is almost reached (Chapter 2).

Women in leadership positions tend to put a greater focus on climate change and environmental sustainability. A study on gender equality and state-level environmentalism found that, across 130 countries, women in government positions were more likely to sign on to international treaties to reduce global warming than men (Norgaard and York, 2005[50]). Promoting the participation of diverse women in leadership positions, as well as climate science, can also inspire young women to participate (Dennehy and Dasgupta, 2017[51]).

Hence, considering women as unique agents in climate action is an imperative that should translate into all areas of climate change action by mainstreaming gender in mitigation, adaptation, finance, and technology and capacity development. Applying tools such as Gender Impact Assessment, Gender Vulnerability and Capacity Assessment (GVA) and Gender-Responsive Budgeting on climate action projects and policy can all contribute to correcting gender imbalances in relation to climate change (UNDP, 2015[52]). For instance, while climate change technologies are not gender-neutral they are sometimes introduced without a gender assessment, accentuating women's and reinforcing gender roles. The operational arm of the UNFCCC Technology Mechanism, the Climate Technology Centre and Network (CTCN), acknowledges these challenges and integrates a gender analysis in their Technology Needs Assessment and Feasibility Studies, accounting in this way for social and financial benefits to women derived from new climate technologies.

12.5. Key actions for advancing the agenda and ongoing work

There are a number of key actions to better address the impact of climate change on women and allow their empowerment to take climate action:

- Providing equal rights to women and ending all forms of discrimination can provide a massive boost to the fight against climate change and strengthen the planet's resilience and sustainability.
- There is also a need to step up evidence gathering and indicators on the impact of climate change on women, especially those in more vulnerable situations, and to consider remedial policy actions. Coordinating with the private sector and civil society that produce quantitative and qualitative work in the field can contribute to this objective.
- More evidence is needed to understand the ways and sectors in which women are already having a positive effect on climate action in order to further support their efforts.
- The integration of gender and climate change considerations in policy decisions is essential, especially in developing countries with large rural populations and high dependence on agriculture. Domestic and international efforts to advance climate mitigation and adaptation in developing

countries should focus more on women-led projects at the local and community level. In particular, there is a need to continue to integrate a joint gender and environmental dimension into development co-operation efforts, and specifically into ODA.

- There is a need to collect better sex-disaggregated data on climate change impacts and climate policy interventions, and to make use of 'Gender Impact Assessments' (GIA). Understanding the current state of adaptation and possible future impacts of climate change requires further work.
- Applying gender budgeting in the field of climate policy can assist governments to monitor the allocation of resources and analyse the gender-differentiated impact.
- It is also necessary to review decision-making processes and support women's leadership in climate-sensitive policies.

References

Achebak, H., D. Devolder and J. Ballester (2019), "Trends in temperature-related age-specific and sex-specific mortality from cardiovascular diseases in Spain: a national time-series analysis", *The Lancet Planetary Health*, Vol. 3/7, pp. e297-e306, http://dx.doi.org/10.1016/S2542-5196(19)30090-7. [10]

Bixby Center (2017), "Bixby_Annual_Report_2017-18". [31]

Bryant, K. (2018), "Farmers and mental distress: 'I'm still a bit ashamed about my story'", *The Guardian*. [18]

Bryner, N., M. Garcia-Lozano and C. Bruch (2017), "Washed Out: Policy and Practical Considerations Affecting Return after Hurricane Katrina and Superstorm Sandy", *Journal of Asian Development*, Vol. 3/1, p. 73, http://dx.doi.org/10.5296/jad.v3i1.10590. [14]

De Araujo Pinheiro, M. (2011), "Women, Vulnerability, Resilience and Natural Disasters: Interview with Marta de Araujo Pinheiro", *Sciences Po*. [16]

Dennehy, T. and N. Dasgupta (2017), "Female peer mentors early in college increase women's positive academic experiences and retention in engineering", *Proceedings of the National Academy of Sciences*, Vol. 114/23, http://dx.doi.org/10.1073/pnas.1613117114. [51]

Easterling, D. et al. (2012), *Changes in Climate Extremes and their Impacts on the Natural Physical Environment*, Cambridge University Press. [2]

Ervin, J. (2018), "In Defense of Nature: Women at the Forefront", *UNDP*, https://www.undp.org/content/undp/en/home/blog/2018/in-defense-of-nature-women-at-the-forefront.html. [48]

Fouillet, A. et al. (2006), "Excess mortality related to the August 2003 heat wave in France", *International Archives of Occupational and Environmental Health*, Vol. 80/1, http://dx.doi.org/10.1007/s00420-006-0089-4. [11]

GenderCC Network (2007), *"There will be no climate justice without gender justice" Gender: Missing Links in Financing Climate Change Adaptation and Mitigation Plans*. [46]

GENDERNET (2020), *Aid Focussed on Gender Equality and Women's Empowerment: A snapshot of current funding and trends over time in support of the implementation of the Beijing Declaration and Platform for Action*, OECD DAC Network on Gender Equality (GENDERNET), http://www.oecd.org/development/gender-development/Aid-Focussed-on-Gender-Equality-and-Women-s-Empowerment-2020.pdf. [33]

Grosclaude, P. et al. (2018), *Etude collaborative Coordination de la publication*. [20]

INSEE (2020), "Statistics France". [40]

IPCC (2012), *Special panel on Climate Change Managing the Risks of Extreme Events and Disasters to Advance Climate Change Adaptation*. [23]

IPSOS (2018), *What does it mean to consumers? 'Natural' An exploration into diets around the world*. [37]

Love, H. and D. Sulikowski (2018), "Of meat and men: Sex differences in implicit and explicit attitudes toward meat", *Frontiers in Psychology*, Vol. 9/APR, http://dx.doi.org/10.3389/fpsyg.2018.00559. [38]

McCarthy, J. (2020), "How Indigenous Activists Are Championing Nature-Based Solutions to Climate Change", *The Global Citizen*, https://www.globalcitizen.org/en/content/conservation-international-indigenous-voices/. [49]

MINEDD (2019), *Pour un Processus de Plan National d'Adaptation (PNA) qui Reponde aux Questions de Genre en Cote d'Ivoire*, Ministère de l'Environnement et du Développement Durable, République de la Côte d'Ivoire, https://napglobalnetwork.org/resource/pour-un-processus-de-plan-national-dadaptation-pna-qui-reponde-aux-questions-de-genre-en-cote-divoire/. [28]

Murtaugh, P. and M. Schlax (2009), "Reproduction and the carbon legacies of individuals", *Global Environmental Change*, Vol. 19/1, pp. 14-20, http://dx.doi.org/10.1016/j.gloenvcha.2008.10.007. [29]

NCRB (2020), *Accidental Deaths and Suicide in India 2019*, National Crime Record Bureau, New Delhi, https://ncrb.gov.in/sites/default/files/ADSI-2019-FULL-REPORT.pdf. [21]

Norgaard, K. and R. York (2005), "Gender Equality and State Environmentalism", *Gender and Society*. [50]

Nuccitelli, D. (2019), "Climate change could cost the U.S. economy hundreds of billions a year by 2090", *Yale Climate Connection*. [4]

OECD (2020), *EPOC Survey on integrating gender in environmental policies*. [26]

OECD (2019), *Climate Change Mitigation through a Well-being Lens "Putting people at the centre of climate action" The Well-being Lens*, http://www.oecd.org/environment. [36]

OECD (2017), *Aid to gender equality and women's empowerment AN OVERVIEW*, http://www.oecd.org/dac/gender-development. [32]

OECD (2016), *Making climate finance work for women: Overview of bilateral ODA to gender and climate change*. [35]

OECD (2008), *2008 annual report on sustainable development work in the oecd*. [41]

Ogra, M. and R. Badola (2015), "Gender and climate change in the Indian Himalayas: Global threats, local vulnerabilities, and livelihood diversification at the Nanda Devi Biosphere Reserve", *Earth System Dynamics*, Vol. 6/2, pp. 505-523, http://dx.doi.org/10.5194/esd-6-505-2015. [9]

ONS UK (2019), "Overview of the UK population: August 2019". [19]

OXFAM (2018), "The Weight of Water on Women: The Long Wake of Hurricane Maria in Puerto Rico", https://www.oxfamamerica.org/explore/research-publications/research-backgrounder-wash-gender-report-puerto-rico/. [15]

Price, R. (2018), *Women-initiated measures to cope with environmental stresses and climate change in South Asia*. [47]

Räty, R. and A. Kanyama (2010), "Energy consumption by gender in some European countries", *Energy Policy*, Vol. 38(1):646-649, http://dx.doi.org/DOI: 10.1016/j.enpol.2009.08.010 ·. [39]

Ravera, F. et al. (2016), "The diversity of gendered adaptation strategies to climate change of Indian farmers: A feminist intersectional approach", *Ambio*, Vol. 45, pp. 335-351, http://dx.doi.org/10.1007/s13280-016-0833-2. [8]

Sanderson, B. and B. O'Neill (2020), "Assessing the costs of historical inaction on climate change", *Scientific Reports*, Vol. 10/1, http://dx.doi.org/10.1038/s41598-020-66275-4. [5]

Sastry, N. (2009), "Tracing the Effects of Hurricane Katrina on the Population of New Orleans", *Sociological Methods & Research*, Vol. 38/1, http://dx.doi.org/10.1177/0049124109339370. [13]

Shivji, S. (2021), *Burdened by Debt and Unable to Eke Out a Living, Many Farmers in India Turn to suicide*, CBC News, New Delhi, https://www.cbc.ca/news/world/india-farmers-suicide-1.5968086. [22]

Sinharoy, S. and B. Caruso (2019), *On World Water Day, gender equality and empowerment require attention*, Elsevier B.V., http://dx.doi.org/10.1016/S2542-5196(19)30021-X. [42]

Smith, K. et al. (2014), *Human Health: Impacts, Adaptation, and Co-Benefits Coordinating Lead Authors: Lead Authors: Contributing Authors*. [30]

Sorensen, C. et al. (2018), "Climate Change and Women's Health: Impacts and Opportunities in India", *GeoHealth*, Vol. 2/10, http://dx.doi.org/10.1029/2018GH000163. [17]

StartClim (2013), "STARTCLIM", http://www.startclim.at/ueber-startclim/ (accessed on 10 November 2020). [12]

Terry, G. (2009), "No climate justice without gender justice: An overview of the issues", *Gender and Development*, Vol. 17/1, pp. 5-18, http://dx.doi.org/10.1080/13552070802696839. [45]

The Grantham Institute (2020), "Why the UK needs a diverse leadership team for COP26", *London School of Economics*, https://www.lse.ac.uk/granthaminstitute/news/why-the-uk-needs-a-diverse-leadership-team-for-cop26/ (accessed on 15 December 2020). [7]

UFCOP (2016), *The Role of Green Infrastructure Solutions in Urban Flood Risk Management*. [25]

UN (2020), "'Staggering' rise in climate emergencies in last 20 years, new disaster research shows", *UN News*, https://news.un.org/en/story/2020/10/1075142. [1]

UN (2020), "Women...In The Shadow of Climate Change". [44]

UNDP (2019), *Gender and NDCs: Country Progress and Kenya Findings. 24-26 April 2019*, Nairobi, Kenya, https://www.international-climate-initiative.com/fileadmin/Dokumente/2020/200302_undp-ndcsp-gender-ndc-country-progress-key-findings.pdf. [27]

UNDP (2016), *Gender Equality in National Climate Action: Planning for Gender-Responsive Nationally Determined Contributions*. [34]

UNDP (2015), *Mainstreaming Gender in Mitigation and Technology Development and Transfer Interventions*, https://www.undp.org/content/dam/undp/library/gender/Gender%20and%20Environment/Mainstreaming%20Gender%20in%20Mitigation%20FNL2.pdf. [52]

UNISDR (2015), *The Human Cost of Weather-Related Disasters 1995-2015.* [3]

WHO (2020), "Gender and disaster", http://origin.searo.who.int/entity/gender/topics/disaster_women/en/ (accessed on 10 November 2020). [24]

WHO (2018), *Climate Change and Health*, WHO, https://www.who.int/news-room/fact-sheets/detail/climate-change-and-health#:~:text=Nevertheless%2C%20a%20WHO%20assessment%2C%20taking,to%20heat%20exposure%20in%20elderly. [6]

Yadav, P., S. Han and J. Rho (2016), "Impact of Environmental Performance on Firm Value for Sustainable Investment: Evidence from Large US Firms", *Business Strategy and the Environment*, Vol. 25/6, http://dx.doi.org/10.1002/bse.1883. [43]

13 Women and SDG14 – Life under water: Conserve and sustainably use the oceans, seas and marine resources for sustainable development

Healthy marine ecosystems are crucial to biodiversity and to counteracting and reducing the impacts of climate change. They also provide sustenance to human communities and support the development of a sustainable blue economy. The growth of litter and toxic substances in the oceans is not only damaging fragile maritime ecosystems but also affecting human health, especially that of children and pregnant women. Ensuring women's access to leadership positions and empowering women action on the oceans are fundamental to allow them to play a key role in protecting marine ecosystems, tackling marine litter and promoting sustainable fishing.

13.1. Key findings

This chapter touches on a number of key interactions between gender equality (SDG 5) and the health of the oceans (SDG 14). It reviews existing evidence and proposes a number of recommendations:

- Tackling marine little is key to healthy oceans and to human health. Pregnant women and children are highly sensitive to toxic materials contained in fish. Microplastics have the ability to cross the placental barrier and affect unborn children.
- Negative feedback loops between human damage to the oceans and human-induced climate change are intensifying and reaching tipping points with potentially devastating consequences. Coastal disasters have a differentiated effect as the growing intensity and frequency of sea storms strongly affect women and children. Studies show that women, boys and girls are 14 times more likely than men to die during a disaster.
- Globally, women occupy only 20% of the workforce in fishing and aquaculture and additionally they tend to hold lower paid jobs in the fishing industry. They are on the other hand more represented in artisanal fishing.
- Globally, in 2016, only 1 in top 100 seafood companies was run by a woman, and 54% had no women on boards. Increasing women's participation in high-level, decision-making roles in the fishing sector, could help towards achieving more sustainable fishing and marine conservation.
- Women can play a key role in protecting marine ecosystems and sustainably use marine resources. Local initiatives involving women are achieving a successful regeneration of mangroves across East African countries, protecting coastal areas and yielding more marine wildlife. Tackling discrimination, ensuring access to finance and developing skills are essential for such initiatives to prosper.
- There is a smaller gender gap in ocean science than in science overall. Female scientists represent on average 38% of the researchers in ocean science, about 10% higher than science overall.
- Gender equality also needs to be mainstreamed in development co-operation targeting the oceans, supporting initiatives to protect coastal areas and developing small-scale, sustainable fishing that benefit local communities and help decrease gender gaps.
- There is a need to improve evidence gathering and data collection on the differentiated impact of oceans degradation on women's and men's health, well-being and employment opportunities, with a focus on the most vulnerable, and addressing intersectionalities.
- Policy solutions to better conserve the oceans require a gender-lens, addressing the gender-specific concerns of degrading oceans, including the impact of coastal storms, the depletion of fish stocks and the increase in marine litter.

13.2. Key interlinkages between gender equality, sustainable management of marine resources, and other SDGs

SDG 14 touches on a vast range of issues – in sync with the very vastness of the ocean itself which covers 71% of the Earth's surface and contains 97% of the Earth's water (UN Atlas of the Oceans, n.d.[1]). Healthy marine ecosystems are crucial to counteracting and reducing the impacts of climate change (SDG 13), as well as providing sustenance (SDG 2). Fish, in particular, provide unique nutritional benefits for neurodevelopment and cardiovascular health (SDG 3). Small-scale fishing, as well as restoration and protection of ecosystems provide decent work opportunities (SDG 8), while desalination plants can help secure the supply of clean water in areas with limited fresh water (SDG 6). There are also new employment and economic opportunities in the conservation and sustainable use of maritime biodiversity (fish, mangroves, coral reefs) and in eco-tourism, as well as opportunities for innovation to reduce and clean up ocean pollution (SDG 9). In addition, there is a growing capacity to harness the thermal and mechanical energy of oceans for affordable and renewable electricity generation (SDG 7).

Humans are highly dependent on maritime ecosystems and resources. The United Nations Atlas of the Oceans records that around 40% of the world's population lives within 100 kilometres (60 miles) of the coast and nearly a billion people rely on the oceans for their livelihoods. Coastal populations and entire industries, such as fisheries and tourism, are particularly exposed to the growing fragility of the oceans (UN Atlas of the Oceans, n.d.[1]). A conservative estimate of the value of ocean economy by the OECD put it at USD 1.5 trillion, or approximately 2.5% of world gross value added (OECD, 2016[2]). Human economic activity in the oceans, in particular fishing and maritime transport, directly affect the state of the oceans. But ultimately, all forms of unsustainable production and consumption end up affecting the oceans. Recent studies show the astonishing rate at which human activity has degraded oceans – with just 13% untouched and only 5% of ocean wilderness falling within marine protected areas (Jones et al., 2018[3]). Human action influences 97% of oceans, pressuring coastal marine ecosystems, water quality, and coastlines (IPBES, 2019[4]).

The growth in plastic litter, mercury and other toxic substances in the oceans is not only damaging fragile maritime ecosystems but also affects human health. Human activity also drives eutrophication, acidification, dead zones, and rising sea levels, negatively affecting marine ecosystems, and in turn human physical and mental health (Viviani, 1992[5]) (WHO Regional Office for Europe and European Commission, 2002[6]) (Falkenberg et al., 2020[7]) (EPA, n.d.[8]). Overfishing affects today one third of global marine stocks (Delpeuch and Hutniczak, 2019[9]).

Negative feedback loops between human damage to the oceans and human-induced climate change are intensifying and reaching tipping points with potentially devastating consequences. For instance, a square kilometre of coastal ecosystem such as mangroves forests can store up to five times more carbon than the equivalent area of mature tropical forests. But these areas are being destroyed three to four times faster than forests, releasing substantial amounts of carbon dioxide into the atmosphere and the ocean, thus contributing to climate change (IUCN, 2020[10]).

There are various links between gender equality and the protection of the oceans. Toxic substances contained in marine litter can get into food systems and affect men's and women's health differently (SDG 4). There may also be gender differences with regards to consumption, production and waste management and the impact they can have on pollution of our oceans (Target 14.1). Men and women may also play differentiated roles in protecting and restoring ecosystems (Target 14.2), and may benefit differently from the economic benefits from sustainable use of marine resources (Target 14.7). Target 14B on supporting small-scale fishers also has an important gender aspect, as many are women. Despite potentially important gender differences, none of the SDG 14 targets address gender equality or the relation of marine resources to the livelihoods of women and men, including the role they can play in food security, employment and poverty reduction.

13.3. Gender effects of marine litter and maritime natural disasters

Both men and women are vulnerable to marine debris, microplastics and chemicals, yet, the health of the oceans has a differentiated effect on their health and well-being. The growing pollution of the oceans, such as plastics and mercury ultimately ends up in the human body. Pregnant women and children are most sensitive to the toxic materials contained in fish. In particular, microplastics have the ability to cross the placental barrier and affect unborn children (Lloyd-Smith and Immig, 2018[11]).

Mercury bioaccumulates in food and deteriorates women's and men's health. In poor coastal communities, pollutants cluster in shorelines and, as supplementary fishers are often women, they are exposed to these dangerous chemicals. Mercury exposure can be managed through dietary advice. A recent study that offered pregnant women dietary guidance for lowering their mercury intake by avoiding large predatory fish showed a significant decrease in mercury levels three months after (Kirk et al., 2017[12]).

Lastly, there is an issue of occurrence and adaptation to the growing intensity of natural disasters. Women living in coastal areas are also most affected by the growing intensity and frequency of sea storms, as studies show that women, boys and girls are 14 times more likely than men to die during a disaster (UNDP, 2016[13]) (UNDP, 2016[14]). The tsunami that took place in Sri Lanka in 2004 made these inequalities apparent as it was easier for men to survive as they climbed trees, which is mainly taught to boys (IUCN, 2008[15]). This led to girls and women in Sri Lanka to having less possibilities of surviving in natural disasters (Oxfam International, 2005[16]).

Feedback loops between climate change, environmental stressors and pressures over diminishing, degrading and/or depleting natural resources, has triggered a rise in gender-based violence. (Camey et al., n.d.[17]).

13.4. The blue economy

An inclusive blue economy offers the opportunity to improve the workplace conditions to make them more favourable to women, move towards unbiased recruitment processes, and support policies and actions that promote female role models. Overall, an inclusive blue economy can support the transition to a more sustainable and gender balanced fishing sector (Shaleh, Fui-Fui and Mustafa, 2020[18]). Policy support is imperative in order to trigger these necessary changes and ensure women achieve their share in stewardship of marine resources. It could also offer the chance to develop businesses that could provide women with economic independence and improve their well-being (Saleem and Abentim, 2019[19]).

13.4.1. Women's employment in the fisheries sector

The health of the ocean equates the health of the planet, with billions of livelihoods directly depending on them. Women represent more than half the workforce in processing, cleaning and trading fish, but in 2014 only represented 19% of all people directly engaged in catching or harvesting of wild fish and in fish farming (UN Women, 2020[20]). According to the UN Food and Agriculture Organisation (FAO), women accounted for just 14% of the 60 million people working in the aquaculture and fisheries sector in 2018 (FAO, 2020[21]). In Asia alone, women reportedly occupy 33% of the aquaculture workforce in China, and 42-80% in freshwater and cage culture in Indonesia and Viet Nam (OECD, 2015[22]).

Women have set roles in traditional fishing communities and often lack the institutional capacity and technical knowledge for boat fishing due to gender norms (UNEP, 2017[23]). Women are often more present on lower paid, seasonal and unstable positions in the fisheries sector (FAO, 2020[21]). Such jobs often do not benefit from health, safety and labour rights protections. Also, women earn on average 64% of men's wages for the same work in aquaculture (UN Women, 2020[20]).

Given that fish is perishable, low-income women without access to storage technology and transport are most vulnerable to losses associated with its wastage (UN Women, 2020[24]). Women account for most (over 90%) of the workers in secondary marine-related activities such as fish processing, marketing and maintenance, which are often low-paid or unpaid jobs (UN Women, 2017[25]). Moreover, the post-harvest processing sector is associated with occupational health hazards. Women shrimp workers in Bangladesh have reported fungal disease of the hands; a study in Australia found significant incidence of urticaria and work-related asthma among seafood workers; and in South Africa, women have claimed to suffer from similar skin problems (Thirumoorthy et al., 2016[26]) (Jeebhay, Lopata and Robins, 2000[27]) (Jeebhay and Lopata, 2012[28]).

Overall, women have much lower economic gains from their participation in the fisheries sector (FAO, 2011[29]) and do not participate fully and equitably in the industry (FAO, 2015[30]). The problem extends across countries, both developing and developed, with different intensity. For instance, a study of women fishers in Norway found that there is an intrinsic subordination of women in the fisheries sector (Gerrard and Kleiber, 2019[31]).

Figure 13.1. Only 20% of women in fishing and aquaculture in OECD countries

2017 data

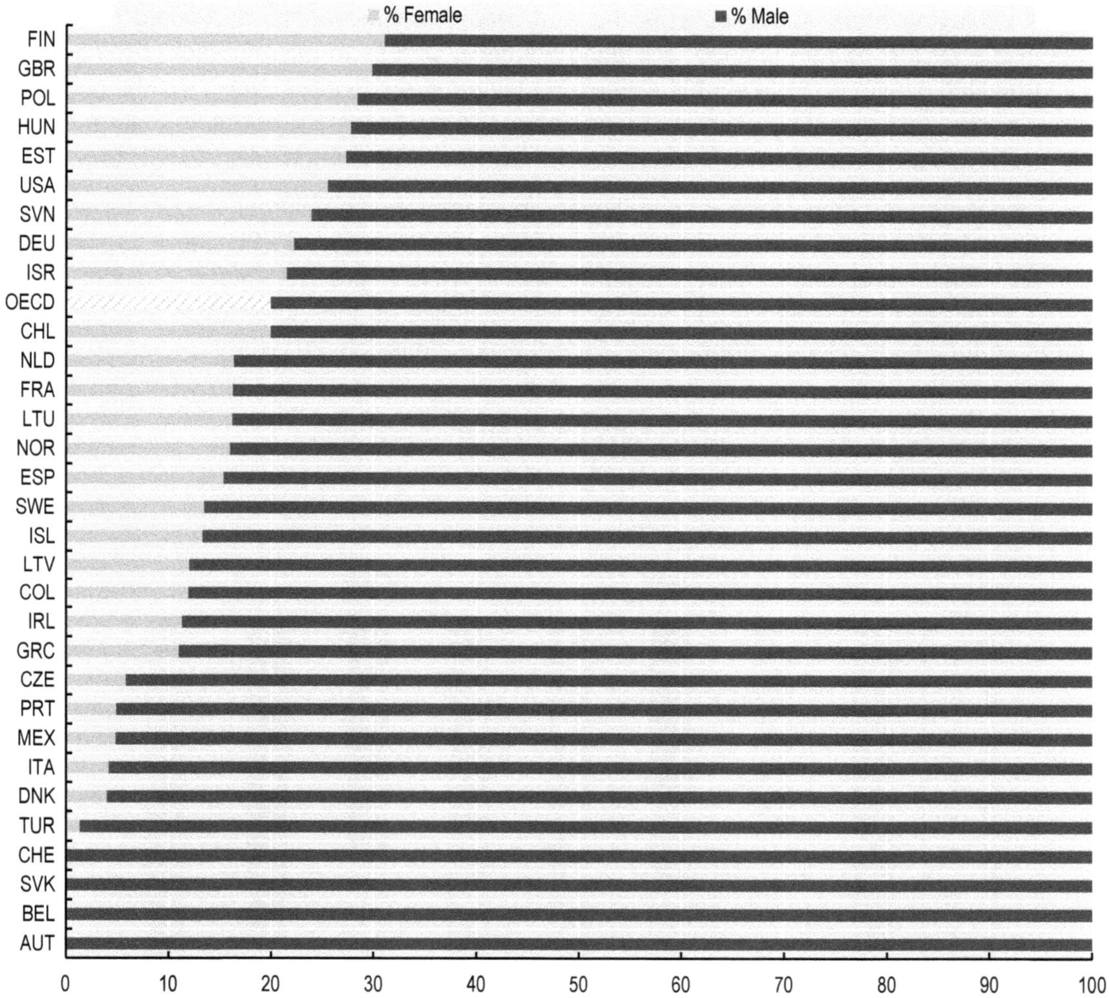

Note: All data for 2017, under "Economic activity (ISIC-Rev.4), 2 digit level: 03 - Fishing and aquaculture", except for Austria and Israel (2016); Belgium and Slovak Republic (2015); and Slovenia (2013). For Chile and Colombia data are under "Economic activity (ISIC-Rev.3.1), 2 digit level: 05 - Fishing, aquaculture and service activities incidental to fishing". Data not available for Australia, Canada, Japan, Korea, Luxembourg and New Zealand.

Source: ILOSTAT (ILO, 2020[32]).

In OECD countries, women occupy only 20% of the workforce in fishing and aquaculture, even though in countries with large coastal areas, such as Finland and the United Kingdom, women are around 30% of the workforce in the sector (Figure 13.1). Men are mostly involved in fish and aquaculture harvesting (81% in 2014 in OECD countries), and women are overwhelmingly involved in secondary fields such a fish processing, marketing and fishing machinery maintenance (90%), which are often low paid or unpaid (European Commission, 2002[33]) (FAO, 2018[34]). Moreover, documentation and research on the subjects of marine industry including shipping, deep sea and offshore exploration tend to be rather gender-blind (UNEP and Water Alliance, 2019[35]).

When it comes to industrialised fishing-related activities, such as fish processing, women are increasingly gaining share of the workforce in the fishing sector. Women, however, are usually covering the low-skilled low-paid jobs (Biswas, FAO and ICSF, 2017[36]).

Globally, in 2016, only 1 in 100 top seafood companies were run by a woman, and 54% had no women on boards. Increasing women's participation in high-level, decision-making roles in the fishing sector, could help towards achieving more sustainable fishing and marine conservation. Spreading out the power imbalances in the sector, by for instance facilitating women's access to microfinance, fishing resources and decision-making positions could enable women to play a more important role in marine conservation. Studies have shown that including women in leadership and management positions fosters community well-being, economic growth and positive outcomes for families' well-being (FAO, 2015[37]).

Women representation in some of the largest fishing conglomerates is minimal, except for some cases where they have implemented quotas in order to achieve a 50% balance (Figure 13.2). The Galician Foundation for Fishing and Shell Fishing, together with FARNET, are EU-funded projects (European Maritime and Fisheries Fund [EMFF]) that help women capitalise on their knowledge and determination through targeted funding and local partnerships (European Commission, 2019[38]).

Figure 13.2. Board representation in fishing conglomerates, by gender

2015 data

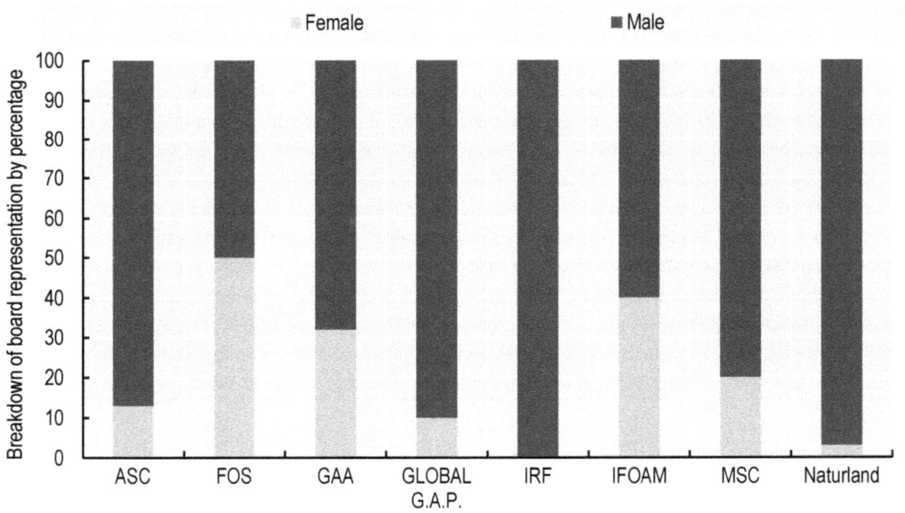

Note: ASC: Aquaculture Stewardship Council; FOS: Friend of the Sea; GAA: Global Aquaculture Alliance; GLOBAL G.A.P. Global Partnership for Good Agricultural Practice; IRF: Iceland Responsible Fisheries; IFOAM: International Federation of Organic Agriculture Movements, MSC: Marine Stewardship Council. Information unavailable for China G.A.P.
Source: (Potts et al., 2016[39]).

Creating strong networks to advocate for women in fisheries is also crucial to ensure their participation in decision-making processes and access to leadership positions. Such networks can emerge from grassroots mobilisation such as the MBKMMVS group of women fish vendors in Mumbai, India, who organised themselves and are now the official managers of their local fish market. Similarly, institutional initiatives such as the African Network for Women Fish Processors and Traders (AWFISHNET) created in

2017, gives a platform for the exchange of best practices, knowledge and technologies, and improve access to markets (FAO, 2017[40]).

13.4.2. Supporting women engaged in small-scale fishing

Half of global fish catches come from small-scale fisheries, which in turn occupy more than 90% of fishers worldwide (FAO, 2020[21]). At the global level, women seem to be more engaged in fisheries-related activities close to the household and when women are directly engaged with fishing, they seem to focus more on small catches of highly nutritious fish and other aquatic animals for immediate household consumption, instead of trade-oriented activities (FAO, 2018[34]).

Women account for a large share of the millions of people who are involved in artisanal fish processing. This usually leads to women's role not being sufficiently recognised, as it is considered as part of domestic/household work and therefore not valued in economic terms, and overlooked in statistical data collection (Biswas, FAO and ICSF, 2017[36]). Women's marginalisation may also be linked to ownership rights of fishing communities, as well as to the impact of climate change on coastal areas (UN WomenWatch, 2009[41]).

Women are affected by both explicit and implicit discrimination in the fisheries sector, which at times can intersect with environmental mismanagement. For instance, in the case of Lake Victoria in Tanzania, only bigger size fish was prioritised, thus excluding women's participation in formal trading activities. As a result, women tend to partake in small size fishing due to specific techniques and lack of access to large boat fishing. This is despite the Lake's fisheries co-management system which sets a quota for the minimum inclusion of women in community-based structures (Nunan and Cepić, 2020[42]). At the same time, the human pressure on the catchment area of the lake and the introduction of alien species has impacted in a negative way on its biodiversity causing eutrophication and increased algal blooms (Njiru et al., 2008[43]). Hence, the intersection of both social and environmental impacts on the lake highlights the importance of having comprehensive strategies for nature restoration and conservation.

Multiple women's empowerment projects in the fisheries sector have resulted in women pooling savings to fund ongoing projects and provide financial security. A number of microfinance initiatives illustrate that women make better use of small loans or credit than men. Women appear more focused on using the money to ensure business sustainability over time, while better protecting marine ecosystems (Galtung, Colonia and Sacramento, 1997[44]). Research looking into the West Madagascar Octopus community-based small-scale fishing, finds that current female involvement in enclosure fisheries management is low considering the financial importance it represents for women. The conclusions recommended women's participation should be strengthened, wherever possible, to encourage and enhance community benefit sharing, thereby increasing buy-in to enclosure fisheries and rethinking community based management initiatives that tend to reinforce gender inequalities, because they are based on traditional, usually male-dominated, decision-making (Louise et al., 2014[45]).

In another example, Kwale women in Kenya have begun a sustainable seaweed farming project that provides them with financial security and maintains steady growth of fish stock in the sea (ODINAFRICA, 2020[46]). Supporting the findings from various reports on the successful examples of Blue Economy in Africa, this project is people-centred and aids overcoming women's marginalisation (Okafor-Yarwood et al., 2020[47]).

FAO has developed Voluntary Guidelines for Sustainable Small-Scale Fisheries in the Context of Food Security and Poverty Eradication that mandate gender mainstreaming, together with building fisheries' resilience to climate change and extreme weather (FAO, 2018[48]). These guidelines constitute the first internationally agreed instrument for the small-scale fisheries sector. They both prioritise gender mainstreaming and support investing in health, literacy, technological education, eradicating forced labour, promoting social security protection and building fisheries' resilience to climate change, and extreme weather. Building on these guidelines, FAO is implementing a five-year Western Africa project that is part of a larger Global Environment Facility financed by the Coastal Fisheries Initiative in Cabo Verde, Côte d'Ivoire and Senegal. FAO studies value chains in order to find ways to improve both fisheries management and post-harvest processes while examining the "invisible" role of women in fisheries (FAO, 2018[48]).

A 2019 IUCN report highlighted the need for more evidence on the interlinkage between women's empowerment, access to finance and sustainable fisheries, based on past and ongoing pilot projects in Ghana, Indonesia and the Philippines. The initiative Mangroves for the Future (MFF) a partner-led initiative to promote investment in coastal ecosystem conservation for sustainable development has developed a gender toolkit for coastal management practitioners (MFF, SEI and SEAFDEC, 2018[49]) Along the Densu River in Ghana, initiatives addressing and strengthening women's empowerment in the fisheries sector resulted in increased monitoring of water conditions and illegal fishing, restoration of mangroves by planting thousands of new seedlings, advocacy and pressure campaigns to thwart plastic waste, increased community efforts to clean fisheries habitats, and the establishment of a village savings and loan group to provide financing for women fish processers (IUCN, 2019[50])

Development co-operation projects financed by Japan specifically target women against poverty in the fishing sector, providing assistance to women in the dried fish business in Sri Lanka. Results show that assistance can help women earn steady incomes while they also carry out sustainable fishing practices (Ministry of Foreign Affairs of Japan, 2014[51]).

13.5. Leveraging women's role to protect the oceans and sustainably develop marine resources

If properly empowered, women can be powerful agents of change, protecting the oceans and sustainably developing marine resources. Initiatives to engage women in sustainable marine activities will help progress towards SDG 14, while also buttressing greater gender equality.

13.5.1. The role of women in tackling marine pollution

There are multiple forms of marine pollution that threaten biodiversity and human health, including sewage related debris (SRD), agricultural runoff and plastic litter. One of the most effective tools for combatting plastic and trash entering the ocean is by improving waste management and women have an important role to play. Partly in the types of products they choose to buy and use, and partly by pioneering alternative, eco-friendly and renewable products based on the female experience (see Chapter 11).

Food, health, clothing or household products are often packaged in or made up of plastic components. Women drive the majority of consumer purchasing and predominately manage their households, meaning that, as consumers, they have a strong impact on perpetuating or curbing plastic waste. An estimated 13 million metric tons of plastic end up in the oceans each year, with land based sources accounting for up to 80% (Le Guern, 2020[52]); (Reddy, 2018[53]).

As explored in Chapter 11 pertaining to sustainable consumption and production, the impact that a change in behaviour can have on environmental sustainability is enormous. Another takeaway from existing research is that women tend to be more environmentally conscious and more willing to take efforts to reduce their carbon footprint and protect the environment (Kassinis et al., 2016[54]). Women's sustainable consumption patterns and engagement in waste management can support the decrease of marine litter through programmes such as those implemented in East Asian Seas (UNEP, COBSEA and SEI, 2019[55]). East Asian Seas enables sustainable, resilient and inclusive blue economies while fighting for cleaner seas.

Beyond female-led efforts to replace widely used necessities with renewable options, is the role they can play in improving waste management, especially in coastal areas. Collective action – such as coastal clean-ups – can have profound effects. A 2019 report by the Ocean Conservatory, focusing on India, Indonesia, the Philippines and Viet Nam, recommends that in order for collective action to tackle the plastic pollution crisis effectively, it should include global, inclusive solutions that tackle global supply chains and engage both men and women (Center for Ocean Conservancy, 2019[56]).

The case of the Mexican coastal town of Celestún, a biodiversity-rich town where women have organised in participatory grassroots recycling organizations, is an example of how women's knowledge and action can be central to creating innovative conservation strategies. While national and international programmes have prioritised protection of wetlands from unsanitary activities in Celestún, they have often neglected dealing with sanitation and solid waste and wastewater management directly. Women have been burdened with the extra care work of looking after the sick due to the rise of diseases linked to poor waste management. Using their local knowledge and community network, women in Celestún organised in grassroots recycling and composting groups which considerably benefited the community's environmental health and reversed much of the beach erosion and wetlands ecosystems' disruption. Key to their success was also national and state-level recognition as key actors in conservation. This example of local mobilisation shows how conservation programmes can benefit from a gender perspective that accounts for gendered division of labour in each specific context and embraces local women's knowledge (UNEP and Water Alliance, 2019[35])

While all these initiatives certainly make a difference, much of the plastic in our oceans and seas is beyond collection, whether it is submerged plastic debris found on the ocean floor and in benthic creatures, or plastic accumulating through rainfall. Women can also play a key role in initiatives to clean the oceans.

13.5.2. The role of women in protecting marine ecosystems

Protecting mangroves and coral reefs can make a major contribution to sustaining life under the seas while helping to combat climate change. Coral reefs and mangrove swamps also provide invaluable protection from cyclones and tsunamis for those living on coasts. Given their success, women-led initiatives to protect coasts and marine life should be promoted and scaled up.

Small-scale local women-led initiatives have achieved a successful regeneration of mangroves in Kenya and other East African countries, protecting coastal areas and yielding more marine wildlife. Accounts of microfinance initiatives show that women prioritise business sustainability in the long term more than men, in turn leading to better protection of marine ecosystems (Stevenson and St-Onge, 2005[57]). A recent UN Environment report has also highlighted the role of women-led initiatives to clean up and protect coastal areas, including via mangrove regeneration in parts of India, Mexico and the Philippines (UN Environment, 2020[58]).

Women are also making an important contribution in ocean science. There is actually a smaller gender gap in ocean science than in science overall. Female scientists represent on average 38% of researchers in ocean science, about 10% higher than science overall (UNESCO, 2017[59]). To cite an example, during the 2018 academic year in Mexico, the participation of women corresponded to 71% of the school staff at the undergraduate level in the academic areas of biology, earth sciences and sustainable management in coastal areas. Likewise, it represented approximately 54% of graduate students related to biology, marine sciences and limnology and sustainability sciences across all educational institutions (UNAM, 2020[60]). However, much more should be done to retain women in science fields, and more particularly in those linked to the ocean and marine environment. This can be achieved by developing mentoring schemes, supporting working environments and conditions that are better adapted for women, and tackling unconscious biases (Kappel, 2014[61]).

13.6. Key actions for advancing the agenda and ongoing work

There are a number of actions that can be taken to promote gender mainstreaming in policies and actions to better protect and conserve the oceans and precious marine life:

- Collect evidence on the impact of oceans degradation on women's health, well-being and employment opportunities, with a focus on the most vulnerable and an intersectionality lens.
- Design policy solutions to better conserve the oceans with a gender-lens, addressing the specific differentiated concerns of degrading oceans, including the impact of coastal storms, the depletion of fish stocks and the increase in marine litter.
- Empower women to contribute to preserve marine ecosystems and sustainably use of marine resources.
- Design and implement legislation that enables and supports associations, organisations and networks of women within the fisheries and aquaculture sector.
- Ensure women's full integration in the blue economy through policy that recognises women's work in harvest and post-harvest and provides access to credit and markets, comprehensive social security and occupational health and safety measures based on women's needs.
- Mainstream gender in development co-operation targeting the sustainable management of oceans, supporting women's initiatives to protect coastal areas (in particular mangrove swamps and coral reefs) and developing small-scale, sustainable fishing that benefit local communities. There is potential in replicating the benefits from small-scale projects to a more global scale.

References

Biswas, N., FAO and ICSF (2017), *Towards gender-equitable small-scale fisheries governance and development : a handbook in support of the implementation of the Voluntary Guidelines for Securing Sustainable Small-scale Fisheries in the Context of Food Security and Poverty Eradication*. [36]

Camey, I. et al. (n.d.), *Gender-based violence and environment linkages: the violence of inequality*, https://twitter.com/IUCN/. [17]

Center for Ocean Conservancy (2019), *Stemming the Tide: Land-based strategies for a plastic-free ocean*. [56]

Delpeuch, C. and B. Hutniczak (2019), "Encouraging policy change for sustainable and resilient fisheries", *OECD Food, Agriculture and Fisheries Papers*, No. 127, OECD Publishing, Paris, https://dx.doi.org/10.1787/31f15060-en. [9]

Department, F. (ed.) (2018), *The state of world fisheries and aquaculture 2018 : meeting the sustainable development goals.*. [34]

EPA (n.d.), *The Effects: Dead Zones and Harmful Algal Blooms*, https://www.epa.gov/nutrientpollution/effects-dead-zones-and-harmful-algal-blooms (accessed on 4 November 2020). [8]

European Commission (2019), "Euronews OCEAN episode 7: Women in fisheries", https://ec.europa.eu/maritimeaffairs/press/euronews-ocean-episode-7-women-fisheries_en (accessed on 22 December 2020). [38]

European Commission (2002), "THE ROLE OF WOMEN IN THE FISHERIES SECTOR", *DIRECTORATE GENERAL FOR FISHERIES* TENDER FISH/2000/01-LOT NO 1, https://ec.europa.eu/fisheries/sites/fisheries/files/docs/body/mainreport_en.pdf (accessed on 3 November 2020). [33]

Falkenberg, L. et al. (2020), "Ocean Acidification and Human Health", *International Journal of Environmental Research and Public Health*, Vol. 17/12, http://dx.doi.org/10.3390/ijerph17124563. [7]

FAO (2020), *The State of World Fisheries and Aquaculture 2020*, FAO, http://dx.doi.org/10.4060/ca9229en. [21]

FAO (2018), *Achieving Blue Growth Building vibrant fisheries and aquaculture communities*. [48]

FAO (2015), *The role of women in the seafood industry*, http://www.globefish.org. [30]

FAO (2011), "Faces of women in global fishery value chains: Female involvement, impact and importance in the fisheries of developed and developing countries", *NORAD/FAO Value Chain Project*. [29]

FAO, F. (2017), *Towards Gender-Equitable Small-Scale Fisheries Governance and Development*, FAO, Rome, http://www.fao.org/3/i7419e/i7419e.pdf. [40]

FAO, F. (2015), *A Review of Women's Access to Fish in Small-Scale Fisheries*, FAO, Rome. [37]

Galtung, J., H. Colonia and D. Sacramento (1997), *HELPING THE POOR TO HELP THEMSE \ k INTERVIEW WITH.* [44]

Gerrard, S. and D. Kleiber (2019), "Women fishers in Norway: few, but significant", *Maritime Studies*, Vol. 18/3, pp. 259-274, http://dx.doi.org/10.1007/s40152-019-00151-4. [31]

ILO (2020), "ILOSTAT database. Data retrieved in June 21, 2020.". [32]

IPBES (2019), *Global Assessment Report on Biodiversity and Ecosystem Services*, http://www.ipbes.net. [4]

IUCN (2020), "Facts and figures on Biodiversity", https://www.iucn.org/content/facts-and-figures-biodiversity. [10]

IUCN (2019), "Fishing for Gender Equality and Sustainability", https://www.iucn.org/news/gender/201910/fishing-equality-and-sustainability (accessed on 3 November 2020). [50]

IUCN (2008), "Disaster Gender Statistics". [15]

Jeebhay, M. and A. Lopata (2012), "Occupational Allergies in Seafood-Processing Workers", in *Advances in Food and Nutrition Research, Advances in Food and Nutrition Research Volume 66*, Elsevier, http://dx.doi.org/10.1016/b978-0-12-394597-6.00002-1. [28]

Jeebhay, M., A. Lopata and T. Robins (2000), "Seafood Processing in South Africa: A Study of Working Practices, Occupational Health Services and Allergic Health Problems in the Industry", *Occupational Medicine*, Vol. 50/6, pp. 406-413, http://dx.doi.org/10.1093/occmed/50.6.406. [27]

Jones, K. et al. (2018), "The Location and Protection Status of Earth's Diminishing Marine Wilderness", *Current Biology*, Vol. 28/15, pp. 2506-2512.e3, http://dx.doi.org/10.1016/j.cub.2018.06.010. [3]

Kappel, E. (2014), *Women in Oceanography: A Decade Later*, http://www.tos.org. [61]

Kassinis, G. et al. (2016), "Gender and Environmental Sustainability: A Longitudinal Analysis", *Corporate Social Responsibility and Environmental Management*, Vol. 23/6, pp. 399-412, http://dx.doi.org/10.1002/csr.1386. [54]

Kirk, L. et al. (2017), "Public health benefits of hair-mercury analysis and dietary advice in lowering methylmercury exposure in pregnant women", *Scandinavian Journal of Public Health*, Vol. 45/4, pp. 444-451, http://dx.doi.org/10.1177/1403494816689310. [12]

Le Guern, C. (2020), "Plastic Pollution: When the Mermaids Cry", *Coastal Care*, https://coastalcare.org/2020/01/plastic-pollution-when-the-mermaids-cry-the-great-plastic-tide-by-claire-le-guern/ (accessed on 3 November 2020). [52]

Lloyd-Smith, M. and J. Immig (2018), *Ocean Pollutants Guide Toxic Threats to Human Health and Marine Life*, http://www.ipen.org. [11]

Louise, S. et al. (2014), *The Role of Women in Community-based Small-Scale Fisheries Management: The Case of the South West Madagascar Octopus Fishery*, https://www.researchgate.net/publication/271472394. [45]

MFF, SEI and SEAFDEC (2018), "Gender-Analysis-Toolkit-for-Coastal-Management-Practitioners". [49]

Ministry of Foreign Affairs of Japan (2014), "Dried fish business empowers women in Sri Lanka – Support for women struggling against poverty in a Sri Lankan fishing village", https://www.mofa.go.jp/policy/oda/white/2014/html/column/column03.html (accessed on 20 December 2020). [51]

Njiru, M. et al. (2008), "An overview of the current status of Lake Victoria fishery: Opportunities, challenges and management strategies", *Lakes & Reservoirs: Research & Management*, Vol. 13/1, pp. 1-12, http://dx.doi.org/10.1111/j.1440-1770.2007.00358.x. [43]

Nunan, F. and D. Cepić (2020), "Women and fisheries co-management: Limits to participation on Lake Victoria", *Fisheries Research*, Vol. 224, p. 105454, http://dx.doi.org/10.1016/j.fishres.2019.105454. [42]

ODINAFRICA (2020), "Seaweed farming helps Kwale women exploit blue economy", http://www.odinafrica.org/about-us/news/185-seaweed-farming-helps-kwale-women-exploit-blue-economy.html (accessed on 22 December 2020). [46]

OECD (2016), *The Ocean Economy in 2030*, OECD Publishing, Paris, https://dx.doi.org/10.1787/9789264251724-en. [2]

OECD (2015), *Green Growth in Fisheries and Aquaculture*, OECD Green Growth Studies, OECD Publishing, Paris, https://dx.doi.org/10.1787/9789264232143-en. [22]

Okafor-Yarwood, I. et al. (2020), "The Blue Economy–Cultural Livelihood–Ecosystem Conservation Triangle: The African Experience", *Frontiers in Marine Science*, Vol. 7, http://dx.doi.org/10.3389/fmars.2020.00586. [47]

Oxfam International (2005), *The tsunami's impact on women*, https://oxfamilibrary.openrepository.com/bitstream/handle/10546/115038/bn-tsunami-impact-on-women-250305-en.pdf?sequence=1&isAllowed=y (accessed on 3 November 2020). [16]

Potts, J. et al. (2016), *State of sustainability initiatives review : standards and the blue economy*. [39]

Reddy, S. (2018), "Plastic Pollution Affects Sea Life Throughout the Ocean", *PEW*, https://www.pewtrusts.org/en/research-and-analysis/articles/2018/09/24/plastic-pollution-affects-sea-life-throughout-the-ocean (accessed on 3 November 2020). [53]

Saleem, M. and E. Abentim (2019), "Blue Growth and Blue Economy in The Context of Development Policies and Priorities in Malaysia". [19]

Shaleh, S., C. Fui-Fui and S. Mustafa (2020), "Gender Roles in Inclusive Blue Economy", http://dx.doi.org/10.1007/978-3-319-70060-1_68-1. [18]

Stevenson, L. and A. St-Onge (2005), *Support for growth-oriented, women entrepreneurs in Ethiopia, Kenya, and Tanzania : an overview report*, Programme on Boosting Employment through Small Enterprise Development, Job Creation and Enterprise Dept., International Labour Office. [57]

Thirumoorthy, A. et al. (2016), "Health Hazard of Women Employed in Small Scale Seafood Processing Units", *Indian Journal of Geo-Marine Sciences*, Vol. 54(4): 574-582. [26]

UN Atlas of the Oceans (n.d.), *UN Atlas of the Oceans*, http://www.oceansatlas.org/facts/en/ (accessed on 4 November 2020). [1]

UN Environment (2020), "New guidelines aim to support mangrove restoration in the Western Indian Ocean", *Ecosystems and Biodiversity*. [58]

UN Women (2020), "Empowering Women through Oceans Conservation". [20]

UN Women (2020), *Women's Economic Empowerment in Fisheries: In the Blue Economy of the Indian Ocean Rim*, UN Women, New York. [24]

UN Women (2017), "SDG 6: Ensure availability and sustainable management of water and sanitation for all", https://www.unwomen.org/en/news/in-focus/women-and-the-sdgs/sdg-6-clean-water-sanitation (accessed on 3 November 2020). [25]

UN WomenWatch (2009), "Women and Climate Factsheet", pp. 1-11, https://www.un.org/womenwatch/feature/climate_change/downloads/Women_and_Climate_Change_Factsheet.pdf. [41]

UNAM (2020), *2020 Agenda Estadística UNAM*, https://www.planeacion.unam.mx/Agenda/2020/pdf/Agenda2020.pdf. [60]

UNDP (2016), *Gender, climate change adaptation and disaster risk reduction*. [13]

UNDP (2016), *Overview of linkages between gender and climate change*. [14]

UNEP (2017), *How are women differently vulnerable?*. [23]

UNEP and Water Alliance, U. (2019), *Gender Mainstreaming in the Management of the Marine and Coastal Ecosystems*, UNEP, Nairobi. [35]

UNEP, COBSEA and SEI (2019), *Marine plastic litter in East Asian Seas: Gender, human rights and economic dimensions*, United Nations Environment Programme, Coordinating Body on the Seas of East Asia, and Stockholm Environment Institute. [55]

UNESCO (2017), "Gender Mainstreaming in Marine Science", *Gender and Science*, http://www.unesco.org/new/en/natural-sciences/priority-areas/gender-and-science/cross-cutting-issues/gender-mainstreaming-in-marine-science/ (accessed on 3 November 2020). [59]

Viviani, R. (1992), "Eutrophication, marine biotoxins, human health", in *Marine Coastal Eutrophication*, Elsevier, http://dx.doi.org/10.1016/B978-0-444-89990-3.50056-0. [5]

WHO Regional Office for Europe and European Commission (2002), *Eutrophication and health*, European Commission. [6]

14 Women and SDG 15 – Life on Land: Protect, restore and promote sustainable use of terrestrial ecosystems, sustainably manage forests, combat desertification halt and reverse land degradation and halt biodiversity loss.

Women in rural societies may be significantly affected by biodiversity loss. In many developing countries, women's role in ensuring water and fuel supplies, as well as collecting wild edible and medicinal plants, makes them most sensitive to deforestation, land degradation and desertification. Lack of ownership rights and access to resources intensifies these negative effects. Women also face major challenges from biodiversity loss in indigenous and rural communities in some developed countries. At the same time, women can be agents of change, leading biodiversity protection, conservation and sustainable farming efforts. Such positive effects can be magnified by buttressing gender equality and tackling gender-based barriers.

14.1. Key findings

This chapter provides a description of the links between gender equality and conservation efforts in relation to forests and, more broadly, to ecosystems. It covers the following questions:

- Women can be significantly affected by biodiversity loss and ecosystems' degradation. Women and indigenous groups living in rural areas can be affected by soil depletion and reduced water supply, which may exacerbate poverty and hunger. Lack of access to land, forests and other natural resources is a major cause of deprivation for women. This is especially important for indigenous communities, given their dependence on shared, ancestral lands.
- Ecosystem degradation resulting from industrial farming, extractive industries and major infrastructure projects is sometimes linked to Gender-based violence (GBV) and many climate and environmental activists suffering violent attacks are women.
- Women in many developing countries are the principal users and managers of land, as farmers and pastoralists with primary responsibility for household food production. Their role in promoting sustainable land management is an opportunity to achieve the dual objective of sustainable land management and gender equality.
- As with other environment-related SDGs, a lack of sex- and gender-disaggregated data is a major concern. SDG 15 has no gender targets. Of the Aichi Biodiversity Targets, only Target 14 overtly addresses gender issues, calling for the needs of women, indigenous peoples and local communities, and the poor and vulnerable, to be taken into account in the restoration and safeguarding of ecosystems. Yet Aichi Target 14 does not include a specific indicator on gender equality, and existing indicators are not sex-disaggregated.
- Women can contribute to the management of "commons" such as forests, mountain resources, and rivers, but they are often excluded from decision-making, including at the local and community level. There is a need to better integrate gender considerations into National Biodiversity Strategies and Action Plans (NBSAPs).
- All countries have a major stake in ensuring that their transboundary policies (trade, investment, and development co-operation) promote the empowerment and engagement of women and indigenous groups in other countries. Business has a responsibility to address gender equality and ensure more sustainable management of natural resources.

14.2. Key interlinkages between gender equality, sustainable use of land resources and other SDGs

Protecting, restoring and promoting the sustainable use of land resources (SDG 15) has a great potential to combat global warming (SDG 13), while land degradation in all its forms (e.g. deforestation, loss of soil and freshwater etc.) is a major contributor to climate change. Forests and trees are vital to the world's clean air and water, annually absorbing one-third of CO_2 emissions from burning fossil fuels (Muller et al., 2018[1]). As shown in Figure 14.1, primary forest cover has decreased by 81 million hectares since 1990, though the rate of loss more than halved in 2010–20 compared with the previous decade (FAO, 2020[2]). This reduces human ability to combat climate change (SDG 13).

Figure 14.1. Global annual forest area net change, by decade, 1990–2020

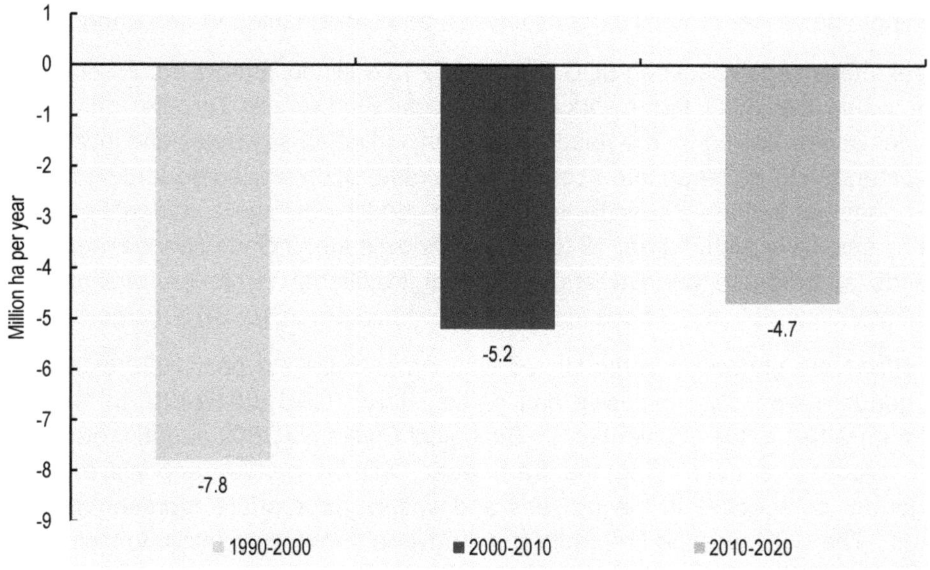

Source: (FAO, 2020[2]).

SDG 15 is also key to food and water security (SDGs 2 and 6), health and well-being (SDG 3) and the provision of affordable energy (SDG 7). In particular, shrinking biodiversity has been linked to zoonosis, which evidence suggests may have been the root cause of the COVID-19 pandemic (OECD, 2020[3]).

A 2018 report by the Intergovernmental Science-Policy Platform on Biodiversity and Ecosystems found that the benefits of land restoration are ten times higher than the cost, and that current rates of land degradation undermine the well-being of at least 3.2 billion people (Brainich et al., 2018[4]). Biodiversity loss in Europe alone costs nearly USD 500 million per year (Carrington, 2018[5]). Globally, among the main culprits of land degradation and biodiversity loss are unsustainable agriculture practices and high consumption lifestyles – areas in which interventions are possible and women's engagement is essential (Section 11.4).

The agriculture, forestry and fisheries sectors depend on the health of terrestrial ecosystems (e.g. tundra, forests, deserts, grasslands) and the plant and animal life that inhabit them to productively supply basic needs and inputs to society and other economic sectors (OECD, 2018[6]). An estimated 45% of the world's population depends on these sectors for their livelihoods (CBD, 2018[7]); one in three workers globally is employed in agriculture (FAO, 2012[8]); (OECD, 2018[9]). While these sectors are crucial to sustain human life and livelihoods, they also exert pressure on the environment, unless conservation and sustainable use efforts are employed (OECD, 2018[9]).

Forests are source of food, medicine and fuel. Forests alone hold more than three-quarters of the world's terrestrial biodiversity, and the top ten most forested countries are in the developing world (FAO, 2020[10]). Protecting biodiversity is essential to advances in medicine. More than 70 000 different plant species are used to manufacture pharmaceuticals, and the majority of the world's plant biodiversity exists within the Global South (Alamgir, 2017[11]).

More sustainable farming methods are key to avoiding further deterioration to land-based ecosystems and to tackling climate change. Promoting conservation and protecting biodiversity in the agriculture, forestry and fisheries sectors are also vital to meet development objectives, including social inclusiveness and gender equality (SDG 5).

Women, especially in traditional societies, are especially affected by biodiversity loss. Lack of women's rights and access to resources intensifies these negative effects. At the same time, women can be agents of change, leading biodiversity protection, conservation and sustainable farming efforts.

Despite the clear interlinkages between SDG 5 and SDG 15 outlined in more detail below, SDG 15 has no gender targets within the SDG framework. Of the Aichi Biodiversity Targets, only Target 14 overtly addresses gender issues, calling for the needs of women, indigenous peoples and local communities, and the poor and vulnerable to be taken into account in the restoration and safeguarding of ecosystems. Yet Aichi Target 14 does not include a specific indicator on gender equality, and identified indicators are not disaggregated by sex. Only Aichi Target 18 (traditional knowledge) includes gender-relevant indicators, in respect to trends in land-use change and tenure in traditional territories of indigenous and local communities, differentiated by sex. These are the same indicators as for SDG Targets 5.a and 1.4.

Reassuringly, efforts are underway in the United Nations to make the post-2020 biodiversity framework "rights-based, gender-responsive, inclusive and participatory" (CBD, 2019[12]). In November 2018, the Conference of the Parties to the Convention on Biological Diversity (CBD) adopted decision 14/34, which states that the process of developing the framework "will be gender-responsive, by systematically integrating a gender perspective in the process and ensure appropriate representation, particularly of women and girls." The CBD was the first multilateral environmental agreement to include a Gender Plan of Action (Global Youth Biodiversity Network, 2016[13]).

14.3. The degradation of terrestrial ecosystems has more intense effects on women

The environmental degradation and shrinking biodiversity caused by large scale farming, deforestation, mining and other human activity disproportionately affect women. In developing countries and indigenous communities, women's role in the provision of water and fuel supplies, as well as in collecting wild edible and medicinal plants, makes them most sensitive to deforestation, land degradation and desertification. Environmental degradation can either spoil or reduce clean water and ecosystem services, forcing women to travel further to collect them for household use. The destruction of forests and 'marginal' land also tends to affect women and indigenous peoples most, as they play a key subsistence function (Fargione et al., 2008[14]).

Women and indigenous groups living in deprived areas are especially affected by degradation of soil and reduced water supply, which has already reduced the productivity of nearly one quarter of the global land surface, further exacerbating poverty and hunger (IPBES, 2019[15]). Heightened financial insecurity, caused by lost agricultural revenue, can worsen the plight of women and children.

Environmental degradation is linked to gender-based violence (GBV) both directly, through corrupt systems of illegal extraction and logging, and indirectly, due to climate change impacts. There are many accounts of sexual exploitation and harassment of women in the illegal logging industry, which hinges on women's informal work status, lack of land rights and historic role as environmental defenders (Castañeda Carney et al., 2020[16]). A 2016 UNICEF study in India found a correlation between a rise in abuse against women and children during droughts, including child labour and trafficking, women forced into prostitution, and femicide. Gender-based violence is related to inability to provide higher dowries to supplement lost income, or inability to conceive due to malnourishment (UNICEF, 2016[17]). In Ethopia, an increase in the number of girls sold into marriage was found in drought-affected areas (UNICEF, 2017[18]).

Women disproportionately suffer health consequences of environmental degradation because of their role in reproduction. Environmental contaminants in water, air and soil – for instance, by-products of the misuse of agricultural inputs like pesticides and fertilisers, or dumping of toxic materials – can act as endocrine disruptors that impair women's reproductive systems, harm the developing bodies of foetuses, or cause toxins to bio-accumulate in breast milk (Stefanidou, Maravelias and Spiliopoulou, 2009[19]).

Beyond the direct environmental effects, large-scale economic activity can also be accompanied by adverse social spillovers to women living in local communities. Extractive industries, in particular, offer a clearer picture of the way in which exploitation of natural resources affect women and men differently, both in terms of opportunity and risk. Global evidence shows that benefits of higher-paying jobs primarily go to men, while women, who are usually excluded from the sector, disproportionately bear the social and environmental risks (World Bank, 2013[20]). Such risks include both negative impacts on water and land resources from extraction, and an increase in gender-based violence, as mentioned above (Macdonald, 2018[21]).

14.4. Constraints on women and indigenous groups' engagement in land, forest management and conservation efforts

Despite women's dependency on natural resources and active engagement as users and custodians (see more under Chapter 6), women in many developing countries face restricted access to productive and financial resources and are marginalised when it comes to decisions about land tenure. Women's limited ownership of land – driven in large part by discriminatory practices – reduces their capacity to change how land is used, hampering their ability to deal with environmental damage (Samandari, 2017[22]). This and informal employment limit women's participation in decision making in farming.

Women in forest-dependent communities play a central role in the management of resources, including collecting non-timber forest products, yet they too are often excluded from decision making (UN Environment, 2016[23]). Social norms, entrenched traditions and personal endowments are usually the main obstacle to greater participation of women in decision-making bodies.

Equal access to land rights could have positive effects in forestland restoration and sustainable management of ecosystems (FAO, 2018[24]). Several cases show that men and women having more equal land-tenure rights may bring about more environmentally sustainable outcomes. For example, in 2010 the Government of Rwanda launched a low-cost land tenure regularisation programme to clarify land ownership and resources following that country's civil war. The programme allowed for female land ownership and inheritance, in parallel to land-related investment. Legally married women (76% of married couples) saw an improvement in their land access rights (Hoza Ngoga, 2019[25]). An evaluation of the programme found that women-headed households largely contributed to investment and maintenance of soil conservation measures, while overall no negative effect on vulnerable groups was recorded (Ali, Deininger and Goldstein, 2014[26]); (Abbott, 2015[27]).

The SDG framework pays specific attention to the question of women's land tenure and ownership. In fact, the only gender-relevant biodiversity and conservation indicators are related to these legal issues (Box 14.1).

Box 14.1. Examples of gender-responsive SDG biodiversity and conservation indicators

- 1.4.2: Proportion of total adult population with secure tenure rights to land, with legally recognised documentation and who perceive their rights to land as secure, by sex and by type of tenure.
- 5.a.1: (a) Proportion of total agricultural population with ownership of secure rights over agricultural land, by sex, and (b) share of women among owners or rights-bearers of agricultural land, by type of tenure.
- 5.a.2: Proportion of countries where the legal framework (including customary law) guarantees women's equal rights to land ownership and/or control.
- 5.c.1: Proportion of countries with systems to track and make public allocation for gender equality and women's empowerment.

Source: (UNEP and IUCN, 2019[28]) (Despot-Belmonte, 2019[29]).

Yet, the OECD's Social Institutions and Gender Index (SIGI) shows that, even if a country's laws provide for equal rights between men and women to own, use, and make decisions regarding land, discriminatory social institutions ensure that rights are far from equal in reality. Preference is still given to men in terms of inheritance of land, names on land titles, and decision-making power over land tenure, including in OECD countries. Laws governing inheritance in France, Israel, Greece, Mexico, Spain, Turkey, and the United Kingdom still contain discriminatory clauses that negatively affect women (OECD, 2019[30]). Globally and across countries, depending on a woman's marital status, her rights may be even further restricted or nullified.

Achieving SDG 5 is a prerequisite for attaining sustainable land management. Studies have shown that involving women in participatory land management can reverse desertification and promote sustainable land use (Agarwal, 2009[31]); (Ray, Mukherjee and Bhattacharya, 2016[32]). Hence, sex-disaggregated data can better reflect the impacts of land degradation on women and men, as well as highlight opportunities for gender-sensitive policies. The UNDCCD Science Policy Interface is doing important work on this by mandating that all land degradation neutrality (NDL) efforts that include monitoring of indicators be sex-disaggregated, warning that findings would be incomplete otherwise (Orr et al., 2017[33]).

14.5. Women's role in conservation efforts and protecting biodiversity

Beyond their role in forest management, women-led groups have been at the forefront of campaigns to protect biodiversity and eliminate pesticides from agriculture. Including gender considerations in National Biodiversity Strategies and Action Plans (NBSAPs) is crucial in developing women's role in conservation efforts while protecting biodiversity.

14.5.1. Women's role in biodiversity conservation and sustainable forest management

There are many examples of how engaging women can strengthen conservation efforts and contribute to SDG 15. A review of 17 studies on women in local resource decision making in the forestry and fisheries sectors (in non-OECD countries) found that the participation of women has a strong positive affect on resource governance and conservation outcomes (Leisher et al., 2016[34]). In Namibia, which collects sex-disaggregated data through its Community-Based Natural Resources Management Programme, evidence from 2012 shows that 30% of conservancy management committee members were women, and that women were mainly involved in the management of indigenous plants (CBD, 2014[35]).

In northeast regions of India, where male migration affects about 15% of local families, women have a more prominent role in subsistence farming and in managing agro-biodiversity. Women in these regions have been engaging in local seed conservation initiatives, including seed exchange, in an attempt to safeguard existing knowledge, diversify agriculture and guarantee food security. In these regions more sustainable agricultural processes were supported both by men and women, who opted for ecosystem-based rather than technology-based solutions and strategies for income generation (Price, 2018[36]).

Another example is Costa Rica's Action Plan of the National Strategy on Climate Change, in which gender is being mainstreamed and women's role is recognised as critical in the restoration of forestlands and ecosystems (UNFCCC, 2015[37]). Costa Rica is introducing a gender approach to agroforestry systems, critical to boosting low-carbon production systems. By creating conservation units that unite small, women-led farms, female producers have the opportunity to strengthen their capacity while achieving lower emissions and maintaining a percentage of the plot with forest coverage.

A gender perspective is also critical for biodiversity and conservation efforts in other OECD countries. For instance, recent research has highlighted the wealth of community forest arrangements in Europe, although the specific role of women has not been addressed (Lawrence et al., 2020[38]). In general, women are underrepresented in the broader forestry management sector. For instance, in Canada, women represented 17% of people employed in the forest industry in 2016.1 In 2018, the Canadian government announced a Gender Equality in Forestry National Action Plan that will work to promote women's careers in the forestry industry.

The role of women in the management of commons requires much greater attention than has been the case up to now. The importance of this issue was at the core of the research of Elinor Ostrom, the first woman to win the Nobel Memorial Prize in Economics for her "analysis of economic governance, especially the commons" (Ostrom, 1990[39]). Ostrom researched how humans interact with ecosystems to maintain long-term sustainable resource yields, developing institutional mechanisms to share the use, management and monitoring of commons, while avoiding ecosystem collapse. Her work emphasised the multifaceted nature of human ecosystem interaction and argued against any singular solution for individual social ecological system problems. Sustainable development requires a community focus that empowers women and indigenous populations to participate and take on leadership positions (Meinzen-Dick, Kovarik and Quisumbing, 2014[40]) (Box 14.2).

Box 14.2. Women's role in managing and using community forests in Nepal

To fight the effects of illegal logging, Nepal has been a pioneer in devolving forest uses and management rights to local communities. Approximately 22 000 community forest user groups (CFUGs), involving 40% of the total population, oversee 32% of the country's forested land. Research from the Center for International Forestry Research (CIFOR) has shown that community forest agreements play a role in forest regeneration, with notable increases in forest cover, firewood and non-timber forest products. A legally recognised self-governing community-led group has also allowed individuals from lower social castes and indigenous groups to benefit from higher access to community forest resources, with positive impact on their livelihoods. In particular, CIFOR research has shown that women, as collectors of non-timber forest products, are the principal beneficiaries of CFUGs. The Chisapani Village CFGU, next to Bardiva National Park, is mostly supplied by women farmers, and women make up the majority of its staff. Following national law, profits from the harvesting of lemongrass and its transformation into essential oil are shared equally among the women.

Source: (Paudyal et al., 2017[41])

Lastly, nature-based solutions to climate problems need to be considered for their role in achieving both conservation and gender equality goals, particularly during the COVID-19 pandemic, which has had a differentiated effect on women. Nature-based projects have also been recognised for their potential to create green jobs (WWF and ILO, 2020[42]). Evidence from Brazil, Cameroon and South Africa has found that agroforestry promotes gender equality, with 40-50% of women becoming involved with agricultural activities (FAO, 2018[43]). Integrating gender considerations in the design and implementation of nature-based solutions could potentially guarantee a wider engagement of women in environment-related employment and also more sustainable solutions, due to women's – and indigenous communities' – knowledge of local land, biodiversity and natural resources.

14.5.2. Women in indigenous communities and their role in protecting ecosystems

There are more than 370 million indigenous people in the world, in some 90 countries (UNDESA, 2009[44]). Over 38 million indigenous peoples live across 12 OECD countries (OECD, 2019[45]). Indigenous communities draw much of their subsistence food, water and energy from the surrounding environment. Indigenous peoples' close links to and dependency on well-functioning ecosystems makes them highly vulnerable to environmental damage and climate change. Deforestation and pollution caused by mass farming, industrial activities and expanding urbanisation all pose grave and growing threats to the livelihoods and survival of their communities. Indigenous peoples are directly affected by the decline in biodiversity (UNEP, 2016[46]). It is estimated that while indigenous people make up 5% of the global population, they protect around 80% of global biodiversity (World Bank, 2021[47]).

Women in traditional and indigenous societies play a central role in ecosystem management, on which they have accumulated traditional knowledge and largely depend for sustenance and medicine. In many communities, men and women hold differentiated knowledge deriving from traditional segregation of responsibilities. Indigenous women have played a fundamental role in environmental conservation and protection throughout the history of their peoples. Historically, in traditional societies, indigenous women and men have often had equal access to lands, animals and resources. Many of these societies were once matriarchal, with women as managers of the household and family, and founding pillars of their societies. This has been changing as "modern" practices and legislation were introduced (UN, 2010[48]).

Addressing the vulnerabilities of women in indigenous groups in both OECD and developing countries is not only a matter of justice and fairness. Their vast wealth of traditional knowledge of the medicinal properties of plants and other benefits that can be drawn from ecosystems, as well as sustainable management of natural resources, is fundamental for the survival of indigenous communities and their ecosystems.

As indigenous peoples increasingly interact with "modern" economies and societies, it is often indigenous men, rather than women, who participate in the decision making and planning of projects related to natural resource management. As a result, valuable knowledge of women and their attitudes towards the environment are often ignored. Furthermore, the move from collective ownership and responsibility to titled land and inheritance laws often leads to the discrimination of women, which reduces incentives to protect the environment. All these negative effects can create cycles of declining productivity and sustainability, environmental degradation and growing food insecurity.

Building on Ostrom's response to the tragedy of the commons (Ostrom, 1990[39]) a place-based approach to indigenous economic development, with the community question at its core, can place women at the centre of governance in order to secure sustainable management of finite resources (OECD, 2020[49]). In practice, national forestry plans often do not address the issue of the rights of indigenous peoples.

Some countries have implemented specific actions to better integrate indigenous communities in national forestry plans. For instance, in 2005, Australia developed a National Indigenous Forestry Strategy so that indigenous communities could participate in building competitive and ecologically sustainable forest industries. The strategy did not have a gender dimension. International organisations are also active on addressing indigenous peoples' rights. The United Nations Environment Programme is specifically supporting women in indigenous communities (Box 14.3).

Box 14.3. UNEP's dedicated focal point for indigenous peoples

In 2002, the UN Permanent Forum on Indigenous Issues (UNPFII) was established as an advisory body to the UN Economic and Social Council (ECOSOC), aimed at recognising the specific importance of indigenous peoples and their communities. Since 2004, the United Nations Environment Programme (UNEP) has had a dedicated focal point that indigenous peoples can contact at any time regarding the organisation's work programmes. In 2012, UNEP produced policy guidance on indigenous peoples which covers the role of women and the involvement of communities in UNEP sustainable development projects.

Source: (UNEP, 2012[50])

14.5.3. Women's activism to protect biodiversity

Women have traditionally been at the forefront of environmental activism and environmental justice movements, rooted in and birthed from their own experiences of social marginalisation. Researchers postulate that power dynamics orient a feminist approach to environmental activism. Men are traditionally at the helm of political and economic structures responsible for environmental damage, and thus may eschew environmental responsibility based on vested interests (Bell, 2016[51]). Women activists tend to be more collaborative, supportive of co-production of knowledge, and forge coalitions to buttress their efforts and solidify solidarity (Berila, 2006[52]). For example, environmental activism in the Central Appalachian coalfields of the United States began with women activists of all races, creeds and social standing coming together during a time of racial segregation to fight for worker's rights in the coal mines. The initial struggle has held strong and expanded to include environmental conservation (e.g. safeguarding groundwater, opposition to mountaintop removal) and shed light on and demanded a response to the social and health impacts of coal mining (black lung disease, poverty etc.).

Where women face barriers to or are kept at bay from formal decision making (i.e. local councils, parliaments), they seek a voice to initiate change through grassroots activism. Women Defenders of the Amazon, who delivered a Mandate of Amazonian Women Defenders of the Jungle of the Bases against Extractivism to Ecuador's president and ministers, or Brazil's National Association of Ancestral Indigenous Women Warriors (ANMIGA), are only two examples of such women-led social mobilisation. But this type of activity can entail great risk to women with little protection for recourse or justice (Chapter 4). Women activists – both environmentalists and environment defenders such as lawyers or journalists – are more prone to attack in that they are seen as breaking social norms by speaking out (De Cicco and Sekyiamah, 2017[53]) (Ervin, 2018[54]). Violence against female environmentalists - such as threats, intimidation, rape or torture - largely goes unnoticed (Ervin, 2018[54]). The international human rights organisation Global Witness reported 167 land and environmental defenders killed in 2018, which averages out to more than three a week (Global Witness, 2019[55]).

14.6. Integrating a gender lens into biodiversity initiatives

The 12th meeting of Conference of the Parties to the Convention on Biological Diversity (CBD COP 12) recognised the importance of gender considerations in achieving the Aichi Biodiversity Targets, introduced a 2015-20 Gender Action Plan, and called for more sex-disaggregated data and monitoring of policies. (CBD, 2014[35]). The Gender Action Plan's major objective is to integrate gender in NBSAPs and is organised in four areas of action: (i) developing a policy framework that can provide the mandate, political support and resources to ensure integration of gender considerations in implementing the Convention; (ii) addressing gender issues in underlying theory, methodology and applied research upon which CBD interventions are based; (iii) working on gender equality in staffing through institutional capacity, staff development, accountability and related equal opportunity policies; and iv) mobilising partners, building partnerships and building on existing efforts, best practices and lessons learned (CBD, 2017[56]).

The Gender Action Plan within the UN Convention to Combat Desertification 2018-2030 Strategic Framework enhances the implementation of the Convention, and therefore serves as a valuable instrument for transforming the livelihoods of millions of women and girls. The Plan recognises the importance of women in the implementation of the Convention, and identifies critical areas for their engagement: (i) awareness-raising and participation in the design and implementation of programmes; (ii) decision-making processes that men and women adopt at the local level in the governance of development, implementation and review of regional and national action programmes (RAPs and NAPs); and (iii) capacity-building, education and public awareness, particularly at local level through the support of local organizationsorganisations (UNCCD, 2018[57]).

NBSAPs are the key mechanism through which signatories to the CBD implement their goals. As such, they provide an important opportunity to integrate women's empowerment and gender considerations into biodiversity management across the agriculture, forestry and fisheries sectors. Recent research analysing the latest 174 NBSAPs finds that while 7% of countries include an objective or goal to advance gender equality, double that number (14%) include gender equality as a guiding principle, and more than double (18%) include gender equality or women's empowerment considerations as part of a key objective, target or goal (CBD, 2016[58]). Between 1993 and 2016, 56% of NBSAPs mentioned keywords such as "gender" or "women", but how women and their participation was defined differs. Around one-third of reports characterised women as "stakeholders" and/or "beneficiaries", 17% referred to women as "vulnerable", and 4% as "agents of change." Multiple countries referenced Aichi Biodiversity Target 14.

Uganda's National Gender Policy (1997) promotes the integration of gender concerns in environmental policy planning, decision making and implementation at all levels to ensure sustainable social and economic development. The country's policies pertaining to wildlife, forestry, fisheries and agriculture sectors each call for attention to gender issues. Similarly, an analysis of Mexico's National Development

Plan 2013-18 shows that inclusion of gender perspectives is a multifaceted necessity and was therefore included in their National Programme for Equality of Opportunities and Non-discrimination against Women (PROIGUALDAD, 2013-18) together with implementation of the CBD. Brazil's national plans address the need for equitable sustainable development and to promote women's land rights, with gender equality included as a cross-cutting element in national environmental policies (CBD, 2016[59]).

In order to help countries successfully integrate gender into environmental strategies and build upon the examples of Uganda, Mexico and Brazil, the CBD has developed a methodology. The initial step involves examining national policies, as well as legal and institutional frameworks for gender equality and biodiversity interaction, followed by identifying the status of women on gender issues and identifying stakeholders. The second step is establishing governance and consultation mechanisms to capture diverse voices, including those of women. The last step is identifying priorities and recommendations and submitting them to lead biodiversity institutions in order to promote change (CBD, 2016[59]).

References in NBSAPs indicate support for women, but stop short of clearly defining women's influence on biodiversity outcomes as leaders in their communities, as consumers and as entrepreneurs. Failure to mention or acknowledge women altogether is a symptom of a bigger problem: presumption that women are a part of management, decision-making processes and solutions, thus a focus on their engagement is unnecessary. Available data tells a different story, and NBSAPs will need to go beyond acknowledgement and tokenism to define more substantive action, for instance identifying what natural resources women need and why, action plans for gender balanced decision making and access to technology and inputs, and commitment of funds to implement initiatives.

Development co-operation data show that there is further potential for mainstreaming gender equality in programming related to biodiversity and conservation projects. Bilateral allocable aid commitments targeting gender equality and women's empowerment as either a significant (secondary) or principal (primary) objective have seen a significant increase from 2015 to 2019 (over USD 10 billion). However, only a small fraction of this bilateral aid is dedicated to biodiversity - that is about 1.2% annually on average for the period 2015-2019 - indicating that the link between gender equality and halting biodiversity loss needs to be strengthened in Official Development Assistance (OECD.Stat, n.d.[60]).

Infrastructure and natural resource management projects at both local and national levels often overlook gendered effects and approaches. For example, the international programme for Reducing Emissions from Deforestation and Forest Degradation (REDD+), which provides payments to developing countries in exchange for conserving their forests, in some cases excluded women in governance frameworks (e.g. Nepal, Cameroon), and resulting decisions overlooked the different needs of men and women (Larson et al., 2015[61]) (Elwell and Williams, 2016[62]).

Action is necessary not only from public authorities but also from non-governmental organisations (NGOs). The World Wide Fund for Nature (WWF) developed interesting and successful initiatives while adopting its Gender Policy in 2011 that aimed to drive stronger integration of a gender perspective in both its conservation work and its internal operations. WWF has been mainstreaming gender equality and women's empowerment in their global work by helping women in developing countries gain better access to education, health care and sustainable livelihoods, as well as to build their self-confidence (WWF, 2020[63]). An example in Nepal empowers marginalised women to actively participate in community adaptation processes by identifying their specific climate vulnerabilities and ensuring that solutions for them are included in local climate adaptation plans (WWF, 2020[63]). These sustainability improvement activities range from rainwater harvesting and improving water use efficiency to introducing climate-adapted vegetable crops in order to help women adapt to climate change while also restoring long-lasting ecosystem support.

14.7. Key actions for advancing the agenda and ongoing work

A number of actions are needed to integrate gender equality and conservation efforts:

- As with other environment-related SDGs, addressing data gaps and strengthening evidence collection and monitoring beyond the existing gender targets and indicators identified in Agenda 2030 should be a first step in correcting the general lack of gender focus in the implementation of SDG 15.
- The current list of biodiversity and conservation targets relevant to gender SDG indicators are limited in scope, and focus mainly on access to land. The SDGs are silent on both the heightened effects of environmental degradation on women (this could be included in SDG Target 15.6) and the potential of engaging women in conservation efforts. Further efforts are needed to embed gender-responsive indicators throughout the post-2020 biodiversity framework, following initial steps by the Conference of the Parties to the Convention on Biological Diversity.
- Tackling gender discrimination and women's empowerment needs to go beyond private land titles and agricultural production to also address the need for women to access shared resources from forests, mountains, rivers and other commons. This is especially important for indigenous communities given their dependence on shared, ancestral lands.
- Gender considerations need to be better integrated into National Biodiversity Strategies and Action Plans (NBSAPs). In particular, there is a need to ensure gender balanced decision making and access to technology and finance for women-led projects.
- All countries have a major stake in ensuring that their transboundary policies (trade, investment, and development co-operation) promote the empowerment and engagement of women and indigenous groups in other countries.
- Multinational enterprises that operate in developing countries, especially those that use the natural resources within them, have a duty to act responsibly and mitigate the negative environmental and social impacts of their activities. Initiatives such as the UN Global Compact and the OECD's Guidelines for Multinational Enterprises play a major role in this regard, but efforts are needed to strengthen monitoring and sanctioning mechanisms.

References

Abbott, P. (2015), "Land Tenure Regularisation in Rwanda: Progress Report for Selected Indicators", http://dx.doi.org/10.13140/RG.2.1.4208.3280. [27]

Agarwal, B. (2009), "Gender and forest conservation: The impact of women's participation in community forest governance", *Ecological Economics*, Vol. 68/11, pp. 2785-2799, http://dx.doi.org/10.1016/j.ecolecon.2009.04.025. [31]

Alamgir, A. (2017), "Therapeutic Use of Medicinal Plants and Their Extracts: Volume 1. Progress in Drug Research", http://dx.doi.org/10.1007/978-3-319-63862-1_1. [11]

Ali, D., K. Deininger and M. Goldstein (2014), "Environmental and gender impacts of land tenure regularization in Africa: Pilot evidence from Rwanda", *Journal of Development Economics*, Vol. 110, pp. 262-275, http://dx.doi.org/10.1016/j.jdeveco.2013.12.009. [26]

Bell, K. (2016), "Bread and roses: A gender perspective on environmental justice and public health", *International Journal of Environmental Research and Public Health*, Vol. 13/10, http://dx.doi.org/10.3390/ijerph13101005. [51]

Berila, B. (2006), "The Links between Environmental Justice and Feminist Pedagogy: An Introduction", *Feminist Teacher*, Vol. 16/2, pp. 93-97, http://dx.doi.org/10.2307/40545982. [52]

Brainich, A. et al. (2018), *The Assessment Report in Land Restoration and Degradation. Summary for Policymakers of the IPBES Report on Land Degradation and Restoration*, http://www.ipbes.net. [4]

Carrington, D. (2018), "What is Biodiversity and why does it matter to us?", *The Guardian*. [5]

Castañeda Carney, I. et al. (2020), *Gender-based violence and environment linkages: The violence of inequality*, IUCN, International Union for Conservation of Nature, http://dx.doi.org/10.2305/IUCN.CH.2020.03.en. [16]

CBD (2019), *Towards a Gender Responsive Post- 2020 Global Biodiversity Framework: Considerations for Gender Mainstreaming*, https://genderandenvironment.org/2015/08/stop-being-so-sensitive-the-shift-from-gender-sensitive-to-gender-responsive-action/. [12]

CBD (2018), "Towards a Sustainable, Participatory and Inclusive Wild Meat", Vol. CBD/COP/14/INF/7, pp. 1-181. [7]

CBD (2017), *2015–2020 Gender Plan of Action Pocket Guide: Summary and Examples*, https://www.cbd.int/gender/doc/CBD-GenderPlanofAction-EN-WEB.pdf. [56]

CBD (2016), *Inclusion and characterization of women and gender equality considerations in National Biodiversity Strategies and Action Plans (NBSAPs) Gender and Biodiversity*, http://www.genderandenvironment.org/EGI. [58]

CBD (2016), *Integrating Gender Considerations in National Biodiversity Strategies and Action Plans Pilot Project Process and Initial Considerations*, http://genderandenvironment.org/works/ccgaps/. [59]

CBD (2014), *Decision Adopted by the Conference of the Parties to the Convention on Biological Diversity. Mainstreaming gender considerations*, UNEP/CBD/COP/DEC/XII/7. [35]

De Cicco, G. and N. Sekyiamah (2017), "Cinq espaces féministes extraordinaires qui nous ont réjoui-e-s en 2017 18 décembre 2017 |", *AWID*, https://www.awid.org/fr/nouvelles-et-analyse/cinq-espaces-feministes-extraordinaires-qui-nous-ont-rejoui-e-s-en-2017 (accessed on 13 October 2020). [53]

Despot-Belmonte, K. (2019), *SDGs context, overview of targets and indicators relevant to gender and biodiversity*, UN Environment, World Conservation Monitoring Centre. [29]

Elwell, N. and Y. Williams (2016), *If You Care About the Environment, You Should Care About Gender*, https://www.wri.org/blog/2016/03/if-you-care-about-environment-you-should-care-about-gender (accessed on 13 November 2020). [62]

Ervin, J. (2018), *In Defense of Nature: Women at the Forefront*, https://www.undp.org/content/undp/en/home/blog/2018/in-defense-of-nature-women-at-the-forefront.html (accessed on 1 September 2020). [54]

FAO (2020), *Global Forest Resources Assessment 2020*, FAO, http://dx.doi.org/10.4060/ca8753en. [2]

FAO (2020), *The State of the World's Forests 2020*, FAO and UNEP, http://dx.doi.org/10.4060/ca8642en. [10]

FAO (2018), *Forest Pathways to Sustainable Development*, FAO, Rome, http://www.fao.org/documents/card/en/c/I9535EN/. [43]

FAO (2018), *Realizing women's rights to land in the law. A guide for reporting on SDG indicator 5.a.2*, Food and Agriculture Organization of the United Nations, Rome. [24]

FAO (2012), *Decent rural employment for food security: A case for action.* [8]

Fargione, J. et al. (2008), "Land clearing and the biofuel carbon debt", *Science*, Vol. 319/5867, pp. 1235-1238, http://dx.doi.org/10.1126/science.1152747. [14]

Global Witness (2019), *Enemies of the State: How Goverments and Business Silence Land and Environmental Defenders*, https://www.globalwitness.org/documents/19766/Enemies_of_the_State.pdf. [55]

Global Youth Biodiversity Network (2016), *CBD in a nutshell*, CBD, Germany, http://www.gybn.org. [13]

Hoza Ngoga, T. (2019), *A quick, cost-effective approach to land tenure regularisation: the case of Rwanda*, International Growth Centre. [25]

IPBES (2019), *The global assessment report on Biodiversity and Ecosystem Services Summary for Policymakers of the IPBES Global Assessment Report on Biodiversity and Ecosystem Services*, http://www.ipbes.net. [15]

Larson, A. et al. (2015), "The role of women in early REDD+ implementation: lessons for future engagement", *International Forestry Review*, Vol. 17/1, p. 43, http://redd-standards.org/. [61]

Lawrence, A. et al. (2020), "Forests in common: Learning from diversity of community forest arrangements in Europe", *Ambio*, http://dx.doi.org/10.1007/s13280-020-01377-x. [38]

Leisher, C. et al. (2016), "Does the gender composition of forest and fishery management groups affect resource governance and conservation outcomes? A systematic map", *Environmental Evidence*, Vol. 5/1, http://dx.doi.org/10.1186/s13750-016-0057-8. [34]

Macdonald, C. (2018), *The Role of Gender in the Extractive Industries*, Oxford University Press, http://dx.doi.org/10.1093/oso/9780198817369.003.0021. [21]

Meinzen-Dick, R., C. Kovarik and A. Quisumbing (2014), "Gender and Sustainability", *Annual Review of Environment and Resources*, Vol. 39/1, pp. 29-55, http://dx.doi.org/10.1146/annurev-environ-101813-013240. [40]

Muller, E. et al. (2018), *The state of the world's forests : forest pathways to sustainable development.* [1]

OECD (2020), *Biodiversity and the economic response to COVID-19: Ensuring a green and resilient recovery.* [3]

OECD (2020), *Linking Indigenous Communities with Regional Development in Canada*, OECD Rural Policy Reviews, OECD Publishing, Paris, https://dx.doi.org/10.1787/fa0f60c6-en. [49]

OECD (2019), *Gender, Institutions and Development Database*, https://oe.cd/ds/GIDDB2019. [30]

OECD (2019), *Linking Indigenous Communities with Regional Development*, OECD Rural Policy Reviews, OECD Publishing, Paris, https://dx.doi.org/10.1787/3203c082-en. [45]

OECD (2018), *Mainstreaming biodiversity for sustainable development.* [9]

OECD (2018), *Mainstreaming Biodiversity for Sustainable Development*, OECD Publishing, Paris, https://dx.doi.org/10.1787/9789264303201-en. [6]

OECD.Stat (n.d.), *Aid projects targeting gender equality and women's empowerment (CRS)*, https://stats.oecd.org/Index.aspx?DataSetCode=DV_DCD_GENDER (accessed on 15 April 2021). [60]

Orr, B. et al. (2017), *Conceptual Framework for Land Degradation Neutrality. A Report of the Science-Policy Interface. United Nations Convention to Combat Desertification (UNCCD)*, UNCCD, https://www.unccd.int/sites/default/files/documents/2019-06/LDN_CF_report_web-english.pdf. [33]

Ostrom, E. (1990), *Governing the commons : the evolution of institutions for collective action*, Cambridge University Press. [39]

Paudyal, K. et al. (2017), "Ecosystem services from community-based forestry in Nepal: Realising local and global benefits", *Land Use Policy*, Vol. 63, pp. 342-355, http://dx.doi.org/10.1016/j.landusepol.2017.01.046. [41]

Price, R. (2018), *Women-initiated measures to cope with environmental stresses and climate change in South Asia.* [36]

Ray, B., P. Mukherjee and R. Bhattacharya (2016), "Attitudes and cooperation: does gender matter in community-based forest management?", *Environment and Development Economics*, Vol. 22/5, pp. 594-623, http://dx.doi.org/10.1017/s1355770x16000358. [32]

Samandari, A. (2017), "Gender-responsive land degradation neutrality", United Nations Convention to Combat Desertification. [22]

Stefanidou, M., C. Maravelias and C. Spiliopoulou (2009), "Human Exposure to Endocrine Disruptors and Breast Milk", *Endocrine, Metabolic & Immune Disorders - Drug Targets*, Vol. 9/3, pp. 269-276, http://dx.doi.org/10.2174/187153009789044374. [19]

UN (2010), *The Millennium Development Goals Report 2010*, United Nations. [48]

UN Environment (2016), *Global Gender and Environment Outlook 2016*, United Nations, New York, https://dx.doi.org/10.18356/0b979453-en. [23]

UNCCD (2018), *Gender Action Plan*, United Nations Convention to Combat Desertification, https://www.unccd.int/publications/gender-action-plan. [57]

UNDESA (2009), *State of the World's Indigenous Peoples*, United Nations, Department of Economic and Social Affairs, Division for Social Policy and Development, Secretariat of the Permanent Forum on Indigenous Issues. [44]

UNEP (2016), *Global gender and environment outlook.* [46]

UNEP (2012), *UNEP and Indigenous Peoples: A Partnership in Caring for the Environment Policy Guidance*, http://www.uncsd2012.org/content/documents/727The%20Future%20We%20Want%2019%20June%201230pm.pdf. [50]

UNEP and IUCN (2019), *Gender and environment statistics: Unlocking information for action and measuring the SDGs*, http://www.un.org/Depts/Cartographic/english/htmain.htm. [28]

UNFCCC (2015), *Least Developed Countries Expert Group: Strengthening gender considerations in adaptation planning and implementation in the least developed countries*, https://www4.unfccc.int/sites/NAPC/Documents%20NAP/UNFCCC_gender_in_NAPs.pdf. [37]

UNICEF (2017), *Horn of Africa: A Call for Action*, https://reliefweb.int/sites/reliefweb.int/files/resources/HOA_CALL_FOR_ACTION_Leaflet_Feb2017_1.pdf. [18]

UNICEF (2016), *A Rapid Assessment of the Impact of Drought on Children and Women in India Coping Crumbles.* [17]

World Bank (2021), *Indigenous Peoples*, https://www.worldbank.org/en/topic/indigenouspeoples#:~:text=While%20Indigenous%20Peoples%20own%2C%20occupy,of%20the%20world%27s%20remaining%20biodiversity.&text=The%20World%20Bank%20works%20with,and%20aspirations%20of%20Indigenous%20Peoples. [47]

World Bank (2013), "Gender in Extractive Industries", https://www.worldbank.org/en/topic/extractiveindustries/brief/gender-in-extractive-industries (accessed on 28 October 2020). [20]

WWF (2020), *Women and Girls Stories*, https://www.worldwildlife.org/stories?initiative_id=women-and-girls (accessed on 10 March 2021). [63]

WWF and ILO (2020), *Nature Hires: How Nature-based Solutions Can Power a Green Jobs Recovery*, 0 World Wide Fund For Nature and International Labour Organization; Gland, Switzerland, https://www.ilo.org/wcmsp5/groups/public/---ed_emp/documents/publication/wcms_757823.pdf. [42]

Notes

[1] https://www.nrcan.gc.ca/our-natural-resources/forests-forestry/state-canadas-forests-report/articles/women-championing-women-forestry/22292

Annex A. Sustainable Development Goal (SDG) Indicators: mapping the gender-environment nexus

Table A.1. Gender- and Environment-related SDG indicators – data availability for OECD countries

Indicator	Indicator Label	Gender-related indicators	Environment-related indicators	Gender-environment nexus indicators	Data availability for OECD countries
1.1.1	Proportion of the population living below the international poverty line by sex, age, employment status and geographic location (urban/rural)	•			
1.2.1	Proportion of population living below the national poverty line, by sex and age	•			
1.2.2	Proportion of men, women and children of all ages living in poverty in all its dimensions according to national definitions	•			
1.3.1	Proportion of population covered by social protection floors/systems, by sex, distinguishing children, unemployed persons, older persons, persons with disabilities, pregnant women, newborns, work-injury victims and the poor and the vulnerable	•			1. [ILO] Proportion of population with severe disabilities receiving disability cash benefit, by sex (%) 2. [ILO] Proportion of mothers with newborns receiving maternity cash benefit (%) 3. [ILO] Proportion of population above statutory pensionable age receiving a pension, by sex (%) 4. [ILO] Proportion of unemployed persons receiving unemployment cash benefit, by sex (%)
1.4.1	Proportion of population living in households with access to basic services	•			
1.4.2	Proportion of total adult population with secure tenure rights to land, (a) with legally recognized documentation, and (b) who perceive their rights to land as secure, by sex and type of tenure	•	•	•	
1.5.1	Number of deaths, missing persons and directly affected persons attributed to disasters per 100,000 population	•	•	•	
1.5.2	Direct economic loss attributed to disasters in relation to global gross domestic product (GDP)		•		
1.5.3	Number of countries that adopt and implement national disaster risk reduction strategies in line with the Sendai Framework for Disaster Risk Reduction 2015–2030		•		

Indicator	Indicator Label	Gender-related indicators	Environment-related indicators	Gender-environment nexus indicators	Data availability for OECD countries
1.5.4	Proportion of local governments that adopt and implement local disaster risk reduction strategies in line with national disaster risk reduction strategies		•		
1.a.1	Total official development assistance grants from all donors that focus on poverty reduction as a share of the recipient country's gross national income				
1.a.2	Proportion of total government spending on essential services (education, health and social protection)				
1.b.1	Pro-poor public social spending				
2.1.1	Prevalence of undernourishment	•			
2.1.2	Prevalence of moderate or severe food insecurity in the population, based on the Food Insecurity Experience Scale (FIES)	•			
2.2.1	Prevalence of stunting (height for age <-2 standard deviation from the median of the World Health Organization (WHO) Child Growth Standards) among children under 5 years of age	•			
2.2.2	Prevalence of malnutrition (weight for height >+2 or <-2 standard deviation from the median of the WHO Child Growth Standards) among children under 5 years of age, by type (wasting and overweight)	•			Obesity rate
2.2.3	Prevalence of anaemia in women aged 15 to 49 years, by pregnancy status (percentage)	•			
2.3.1	Volume of production per labour unit by classes of farming/pastoral/forestry enterprise size		•		
2.3.2	Average income of small-scale food producers, by sex and indigenous status	•	•	•	
2.4.1	Proportion of agricultural area under productive and sustainable agriculture		•		
2.5.1	Number of plant and animal genetic resources for food and agriculture secured in either medium- or long-term conservation facilities		•		
2.5.2	Proportion of local breeds classified as being at risk of extinction		•		
2.a.1	The agriculture orientation index for government expenditures		•		
2.a.2	Total official flows (official development assistance plus other official flows) to the agriculture sector		•		
2.b.1	Agricultural export subsidies				
2.c.1	Indicator of food price anomalies				
3.1.1	Maternal mortality ratio	•			Maternal mortality ratio
3.1.2	Proportion of births attended by skilled health personnel	•			Proportion of births attended by skilled health personnel (%)
3.2.1	Under-5 mortality rate	•			Infant mortality rate (deaths per 1 000 live births)
3.2.2	Neonatal mortality rate	•			
3.3.1	Number of new HIV infections per 1,000	•			Number of new HIV infections per 1

Indicator	Indicator Label	Gender-related indicators	Environment-related indicators	Gender-environment nexus indicators	Data availability for OECD countries
	uninfected population, by sex, age and key populations				000 uninfected population, by sex and age (per 1 000 uninfected population)
3.3.2	Tuberculosis incidence per 100,000 population	•			Death rate due to Tuberculosis
3.3.3	Malaria incidence per 1,000 population	•			
3.3.4	Hepatitis B incidence per 100,000 population	•			
3.3.5	Number of people requiring interventions against neglected tropical diseases	•			
3.4.1	Mortality rate attributed to cardiovascular disease, cancer, diabetes or chronic respiratory disease	•			Mortality rate attributed to cardiovascular disease, cancer, diabetes or chronic respiratory disease (probability)
3.4.2	Suicide mortality rate	•			Suicide mortality rate, by sex (deaths per 100 000 population)
3.5.1	Coverage of treatment interventions (pharmacological, psychosocial and rehabilitation and aftercare services) for substance use disorders	•			
3.5.2	Alcohol per capita consumption (aged 15 years and older) within a calendar year in litres of pure alcohol	•			
3.6.1	Death rate due to road traffic injuries	•			Death rate due to Transport Accident
3.7.1	Proportion of women of reproductive age (aged 15–49 years) who have their need for family planning satisfied with modern methods	•			
3.7.2	Adolescent birth rate (aged 10–14 years; aged 15–19 years) per 1,000 women in that age group	•			Adolescent birth rate (per 1 000 women aged 15-19 years)
3.8.1	Coverage of essential health services	•			
3.8.2	Proportion of population with large household expenditures on health as a share of total household expenditure or income	•			
3.9.1	Mortality rate attributed to household and ambient air pollution	•	•	•	
3.9.2	Mortality rate attributed to unsafe water, unsafe sanitation and lack of hygiene (exposure to unsafe Water, Sanitation and Hygiene for All (WASH) services)	•	•	•	
3.9.3	Mortality rate attributed to unintentional poisoning	•	•	•	Mortality rate attributed to unintentional poisonings, by sex (deaths per 100 000 population)
3.a.1	Age-standardized prevalence of current tobacco use among persons aged 15 years and older	•			Age-standardized prevalence of current tobacco use among persons aged 15 years and older, by sex (%)
3.b.1	Proportion of the target population covered by all vaccines included in their national programme	•			
3.b.2	Total net official development assistance to medical research and basic health sectors				
3.b.3	Proportion of health facilities that have a core set of relevant essential medicines available and affordable on a sustainable				

Indicator	Indicator Label	Gender-related indicators	Environment-related indicators	Gender-environment nexus indicators	Data availability for OECD countries
	basis				
3.c.1	Health worker density and distribution				
3.d.1	International Health Regulations (IHR) capacity and health emergency preparedness				
3.d.2	Percentage of bloodstream infections due to selected antimicrobial-resistant organisms				
4.1.1	Proportion of children and young people (a) in grades 2/3; (b) at the end of primary; and (c) at the end of lower secondary achieving at least a minimum proficiency level in (i) reading and (ii) mathematics, by sex	•			1. Minimum proficiency in mathematics, by education level and sex (%) (GRAD23) 2. Minimum proficiency in mathematics, by education level and sex (%) (LOWSEC) 3. Minimum proficiency in reading, by education level and sex (%) (GRAD23) 4. Minimum proficiency in reading, by education level and sex (%) (LOWSEC)
4.1.2	Completion rate (primary education, lower secondary education, upper secondary education)	•			
4.2.1	Proportion of children aged 24-59 months who are developmentally on track in health, learning and psychosocial well-being, by sex	•			
4.2.2	Participation rate in organized learning (one year before the official primary entry age), by sex	•			Participation rate in organized learning (one year before the official primary entry age), by sex (%)
4.3.1	Participation rate of youth and adults in formal and non-formal education and training in the previous 12 months, by sex	•			Participation rate in formal and non-formal education and training, by sex (%)
4.4.1	Proportion of youth and adults with information and communications technology (ICT) skills, by type of skill	•			Proportion of youth and adults with information and communications technology (ICT) skills, by sex and type of skill (%) (ARSP)
4.5.1	Parity indices (female/male, rural/urban, bottom/top wealth quintile and others such as disability status, indigenous peoples and conflict-affected, as data become available) for all education indicators on this list that can be disaggregated	•			1. Gender parity index achieving at least a fixed level of proficiency in functional literacy skills (ratio) (LITE) 2. Gender parity index achieving at least a fixed level of proficiency in functional literacy skills (ratio) (NUME) 3. Gender parity index for youth/adults with information and communications technology (ICT) skills, by type of skill (ratio) (ARSP) 4. Gender parity index for youth/adults with information and communications technology (ICT) skills, by type of skill (ratio) (CMFL) 5. Gender parity index for youth/adults with information and communications technology (ICT) skills, by type of skill (ratio) (COPA) 6. Gender parity index for youth/adults with information and communications technology (ICT) skills, by type of skill (ratio) (EPRS) 7. Gender parity index for youth/adults with information and communications technology (ICT) skills, by type of skill (ratio) (PCPR) 8.

Indicator	Indicator Label	Gender-related indicators	Environment-related indicators	Gender-environment nexus indicators	Data availability for OECD countries
					Gender parity index for youth/adults with information and communications technology (ICT) skills, by type of skill (ratio) (SOFT) 9. Gender parity index for youth/adults with information and communications technology (ICT) skills, by type of skill (ratio) (TRAF) 10. Gender parity index for achievement in mathematics, by education level (ratio) (GRAD23) 11. Gender parity index for achievement in mathematics, by education level (ratio) (LOWSEC) 12. Gender parity index for achievement in mathematics, by education level (ratio) (PRIMAR) 13. Gender parity index for participation rate in formal and non-formal education and training (ratio) 14. Gender parity index for achievement in reading, by education level (ratio) (GRAD23) 15. Gender parity index for achievement in reading, by education level (ratio) (LOWSEC) 16. Gender parity index for participation rate in organized learning (one year before the official primary entry age), (ratio)
4.6.1	Proportion of population in a given age group achieving at least a fixed level of proficiency in functional (a) literacy and (b) numeracy skills, by sex	•			1. Proportion of population achieving at least a fixed level of proficiency in functional skills, by sex, age and type of skill (%) (LITE) 2. Proportion of population achieving at least a fixed level of proficiency in functional skills, by sex, age and type of skill (%) (NUME)
4.7.1	Extent to which (i) global citizenship education and (ii) education for sustainable development are mainstreamed in (a) national education policies; (b) curricula; (c) teacher education; and (d) student assessment				
4.a.1	Proportion of schools offering basic services, by type of service				
4.b.1	Volume of official development assistance flows for scholarships by sector and type of study				
4.c.1	Proportion of teachers with the minimum required qualifications, by education level	•			
5.1.1	Whether or not legal frameworks are in place to promote, enforce and monitor equality and non-discrimination on the basis of sex	•			1. Legal frameworks that promote, enforce and monitor gender equality (percentage of achievement, 0 - 100) -- Area 3: employment and economic benefits 2. Legal frameworks that promote, enforce and monitor gender equality (percentage of achievement, 0 - 100) -- Area 1: overarching legal frameworks and public life 3. Legal frameworks that promote, enforce and monitor gender equality (percentage of achievement, 0 - 100)

Indicator	Indicator Label	Gender-related indicators	Environment-related indicators	Gender-environment nexus indicators	Data availability for OECD countries
					-- Area 4: marriage and family 4. Legal frameworks that promote, enforce and monitor gender equality (percentage of achievement, 0 - 100) -- Area 2: violence against women
5.2.1	Proportion of ever-partnered women and girls aged 15 years and older subjected to physical, sexual or psychological violence by a current or former intimate partner in the previous 12 months, by form of violence and by age	•			Proportion of ever-partnered women and girls subjected to physical and/or sexual violence by a current or former intimate partner in the previous 12 months, by age (%)
5.2.2	Proportion of women and girls aged 15 years and older subjected to sexual violence by persons other than an intimate partner in the previous 12 months, by age and place of occurrence	•			
5.3.1	Proportion of women aged 20–24 years who were married or in a union before age 15 and before age 18	•			
5.3.2	Proportion of girls and women aged 15–49 years who have undergone female genital mutilation/cutting, by age	•			
5.4.1	Proportion of time spent on unpaid domestic and care work, by sex, age and location	•			1. Proportion of time spent on unpaid domestic chores and care work, by sex, age and location (%) (gender abs. diff.) 2. Proportion of time spent on unpaid care work, by sex, age and location (%) (gender abs. diff.) 3. Proportion of time spent on unpaid domestic chores, by sex, age and location (%) (gender abs. diff.)
5.5.1	Proportion of seats held by women in (a) national parliaments and (b) local governments	•			1. Proportion of elected seats held by women in deliberative bodies of local government (%) 2. Proportion of seats held by women in national parliaments (% of total number of seats)
5.5.2	Proportion of women in managerial positions	•			1. Proportion of women in managerial positions (%) 2. Proportion of women in senior and middle management positions (%) 3. Female share of seats on boards of the largest publicly listed companies
5.6.1	Proportion of women aged 15–49 years who make their own informed decisions regarding sexual relations, contraceptive use and reproductive health care	•			
5.6.2	Number of countries with laws and regulations that guarantee full and equal access to women and men aged 15 years and older to sexual and reproductive health care, information and education	•			
5.a.1	(a) Proportion of total agricultural population with ownership or secure rights over agricultural land, by sex; and (b) share of women among owners or rights-bearers of agricultural land, by type of tenure	•	•	•	

Indicator	Indicator Label	Gender-related indicators	Environment-related indicators	Gender-environment nexus indicators	Data availability for OECD countries
5.a.2	Proportion of countries where the legal framework (including customary law) guarantees women's equal rights to land ownership and/or control	•	•	•	
5.b.1	Proportion of individuals who own a mobile telephone, by sex	•			Proportion of individuals who own a mobile telephone, by sex (%)
5.c.1	Proportion of countries with systems to track and make public allocations for gender equality and women's empowerment	•			
6.1.1	Proportion of population using safely managed drinking water services	•	•	•	
6.2.1	Proportion of population using (a) safely managed sanitation services and (b) a hand-washing facility with soap and water	•	•	•	
6.3.1	Proportion of domestic and industrial wastewater flows safely treated		•		
6.3.2	Proportion of bodies of water with good ambient water quality		•		
6.4.1	Change in water-use efficiency over time		•		
6.4.2	Level of water stress: freshwater withdrawal as a proportion of available freshwater resources		•		
6.5.1	Degree of integrated water resources management		•		
6.5.2	Proportion of transboundary basin area with an operational arrangement for water cooperation		•		
6.6.1	Change in the extent of water-related ecosystems over time		•		
6.a.1	Amount of water- and sanitation-related official development assistance that is part of a government-coordinated spending plan		•		
6.b.1	Proportion of local administrative units with established and operational policies and procedures for participation of local communities in water and sanitation management		•		
7.1.1	Proportion of population with access to electricity	•	•	•	
7.1.2	Proportion of population with primary reliance on clean fuels and technology	•	•	•	
7.2.1	Renewable energy share in the total final energy consumption		•		
7.3.1	Energy intensity measured in terms of primary energy and GDP		•		
7.a.1	International financial flows to developing countries in support of clean energy research and development and renewable energy production, including in hybrid systems		•		
7.b.1	Installed renewable energy-generating capacity in developing countries (in watts per capita)		•		
8.1.1	Annual growth rate of real GDP per capita				

Indicator	Indicator Label	Gender-related indicators	Environment-related indicators	Gender-environment nexus indicators	Data availability for OECD countries
8.2.1	Annual growth rate of real GDP per employed person				
8.3.1	Proportion of informal employment in total employment, by sector and sex	•	•	•	
8.4.1	Material footprint, material footprint per capita, and material footprint per GDP		•		
8.4.2	Domestic material consumption, domestic material consumption per capita, and domestic material consumption per GDP		•		
8.5.1	Average hourly earnings of employees, by sex, age, occupation and persons with disabilities	•			1. Gender gap in self-employed earnings 2. Average hourly earnings of managers (ISCO-08) (local currency) 3. Gender wage gap
8.5.2	Unemployment rate, by sex, age and persons with disabilities	•			1. Labour Force participation rate 2. Unemployment rate, by sex and age (%) 3. Unemployment rate, by sex and disability (%)
8.6.1	Proportion of youth (aged 15–24 years) not in education, employment or training	•			Proportion of youth not in education, employment or training, by sex and age (%)
8.7.1	Proportion and number of children aged 5–17 years engaged in child labour, by sex and age	•			
8.8.1	Fatal and non-fatal occupational injuries per 100,000 workers, by sex and migrant status	•			1. Fatal occupational injuries among employees, by sex and migrant status (per 100 000 employees) 2. Non-fatal occupational injuries among employees, by sex and migrant status (per 100 000 employees)
8.8.2	Level of national compliance with labour rights (freedom of association and collective bargaining) based on International Labour Organization (ILO) textual sources and national legislation, by sex and migrant status	•			
8.9.1	Tourism direct GDP as a proportion of total GDP and in growth rate		•		
8.10.1	(a) Number of commercial bank branches per 100,000 adults and (b) number of automated teller machines (ATMs) per 100,000 adults				
8.10.2	Proportion of adults (15 years and older) with an account at a bank or other financial institution or with a mobile-money-service provider	•			Proportion of adults (15 years and older) with an account at a financial institution or mobile-money-service provider, by sex (% of adults aged 15 years and older)
8.a.1	Aid for Trade commitments and disbursements				
8.b.1	Existence of a developed and operationalized national strategy for youth employment, as a distinct strategy or as part of a national employment strategy				
9.1.1	Proportion of the rural population who live within 2 km of an all-season road	•	•	•	
9.1.2	Passenger and freight volumes, by mode of transport		•		
9.2.1	Manufacturing value added as a		•		

Indicator	Indicator Label	Gender-related indicators	Environment-related indicators	Gender-environment nexus indicators	Data availability for OECD countries
	proportion of GDP and per capita				
9.2.2	Manufacturing employment as a proportion of total employment		•		
9.3.1	Proportion of small-scale industries in total industry value added		•		
9.3.2	Proportion of small-scale industries with a loan or line of credit		•		
9.4.1	CO2 emission per unit of value added		•		
9.5.1	Research and development expenditure as a proportion of GDP		•		
9.5.2	Researchers (in full-time equivalent) per million inhabitants	•	•	•	1. Researcher per million inhabitants (FTE) 2. Share of women inventors
9.a.1	Total official international support (official development assistance plus other official flows) to infrastructure		•		
9.b.1	Proportion of medium and high-tech industry value added in total value added		•		
9.c.1	Proportion of population covered by a mobile network, by technology	•	•	•	
10.1.1	Growth rates of household expenditure or income per capita among the bottom 40 per cent of the population and the total population	•			
10.2.1	Proportion of people living below 50 per cent of median income, by sex, age and persons with disabilities	•			
10.3.1	Proportion of population reporting having personally felt discriminated against or harassed in the previous 12 months on the basis of a ground of discrimination prohibited under international human rights law	•			
10.4.1	Labour share of GDP				
10.4.2	Redistributive impact of fiscal policy				
10.5.1	Financial Soundness Indicators				
10.6.1	Proportion of members and voting rights of developing countries in international organizations				
10.7.1	Recruitment cost borne by employee as a proportion of monthly income earned in country of destination				
10.7.2	Number of countries with migration policies that facilitate orderly, safe, regular and responsible migration and mobility of people				
10.7.3	Number of people who died or disappeared in the process of migration towards an international destination	•			
10.7.4	Proportion of the population who are refugees, by country of origin	•			
10.a.1	Proportion of tariff lines applied to imports from least developed countries and developing countries with zero-tariff				
10.b.1	Total resource flows for development, by recipient and donor countries and type of flow (e.g. official development assistance,				

Indicator	Indicator Label	Gender-related indicators	Environment-related indicators	Gender-environment nexus indicators	Data availability for OECD countries
	foreign direct investment and other flows)				
10.c.1	Remittance costs as a proportion of the amount remitted				
11.1.1	Proportion of urban population living in slums, informal settlements or inadequate housing	•	•	•	
11.2.1	Proportion of population that has convenient access to public transport, by sex, age and persons with disabilities	•	•	•	
11.3.1	Ratio of land consumption rate to population growth rate		•		
11.3.2	Proportion of cities with a direct participation structure of civil society in urban planning and management that operate regularly and democratically		•		
11.4.1	Total per capita expenditure on the preservation, protection and conservation of all cultural and natural heritage, by source of funding (public, private), type of heritage (cultural, natural) and level of government (national, regional, and local/municipal)		•		
11.5.1	Number of deaths, missing persons and directly affected persons attributed to disasters per 100,000 population	•	•	•	
11.5.2	Direct economic loss in relation to global GDP, damage to critical infrastructure and number of disruptions to basic services, attributed to disasters		•		
11.6.1	Proportion of municipal solid waste collected and managed in controlled facilities out of total municipal waste generated, by cities		•		
11.6.2	Annual mean levels of fine particulate matter (e.g. PM2.5 and PM10) in cities (population weighted)		•		
11.7.1	Average share of the built-up area of cities that is open space for public use for all, by sex, age and persons with disabilities	•	•	•	
11.7.2	Proportion of persons victim of physical or sexual harassment, by sex, age, disability status and place of occurrence, in the previous 12 months	•	•	•	
11.a.1	Number of countries that have national urban policies or regional development plans that (a) respond to population dynamics; (b) ensure balanced territorial development; and (c) increase local fiscal space		•		
11.b.1	Number of countries that adopt and implement national disaster risk reduction strategies in line with the Sendai Framework for Disaster Risk Reduction 2015–2030		•		
11.b.2	Proportion of local governments that adopt and implement local disaster risk reduction strategies in line with national		•		

Indicator	Indicator Label	Gender-related indicators	Environment-related indicators	Gender-environment nexus indicators	Data availability for OECD countries
	disaster risk reduction strategies				
12.1.1	Number of countries developing, adopting or implementing policy instruments aimed at supporting the shift to sustainable consumption and production		•		
12.2.1	Material footprint, material footprint per capita, and material footprint per GDP		•		
12.2.2	Domestic material consumption, domestic material consumption per capita, and domestic material consumption per GDP		•		
12.3.1	(a) Food loss index and (b) food waste index		•		
12.4.1	Number of parties to international multilateral environmental agreements on hazardous waste, and other chemicals that meet their commitments and obligations in transmitting information as required by each relevant agreement		•		
12.4.2	(a) Hazardous waste generated per capita; and (b) proportion of hazardous waste treated, by type of treatment		•		
12.5.1	National recycling rate, tons of material recycled		•		
12.6.1	Number of companies publishing sustainability reports		•		
12.7.1	Degree of sustainable public procurement policies and action plan implementation		•		
12.8.1	Extent to which (i) global citizenship education and (ii) education for sustainable development are mainstreamed in (a) national education policies; (b) curricula; (c) teacher education; and (d) student assessment		•		
12.a.1	Installed renewable energy-generating capacity in developing countries (in watts per capita)		•		
12.b.1	Implementation of standard accounting tools to monitor the economic and environmental aspects of tourism sustainability		•		
12.c.1	Amount of fossil-fuel subsidies per unit of GDP (production and consumption)i		•		
13.1.1	Number of deaths, missing persons and directly affected persons attributed to disasters per 100,000 population	•	•	•	
13.1.2	Number of countries that adopt and implement national disaster risk reduction strategies in line with the Sendai Framework for Disaster Risk Reduction 2015–2030		•		
13.1.3	Proportion of local governments that adopt and implement local disaster risk reduction strategies in line with national disaster risk reduction strategies		•		
13.2.1	Number of countries with nationally determined contributions, long-term strategies, national adaptation plans,		•		

Indicator	Indicator Label	Gender-related indicators	Environment-related indicators	Gender-environment nexus indicators	Data availability for OECD countries
	strategies as reported in adaptation communications and national communications				
13.2.2	Total greenhouse gas emissions per year		•		
13.3.1	Extent to which (i) global citizenship education and (ii) education for sustainable development are mainstreamed in (a) national education policies; (b) curricula; (c) teacher education; and (d) student assessment		•		
13.a.1	Amounts provided and mobilized in United States dollars per year in relation to the continued existing collective mobilization goal of the $100 billion commitment through to 2025		•		
13.b.1	Number of least developed countries and small island developing States with nationally determined contributions, long-term strategies, national adaptation plans, strategies as reported in adaptation communications and national communications		•		
14.1.1	(a) Index of coastal eutrophication; and (b) plastic debris density		•		
14.2.1	Number of countries using ecosystem-based approaches to managing marine areas		•		
14.3.1	Average marine acidity (pH) measured at agreed suite of representative sampling stations		•		
14.4.1	Proportion of fish stocks within biologically sustainable levels		•		
14.5.1	Coverage of protected areas in relation to marine areas		•		
14.6.1	Degree of implementation of international instruments aiming to combat illegal, unreported and unregulated fishing		•		
14.7.1	Sustainable fisheries as a proportion of GDP in small island developing States, least developed countries and all countries		•		
14.a.1	Proportion of total research budget allocated to research in the field of marine technology		•		
14.b.1	Degree of application of a legal/regulatory/ policy/institutional framework which recognizes and protects access rights for small-scale fisheries		•		
14.c.1	Number of countries making progress in ratifying, accepting and implementing through legal, policy and institutional frameworks, ocean-related instruments that implement international law, as reflected in the United Nations Convention on the Law of the Sea, for the conservation and sustainable use of the oceans and their resources		•		

Indicator	Indicator Label	Gender-related indicators	Environment-related indicators	Gender-environment nexus indicators	Data availability for OECD countries
15.1.1	Forest area as a proportion of total land area		•		
15.1.2	Proportion of important sites for terrestrial and freshwater biodiversity that are covered by protected areas, by ecosystem type		•		
15.2.1	Progress towards sustainable forest management		•		
15.3.1	Proportion of land that is degraded over total land area		•		
15.4.1	Coverage by protected areas of important sites for mountain biodiversity		•		
15.4.2	Mountain Green Cover Index		•		
15.5.1	Red List Index		•		
15.6.1	Number of countries that have adopted legislative, administrative and policy frameworks to ensure fair and equitable sharing of benefits		•		
15.7.1	Proportion of traded wildlife that was poached or illicitly trafficked		•		
15.8.1	Proportion of countries adopting relevant national legislation and adequately resourcing the prevention or control of invasive alien species		•		
15.9.1	(a) Number of countries that have established national targets in accordance with or similar to Aichi Biodiversity Target 2 of the Strategic Plan for Biodiversity 2011–2020 in their national biodiversity strategy and action plans and the progress reported towards these targets; and (b) integration of biodiversity into national accounting and reporting systems, defined as implementation of the System of Environmental-Economic Accounting		•		
15.a.1	(a) Official development assistance on conservation and sustainable use of biodiversity; and (b) revenue generated and finance mobilized from biodiversity-relevant economic instruments		•		
15.b.1	(a) Official development assistance on conservation and sustainable use of biodiversity; and (b) revenue generated and finance mobilized from biodiversity-relevant economic instruments		•		
15.c.1	Proportion of traded wildlife that was poached or illicitly trafficked		•		
16.1.1	Number of victims of intentional homicide per 100,000 population, by sex and age	•			Number of victims of intentional homicide per 100 000 population, by sex (victims per 100 000 population)
16.1.2	Conflict-related deaths per 100,000 population, by sex, age and cause	•			
16.1.3	Proportion of population subjected to (a) physical violence, (b) psychological violence and (c) sexual violence in the previous 12 months	•			Proportion of population subjected to robbery in the previous 12 months, by sex (%)

Indicator	Indicator Label	Gender-related indicators	Environment-related indicators	Gender-environment nexus indicators	Data availability for OECD countries
16.1.4	Proportion of population that feel safe walking alone around the area they live	•			Feel safe walking alone at night
16.2.1	Proportion of children aged 1–17 years who experienced any physical punishment and/or psychological aggression by caregivers in the past month	•			
16.2.2	Number of victims of human trafficking per 100,000 population, by sex, age and form of exploitation	•			
16.2.3	Proportion of young women and men aged 18–29 years who experienced sexual violence by age 18	•			
16.3.1	Proportion of victims of violence in the previous 12 months who reported their victimization to competent authorities or other officially recognized conflict resolution mechanisms	•			
16.3.2	Unsentenced detainees as a proportion of overall prison population	•			
16.3.3	Proportion of the population who have experienced a dispute in the past two years and who accessed a formal or informal dispute resolution mechanism, by type of mechanism	•			
16.4.1	Total value of inward and outward illicit financial flows (in current United States dollars)				
16.4.2	Proportion of seized, found or surrendered arms whose illicit origin or context has been traced or established by a competent authority in line with international instruments				
16.5.1	Proportion of persons who had at least one contact with a public official and who paid a bribe to a public official, or were asked for a bribe by those public officials, during the previous 12 months	•			
16.5.2	Proportion of businesses that had at least one contact with a public official and that paid a bribe to a public official, or were asked for a bribe by those public officials during the previous 12 months				
16.6.1	Primary government expenditures as a proportion of original approved budget, by sector (or by budget codes or similar)				
16.6.2	Proportion of population satisfied with their last experience of public services	•			
16.7.1	Proportions of positions in national and local institutions, including (a) the legislatures; (b) the public service; and (c) the judiciary, compared to national distributions, by sex, age, persons with disabilities and population groups	•			
16.7.2	Proportion of population who believe decision-making is inclusive and responsive, by sex, age, disability and population group	•			

Indicator	Indicator Label	Gender-related indicators	Environment-related indicators	Gender-environment nexus indicators	Data availability for OECD countries
16.8.1	Proportion of members and voting rights of developing countries in international organizations				
16.9.1	Proportion of children under 5 years of age whose births have been registered with a civil authority, by age				
16.10.1	Number of verified cases of killing, kidnapping, enforced disappearance, arbitrary detention and torture of journalists, associated media personnel, trade unionists and human rights advocates in the previous 12 months	•			
16.10.2	Number of countries that adopt and implement constitutional, statutory and/or policy guarantees for public access to information				
16.a.1	Existence of independent national human rights institutions in compliance with the Paris Principles				
16.b.1	Proportion of population reporting having personally felt discriminated against or harassed in the previous 12 months on the basis of a ground of discrimination prohibited under international human rights law	•			
17.1.1	Total government revenue as a proportion of GDP, by source				
17.1.2	Proportion of domestic budget funded by domestic taxes				
17.2.1	Net official development assistance, total and to least developed countries, as a proportion of the Organization for Economic Cooperation and Development (OECD) Development Assistance Committee donors' gross national income (GNI)				
17.3.1	Foreign direct investment, official development assistance and South-South cooperation as a proportion of gross national income				
17.3.2	Volume of remittances (in United States dollars) as a proportion of total GDP				
17.4.1	Debt service as a proportion of exports of goods and services				
17.5.1	Number of countries that adopt and implement investment promotion regimes for developing countries, including the least developed countries				
17.6.1	Fixed Internet broadband subscriptions per 100 inhabitants, by speed5				
17.7.1	Total amount of funding for developing countries to promote the development, transfer, dissemination and diffusion of environmentally sound technologies		•		
17.8.1	Proportion of individuals using the Internet	•			Share of the population using internet - last 3 months
17.9.1	Dollar value of financial and technical				

Indicator	Indicator Label	Gender-related indicators	Environment-related indicators	Gender-environment nexus indicators	Data availability for OECD countries
	assistance (including through North-South, South-South and triangular cooperation) committed to developing countries				
17.10.1	Worldwide weighted tariff-average				
17.11.1	Developing countries' and least developed countries' share of global exports				
17.12.1	Weighted average tariffs faced by developing countries, least developed countries and small island developing States				
17.13.1	Macroeconomic Dashboard				
17.14.1	Number of countries with mechanisms in place to enhance policy coherence of sustainable development		•		
17.15.1	Extent of use of country-owned results frameworks and planning tools by providers of development cooperation				
17.16.1	Number of countries reporting progress in multi-stakeholder development effectiveness monitoring frameworks that support the achievement of the sustainable development goals				
17.17.1	Amount in United States dollars committed to public-private partnerships for infrastructure		•		
17.18.1	Statistical capacity indicator for Sustainable Development Goal monitoring				
17.18.2	Number of countries that have national statistical legislation that complies with the Fundamental Principles of Official Statistics				
17.18.3	Number of countries with a national statistical plan that is fully funded and under implementation, by source of funding				
17.19.1	Dollar value of all resources made available to strengthen statistical capacity in developing countries				
17.19.2	Proportion of countries that (a) have conducted at least one population and housing census in the last 10 years; and (b) have achieved 100 per cent birth registration and 80 per cent death registration				

Source: Authors' own computations based on UN Global Indicator Framework for the SDGs for determining the environment-related indicators; (Cohen and Shinwell, 2020[1]) analysis provided for gender-related indicators

References

Cohen, G. and M. Shinwell (2020), "How far are OECD countries from achieving SDG targets for women and girls? : Applying a gender lens to measuring distance to SDG targets", *OECD Statistics Working Papers*, No. 2020/02, OECD Publishing, Paris, https://dx.doi.org/10.1787/17a25070-en. [1]

www.ingramcontent.com/pod-product-compliance
Ingram Content Group UK Ltd.
Pitfield, Milton Keynes, MK11 3LW, UK
UKHW051457290926
15471UKWH00008B/1258

9 789264 964136